A BIRDWATCHING

FRANCE

NORTH OF THE LOIRE

J.CROZIER

ILLUSTRATED BY DAN POWELL

ARLEQUIN PRESS

ISBN 1 900159 76 7

First published 2003

Arlequin Press, 26 Broomfield Road, Chelmsford, Essex CM1 1SW
Telephone: 01245 267771
© Jacqueline Crozier

A catalogue record for this book is available.

CONTENTS

INTRODUCTION

BIRDING AREAS

BRITTANY

NORMANDY AND THE CHANNEL COAST

PARIS REGION

NORTH CENTRAL REGION

North of Paris

SOUTH CENTRAL REGION

THE MOUNTAINOUS EAST

Park/ Hautes Vosges

CHECK LISTS

A BIRDWATCHING GUIDE TO NORTHERN FRANCE

INTRODUCTION

France is one of the largest countries in Europe; roughly four times the size of England, but with only a slightly larger population than the whole of Great Britain. It has, therefore, more farmland, more woodland and large rural areas with a very low population density. Its climate ranges from Mediterranean to Alpine, wet, windy Atlantic to cold Continental. Within all these very different climatic regions, there are also a great variety of habitats: wetlands, rivers, lakes, coastal lagoons, deciduous and coniferous forests, lowland and mountain heaths, urban areas and agricultural land.

Bird species reflect the country's size and diversity. For example, the southern mountains hold quite different bird populations from the more northerly ones. Bird species in the Jura and Vosges are surprisingly distinct from those in the Pyrenees. France has long Atlantic and Mediterranean coastlines, and whilst many wetlands along both coasts are of international importance for the number and variety of migratory and wintering birds that use them, there is a noticeable difference in the bird species breeding in, say, the Camargue marshes compared to those on the rocky cliffs and islands around Brittany. The northeast has affinities with central and northern Europe, the southwest with Spain.

Clearly the majority of bird species found in the northern half of the country can also be found in Britain and for this reason many birders will head south to the Mediterranean or Pyrenees. But northern France should not be ignored as besides its accessibility from southern Britain, it holds some surprises: there are breeding Spoonbills, Kentish Plovers, Bluethroats, Crested Larks, Crested Tits, Zitting Cisticolas, Savi's, Melodious and Bonelli's Warblers near the Channel coast; Black, Grey-headed and Middle Spotted Woodpeckers are widely distributed and can be found in both large and small woods throughout most of the north, as can Honey Buzzard and Golden Oriole; a few Black Storks and Collared Flycatchers breed in the north-east and fewer Rock Sparrows in the west; there are even Bee-eaters and Hoopoes near Paris. Additionally, species that are either non-existent or very local in Britain such as all three harrier species, Black Redstart, Serin, Cirl and Corn Buntings and Short-toed Treecreeper, to name but a few, are more common and widespread in northern France. The list could continue but the above will give some idea of the difference species to be found on the other side of the Channel.

Anyone with an interest in sea-watching should try the Channel coast of France. Day-trips or a week-end visit are easy and inexpensive out-of-season. Birds fly closer to land, numbers can be impressive and many rarities turn up, making for better seawatching than from the south and east coasts of England. Those seeking rarities will soon discover that more and more Nearctic vagrants are being found along the west coast, and they should try the Île d'Ouessant, France's Isles of Scilly, while eastern "overshoots" and Siberian "waifs" turn up regularly throughout the country. As the number of French birdwatchers grows, so does the French bird list but, compared to Britain, birders are very few in number.

Readers driving through France or who own homes there, may be pleasantly surprised if they stop off at some of the spring or autumn sites in northern France. The best winter sites, the starred ones, are worth a special visit but even the others should prove of interest to birders working in the area or driving to a skiing holiday, for example.

Great stretches of France are still largely rural but agriculture is big business nowadays and increasingly intensive. Modern agricultural practices discourage birdlife but away from the Paris Basin, there are still very wild and unspoilt areas where traditional farming methods sustain wildlife, especially in the mountainous regions in the east. Tourism and a growing demand for "adventure" sports may be greater threats in these regions. Elsewhere France's huge army of "hunters" with their powerful parliamentary lobby and demands for a an ever longer (July to March) shooting season is another threat to bird populations, with an additional danger posed by the hundred of tons of lead left by their shot each winter. However, after almost 20 years of lobbying by the LPO (la Ligue pour la Protection des Oiseaux), and other conservation bodies, France has recently awarded official protection to 71 bird species. Just how effective this protection will prove to be has yet to be tested.

On the positive side more and more small reserves are being created every year, often managed by LPO regional groups and the LPO are encouraging farmers to manage their land for Little Bustards and Harriers. Each year some 400 volunteers search for Harrier nests and then guard over 1500 nest sites until the young fly. So in spite of the dramatic decline in a few species such as Little Bustard or Bonelli's Eagle, anyone birding France for the first time will still be amazed by the variety of species to be found in France as well as the sheer numbers of birds in many coastal and wetland reserves.

273 (51%) of the 535 European bird species breed in France and 350 species regularly winter there or pass through on migration*. The numbers of wintering ducks and coot, close to a million, makes France the third most important country in Europe (only just behind Britain and the Netherlands) for wintering wildfowl. A total of 512 species have been observed at least once and almost 400 are observed regularly. France's situation in Europe makes it a very important migration route. For example, the total population of Spoonbills breeding in Holland crosses France on their way to Spain or West Africa, as do more than 60,000 Cranes coming from Scandinavia, Germany and the Baltic while all northern Europe's White Storks migrate either down the Atlantic coast or the Rhône Valley. Besides common migrants, many rare or endangered species migrate though France: Black Stork, Corncrake, Little Bittern, Black Tern, Booted Eagle, Osprey and Red Kite among many others.

Species new to France and rarities turn up every year, often at the countless headlands and coves around Brittany and Normandy, many of them just waiting to be explored by keen birders. In fact, whatever your involvement in birds and birdwatching, from casual to professional, there is a great deal to interest you in northern France.

* Figures taken from "Zones Importantes pour la Conservation des Oiseaux en France" published by the Ministry of the Environment and BirdLife International and "Inventaire des Oiseaux de France" Dubois et al, Nathan.

Area covered by this book

The area covered by this book is roughly half of France north of a line running from the south bank of the Loire estuary on the Atlantic coast to Lake Geneva (Lac Léman) in the east. This division is partly climatic and geographic, as can be seen by the bird populations (for example, very few if any Fulmars, Black Storks, Grey-headed Woodpeckers, Collared Flycatchers, Icterine Warblers or Rooks breed south of this line [though the latter are rapidly expanding their range] while Short-toed Eagle, Scops and Eagle Owls, Rock Thrush, Tawny and Water Pipits, Ortolan Bunting, Crag Martin, Fan-tailed, Orphean, Sardinian and Sub-alpine Warblers rarely occur north of it) and partly for convenience when grouping sites. It should be noted that there is also a east-west divide within this area with certain bird species: Nutcracker, Black Grouse, Fieldfare, Marsh Warbler, Willow Tit, Pied and Collared Flycatchers, for example, breeding only or predominantly in the east.

Division into areas and sites: France is divided into départements (departments or counties) and larger administrative regions. A region such as Normandy has six departments (Manche, Calvados, Orne, Eure et Loir, Eure and Seine Maritime). Sometimes names can be confusing; the Loire department is on the opposite side of France to the Pays de Loire region. As departments possibly mean little to many British readers who could not find them easily on a map, this guide is divided into much more general regions (the Channel Coast and the Mountainous East for example) or sites are grouped around main towns (Calais area). If sites were listed under departments or even regions, then it would be easy to miss visiting a good site nearby because it occurs in another department. However, a map showing the departments and regions is on page 18 as this can be a useful reference when travelling in France. **Site Maps**: The large regions into which the book is divided are shown on the map of northern France on page 19. The section on each region opens with a sketch map showing numbered birding areas. Large areas are often divided into two or more sites and/or different itineraries described. The description of each area or site is accompanied by sketch maps where necessary, giving all the detail necessary to find the site. Because France is such an important country for migration, where a site is mainly of interest in spring and autumn when birds are on passage, then it is marked on the maps with **M** after its number. This does not mean that there is nothing of interest to see at other times of the year, but that its main importance is as a migration site. Predominantly seawatching sites are marked **S**.

Important Sites: *starred sites are those found to be the best in an area; the ones with the longest species list. If short of time, visit these first. However, check their "When to visit" section as some are at their best only at a certain time of year. If searching for a particular bird, look through "Special species" at the end of the guide, as a smaller or less important site may be a better bet for some less common species.

Distances and areas: Distances are given in kilometres, as these are the measurement shown on maps and road signs but for drivers with British cars a conversion table is given below. Occasionally the distances shown on the trip meters of different cars may show minor variations. Only very rarely is an exact distance crucial to find a site, usually a road junction or landmark is additionally given to help readers find the correct spot or turning.

The area of most reserves is given in hectares. 1 hectare = 2.471 acres.

Conversion Table Miles/Kilometres					
Kilometres	**=**	**Miles**	**Miles**	**=**	**Kilometres**
0.1	=	0.06213	0.1	=	0.16093
0.2	=	0.12426	0.2	=	0.32186
0.3	=	0.18639	0.3	=	0.48279
0.4	=	0.24852	0.4	=	0.64372
0.5	=	0.31065	0.5	=	0.80465
0.6	=	0.37278	0.6	=	0.96558
0.7	=	0.43491	0.7	=	1.12651
0.8	=	0.49704	0.8	=	1.28744
0.9	=	0.55917	0.9	=	1.44837
1	=	0.62130	1	=	1.60930
2	=	1.24260	2	=	3.21860
3	=	1.86390	3	=	4.82790
4	=	2.48520	4	=	6.43720
5	=	3.10650	5	=	8.04650
6	=	3.72780	6	=	9.65580
7	=	4.34910	7	=	11.26510
8	=	4.97040	8	=	12.87440
9	=	5.59170	9	=	14.48370
10	=	6.21300	10	=	16.09300

Species:

The more important species, or those of most interest to British birders, are listed in **bold type** under the description of each site. Obviously it is not possible to list all the species recorded for every site and so commoner birds, likely to be found in the habitat described, have been omitted. The text usually states whether the birds are to be seen in winter or summer but any reader unsure whether a species is resident or a passage or seasonal visitor should look it up in the check-list at the end of the book or consult a field guide.

Special Species:

The section on page 226 gives details of behaviour and habitat of those species likely to be of most interest to a non-French birder and suggests some sites where they are most likely to be seen. For example, if you particularly want to see Collared Flycatcher, look up this species in the "Special Birds" section at the back of the book where you will read that they are easiest to locate between mid-April to June but become quiet and very difficult to find after this, that they favour a very restricted and local habitat of mature oak woods and that the Lorraine forest sites are the only sure places to find them. Then turn to The Mountainous East section and read the detailed instructions as to location given under these sites.

Little Bustard

Tapes of bird-song:

The use of pre-recorded tapes or CDs to attract birds is subject to much debate and arouses strong feelings on both sides. Whilst there is no doubt that many species (especially woodpeckers, owls and most warblers) react immediately to their calls being played and fly close to investigate, tapes should always be used with the greatest sensitivity and NEVER in the breeding season. It is besides counter-productive to play a recording more than once, or twice at the very most, as birds are never fooled for long. Once they have "sussed" you out, they will not continue to respond. Tapes are most useful for familiarising yourself with calls before visiting an area where the species you wish to see are to be found. Calls and songs are by far the easiest way of locating birds. For example, you would be very lucky to find a Tengmalm's Owl or Grey-headed Woodpecker if you did not recognise their calls.

Wildlife Reserves and Protected Areas in France:

There are some 150 Nature Reserves (*Réserves Naturelles*) in France, covering over 280,000 hectares. Many of them are situated inside one of the six huge National Parks (*Parcs Nationaux*), which cover some 3830 square kilometres - but this is still only 0.7%

of the country. On average five new Reserves are added to this network annually. Their specific purpose is to conserve the flora and fauna within the reserve. Some belong to the State, some are owned and run by local authorities, others managed by voluntary organisations, such as local naturalist groups or the LPO. Some belong to the *Espaces Naturels de France,* a non-profit making organisation. Many coastal reserves are owned by the *Conservatoire du Littoral* (Coastal Protection Society), a Government organisation dedicated to protecting the remaining natural areas of coastline and lakesides. It acquires such areas to ensure that they are preserved for future generations. 12% of the French coastline (750 km) is currently protected in this way but only small areas are reserves. Others, called *Réserve Volontaire,* are privately owned, sometimes by the Local Authority, and generally managed by the local branch of *Espaces Naturels de France* or the LPO. They are not always open to the public and indeed sometimes hardly accessible; certainly not all of them are of interest to bird watchers as they may be protecting invertebrates, orchids or a cave-system. When a reserve forms part of a site described in this book, it is either one that can be visited (though possibly only at certain limited times which are given) or parts of it can be viewed from public roads or footpaths.

As well as National Parks and Nature Reserves, there are also a large number (26) of natural regional parks or PNRs *(Parcs Naturels Régionaux)* such as the Normandie-Maine and Haut-Jura; these cover some 7% of the country's surface. These are not intended primarily to protect wildlife but to maintain traditional human activities within a natural setting. Some sites will be found within these parks but often there is little or no protection (hunting is generally allowed) and/or too many tourists so they are not necessarily the best places for birds.

Important Bird Areas

There are also areas designated as IBAs (Important Bird Areas) by BirdLife International, which are priority sites for conservation. In French these are known as ZICOs *(Zones Importantes pour la Conservation des Oiseaux).* As with other Important Bird Areas all over the world these are not automatically protected areas and although many of them are situated within Parks, both National and Regional, or form part of Nature Reserves, others have no protection whatsoever and are threatened by hunting, urbanisation, tourism or intensive agriculture. ZICOs range in size from a tiny airfield or lake of less than 600 hectares to a vast Ramsar wetland like the Camargue of nearly 80,000 hectares. Their inclusion as a ZICO depends on the rarity and/or number of bird species found there and French conservationists are working to have as many as possible designated a protected area. Currently, France is not doing very well at protecting bird habitat, and comes bottom in the European league table for the percentage of its territory (1.5%) designated as areas with special protection (ZPS) and most protected areas are along the sea coasts. Very few forested or agricultural areas are protected, putting at risk such birds as Woodpecker species, Black Stork, Hazelhen, Capercaillie, Ortolan Bunting and Corncrake.

A study of the location of French IBAs shows that the majority are to be found around the borders of the "Hexagon"; that is, along the sea coasts and the mountain ranges. Far fewer are in the centre and these are all forest or wetland areas, rivers or lakes (man-made or natural). This distribution pattern is clearly reflected in the choice of sites in this guide. Furthermore, some lakes sites, mainly those of importance for the number of duck wintering there, have been excluded because the species found there are ones that are easy to see in Great Britain and therefore of less interest to British birders. Only a limited number of forest sites have been described, mainly because there are so many that it would be impossible to include them all. Those that have been included are either close to other sites, and therefore convenient to visit when in the area or ones that have a high density of certain species (i.e. Black or Middle Spotted Woodpeckers), so the chances of finding them are good. In fact, most of the forest species listed for specific forests can be found in almost all of the woodland in Northern France, and readers may well find the species they are looking for in any forest with the right habitat (see notes under "Special Species" at the end of this book).

France is one of the most heavily wooded countries in the European Union, with some 28% of its land covered with forest. Over 100 IBAs are forested or have forests within the zone. Some are private but the majority come under the aegis of the *Office National des Forêts,* which is State controlled and more or less the equivalent of he Forestry Commission. It manages over four million hectares of forests either for the State or for Local Authorities and this land may also include dunes, moorland, marshland and maquis. *Forêts Domaniales* are state forests, *Forêts Communales* communal ones, belonging to the Local Authority and both are clearly signed as such at every entrance. *The Code Forestier* ensures their protection in perpetuity. Unless there are signs to the contrary, or they are barred, it is possible to walk along most forestry tracks in *Dominale* or *Communale* forests. Hunting is allowed in many of them, so be very careful from autumn to spring; cyclists and walkers are accidentally shot every year. The storms in December 1999 blew down an estimated 350 million trees and some of the forest sites described have been badly hit, especially in Lorraine and around Paris. Huge efforts have been made to clear the fallen trees but there are still areas that are closed to the public because of danger from falling branches, etc. How the damage has affected bird life in these woodlands may take years to assess.

Contrary to what seems logical to many British birders, Hunting Reserves *(Reserves de Chasse)* are areas where shooting is NOT allowed - at least for a certain number of years - to allow game populations to recover. After that period of time, hunting starts again and another patch becomes a reserve. The *Office National de la Chasse* employs wardens and carries out studies on certain games birds, Capercaillie, Ptarmigan, Woodcock, partridges, as well as on deer and other game. Unfortunately, in northern France, shooting birds is widespread and very popular; hunter's rights and traditions are fiercely defended. As many sites are forest or wetland ones, this can cause problems for bird watchers. Even "no-hunting" reserves *(Reserves de Chasse)* are shot over; the hunters ignoring any notices. On coastal marshes, the only really safe places to birdwatch are in paying (private) reserves. You are certainly likely to see more birds there, for when disturbed by hunter's birds tend to take refuge within the reserves. Woods and forests display notices during the hunting season, listing which days shooting takes place, usually weekends and one or two days mid-week. Never leave the road on these days. When wild boar or deer are being hunted with dogs, there are usually notices in the road warning you not to go beyond this point. Do not ignore these notices as every year quite a few people are wounded or accidentally killed by hunters.

Bird Parks *(Parc Ornithologique* or *Parc des Oiseaux)* can cover a variety of avian enclosures varying from exotic birds in cages or a falconry display to a centre for injured birds or a well-managed reserve with hides. Very often, they are a combination; there may be birds in enclosures as well as a stretch of wetland managed for wild birds. Often they are good reserves, so do not be put off by the name. Any mentioned in this book provide acceptable birdwatching and it is worth investigating any others you come across.

Bird organisations, web-sites and twitch lines:

France has a tiny percentage of the number of bird-watchers found in Great Britain (or indeed Holland or Scandinavia). The LPO *(la Ligue pour la Protection des Oiseaux),* the equivalent of the RSPB, is BirdLife's representative for France but has only about

30,000 members. In spite of this, it runs a "twitch line" on 01 43 06 72 50 where you can listen to the latest rarity sightings - provided that you can understand rapid French and know the French names for birds (see checklist at the end of this book). Many keen birders seem to live around Paris, near the LPO's headquarters at Rochefort or in the Camargue so a fair proportion of sightings come from these areas as well as reports from sea-watchers along the Channel coasts and Brittany (in autumn this is the French equivalent of the Scilly isles). However, there are active LPO regional groups that also record local sightings as well as organising guided walks around reserves in their area. Contact them if you are in their region. Alsace: 03 89 81 05 34; Champagne-Ardennes: 03 26 72 51 39; Franche-Comté: 03 84 76 04 50; Lorraine: 03 83 23 31 47; Loire-Atlantique/Vendée: 02 51 62 07 93; Île-de-France: 01 49 84 07 90; Rhône-Alpes: 04 76 00 04 47

The LPO publishes two full-colour magazines (Ornithos with English summaries and L'Oiseau), runs reserves, raises money to buy more land for reserves, cares for injured birds with centres for oiled birds in Brittany and for raptors in the Auvergne, has a continuing programme of protection for threatened species, (such as Montagu's Harriers, Storks, Little Bustard, Corncrakes) and fights the excesses and demands of the hunting-lobby (including taking to court hunters who have shot protected species). If you want to find out when any reserves they run are open, contact them at the address below or telephone 05 46 29 50 74. The British representatives of the LPO are currently Ken and Lys Hall, LPO (UK), The Anchorage, the Chalks, Chew Magna, Bristol, BS18 8SN. Tel: 01275 332980 Fax: 01275 332559.

The French equivalent of the British rarities committee is the Comité d'Homologation National (CHN), Corderie Royale, B.P. 263, 17305 Rochefort Cedex. Detailed reports of rarity sightings should be sent to them in the same way as ones are presented to the British committee. CHN will have the names and addresses of regional recorders who also like to be informed of rare birds in their areas.

Internet sites:
France is accumulating web sites at the same rate as other European countries, and bird and birding sites, especially chat sites, are proliferating. Below is a list of some of the best and most helpful for northern France but more are being added constantly while others disappear. The LPO magazine L'Oiseau lists new ones in most of its issues. Some web sites are also listed under the general information on each region covered in this guide. Most of the LPO sites are excellent. A few I have had difficulty accessing.

LPO France www.lpo-birdlife.assoc.fr
LPO Alsace www.orni.to
LPO Anjou www.lpo-anjou.org
LPO Bretagne http://perso.wanadoo.fr/lpo.bretagne
LPO Champagne-Ardenne www.lpochampagneardenne.com
LPO Haute Normandie http://perso.wanadoo.fr/hnne/lpo-hn/index.html
LPO Île-de-France http://perso.wanadoo.fr/lpo-paris/
LPO Touraine www.multimania.com/lpotouraine
LPO Vendée www.vendee.lpo-birdlife.assoc.fr/
ANVL: association of naturalists of the Loing valley and Fontainebleau
http://perso.club-internet:fr/anvl
Bretagne Vivante SEPNB www.bretagne-vivante.asso.fr
Centre Ornithologique Île-de-France: www.perso.club-internet.fr/corif/
European Crane Working Group: www.grus-grus.com
Picardie Nature: http://www.picardie-nature.org
Clipon Seawatching: http://users.skynet.be/digibirders/Clipon.htm

Updating of sites:
Though every effort has been make to ensure that site information is currently correct, by its very nature a guide such as this constantly needs updating. New roads, building, tourist development or changes in farming practices may very rapidly alter sites and the bird populations they contain. The author and publisher would be very grateful if readers would let them know of any changes to or problems with sites. In addition, readers may find that some of their favourite sites have been omitted. If they would care to send us details, they will be visited, included in future editions and their help acknowledged.

TRAVEL INFORMATION
Getting there
It has never been so easy to get to northern France. Competition between ferries, eurotunnel and the low-price airlines ensures a choice of routes, competitive fares and many reductions, especially for short trips.

BY FERRY Most of the Channel, Normany and Brittany passenger ports are covered by one or more of the following companies. Crossing times vary from 75 minutes on the short crossings to overnight on some of the Brittany and Normandy routes. Costs vary according to season/demand and there are often special rates for one-day or short stay crossings. All carry cars.

P & O European Ferries (Portsmouth): 0870 2424 999 www.poferries.com sail Portsmouth - Cherbourg, Portsmouth -Le Havre

P & O Stena Line: 0870 600 0600 www.posl.com cross Dover - Calais 35 times a day. This route is also offered by SeaFrance 08705 711711 www.seafrance.com and Hoverspeed.

Brittany Ferries: 0870 366 5333 www.brittanyferies.com. Portsmouth - St. Malo, Portsmouth - Caen, Poole-Cherbourg, Plymouth-Roscoff

Condor Ferries: 0845 345 2000 www.condorferries.co.uk. One crossing a day Poole to St. Malo via Guernsey or Jersey.

Norfolkline: 0870 870 1020 www.norfolkline.com cross Dover - Dunkirk. No foot passengers.

Hoverspeed: 08705 240241 www.hoverspeed.co.uk cross Newhaven-Dieppe, Dover - Calais, Dover- Ostend

Try www.ferrybooker.com website for information on all ferry crossings.

BY AIR Low-cost airlines are opening up new routes to northern France all the time, making fly-drive a reasonable proposition. Currently Buzz (www.buzzaway.com 0870 240 7070) has daily flights from London Stanstead to Dijon, Caen, Brest, Tours, La Rochelle, Paris and Poitiers and twice daily to Rouen. Ryanair (www.ryanair.co.uk; 0541 569 569) flies from Stanstead to Dinard with cheap connections from Glasgow to Stanstead. Go fly to Nantes from Stanstead. Some cheaper flights are summer only. Car hire can be arranged when you book a flight.

Air France has internal flights to all the large towns in the area. Flights from the UK are normally via Paris but Strasbourg is direct.

BY RAIL The Eurotunnel 08705 353535 makes rail, either with or without your car, a quick option. www.eurotunnel.com. Eurotunnel has recently launched a new idea in last minute cross-Channel travel. Book a crossing and accommodation, even meals, etc. can be arranged by visiting Before u go @eurotunnel.com at their UK terminal.

Rail Europe (08705 848848 www.raileurope.co.uk is SNCF's main agent in the UK with information and ticket sales. www.sncf.fr is French Railways official website with special offers and on-line booking

BY COACH Eurolines runs express coaches from London Victoria Coach Station to 70 destinations in France. 08705 143219 www.gobycoach.com

If you do not have time to check out all the companies individually or want advice on the best and easiest way to get to France, try "where on earth travel" 01584 891 625 enquiries@whereonearthetravel.co.uk for competitive prices for travel arrangements, hotel bookings, car-hire etc. or www.frenchtourist office.net Tel UK: 01474 871992 or France 05 53 91 65 45 for competitive travel prices and low priced accommodation.

Getting around

BY CAR   This book is intended for birdwatchers and people interested in wildlife generally, and it is assumed that they are either spending a holiday in one area or touring different parts of the country and either way would also like to visit some good birding spots. It would be difficult to reach many of the sites, which are usually way off the beaten track, without your own transport and most directions assume readers are travelling by car. The exceptions are channel port sites some of which could be visited by foot passengers.

Roads, especially rural ones, are much less busy than in Britain and the motorways (except around Paris and other large cities) carry very little traffic compared to Britain and some northern European countries. However, motorways are toll roads. Credit cards are accepted except on some very short, new stretches when you may have to pay about €1 in cash. French motorways have many more petrol stations with pleasant restaurants, picnic and play areas than British ones. Additionally there are frequent aires along motorways with toilet and picnic facilities, often in very attractive surroundings. Some even have nature trails! Not all petrol stations will accept British credit cards, so beware of the 24 hour ones where you can only pay with a card outside normal opening hours. Such filling stations are often ones attached to supermarkets and are frequently the cheapest. Motorway petrol stations are the most expensive but will always accept any credit cards.

Bison Futé is an organisation that provides information on traffic flow and road conditions at busy times of the year. It also suggests "itinéraires bis", alternative routes along less busy roads often through attractive countryside. These are indicated by green signposts and maps showing these routes are available at motorway tollbooths during holiday periods. They are worth taking at any time of the year if you prefer driving along quiet roads.   Their web site is http://www.equipement.gouv.fr. Access "ROUTE" to check traffic conditions in advance.

PUBLIC TRANSPORT: There are good high-speed rail links between large towns and the nearest stations to major birding areas have often been given in the introduction to that region. However rural public transport is normally limited to the school bus run or a twice-daily bus service to the nearest town on market days, so buses may only run once a day - or week! Where it is possible to use public transport, this is stated. See SNCF's website (details above).

CYCLING: When it is feasible to cycle, either by hiring bicycles or taking your own, this is mentioned in the text. Most parts of northern France, especially along the Channel coast, Normandy, the Belgian frontier area and around the Champagne lakes are ideal for combining a birdwatching and cycling holiday. There are many more cycle tracks than there are in Great Britain and it is a popular leisure activity for families. Any tourist office will have leaflets, addresses and helpful advice for cyclists. For example, the National Regional Park des Caps et Marais d'Opale produces 8 "Cycloguides" giving detailed itineraries for the area stretching from Cap Gris-Nez to Saint Omer. Other Parks produce similar leaflets and they are always available from any tourist office or Maison de Parc.

Cycles can accompany you as luggage on TGV or InterCity trains in France only if they are folding models fitting into a 120 x 90 cm cover. Ordinary models must be checked into the rail depot and will travel independently of you, arriving anything between two to five days later (especially over a weekend). This service costs approximately €31. You can take cycles on some regional and local trains free of charge but each train carries only three cycles and the routes are limited. The Rail Express call centre (0990 848848) can tell you whether a specific line has trains with facilities for carrying bicycles. It is also necessary to obtain an up-to-date SNCF timetable and look for services with the bicycle symbol. The regional timetables are published twice yearly. They are available from European Rail Timetables (01909 485855).

WALKING: Long-distance walkers and climbers have their own guidebooks and maps, and many of the sites featured in this book are on or near the network of GR's (Sentiers de Grande Randonnée or long-distance footpaths) that criss-cross France. The Comité National des Sentiers de Grande Randonnée, 8 Avenue Marceau, 75008, Paris publishes guides to these footpaths. Where a birdwatcher can walk along these profitably for short or longer distances, this is also mentioned in the text, but this book is not intended primarily for the long-distance hiker. There are local footpaths near many of the sites featured and they are described if they lead to good birdwatching spots. However, anyone using them for long periods, especially in mountain areas, should purchase walking maps locally.

All long-distance GR footpaths are waymarked with the following internationally recognised codes:

Red and white with arrow = Straight on

Red and white with bent arrow = Follow the direction of arrow

Red and white with a cross over the marks = Not this way. Return to last junction and find the correct sign.

Local footpaths PR (Petite Randonnée) use different colour codes, often yellow.

Accommodation:

It is very rare not to be able to find a small, overnight hotel (cheap by British standards but remember that prices are per room, not per person), however remote the area. The exception is high-season holiday periods (which include winter in the mountain regions) when hotels will be full, or totally out-of-season, when they may be closed. There are an increasing number of cheap chains (Formule I, Première Classe, Etap, Campanile) to be found throughout France, mainly on the outskirts of the larger towns, often beside a motorway, and these are open all year round. Whilst these only charge between €22 -€38 per night for a double-room, they are not usually to be found near any of the sites in this book, though they can be very useful when touring or on the way to a birding destination. Mercure and Ibis are slightly more expensive hotels, also to be found throughout the country, often near motorways. These hotels have a joint agency www.accorhotels.com that can be useful, but it is rarely necessary to book in advance; they are more likely to be full weekdays than at weekends.

In rural areas, the Logis de France group of (usually) small, family-run hotels are excellent value and normally serve very good regional food. A book and map showing all their hotels can be obtained from 83, avenue d'Italie, 75013, Paris (Tel: 01 45 84 70 00 Fax: 01 45 83 59 66) or you can use their Internet site www.logis-de-france.fr. to find where hotels are situated and then make your bookings. Their Central Reservation telephone number is 01 45 84 83 84 or e-mail: info@logis-de-france.fr. Logis are frequently situated in small villages near Regional or National Parks, and one or several Logis will be found near almost all of the sites described in this book. They can be very useful for birdwatchers.

Gîtes ruraux are holiday homes to rent in country areas, useful for a family holiday or if staying in one place for a week or so. The Gîtes Panda are rural gîtes recommended by the WWF, often in or near reserves. There is a contact address for each department, which any French tourist office can supply but the easiest way to find out details of gîtes is through the Internet: Http://www.gites-de-france.fr. The head office is the Maison de Gîtes de France et du Tourisme Vert, 59, rue Saint-Lazare, 75439 Paris Cedex 09. Tel: 01 49 70 75 75 Fax: 01 42 81 28 53 and they publish an annual Guide des Gîtes Ruraux an another for Gîtes Panda. Phone for current prices.

Chambres d'hôtes are the French equivalent of Bed and Breakfast. These can now be found everywhere in France, especially in rural areas; they must meet certain standards and the ones listed in the official guide (current price about €22, available from the address above) are very good and fulfil all the sanitary regulations. You will see the signs at farm entrances and on village houses. Some are also designated table d'hôtes, which means that you can have lunch or dinner there. These are generally farms as all products must be reared and processed by the farmer, except the wine, which is local - and may be a little difficult to drink! Local tourist offices will give you details of ones in the area but outside holiday periods there is usually no need to book in advance.

Camping   There are an enormous number of campsites in France, especially in tourist areas where most of the sites in this book are to be found. Even quite small villages usually have a municipal campsite with electricity, water and toilets. Some of the large campsites near the coast are very sophisticated with every facility but are very full in summer. Only in early spring and autumn may it be more difficult to find a campsite open. Staying in a caravan/camping car outside campsites is forbidden in many areas. The French Camping-Caravanning Federation sells an annually updated guide to sites. Its address is 78 rue de Rivoli, 75004 Paris. Tel: 01 42 72 8   All local tourist offices will have a list of nearby campsites and will check vacancies for you.

Health and emergencies

As France is part of the European Union, visitors from the UK should take form E111 from the Department of Health with them if they wish for reciprocal medical treatment. Otherwise make sure you are covered by a good travel and holiday policy. Emergency services for doctors, dentists and pharmacists can be contacted by dialling 15 (toll free). If involved in an accident, you dial 17 for police, 112 or 15 for medical help, 18 for the fire-service.

As the British do not have identity cards it is advisable to carry your passport with you in case the police stop you even though within the EU you theoretically need only produce valid identification. A passport is naturally essential for non-EU citizens. In case of emergencies there are British Consulates in Lille (Tel: 03 20 12 82 72) and Paris. The Consulate-General in Paris shares a telephone number with the Embassy: 1 44 51 31 00. The address is 18bis rue d'Anjou, 75008 Paris. Office hours are 07.30-11.00/12.30-16.00 in summer and 08.30-12.00/13.30-17.00 in winter. The Embassy is at 35 rue du Faubourg St. Honoré, 75383 Paris Cedex 08. There are also Honorary Consuls in Tours (02 47 43 50 58), Le Havre (c/o P & O Portsmouth 02 35 19 78 88), Calais (03 21 96 33 76), Dunkirk (03 28 66 11 98), Amiens (03 22 72 08 48), Nantes (02 51 72 72 60), St. Malo-Dinard (02 99 46 26 64), Boulogne (03 21 87 16 80), Cherbourg (c/o P & O European Ferries 02 33 88 65 60). In Strasbourg there is a UK Delegation to the Council of Europe (333) (88) 35 00 78

Opening Hours:

In small towns, many shops close from 12.00 to 14.00 and then stay open until (normally) 19.00. Large supermarkets on the outskirts of towns usually stay open during lunchtimes. They also close at 19.00 or 19.30, with late-night opening normally Friday. Only the very largest will be open on Sundays and virtually none are 24 hour. Most banks also close between mid-day and 14.00 but stay open until 18.00, except for Saturdays, which are mornings only and Mondays, when many are closed all day. Opening times do, however, vary from region to region.

Lunch and evening meals are served at standard European hours, 12.00 - 14.00 for lunch and 19.30 - 21 or 22.00 for dinner. Bars, which also serve tea, coffee and soft drinks, and can usually produce a croissant for breakfast and a sandwich or light snack, are open all day until late in the evening. In Brittany and most of Normandy, crêperies serving both sweet and savoury pancakes (crêpes) and galettes (a pancake made with buckwheat flour) are numerous, reasonably cheap and popular.

Telephone numbers:

French numbers quoted in the text (e.g. tourist or LPO offices) are shown as you would dial them within France, on the assumption that most readers would call when in the country. If dialling from outside France, then leave off the first 0 and precede it with 0033.

If you do not own a mobile phone, remember to purchase a phone card when you enter France (available from most newsagents, STA branches), as very few public telephones now take coins. In the country, there is often a telephone for public use in the local bar.

Maps:

Blay-foldex series includes the whole of France 1/1,000,000, which is useful for planning a tour and 15 regional maps 1/250,000 (2 cm=5 km) which cover the country in sensible divisions and give enough detail to find your way to sites if used in conjunction with the sketch maps in this book. They are obtainable from almost any motorway shop and most petrol stations, though usually only the ones covering that area. The Michelin yellow series 1/200,000 (1cm=2 km) gives more detail but using them means buying more maps, although the annually produced *Michelin Atlas Routier et Touristique* has the whole of France in one large book, on the same scale of 1/200,000 (1 cm= 2 km).

It costs about €18 (£12) and is obtainable from any motorway shop, most book-shops and newsagents *Maison de la Presse*. Again, it should be possible to find all the sites using this scale Michelin map plus the sketchmaps in this guide. The Atlas is certainly the most economic option if touring.

Michelin also has a very useful website, www.viamichelin.com for working out the best routes from a to b or for homing in on a site.

The National Geographical Institute (IGN) topographic maps 1/100,000 (1cm=1km) cover the country in 72 maps and are excellent if you need more details for any area. Walkers will need the larger scale IGN walking maps (cartes de randonnées) 1/.50,000 or even 1/25,000. The ones covering the local area can be bought from any *Maison de la Presse*. Each scale has its own colour: for example 1/25,000 maps are from the "série bleue" and 1/100,000 from the *série verte*, so if you know the number you can ask for an "IGN *série bleue numero...*"

Tide Tables

Good birding at most of the coastal sites, especially those in Brittany and Normandy, depends on the state of the tides as they rise and fall to great levels. It is important to bear this in mind when planning coastal visits, as birds can be so far away as to be invisible at low tide! Tide tables are available from local Maisons de la Presse newsagents, are published in local papers, displayed in Tourist Information centres and can be found on websites www.easttide.co.uk and www.ukho.gov.uk. www.quicktide.co.uk produce a QuickTide card that can dial up daily high tides.

VOCABULARY

The short list below is composed mainly of geographical terms that may be encountered on maps or Reserve information boards. For French bird names see check list at back of book.

Anse:	a cove
Bac:	a ferry
Balisage:	waymarking of footpaths
Barrage:	dam
Base de loisirs:	leisure centre, usually refers to a marina or water sports centre
Bocage:	mosaic of small fields surrounded by hedgerows
Bois:	wood
Boucle:	river meander
Chambre(s) d'Hôte(s):	bed and breakfast
Chasse:	hunting i.e. shooting, sometimes with dogs (see Reserve de chasse). There are a few packs that hunt deer on horseback.
Digue:	embankment or dyke
Écluse:	canal lock or sluice gate
Étang:	can be a pool or pond, usually shallow (any piece of water smaller than a lake: *lac*) including fresh or brackish lagoons near the coast as well as man-made lakes used for fish-farming. Other words for stretches of water include *bassin*, *pièce* (or plan) *de l'eau* (often ornamental, in a park), *mare* (in a village) and *réservoir*
Falaise:	cliff, sheer rock face
Havre, hâble, haben, hafen:	(place names that occur frequently in the north) all mean port
Loisirs:	leisure activities
Manche (la):	the Channel
Marais:	marsh.
Mollières:	water meadows, often flooded in winter (Riet in Alsace)
Observatoire:	Hide
Parcours:	circuit or route; journey; often a circular nature trail with information boards
Péage:	toll on motorway, either to take a ticket or to pay. If you want to .. avoid paying, there is nearly always an exit just before the tolls leading onto a Route National or N road.
Phare:	lighthouse
Plage:	beach
Plan d'eau:	lake or reservoir - often used for stretches of water where leisure activities are permitted
Pointe:	headland, foreland
Pont:	bridge
Presque'île:	peninsular
Rade:	roadstead where ships can anchor
Reserve de Chasse:	no-hunting area
Riet:	see Mollières
Renseignements:	further information, queries (on reserve information boards often followed by telephone number)
Sauf riverains:	Residents only. May refer to parking or entry to narrow street or village
Sentier:	footpath. *Sentier littoral*: coastal footpath, sometimes part of a GR: *Grande randonnée*: long-distance footpath. Circular nature trails with information boards are sometimes labelled *Parcours*: circuit or route
Tourbière:	peat bog
Voie sans issue:	dead-end

France Showing Regions and Departments

01 Ain	23 Creuse	47 Lot-et-Garonne	71 Saône-et-Loire
02 Aisne	24 Dordogne	48 Lozère	72 Sarthe
03 Allier	25 Doubs	49 Maine-et-Loire	73 Savoie
04 Alpes de	26 Drôme	50 Manche	74 Haute-Savoie
Haute-Provence	27 Eure	51 Marne	75 Paris
05 Hautes-Alps	28 Eures-et-Loir	52 Haute-Marne	76 Seine-Maritime
06 Alpes-Maritimes	29 Finistère	53 Mayenne	77 Seine-ey-Marne
07 Ardèche	30 Gard	54 Meurthe-et-Moselle	78 Yvelines
08 Ardennes	31 Haute-Garonne	55 Meuse	79 Deux-Sèvres
09 Ariège	32 Gers	56 Morbihan	80 Somme
10 Aube	33 Gironde	57 Moselle	81 Tarn
11 Aude	34 Hérault	58 Nièvre	82 Tarn-et-Garonne
12 Aveyron	35 Ille-etVilaine	59 Nord	83 Var
13 Bouches-du-Rhône	36 Indre	60 Oise	84 Vaucluse
14 Valvados	37 Indre-et-Loire	61 Orne	85 Vendée
15 Cantal	38 Isére	62 Pas-de-Calais	86 Vienne
16 Charente	39 Jura	63 Puy-de-Dôme	87 Haute-Vienne
17 Charente-Maritime	40 Landes	64 Pyrènèes-Atlantiques	88 Vosges
18 Cher	41 Loir-et-Cher	65 Hautes-Pyrènèes	89 Yonne
19 Corrèze	42 Loire	66 Pyrènèes Orientales	90 Territoire de Belfort
2A Corse du Sud	43 Haute-Loire	67 Bas-Rhin	91 Essonne
2B Haute-Corse	44 Loire-Atlantique	68 Haut-Rhin	92, 93 et 94: petite
21 Côte d'Or	45 Loiret	69 Rhône	ceinture de Paris
22 Côtes d'Armor	46 Lot	70 Haute-Saône	95 Val d'Oise

Birding Regions - division into:

BRITTANY The peninsular west of a line running from Mont St. Michel to St. Nazaire. This includes a small part of the Pays de Loire department near the coast north of the River Loire that conveniently and geographically forms part of the Brittany peninsular.

NORMANDY AND THE CHANNEL COAST As most of the coastal sites stretching from north Normandy to the Belgian frontier are similar as regards species, passage, seawatching conditions, etc., this region covers all the Normandy coastline as well as the short coastal strip of Picardie east to Amiens and the western half of Nord-Pas-de-Calais east to Lille.

PARIS REGION covers an area extending roughly 60 km around the capital; it therefore includes the Île de France as well as small parts of surrounding departments

NORTH CENTRAL REGION includes non-coastal Picardie, western Lorraine and the north of Champagne-Ardenne

SOUTH CENTRAL REGION comprises the inland area south of Paris: Pays de la Loire north of the River Loire, southern Champagne and most of Centre and Burgundy.

THE MOUNTAINOUS EAST includes all of Alsace and Franche Comté as well as the eastern part of Lorraine

Northern France – Showing this Guide's division into birding regions

NORTHERN FRANCE SITE CALENDAR

January   **All coastal sites** for divers, sea duck and waterbirds. Wintering geese, ducks and waders at sites around the **Brittany and Normandy peninsulas** in gulfs and bays. The **Brière Natural Park** attracts many winter visitors.
Alsace, the Champagne and Lorraine lakes: **Lac du Der** and **Foret d'Orient, Madine, Lindre** for wintering duck and Cranes, possibly White-tailed Eagles. Hard weather will bring many more northern duck and geese to the River Rhine sites in Alsace as well as many inland lakes and coastal bays both this month and next. Thrush and finch flocks throughout the country.
Crossbills active in conifer forests; Citril Finches flocking at lower altitudes in the **Vosges** and the possibility of Snow Finch near the **Hohneck**.

February   Storks already back at some coastal sites; others migrating north. Buzzard and Goshawk displaying over forests. By the end of the month most Woodpeckers are becoming territorial and so easy to locate in woodland sites while Buzzards and accipiters display overhead. Ravens nesting on Brittany sea cliffs. Cranes return north from the middle of the month; they cross the Pyrenean passes during good weather and may be seen flying north. Their numbers increase at the **Champagne lakes**. Geese and plovers start leaving the **Channel coastal sites**. Best month to observe Tundra Bean Geese in **Alsace, Champagne** and **Lorraine** before they depart mid February to mid-March.

March   Stork and Crane migration continues, as do raptor displays. **Channel coastal sites** for geese, dabbling ducks, waders and other migrants returning north. Spoonbill migration north peaks during the second week, try Croisic at the mouth of the Loire, **Le Havre** and other **Normandy** sites and the **Channel coast** sites in **Pas-de-Calais**. Bluethroats are also on passage at the same sites.
Possibly the best month for finding Woodpeckers, which continue to call and for spotting Hawfinch in woodland sites.

Golden Orioles

Black Kites are early migrants; look out for them following rivers north. The first Stone Curlews are back on the **River Loire** sandbanks by mid-month. Hoopoes return to breeding sites.

April   Bluethroats' passage continues through the month along the **Channel coast sites**. Look for them this month and the next in **Brittany,** round the **Guérande saltpans** and in the **Brière marshes**. Summer breeders arrive through-out month at all lower altitude sites. Warblers, **Golden Orioles** and **Night-ingales** singing. Many species holding territory and early breeders already nesting. Gargany may be spotted at the coast or on inland lakes such as **Marcilly Lake in the Sologne**, the **Champagne lakes, Lake Madine** in **Lorraine,** the **Rhine** sites in **Alsace** and the flooded meadows round Angers.

Last week: best time for **coastal sites** - waders, migrants and summer breeders. Look for the first marsh terns over lakes. Bee-eaters start to arrive back at colonies.n Migration sites (along the **River Loire, inland lakes**) for large flocks of Black Kites, hirundines and many passerines during the first half of the month. Montagu's Harriers return to breeding sites throughout the month. .

May   First week: **Sologne, Champagne** and **Lorraine lakes, River Loire** for terns, bitterns and herons. . Best period to find Collared Flycatchers in **Lorraine**. Marsh terns may be seen over most large wetlands and lakes. Common Terns starting to breed along the River Loire. Reed and Savi's Warblers singing in reed beds in the **Brière marshes** and **Romelaere**. **All coastal sites** also good. Migration of Honey Buzzards throughout month to woodland breeding sites. Last two weeks are the best period for summer and resident breeders at **Vosges** and **Jura** sites as higher sites normally accessible for Rock Thrush, Citril Finch, Water Pipit and Ring Ouzel. Late migrants such as Marsh Warbler and Spotted Flycatcher arrive.

June   Ideal period for all **mountain sites** in the east, also **coastal breeding** sites of Fulmars, Kittiwakes, Puffins in Brittany and Normandy. Icterine and Melodious Warblers feeding young.

July   Birds still active in the highest areas of the **Vosges** and **Jura mountains**. Juvenile Crossbills and Citril Finch disperse. At the end of the month the first waders return from the Arctic to wetland sites down the **North Sea** and **Channel coasts**. Black Kites start to migrate south.

August   The quietest months for birds inland, the busiest for tourists. Seabird passage down the **Channel** and **Atlantic coasts** gathers momentum throughout the month; **Gannets** and **shearwaters** numerous, many **skuas. Nutcrackers** easy to see in the **eastern mountains**. During the last week, post-breeding migration gathers momentum; large numbers of Black Kites and Honey Buzzards fly down the river migration routes. Spoonbill and Bluethroat migration south down the **Channel coast** peaks during the last ten days of the month. White Storks and a few Black pass through on migration this month. The numbers of waders along the **western coasts** increases.

September   Migration and seabird passage continues throughout month. Ospreys can be seen along the main river valleys and at wetland sites (**Rivers Loire, Allier** and **Rhine sites**, the **Solonge, Lac de Der** and **Forêt d'Orient**). Peak sea-watching period for **shearwaters, Gannets, skuas**, terns along the **Channel coast** and the **Vilaine Estuary**. The end of the month (and the beginning of the next) is the best time to search for Nearctic rarities on **Normandy** and **Brittany headlands** and the **Île d'Ouessant,** especially after westerly gales.

<u>October</u>   Good numbers of waders at the **Champagne** and **Lorraine lakes** from mid-September to mid-November; often up to 80 or so Great White Egrets there. Still good for seawatching as migration continues down the **Channel coast**. American vagrants still turning up in **Brittany**; waders at **coastal** sites. Northern populations of Stone Curlews and the few remaining Little Bustards begin to flock and move south. Look for them on the plains north of **Orléans** and **along the Loire**. **Cranes** start migrating. **Redwing, Fieldfare, Siskin, Brambling** and **Redpoll** start arriving.

<u>November</u>   Crane passage peaks. By the last week there are large numbers of Cranes at **Lac de Der**, **Lorraine** and Alsace sites.   Red Kite still moving south.   The first wintering **ducks** and **Brent Geese** arrive in number in Brittany and at Channel coastal sites; **Greylag** and **Tundra Geese** start arriving at the Champagne and Lorraine lakes. Migrating and wintering **Woodcock** make this the most likely month to come across them in any wooded area, especially from Paris eastwards.

<u>December</u>   First week: **Cranes** still at above sites. **Geese** and **swans** at wintering sites. Intense cold will bring large numbers of **sawbills, Goldeneye, Smew, Eider** and **geese** to the Atlantic coast and any unfrozen inland lakes. Divers and **sea ducks** offshore at **Channel coast** sites. **Snow Bunting, Twite** and **Horned Lark** may be seen along the Channel coast.

White-tailed Eagles return to the **Champagne lakes** most winters and sometimes one or two Spotted Eagles to **Lorraine**.

Please note that the calendar suggests ideal times to visit various sites, though extreme weather conditions may affect timing.   Except for specific periods mentioned, most species will be in these sites for some time before and after the suggested month.

I would like to thank the LPO and all those people, friends, wardens and other birdwatchers, who have helped with information on sites and birds, but most especially Brian Dore for the hours of driving and checking not only the sites but also the text of this book and also Stephanie Coghlan for Brittany Section.

BRITTANY

Area 1   St. Nazaire
Site i.   Guérande and le Croisic salt marshes *
Site ii.   Brière marshes *
Site iii.   Vilaine Estuary * (M) (S)

Area 2.   Vannes/ Golfe du Morbihan
Site i.   Marais de Pen-en-Toul
Site ii.   La Pointe d' Arradon
Site iii.   Étang au Duc
Site iv.   Séné marshes-Falguérec Reserve. *
Site v.   Duer marshes *
Site vi.   Suscinio marshes and Penvins headland (S)
Site vii.   St. Pierre Lopérec
Site viii.   Kervilhen marsh
Site ix.   Quiberon peninsula and Belle Île

Area 3.   Quimper
Site i.   Cap Sizun/Reserve de Goulven *
Site ii.   agunes de Lespoul Nature Reserve
Site iii.   Audierne Bay/Trunvel Reserve *
Site iv.   Seawatching headlands (S)

Area 4.   Brest
Site i.   North Shore
Site ii.   South Shore

Area 5.   Île d'Ouessant * (M)

Area 6.   Roscoff/Morlaix
Site i.   Morlaix and Carantec Bays
Site ii.   Goulven Bay *
Site iii.   Seawatching sites (S)

Area 7   Sept Îles Reserve *

Area 8.   St. Malo/Dinard
Site i.   St. Brieuc Bay
Site ii.   Cap Fréhel and Cap d'Erquy (S)
Site iii.   Beaussais and Lancieux Bays
Site iv.   Rance Estuary
Site v.   St. Malo
Site vi.   Pointe du Grouin (S)
Site vii.   Mont St. Michel Bay west

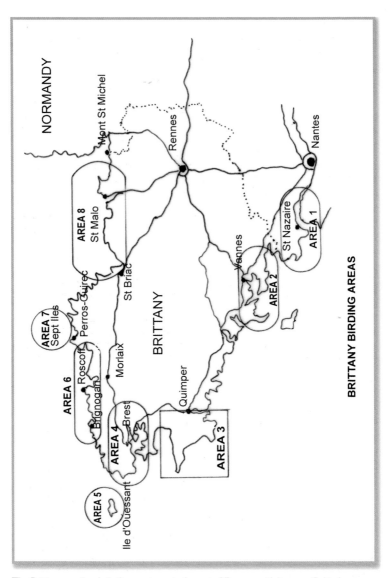

BRITTANY BIRDING AREAS

NORMANDY

Mont St Michel

Rennes

Nantes

St Nazaire

AREA 1

AREA 8
St Malo

Vannes

AREA 2

St Briac

BRITTANY

AREA 7
Sept Iles

Perros-Guirec

Morlaix

Quimper

AREA 6

Roscoff

Brignogan

AREA 4

Brest

AREA 3

AREA 5

Ile d'Ouessant

The Brittany peninsula is the most westerly part of France, with its own Celtic language, customs and cuisine. Both geographically and culturally, it is quite different from the rest of France. Brittany has over 1,200 kilometres of coastline with hundreds of rocky islands off-shore and is physically divided into the coastal region, the Armor, meaning the "country near the sea", rocky in the north and west and sandy in the south, and the hillier and more wooded centre, the Argoat, meaning the "county of the wood", in modern times now reduced to scattered remnants of forest. Most of the best bird sites are to be found around the coast, the rocky stretches of which are known by the colour of the rock so there is the Côte de Granit Rose and the Côte d'Emeraude stretching along Brittany's north coast in the department of Côtes d'Armor.

To French birders, Brittany is best known for its seabird colonies, such as those on Les Sept Îles, and the rarities that turn up during migration, especially on the Île d'Ouessant, the French equivalent of the Isles of Scilly, as well as for the large numbers of geese and duck that winter in its bays. However, in the south of the peninsula (actually just in the Loire Atlantic department) are the Brière marshes, second only in size to the Camargue, where Black and Whiskered Terns, Purple Heron, Bittern, Marsh Harrier, Bluethroat, Bearded Tit and Savi's Warbler all breed. These marshes are, in fact, the last remaining site in northern France where Savi's Warblers breed in any number. On the north and west coasts seabirds such as Puffin, Guillemot and Razorbill are at the southern limits of their breeding range and the western sea cliffs are also the only sites for Red-billed Chough in northern France. Bluethroat and Fan-tailed Warbler are most easily observed on the south coast of Brittany but the six species of woodpecker, widely distributed across most of northern France, can only be found in the extreme east of Brittany.

Many of the reserves in Brittany are managed by the SEPNB (Société pour l'Étude et la Protection de la Nature en Bretagne).

Major sites only are covered in this book. For a more comprehensive coverage of the region refer to a companion guide in this series: Stephanie Coghlan's "A Birdwatching Guide to Brittany".

Maps: Michelin yellow maps 58, 59 and 63 1/200,000 (1 cm = 2 km) cover the region with some overlap. Red Michelin 230 covers all of Brittany, as does Blay-foldex no. 1. but the scale is too small except for planning a trip. A yellow Michelin plus the sketch maps should enable you to find all sites below. Be warned, place names vary from map to map and road-signs may be different again; it all depends if they have been "Frenchified" or are in Breton.

Area 1. ST. NAZAIRE

Site i.

GUÉRANDE and **LE CROISIC** salt-marshes, mudflats and saltpans lie some 12 km west of St. Nazaire, a few kilometres from La Baule. Enclosed by sand-bars and the rocky coastline around Le Croisic, this is an interesting site throughout the year.

WHEN TO VISIT: In winter there are large number of **Brent Geese** and duck (**Shelduck, Pintail, Wigeon, Teal, Goldeneye, Red-breasted Merganser**), five **grebe** species (though Red-necked and Slavonian are rare), **egrets, Avocet** and **Oystercatcher. Divers** and **sea duck** can be seen at the coast. **Marsh Harrier** can be seen throughout the year.

From March many more **wader** species begin to arrive; **Spoonbill** on passage. **Black-winged Stilt, Avocet** and **Common Tern** breed, together with good numbers of Bluethroat (easiest observed April and May, when they are singing).

August and September are the best months for watching **shearwater** (mainly Balearic), **Gannet, Kittiwake** and **skua** passage off the Pointe de Croisic. **Gull** numbers build up at roosts. Autumn migration brings many more **waders** and **Spoonbill** back to the saltpans.

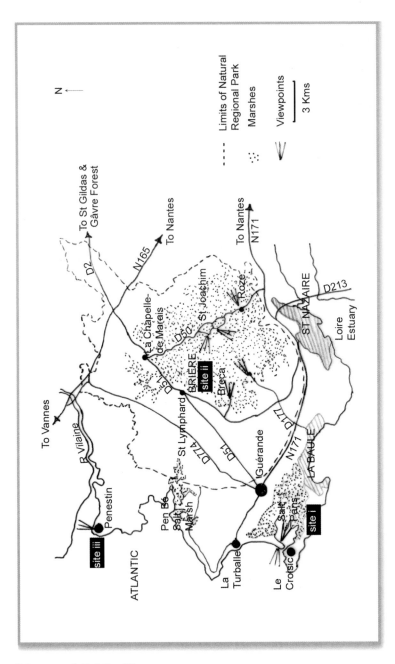

Brittany area I site i, ii and iii

ACCESS: The northern edge of the salt-pans can be explored from the D92 between SAILLÉ and MAISONS BRÛLÉES Take the D774 south of GUÉRANDE and turn right (west) at the roundabout at Saillé by-pass onto the unsigned road (the opposite direction to the village). There are plenty of places along this quiet road to park and check the saltpans. Many are private but it is often possible to walk along the banks for a short distance (beware hidden holes). There is a LPO visitors' centre at the Maison de Sel, just outside Kerignon, where there is information on salt-making and the area.

At LERGAT the D92 swings south towards PEN BRON. **Spoonbills** seem to favour the pans in this area and it is also good for **Bluethroat** (though they may be anywhere). There are short stretches of pinewoods and gorse scrub along this road that are good for passerines, especially in spring. Park by the dunes just after the pinewood to scope the sea for **divers, Scoter, Eider, grebes** in winter. Park just before the barrier to Pen Bron medical centre and look over the bay and mud-flats on the left. Best on a rising or high tide. Excellent for **geese, duck, waders** and **Black-necked Grebe** from autumn to spring.

The southern parts of the salt marsh can be reached from two minor roads leading off the D92 some 2 and 2.8 km from the Saillé roundabout and leading to BATZ-sur-Mer. The area around the Sissable turning (now accessible only to owners) is another good area for **Bluethroat**. The track to Sissable is very rough but worth walking down for a short distance.

The rocky coastline around the Pointe du Croisic can be reached from BATZ-sur-Mer. Turn right onto the N171 towards LE CROISIC and at the roundabout at the entrance to the town follow the Côte sauvage signs for the D45 which runs around the headland, with several seawatching viewpoints, especially from the Point. There are Turnstone and other waders on the rocks. There is also good birdwatching from the Jetty and port in Le Croisic, especially for gulls and terns but also **divers, sawbills, sea duck** and **waders**, when a rising tide drives birds towards the mudflats.

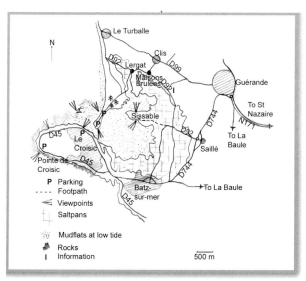

Brittany area 1 site i. Guérande and Le Croisic saltmarshes

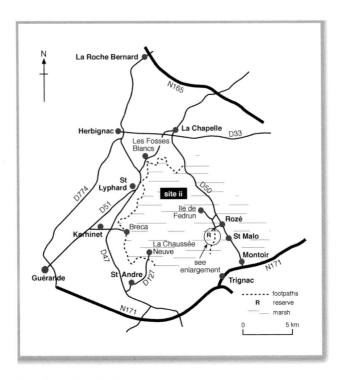

Brittany area I site ii. Brière marshes

The **BRIÈRE MARSHES,** which form part of the Regional Nature Park of Brière, cover a very large area north of the N171 between Trignac and Guérande. The second smallest N. R. Park in France, Brière covers 40,000 hectares and the Brière marshes in the centre 9,700 hectares. There are more marshes in the east of the Park, all surrounded by water meadows and criss-crossed by drainage ditches and canals. The Brière is France's largest wetland after the Camargue and is a Ramsar site.

The Maison du Park is at 177 Île de Fédrun, 44720 Saint Joachim (Off the D50). Tel: 02 400 91 68 68   Website: www.parc-naturel-briere.fr e-mail: info@parc-naturel-briere.fr WHEN TO VISIT: spring (late March - June) is the best season. Brière is the best site in northern France for **Savi's Warbler** and **Black Tern**. Both migration periods are good and there are always numbers of waterbirds in winter.

Among the 40 plus species that breed in the reedbeds and marshes are **Bittern, Purple Heron, Garganey, Redshank, Black-tailed Godwit, Snipe, Water Rail, Spotted Crake, Marsh Harrier, Black** and a few **Whiskered Tern, Bluethroat, Sedge, Reed, Great Reed, Savi's, Grasshopper** and **Cetti's Warblers, Reed Bunting.** Many more species, especially waders, occur on passage and a few winter there. **Spoonbill** can be seen on passage. Wintering duck include **Pochard, Tufted Duck, Wigeon, Teal** and **Pintail** and at this season **Sacred Ibis** regularly feed with **Little Egrets**; they can sometimes even be seen from the N171

ACCESS: The D47/D51 and the D50 run north from the D171 along the west and east sides of the marshes respectively, meeting at LA CHAPELLE-des-Marais, where there is an map showing footpaths in the Information Centre car park. The best way to cover the area is to drive along these two roads, scanning from any lay-by overlooking the marshes and noting any farm tracks leading off that you can walk along, as well as visiting the sites described below where there are footpaths. Note that these roads are very busy at weekends and during the summer.

The northern half of the D50 from La CHAPELLE to ST. JOACHIM has several viewpoints along the 8 km stretch. At St. Joachim, turn off the D50 west to the ÎLE DE FÉDRUN, a traditional village and museum with some viewpoints over the marshes. Boat trips run from here.

Further south on the D50 just north of ST. MALO-de-Guersac turn off to the Parc Animalier at ROZÉ where there are hides, viewing platforms and a visitors centre. Entrance currently €2.80. Park near the Café du Pont opposite the Information Centre which is open 10.00-13.30 and 15.00-18.30. Cross the canal bridge and walk with the canal on your right and the marsh on the left. This is a good birding area and it is worth taking the circular trail in the Parc.

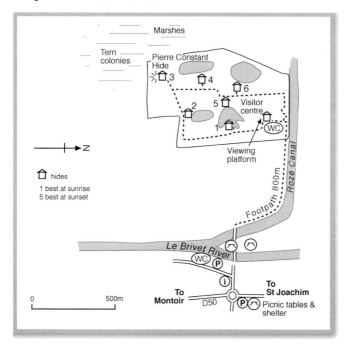

Brittany area I site ii Enlargement of Rozé Reserve in Brière marshes

Off the D47, at LA CHAUSSÉE NEUVE in the south-west of the Park, way-marked footpaths and a viewing mound (telescope useful) lead off from the parking area. Access depends on water levels and they can still be flooded as late as May. In addition boats can be hired with or without a guide. Beware getting lost. Guides are knowledgeable and speak English. It costs approximately €15-16 per person. Contact A. Mahé, la Chausée Neuve,

44117 St. Andre des Eaux. Tel: 02 40 91 59. Booking advisable during holiday periods.
ACCESS: Turn off the N171 at St. Nazaire exit 3 and take the D47, turning off it to ST. ANDRE-des-Eaux and following the D127 signed to the Parc and Porte de Brière to LA CHAUSÉE NEUVE.

Other good birding areas up the D47 include BRÉCA, turn off east 6.5 km north of the St. André junction, where there a footbridge giving access to the canal footpath. Boats can also be hired there.

A GR footpath runs east of the D47, and can be joined at ST. LYPHARD, BRÉCA or the D127 south of LA CHAUSÉE NEUVE. It is also likely to be flooded in winter a nd spring.

Other fauna and flora: Otter and Water Rat occur in the Brière but are not as common as the introduced Coypu and Muskrat, both of which can be a menace damaging river banks and destroying plant life. Amphibians and reptiles are numerous and include Edible, Agile, Parsley and Common Tree Frogs, Fire Salamander, Marbled and Warty Newts together with their hybrid, Blasius' Newt, Green and Viviparous Lizards, Slow Worm and several species of snake. It is a good area for dragonflies and butterflies include Camberwell Beauty and Swallowtail. There is a typical marsh flora, most striking in May when the Yellow Iris is in flower.

<u>Accommodation</u>: The campsite in St. Lyphard has been recommended by birders as beyond the river there is of good birding area of willow woodland leading into reedbeds. There are also restaurants and a couple of pleasant hotel here (closed in winter). There is also a Logis at Pontchâteau on the east side of the marshes and plenty of campsites and hotels on the coast around St. Nazaire and La Baule.

Site iii.
LA VILAINE ESTUARY is an excellent sea-watching site in autumn and good for duck in winter. There are also many waders on the mudflats on passage. It is an IBA for the large numbers of **geese**, **duck** and **waders** that winter there, more than 20,000 on a regular basis.

The River Vilaine runs almost due west towards its mouth and the estuary opens out below the south coast of the Brittany peninsula, between the Brière marshes and Morbihan, to its east. On the north and south banks of the estuary are rocky coasts around the Pennlan headland on the north and the Halguen and Cofrenau headlands on the south bank. Further south is the Falaise de la Mine d'Or (or Golden Cliff) a strange ochre-coloured cliff with a high mica-schist content that causes it to glow in the setting sun. 18 metres high and 2.3 kilometres long it towers above a sandy beach and is also a sea-watch point. Also on the south bank are some inter-tidal mudflats and marshes

WHEN TO VISIT: Vilaine is essentially an autumn and winter site. From August to October **Balearic Shearwater** flock in large numbers in the evening, especially at high tides. Numerous waders, notably **Dunlin, Curlew** and **Ringed Plover** congregate on the mud-flats.

There can be large flocks of **gulls** and **Common, Little, Sandwich** and **Roseate Terns** from September onwards.

In mid-September **Sabine's Gull** occasionally stops off at the mouth of the estuary.

From September to November, **Arctic** and **Pomarine Skuas** occur at the mouth of the Vilaine. A few **Great Skuas** can be seen between September and November in suitable weather. All the above are best seen from the sea-watching points on the south side of the estuary.

In winter, up to 2000 **Avocet** and 1000 **Curlew** winter in the estuary. Some 3000 **Brent Geese**, many dabbling (**Wigeon, Pintail**) and diving duck (**Common Scoter**, a few **Velvet Scoter, Pochard, Tufted Duck, Scaup**) can be seen on the mudflats and below the Pennlan headland, which is the latter's main wintering site in France; between 2000-5000 may congregate there. Flocks of **Divers** and **Great Crested Grebe** can gather off the Golden Cliff.

ACCESS: On the north side of the Estuary, 500 metres east of the POINTE DE PENNLAN (follow the D5 south from BILLIERS) is a good sea-watching point with parking at LES GRANGES, You can walk east along the cliff path for good views over the estuary. The recommended time to visit is about mid tide. In winter this is the best place to observe **Scaup**.

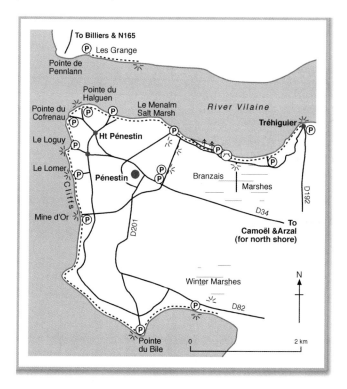

Brittany area I Site iii La Vilaine Estuary

On the south bank, the cliff between the POINTE DU HALGUEN and the POINTE DU COFRENAU is a good sea-watching site. The best time here is high tide. From HAUTE PÉNESTIN take the road towards Logui. LE LOGUI on maps, LOGUY on signposts. Park before you reach the beach, then walk following the first creek to the north for the recommended place to watch. The Pointe du Halguen is also noted for the concentrations of seabirds that occur in autumn. Sabine's Gull turns up regularly and there are often dozens of skuas. There are also Dartford Warblers in the gorse bushes in the car park and Cirl Buntings in the hedges.

To reach the Golden Cliff (LA MINE D'OR) either take the D201 south-west from PÉNESTIN and follow the signs or follow the brown coastal road signs south from the Pointe de Cofrenau.

LE BRANZAIS (delete words in brackets) marshes lie off the D34 north-east of Pénestin. Turn north (right) in Pénestin, following the brown signs for the coastal road, towards TRÉHIGUIER. In about 300 metres, park at the wood with picnic tables or nearer Pénestin at the Marché car-parks or walk the roadside to view the reed beds and salt-flats which have Little Egret, Little Grebe, Grey Heron, duck species, Kingfisher, Mute Swan and Marsh Harrier throughout the year. Bluethroat may be seen in spring and many wader species in autumn and winter.

Accommodation: There are hotels and campsites at Pénestin

Area 2. **VANNES/GULF OF MORBIHAN**

THE GULF OF MORBIHAN is a huge bay surrounded by rocky coasts, mudflats, saltmarsh, sand and shingle beaches. It is a maze of peninsulas and small islands (some of which can be visited), linked to the sea by a narrow channel on the south-west. The entrance can be viewed from the west side at the POINTE DE KERPENHIR and on the east at Port Navalo and Bilgroix. Given its size (the name in Breton means "small or little sea"), the fact that the coast is often not easily accessible and that tide levels are vital for good sightings, it is not an easy area to bird. However there are some excellent viewpoints, marshes and nature reserves scattered throughout the region. It is a Ramsar Site and an IBA, one of the 15 foremost such sites in Western Europe for wintering flocks of **Brent Geese** (8000 plus), **Shelduck** (2,500-4,250), **Wigeon** (7-15,000), **Pintail** (1-2000), **Red-breasted Merganser** (2000), **Grey Plover** (1-2000), **Dunlin** (15-30,000), **Avocet** (500-900), **Black-necked Grebe** (900-1500) and **gulls** among other species, with many more on passage. The whole area is famous not just for the large number of birds wintering in the gulf, but also for the SÉNÉ and DUER marshes and old salt pans that attract breeding birds in summer (**Avocet, Black-winged Stilt, Redshank, Bluethroat**) and passage migrants, such as Spoonbills and Bluethroat, in spring. WHEN TO VISIT: Best in autumn and winter. Dabbling duck numbers (mainly **Wigeon, Shoveler, Pintail, Teal, Shelduck, Mallard**) build up from September-February; diving duck (**Red-breasted Merganser, Goldeneye**) from November-March; **Black-necked** and **Great Crested Grebes** August-March; **gulls, cormorants** July-March. The recommended best time to visit is 3 hours before or after low tide. The tide tables refer to VANNES/PENBOCH. If you are using tide tables for outside the Gulf, high tide appears to be about 2-3 hours later and the tide is full for about an hour due to the narrowness of the entrance. During the year different sites have different importance. The following sites are recommended by SEPNB in the following months:

March-August	Séné - Falguérec site iv
	Marais de Suscinio site vi
	Pointe de Penvins site vi.
	Marais de Pen-en-Toul site i.
September- March	Pen Cadenic (see Penvins site vi)
	Le Pont d'Banastère (see Penvins site vi)
	L'Anse de Kergeorget near Duer site v
	St. Colombier/Duer Marsh site v.
	Île Tascon (off D780. Linked to mainland by causeway from Lasné, covered at high tide)

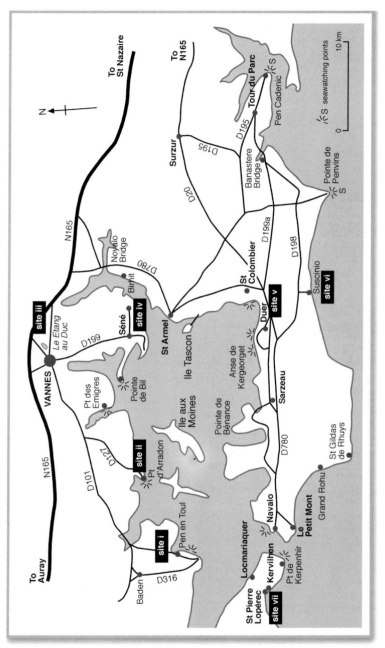

Brittany area 2 Gulf of Morblan/Vannes sites i - vii

In winter (November-February), in addition to the above, almost any minor road leading to the shore of the Gulf, especially off the D780, can be good for wintering flocks and are worth checking if you have time.

On the north side of the Gulf there are three good sites; the first a breeding site, the other two for wintering birds:

Site i.

MARAIS DE PEN-EN-TOUL. This inland marsh lies south-west of Vannes. It is only open during the non-breeding season for a circular walk. In the breeding season, view the old saltpans from the entrance area just past the Hut. Best in spring and summer.

ACCESS: Take the D101 south-west from Vannes signed to Baden. In 8 km (just after crossing an inlet) turn off onto the D316 following signs to LAMOR BADEN south of the hamlet of LOCQUÈLTAS, park after the bridge opposite a large house with blue shutters with a white Z. A hotel advertising sign marks the start of the track.

Site ii.

LA POINTE D'ARRADON is good from November to February.

ACCESS: This site is on the West of the Gulf, south-west of Vannes. Turn off the D101 to Arradon and follow the bypass south to the Pointe.

Site iii.

ÉTANG AU DUC is a small inland urban site in the east of Vannes itself, best from November to February.

ACCESS: Turn off the N165 going west on to the D779. Coming from the west turn off at Vannes east. Follow signs to LE HESKENNE and Vannes centre. At a crossroads turn right. The Étang is immediately on the right.

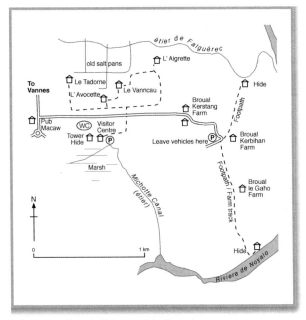

Brittany area 2 site iv. Marais de Sene Reserve

On the east of the Gulf, going south from Vannes, are some of the best areas:

Site iv.
SÉNÉ MARSH - FALGUÉREC RESERVE are forty hectares of former salt-pans, part of the 410 hectares of the Séné Marshes Nature Reserve, now converted into an international site for migratory and breeding water birds including **Avocet, Black-winged Stilt, Sacred Ibis, Shelduck, Bluethroat, Bar-tailed Godwit, Redshank, Black Tern, Turtle Dove**. Recently **Black Woodpecker** has been recorded for only the third time in this part of Brittany. In early autumn this is a good site for waders, gulls, tern and **Spoonbill**.
ACCESS: The reserve lies 5 km south-east of Vannes and is signposted from the D779. Just outside Séné follows signs to Reserve FALGUÉREC to the east. There is a large car park on the right with a new Information Centre (entrance fee €3.80) with viewing platform and a tower hide (always open) overlooking the new scrapes and footpaths leading to other viewpoints in the Petit Falguérec part of the Reserve. There is another parking area 300 metres further down the road from where trails lead to two more hides (no charge and always open). E-mail: reserve.sene@wanadoo.fr

Site v.
The DUER MARSHES are being progressively restored to attract birds and to build up plant diversity. Some of the species to be seen throughout the year are: **Brent Goose, Teal, Gadwall, Sacred Ibis, Lapwing, Spoonbill, Black-winged Stilt, Spotted Redshank, Little Egret, Sedge Warbler, Yellow Wagtail, Serin**. Also there are four acres of easily accessible woodland with a tower hide, good for the more common woodland species.
ACCESS: These old saltpans and saltmarsh lie north of SARZEAU on the D780 just after passing ST. COLOMBIER, 12 km from the junction with the N165 east of Vannes. The marsh can be seen from the roadside viewpoint at St. Colombier, signed ZONE ORNITHOLOGIQUE. There is a lay-by for parking, a picnic table and information board. From here you can walk to hide 1 overlooking the salt marsh and the Gulf. On a rising tide Brent Geese and duck flock together reasonably close inshore. For the Mudflats Viewpoint turn off immediately after a reserve sign onto a very minor road. In 50 metres, there is a parking place and information board.
Driving further along the D780 take the next minor road to DUER and park at the pool and green. From the Duer parking you can walk to the right through a gate along the edge of the marsh back to the previous hide 1, or you can walk left, through the woodland to the tower hide.
A third parking place is found by continuing through the village towards the sea, where there are picnic tables and views over the Gulf. A footpath to the north is signed to hide 2 (tower) and south along KERGEORGET COVE, which is also a good site for wintering duck and geese on an incoming tide. Kergeorget Cove or the Anse de Kergeorget is not marked as such on the maps but lies west of Duer. From this village take a minor road to KERBODEC. It passes a megalith and the Château Kergeorget. From Kerbodec a footpath leads to the shore. The area is a No Hunting Reserve and attracts large daytime roosting flocks. The best time here is on a rising tide. One hour plus one to two and a half hours after low tide.

Site vi.
The SUSCINIO MARSHES and old saltpans lie on the south coast surrounding the CHATEAU DU SUSCINIO. A variety of habitat makes for a varied bird list of interest throughout the year and the dunes are a good site for **Kentish Plover** Other species include **Shelduck, Black-winged Stilt, Lapwing, Turnstone, Common Tern,**

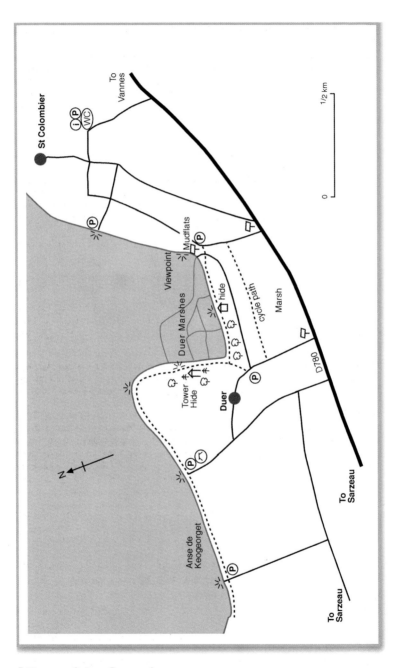

Brittany area 2 site v. Duer marshes

Yellow Wagtail, Skylark, Reed and **Sedge Warblers, Zitting Cisticola, Linnet, Reed Bunting**.

ACCESS: Leave the D780 at SARZEAU and take the D198 for some 3 km. Follow the signs to the Château where you can park or drive to the cove and park by the sea.

The grounds of the castle and its moat attract birds, and you can walk from here through the lane which passes between reed beds to the dune slacks and finally to the sandy cove. A similar walk can be made along the shore to LANDUEAC and return through the lanes to the car park or to the shore.

East of the Suscinio, marsh is a good sea-watching site at the POINTE DE PENVINS. Return to the D198 and turn right for 3 km to Penvins. Follow the signs to the Pointe where there is parking, WC and picnic site.

This site is well-known to local birders, who find it best after autumn and winter gales. **Skuas** and **petrels** are observed regularly, **Sabine's Gull** quite frequently and sometimes phalaropes. The east bay attracts feeding waders, the headland has roosts on the rocks, migrants in the bushes and hedges around the chapel and **larks, pipits** and **wheatears** on the open headland fields

Two winter sites (November to February) can be found just north-east of Penvins. BANASTÈRE BRIDGE is reached by turning of the D780 just at the edge of St. Colombier after the Tourist Information and follow the road to the cross roads at La Belle Croix. Turn right onto the D199 and then the D324 to Banastère. Parking either side of the bridge. Best on a rising tide.

PEN CADENIC lies north-east of Banastère bridge. Drive to the Tour du Parc and take the D195 to Pen Cadenic hamlet which overlooks the confluence of the Rivers Penerf and Sarzeau. Seawatching from the oyster and fish farming port (smelly). Gull and wader roosts on offshore islands. Check the tides.

West of the Gulf of Morbihan, between the entrance to the Gulf and the Quiberon peninsula are two more sites overlooking Quiberon Bay, which is another IBA for wintering waterbirds, especially **Brent Geese, Dunlin** and **Turnstone** on passage.

<u>Site vii.</u>

ST. PIERRE LOPÉREC has a good selection of passerines as well as waterbirds.
ACCESS: Turn off the D781 to LOCMARIAQUER at the parking and information board and follow signs to ST. PIERRE. In about 3 km park at a large shaded car park. There are walks to the bay and peninsula and through wetlands. You can walk in an anticlockwise circle across a boardwalk and follow paths and roads back to the car park.

<u>Site viii.</u>

At **KERVILHEN**, between Carnac and Locmariaquer is an old salt marsh and a wet zone with thickets and plantations. There is parking and a hide from where **Little Egret, duck species, waders, Little Grebe, gulls** and **warblers** on passage may be observed.
ACCESS: From the D186 coastal road east of CARNAC turn south at LA TRINITÉ MER following signs to PLAGE DE KERVILLEN (note alternative spelling).

<u>Site ix</u>

The **PRESQU'ÎLE DE QUIBERON** is a rocky peninsula connected by a narrow neck to the mainland. The best birding area is along the C_te Sauvage or wild coast, which is open with low heaths, from PORTIVY to PORT MARIA on the west coast of the peninsula (the east coast has sandy beaches). Turn west from the D768 after crossing the neck of the peninsula, go through Portivy to Pointe du Perche and then take the D186 coast road south to Quiberon. This coastal road has many parking places and

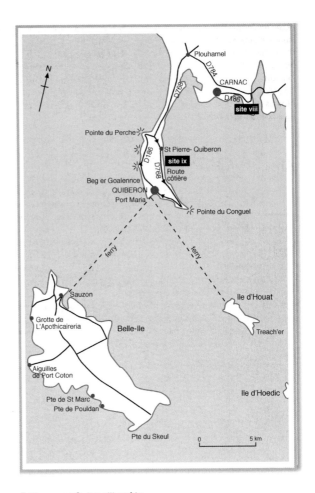

Brittany area 2 sites viii and ix.

viewpoints over the rocky coast. From the POINTE DU CONGUEL there is a panorama over the Quiberon Bay and its islands. Apart from sea-watching, **Northern Wheatear, Rock Pipit, Linnet** and passing migrants that like short turf can be found here.

From Port Maria in Quiberon town there are ferries to BELLE-ÎLE, which is a SEPNB reserve for some of Brittany's cliff nesting birds: **Fulmar, Rock Dove, Raven, Red-billed Chough, Shag** and **gulls**. The best stretch of cliffs is on the south coast, between the Pointe de Saint-Marc and Pointe de Pouldon. Ferry crossings run frequently during the high season, take 45 minutes and cost about €22,20 for adults. Cars, which must be booked in advance, cost €109,20 Belle-Île Tourist Office tel: 02 97 31 81 93.

The smaller, nearer ÎLE D'HOUAT, another reserve, can also be reached from Port Maria. One or two boats a day.

Accommodation: This is a popular holiday area and there are numerous campsites (mostly summer only when they become very full). Vannes has hotels in all categories, including the cheaper chains, and is the best place to stay in winter. Quiberon also has plenty of hotels in all price ranges, most closed in winter and fully booked in summer. On Belle-Île, the Hôtel Vauban just above the Port du Palais has been recommended. Tel: 02 97 31 45 42 Rooms €61-70 Closed end November-February and on Île aux Moines within the Bay the small (6 room) Hôtel de l'Isle, rue du Commerce, 56780 Île-aux-Moines is open from 1/2 to 11/11.

Area 3. QUIMPER

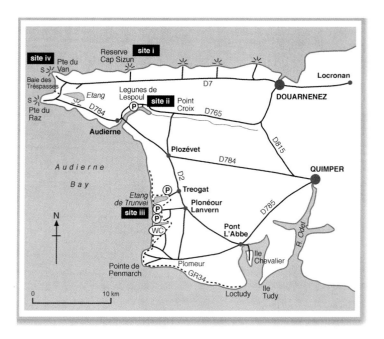

Brittany area 3

Along the south coast, the area from Auray to Quimper is a very attractive region popular with tourists. It is full of small bays, wooded valleys and inlets and has many coastal areas attractive to birds. Many rivers drain into theis stretch of the coast, including the Scorff, Blavet, Odet and Aven. These wooded river valleys are very scenic, but while attractive to birds are difficult to access for birders, although they are accessible by road viewpoints. River cruises are available in the main holiday season. Between the rias are coastal dunes backed by shallow lagoons and scrubby forest. The major sites in this area, however, are on the Douarnenez peninsula west of Quimper.

Site i.

CAPE SIZUN RESERVE (also referred to as RÉSERVE DE GOULIEN or RÉSERVE MICHEL-HERVÉ JULIEN) is a very wild granite cape, formed of rocky headlands, coves and creeks, home to colonies of breeding seabirds and cliff-nesting species: **Shag, Guillemot** (some 70 pairs), **Fulmar, Lesser and Great Black-backed Gulls, Kittiwake** (one of France's strongest colonies 900 pairs), **Raven, Red-billed Chough, Rock Dove.** Other species to be found here include Marsh Harrier, Linnet, Skylark, Stonechat, Yellowhammer, Whitethroat. The bird sanctuary created by the SEPNB in 1959 in the parish of Goulien contains some of the area's richest cliffs and islands and supports several important seabird colonies. Unfortunately pollution and oil spills have decimated the former seabird colonies. Puffins disappeared in 1980 and Razorbills are on the brink.

There is a marked footpath with viewpoints; it takes about an hour to walk round the circuit with stops. A leaflet with sketchmap showing colonies is available from the information centre. Guillemots can be seen from the Kastell ar Roc'h cliff. The GR34 coastal footpath passes through so you can walk west and east to other

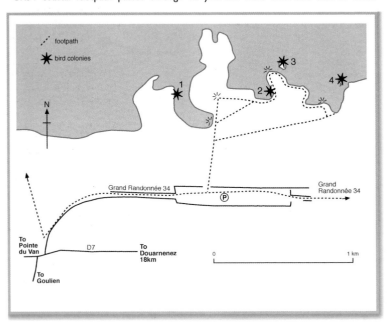

(Brittany area 3 Site i Cape Sizun Reserve) Colonies 1. Kastell at Roc'h - Guillemots 2. Herring Gulls, Fulmars, Kittiwakes 3 & 4 Great Black-backed Gulls, Shags

headlands. The walk along the cliff footpath to the west is best. Walk back along the entrance road to a green sign and follow the green arrows. There is the possibility of a circular walk if you have the time.

WHEN TO VISIT: Best between mid April to early July. The centre is open March 15 to August 31, 10-12h. / 14-18h. There are guided walks during July and August that last about 3 hours. Tel: 02 98 70 13 53 for more information.

ACCESS: The Cape lies off the D 7 15 km west of Douarnenez. The turning is signed. It is also sign-posted from Audierne. Look for Réserve Michel-Hervé Julien.

<u>Site ii.</u>
The **LAGUNES DE LESPOUL**, old sewage lagoons converted to a Nature Reserve, lie between the towns of Audierne and Pont Croix, on the north bank of the tidal river Goyen.

There is a one-way system to drive around and a series of lagoons which can be watched from your vehicle to avoid disturbance. Access is also possible on foot along the riverbank. Common birds include **Shelduck, Grey Heron, Little Egret**, hirundines in summer, duck and gulls in winter and almost anything on passage.

ACCESS: The Reserve can be reached from the D765. Travelling west look for a sign Marbrerie Monlien, Abattoir. The exit is almost opposite. The entrance is through the car park further along on the left

<u>Site iii.</u>
TRUNVEL RESERVE, near the centre of **AUDIERNE BAY**, is the most important birding area in the region. It is a site of major importance for breeding and migrating wetland warblers (several hundred Aquatic Warblers can turn up here in autumn) and has a ringing station open during the autumn. It is also one of the best sites in Brittany for summer breeding birds including **Bittern, Purple Heron, Little Bittern, Kentish Plover** (in the dunes), **Bearded Tit, Zitting Cisticola, Dartford Warbler, Reed** and **Sedge Warblers, Reed Bunting, Hoopoe** and **Bee-Eater**, attracted by the variety of habitat on the reserve: excellent reed beds, a dune system, coastal marsh and open water.

There are three main areas to visit if you wish to cover all the various habitats and see as many species as possible. They are: 1. The Étang de Trunvel   2. Kermabec beach   3. The Maison de la Baie near St. Vio. If short of time, then Trunvel is possibly the best area.

WHEN TO VISIT: This is a year-round site. Besides the breeding birds listed above, **waders** on passage can be seen in spring and autumn. Mid-August to mid-September is the peak period for **Aquatic Warbler** and other migrating passerines. Winter is also an interesting season with many species of **duck**, as well as **Bittern, Merlin, Marsh** and **Hen Harriers, Bearded Tit** (the easiest time to see them), **Dartford Warbler**.

ACCESS: 1. <u>Trunvel</u>. Turn off the D235 km north of Plonéour-Lanvern in the centre of TRÉOGOAT. Follow the signs to TRUNVEL. As you approach the village, on a sharp bend is a car-park on the left with distant views over the Étang. Off-season you can also park in the village on the green area by the rubbish bins.

Walk down the road towards the village. Past the last building it becomes a track with a good hedge and bushes for migrants on the lakeside of the road. 100 metres further on the left at a sharp bend is a hide/ observatoire which gives good views over the Étang de Trunvel. Telescopes useful.

Further along the track going west through more migrant bushes is the Ringing Station/Station de Baguage, which a notice claims opens mornings 1/07-31/10. However, the ringers are not always there every morning during the season due to poor weather or lack of manpower. If it is open, interested birders will be made welcome (delete all words in brackets.

2. **Kermabec Beach**. Take the D2 at the crossroads in Plonéour-Lanvern. Fork left onto the D156 to TRÉGUENNEC and follow this road to the sea, just over 6 km. Kermabec beach is not marked on Michelin maps but is at the end of the D156 and there is a car park.

If you have been to Trunvel first then it is possible to reach Tréguennec on small country roads.

From KERMABEC car park several walks are possible. Birds likely to be seen in summer include Marsh Harrier, Lapwing, Kentish Plover, Hoopoe, Yellow Wagtail, Zitting Cisticola, Bearded Tit, Stonechat, Skylark, Meadow Pipit, Corn Bunting, Linnet, Northern Wheatear.

> i.   Walk north along the shore for 1 km approximately, until you reach the outlet of the Étang. Check the shore for roosting gulls and waders, or waders feeding by the waves and especially for breeding **Kentish Plover**. Return inside the dunes following a line of posts just behind the dunes. This gives good but distant views into two étangs (telescope useful). Return to the car park.

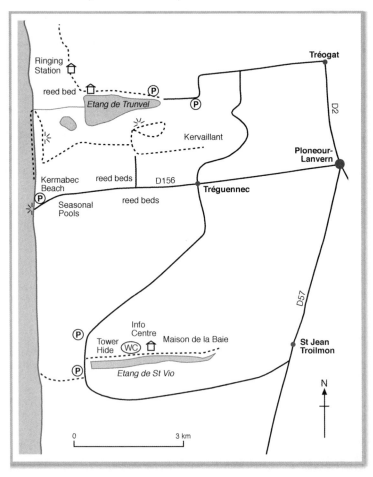

Brittany area 3 Site iii. Trunvel Resewrve

ii.   Walk out of the car park east, back towards Kermabec along the road. Check the small pools (if wet) behind the car park and beside the road and the surrounding fields. About 10 minutes up the road turn off onto a cart track, signed to KERVAILLANT 1.5 km. Good bushes for migrants in autumn. When the cart track swings right, carry straight on to reach the higher ground, from where you can obtain good views of the Étang de Trunvel. This track is greener than the cart track and can be followed in a circuit round the top of the little hill. Return the same way, but just before you reach the cart track again, look on your right for an indistinct track, after crossing a wet ditch, leading towards the sea. This skirts the reeds and meets a line of posts that mark the edge of the reserve. Follow these until you meet an old sign with very faded lettering marking the reserve. Look from this sign for the car park, marked by a new sign at its edge.

iii.   You can do this walk in reverse, depending on the light, by finding the sign in the car park, which says BAIE D'AUDIERNE, KERMABEC. Walk to the old sign and then follow the posts across the edge of the marsh. When the posts run out walk straight on. Cross the ditch to the dirt road and turn left to the viewpoint or right to return via the lane and the road.

3. Maison de la Baie   There is an information centre, Maison de la Baie d'Audierne, at ST. VIO, in an old converted farm, where there is parking. It is open July and August when guided walks and activities for children are available. Nearby is a viewing tower with special bushes planted for migrants, surrounded by short trails around the area. The coastal footpath, GR34, passes through and there is a track beside the Etang de Vio, passing close to the water and reedbeds. Further along the road are other places to park and you can walk out onto the marsh towards the sea to the Loc'h Stang area via a fenced track The Warden may be able to tell you if any Bee-eaters are breeding nearby this year. St. Vio can be reached by turning south off the B156 at Tréguennec for 3 km. Equally it can be reached from KERMABEC; turn right and follow the signs.

Site iv.
SEAWATCHING SITES AT THE POINTES DU RAZ AND DU VAN.
The two headlands at the westernmost tip of the peninsula have excellent seawatching possibilities in autumn (for weather conditions and timing check information under "Seawatching sites north of Le Havre" Normandy and the Channel coast site vi) and could be good sites for passerines as well as seabirds during spring and autumn migration.

POINTE DU RAZ is reputed to be the most westerly point in France and therefore a very popular tourist site with a high daily charge for parking. (In fact the Pointe de Corsen is further west). There is a footpath around the site.

The POINT DU VAN is much quieter, if not as spectacular but there is a car park and WC, a circular walk around the cliff, heathland and an interesting chapel.

Outside the   migration periods, expect to see **Fulmar, Great** and **Lesser Black-backed Gulls, Kittiwake, Red-billed Chough, Wheatear, Skylark, Black Redstart, Stonechat.**

ACCESS: Both headlands can be reached by following signs from the D7 west from Douarnenez or from the D784 west from Audierne.

Accommodation: Another popular area with plenty of summer accommodation. There are hotels and campsites at Audierne, Plogoff and Douarnenez as well as two hotels between the Points du Raz and du Van, at the Baie des Trépassés where there is a reed bed and pool (gull species, Marsh Harrier), giving opportunities for early morning and evening bird watching. Both can be recommended but are closed October-April. Tel: Hotel de la Baie des Trépassés 02 98 70 61 34; Relais de la Pointe du Van 02 98 70 62 79

Area 4. **BREST HARBOUR**

Brest Harbour or Rade de Brest is a very large, deep and spectacular harbour, surrounded by rocky coastlines, beaches and mudflats. Thousands of waterbirds winter here, notably up to 2000 **Black-necked Grebe** as well as large numbers of **Wigeon** and **Dunlin**. The south side of the harbour is formed by the north coast of the three-headed Crozon Peninsula, very scenic with dramatic cliffs holding colonies of breeding seabirds, **Razorbill, Guillemot** and **Red-billed Chough** and with the potential for attracting rare migrants.

The central part of the Department of Finistère from the Crozon peninsula to the Mont d'Arrée and Huelgoat has been designated the Parc Natural Regional d'Armorique, which has visitor centres and nature reserves such as that at Venec (Brennilis) where European beavers have been reintroduced. On the uplands **Curlew, Hen** and **Montagu's Harriers breed**.

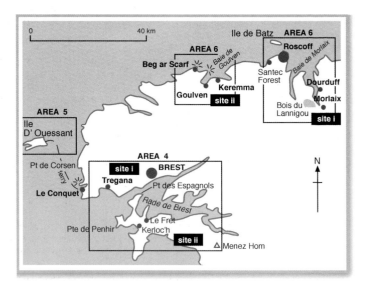

Brittany areas 4 - 6

Site i.
THE NORTH SHORE WEST OF BREST. Going west from Brest on the D789 you can turn off after about 12 km to the POINTS DU GRAND and PETIT MINOU, which look towards the narrow harbour entrance. Back on the D789 and a couple of kilometres further west turn off south at the signs for TREGANNA. Here there is a

large car park with maps and an orientation board, cliff walks, a beach and views across to the Roscanvel Peninsula. The coastal footpath GR 34 links these three viewpoints, giving a 5-6 km walk.

Continuing further west along the D789, as you reach LE CONQUET (ferry port for Île d'Ouessant area 5), the ria becomes wooded and has gull and wader roosts on its upper reaches. Turn north on the D28 and follow signs to LES BLANCS SABLONS, then take sign for Presqu'île not Plage. The parking for the beach is at FORT LOUIS. Further along this road is Pointe (or Presqu'île) de KERMORVAN. It is on the north side of the inlet and about 4 km from le Conquet by road. This can be a good seawatching site; in addition there are walks on the headland.

Continuing north from LE CONQUET along the coast road, or by turning west off the D28 at Ploumoguer, you will come to the POINTE DE CORSEN (well signed). This is the most westerly point on mainland France, with views out to Île d'Ouessant and Île Molène.

It is another seawatching point, best during migration or you can walk the coastal footpath GR34 in either direction from here. There are other headlands for seawatching further north up this stretch of coast but too often (because of reefs, the geography) birds are too far out for good views. Ouessant (see below) is so much better.

Site ii.

THE SOUTH SHORE From the south, the entrance to the Crozon peninsula is via CHÂTEAULIN on the D887 past Ménez Hom and Col du Ménez. Take a minor road, the D83, to the top of the hill for views over the peninsula and the Armorique Natural Park. The road continues to CROZON. From Brest, leave the N165 dual-carriageway at LE FAOU and take the D791 to Crozon.

North from Crozon lies the POINTE DES ESPAGNOLS overlooking Brest. The D355 coastal road circuits the peninsula. The west side has many old and current military establishments and so the coastal walks are limited. This is the most scenic road. There are however several lay-bys with bushes which are suitable for migrants in spring and autumn particularly and for views over the bay. Best to view early and late in the day. At the Pointe itself is a fortified headland with blackthorn and gorse scrub, which is a good seawatching point. On the east side of the peninsula, there are two small saltmarshes at Quélern and le Fret which could hold waders, duck and gulls at high tide. Be careful when using a telescope or binoculars in this area as l'Île Longue is a nuclear submarine base and the gendarmes are very wary of people with 'scopes and binoculars. 5 km along the D355 from Crozon turn right for LE FRET. The Étang du Fret is a lake that is protected from the sea by a shingle bar now holding the road. There is parking at the north end and footpaths around the area. The paths are board-walked in parts.

Take the D8 west from Crozon for some 6 km to KERLOC'H, a large reed-filled lake that is blocked from the sea by a sand shingle bar that carries the road. There is parking here for the beach and the Customs footpath but the views over the lake are only of the reeds.

The open water can be seen most easily by accessing the footpath, which uses the old railway line. This is the Circuit entre Deux Mers and is waymarked in yellow. You can reach the footpath from near Crozon to follow the whole track or from the Chapel de St. Philibert (turn off the D8 at a stone crucifix - parking is limited here) or by navigating to the north side of the path to Perros. Park and cross the old bridge and walk right to path above the old railway line which has distant views of the clear water. The old railway cutting is a sheltered walk and should be good for migrants in autumn and spring. *Other fauna*: This is a good area for butterflies: Marbled White, Glanville

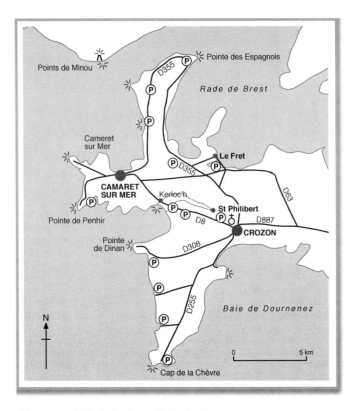

Brittany area 4 site ii The Crozon Peninsula

Fritillary, Small Heath, etc. and many species of dragonfly have been recorded at Kerloc'h though access to the actual water is difficult.

Accommodation: Brest is a modern city, with a local airport, also with flights to the islands from Guipavas airport. It is also served by TGV from Paris. There are many hotels in all price ranges. Away from the city, there are Logis de France at Crozon, e Fret, le Faou and, on the north shore, Plougonvelin.

Area 5. ÎLE D'OUESSANT

Île d'Ouessant (or Ushant in English) is the most westerly island in France, situated between the Atlantic and the Channel. It is the "Mecca" of French birdwatching and France's equivalent of the Isles of Scilly as far as Nearctic and eastern migrants are concerned and the French consider that it may even have the edge over the Scillies! Since 1984, it has been France's only permanent coastal bird observatory for studying migration. In addition to its interest during migration periods, it also has good seabird colonies: **Fulmar, Storm Petrel, Manx Shearwater, Shag, Great** and **Lesser**

Black-backed Gull, and **Chough** as well as excellent seawatching with an often spectacular passage of **shearwaters** (5-6 species) in autumn, as well as good numbers of **petrels, Gannets, skuas** and other seabirds.

The island was once heavily populated and intensively farmed but the central fields are slowly returning to wet scrub with some grazing land. There are coastal paths around the island and it is criss-crossed by many lanes to allow access to the four peninsulas on this almost rhomboid island.

Brittany area 5 Île d'Ouessant

ACCESS: Daily ferries: Penn ar Bed Maritime Co.   Tel: 02 98 80 80 80 from BREST leaves at 08.30 from the Port du Commerce. 2 1/2 hour crossing.

Pen ar Bed Maritime Co. from LE CONQUET leaves at 09.45 approx and. costs €28-29 (all prices are approximate).

Return ferry for LE CONQUET and BREST leaves daily at 17.00 h and on Sundays at 19.00.   In summer there are also ferries from CAMARET south of BREST on the Crozon peninsula. Cost €24 Tel: 02 98 27 88 22

Reservations necessary at all ports. Check in 30 minutes before departure. Booking can also be made at any Tourist Office in the west.

Flights: Finist'Air - Aeroport de Brest - Guipavas - 29490 Tel: 02 98 27 88 22 Fax: 02 98 84 64 60

Daily at 08.30 and 16.45. Duration 15 mins. Cost €55 each way. Reservations necessary. You only pay for your ticket on departure (Visa taken). Cost is for 1 - 2 persons, reductions for groups of 3 or more booking together. Tax included. Check-in

30 minutes before departure. Return at 09.00 and 17.15. Reservations necessary. No check-in on Ouessant; just turn up and wait for the incoming flight at the Reception Hall. Pay for your return flight on arrival back at Guipavas.

Finist'Air has its own terminal there, which is the white hangar to your right as you face the main arrivals hall from the car park (There is a charge for parking - Visa accepted).

Maps: Available from the newspaper shop in Lampaul, Tourist Office and ferry company. A more detailed birding map with coloured circles marking good breeding and migrant spots is available from the Bird Observatory (open daily) and from the Park Office (open daily in the summer, restricted hours in the autumn).

All the villages, hamlets and houses are marked with name boards/wooden signs with black lettering to help your orientation.

Information Boards: In autumn a "birds recorded" list is posted daily at the Bird Observatory inside the porch near reception, and in the National Park Office in Lampaul, which you can find below the church on the corner of the road leading to the airport. However, the names of rare migrants are in French only or just initials (PGS is Yellow-browed Warbler, for instance). However, most birders speak some English but it is worth checking the scientific name to avoid confusion.

Bicycle Hire: If you are considering hiring a bicycle there are at least three companies offering them based at Port de Stiff and at Lampaul, the main town. They will transport your luggage to your accommodation for you and pick it up on your return.

You can hire by the hour, half or full day, or longer.

Warning: Please bear in mind that for your personal safety and to prevent damage to the cliff paths you are forbidden to cycle on the coastal path/ Sentier Côtier by the Park regulations.

Taxis And Minibuses: These meet the ferries and usually the flights. Telephone numbers available at the airport if they do not arrive. Do not forget your telephone card.

What To Bring: There are at least three supermarkets, a baker's and two butcher/delicatessen's in Lampaul, if you are staying at the Observatory (see below) or self-catering. Meals are available at the two Crêperies in the summer but only bars and hotels offer food in the autumn. Rubber boots are worn by all the birders and can be very useful. A torch can also be useful as there is little street lighting.

WHEN TO VISIT: Ouessant is of interest at every season but obviously late summer and autumn are the most popular periods. The spring passage is not as good as the autumn one.

In **summer** the breeding sites are in the east of the island, north and south of the PORT DU STIFF (where the ferry arrives) and the ILE DE KELLER off the north coast. If you are on a summer day trip you can walk to these areas as you have up to 6 hours between ferries. In addition to the breeding birds listed above, you should expect to see **Kittiwake, Puffin** (though numbers have declined dramatically and there are only one or two pairs on Ouessant now), **Oystercatcher, Razorbill, Guillemot, Montagu's** and **Marsh Harriers, Dartford Warbler, Stonechat, Raven**.

In **autumn** expect to see the same birds as above, many migrant passerines, seabird passage off the coast and the possibility of rarities and vagrants turning up.

Near the observatory there are several places worth checking for migrants: near the wooden windmill are bushes, willow scrub and a damp area; south of the observatory is the hamlet of COAT AR REUN where small gardens can attract migrants; at POINTE DE PERN you can watch for migrants and wintering birds such as **Snow Bunting** and **Purple Sandpiper**; the fields to the north of the observatory and around the PHARE DE CREAC'H (lighthouse) can be good for migrants and flocks of **Red-billed Chough**. In the evening it is well worth visiting the lighthouse to look for migrants and for possible **Short-eared Owl** hunting in the lights. In September and October, **Gannets, skuas, shearwaters** and **petrels** pass offshore; **Sabine's Gull** is possible.

North of the observatory is the small bay of YUSIN, which is sheltered and suitable for waders and coastal migrants feeding on seaweed: **Turnstone, American Golden Plover, Little Egret, Rock Pipit, Oystercatcher, Curlew.**

STANG MAUR is a wet, scrubby, badly-drained valley that attracts rarities. Only the correctly shod should tackle this one (wellingtons essential). It is very rough underfoot. Even the coastal path is rough. Stang Maur has attracted **Red-breasted Flycatcher, Blackpoll Warbler, Great Snipe,** and **Scarlet Tanager** amongst others, so it can be worth it. In LAMPAUL itself there is a valley running east-west that attracts migrants. It lies south of the cemetery but access is difficult. The small wood below the cemetery may also be good; Yellow-browed Warbler has been found here.

Further along the road towards the Pointe Penn ar Vilen is a small reedbed STANG KORZ. You can walk east alongside this valley to check out the area. At the hamlet turn right and in a short while check out the willows in the wet area where the road crosses the head of the valley. The birders wear wellingtons and wade into this wet area looking for migrants.

The short turf of the AIRFIELD can attract **Dotterel, Buff-breasted Sandpiper, Wheatear**, etc.

In the east of the island PENN ARLAND is the only substantial wooded valley. It is a good autumn site for small insectivorous passerines. The road runs down to the small sandy bay and harbour. There are bushes on both sides of the road and a wet trail in part of the woodlands. A sandy track runs parallel with the tarmac road so you can do a circular walk on your return.

The Cromlech on the headland east of Penn Arland is also a good area for migrants. **Dartford Warblers** nest in the gorse.

In the centre of the island are some reservoirs at Kernigan around which there can be migrants and the wet, scrubby valley at STAR AR MARDY.

The northern headland at ENEZ KADORAN (or Pointe de Cadoran) is also a good area for migrants, as well as breeding seabird colonies in summer.

PORZ DOUN, the furthest south-west point on the island, is a good site for waders.

Seawatching can be good from CREAC'H headland, especially in September and October when there is a good passage of seabirds. It is more sheltered near the lighthouse.

PENN headland south of Porz Cuvet and PENN AR ROC'H due south of Lampaul are recommended sites but offer no shelter. At ENEZ KADORAN in the north there is also seawatching on the cliffs looking for west-bound migrants.

Other fauna: Both Common or Harbour Seals Phoca vitulina and the much rarer Grey Seals Halichoerus grypus can be seen from the island.

Accommodation: There are a few small hotels, a campsite, self-catering cottages, Chambres d'Hôtes (B & B). For all of these contact the Tourist Office, Place de l'Eglise, 29242 Ouessant. Tel: 02 98 48 85 83. e-mail: otouessant@ aol.com. The Hotel Roc'h ar Mor at Lampaul Tel: 02 98 48 80 19 has been recommended (rooms €48 - 75). Closed January and end November. Reservations for all accommodation is necessary at all seasons

There is also accommodation at the Observatory, which is called the Centre d'Étude du Milieu (CEMO) 29242 Ouessant. Tel: 02 98 48 82 65 Fax: 02 98 48 87 39

It is in the west about 1 km from Lampaul and offers communal kitchen, washrooms and showers and 4-bedded rooms or larger dormitories. Linen is available to hire or bring a sheet sleeping bag. Down sleeping bags are not necessary as the building is well heated.

There is an international clientele and it is a friendly place to stay if you are interested in searching for migrants in spring and autumn.

Area 6. **ROSCOFF/MORLAIX**

MORLAIX and **CARENTEC BAYS** lie south-east of the Port of Roscoff, and north of Morlaix. Both are important for wintering waterbirds as well as for some large tern colonies. Thousands of **Brent Geese, Oystercatchers, Dunlin** and **Turnstone** winter there, while **Sandwich, Common** and **Roseate Terns** all breed, as well as **Shag, Cormorant, Little Egret,** several pars of **Red-billed Chough** and **Storm Petrel**. Thousands Of **Black-headed Gulls** winter in the bay and there are breeding colonies of **Lesser** and Great **Black-backed Gulls**.

Both estuary and bay have mudflats, sand and shingle beaches, rocky cliffs and small islands. It is a vast area and quite difficult to access. Indeed landing on the breeding bird granite islets scattered throughout the bay is forbidden from April to August.

ACCESS: At DOURDUFF, on the south-east side of Morlaix Bay there is a hide overlooking the river, which is signposted from the D76. A rising tide is essential to get the best from the visit. It can be a good site for **Roseate Terns** in late summer.

The D73 running north from Morlaix gives several views over the west bank of the estuary, especially north of the village of LOCQUÉNOLÉ. At CARANTEC turn right to the lighthouse and headland at POINTE DE PEN-AL-LANN for good views across the bay. To the north of the Carantec peninsula, between the two estuaries, is ÎLE CALLOT, made up of granite linked by dunes. The northern part is the wildest with its sandy creeks and rocky headlands. It takes about 2 hours to walk round and is accessible from the Grève Blanche port by car for 2-3 hours at low tide. **WARNING:** Check the tides carefully as the road is submerged at high tide. There are many views over the bay and its birds.

At ST. P-DE-LÉON on the west side of the bay there are views from ROCHER STE. ANNE

Site ii.

GOULVEN BAY, some 25 km west of Roscoff, is a large north-facing bay with two "arms": Goulven Bay to the west and Kernic Bay to the east, separated by the Keremma sand dunes, a Reserve managed by the Conservatoire du Littoral. The site is best known for the thousands of waders that it holds on passage and in winter, notably Ringed Plover, Sanderling, Bar-tailed Godwit, Redshank, Turnstone, Dunlin and Lapwing but there may also be Purple Sandpiper, Knot, Sanderling, Spotted Redshank, Kentish Plover and many other species. Beg ar Scarf headland north-west of the bay can be good both for migrating passerines and seawatching in autumn.

WHEN TO VISIT: Autumn is best for migrant passerines, waders and seawatching, though the spring passage can also be good. In winter there are duck (Wigeon, Shoveler, Teal, Shelduck, Goldeneye) besides overwintering waders. Birds are seen best during the hour or so before a good high tide.

ACCESS: The bay lies west from PLOUESCAT, through Goulven and past Plounéour-Trèz to Beg ar Scaf headland (not named on Michelin maps). There are several parking and access areas working west starting with

KEREMMA DUNES. There is a carpark and Information Centre at KEREMMA signed from the D10 coast road. The Maison des Dunes is only open during July and August, when there are activities and guided walks.

From here it is possible to take walks through the dune area to the sea and along the old railway line through saltmarsh and fields to LA DIGUE.

Working west to Goulven on the south side of the bay there are a series of car parks. LEZ AR MAR Watch out for the white posts with red bands near the top near a sandy coloured building with a sign   Lez ar Mar. Turn up the dirt track to park.

LA DIGUE You can also park at La Digue and walk along the embankment over-looking the bay and the reed-filled étang. You need to be here at low tide for the mudflats to be exposed.

GOULVEN VIEWPOINT   Another good parking place is at the old railway station car park. Turn off the Goulven bypass opposite the sign to La Crêperie du Goulven. There is a good view from an old concrete platform just past the Reserve sign (a good place to scope from). From here you can walk back to La Digue, which is recommended on a low to rising tide to see the salt-flats, or onwards towards the head of the bay.   Timing here is important. The birds are driven into the area on the rising tide. Plan your visit to watch from mid to a good high tide. Tide tables Horaire de Mer are available from any Maison de la Presse (newsagents), in the local paper and on boards in ports.

At the HEAD OF THE BAY there is parking space in a lay-by on the west side of the

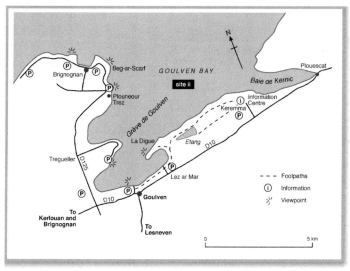

Brittany area 6 Site ii Goulven Bay

D125. This is the wrong side of the road for the bay and offers no cover but this area has waders, geese, duck and terns roosting at high tide.

POINTE ORNITHOLOGIQUE   The best viewpoint for a high tide roost is at TRÉGUELLER, signposted Pointe Ornithologique. Take the first right from the D125 and drive right down to the sea below the small farm and watch from the car to prevent disturbance. There is a tarmac road and rough circular turn round at the beach but parking is a problem. Wait patiently at very high tides for the birds to assemble and be pushed off other areas into this part of the bay. On lower tides it is less spectacular. Dog walkers can also disturb the birds.

Further along the road going north through PLOUNÉOUR-TRÈZ, follow the signs to the beaches- Plages. There are many parking points and views over the bay. At high tide check the rocks in the bay for roosts.

FOOTBALL CLUB CAR PARK near Lidivic beach. Opposite the Football Club there is a large car park. Walk over the dunes to the sea. At high tide there are many rocks offshore which act as roost points. At low tide there can be waders feeding on the sands.

BEG AR SCARF HEAD (see site below). Take the minor road through Soulougan to reach this headland, where there may be large numbers of passerines during autumn migration and is also a good seawatching point at this period when westerlies blow in from the Atlantic.

Site iii.
The best SEAWATCHING in this area is from the newish sémaphore (signal station) at BRIGNOGAN. Post-nuptial passage is the most remarkable, from the last week in August to the middle of September. Terns (4/5 species), skuas (4 species) and shearwaters (4/5 species) are the most numerous but 30-40 different species may be seen. Sabine's Gull is regular in reasonable numbers.

The lighthouse on the nearby headland to the west, the Pointe de Pontusval, is another possible site as is the Beg ar Scarf headland (see above) but neither have proved as good as the signal station site.

ACCESS: The new sémaphore is situated at the most northerly point of the commune,

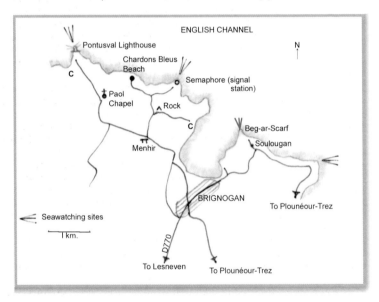

Brittany Area 6 Site iii Brignogan Seawatching Site

about 2 km from Brignogan and a few hundred metres east of the Paol chapel and a large menhir, well signed from the centre of the town. Large boulders below the station shelter observers from the wind.

To the east of Brignogan, the **ÎLE DE BATZ**, 2 km north of Roscoff, is another seawatching spot, especially for skuas on passage, but it is less convenient than mainland sites and not easy to find a good viewpoint once there. The north-west coast of the island is the best for seawatching.

ACCESS: Boats (Armein, vedettes de l'Île de Batz Tel: 02 98 61 77 75) leave from the outer harbour in Roscoff with alternative low and high tide departure points. The crossing takes about 15 minutes, currently costs 6€ and there are regular sailings about once an hour. Tickets available on boats. There is a 34 room hotel on Batz, the Grand Hôtel Morvan, Port Kernoc, 29253, open from 1/02 to 30/11

Flora: The Keremma reserve has a good dune flora including sheets of Pyramidal Orchids in June and Batz has an exotic tropical garden.

Area 7. **SEPT-ÎLES RESERVE and ÎLE GRANDE**

The *Réserve naturelle des Sept-Îles lies* several kilometres north of the coast, between Perros-Guirec and Trégastel. The archipelago comprises five islands: Île aux Moines (10 ha), Bono (21 ha), Malban (1 ha), Rouzic (3 ha), Plate (5 ha) and numerous smaller islets and rock stacks, all of interest for their breeding seabirds; the Reserve forms the largest seabird colony in France. 27 species nest throughout the islands, 13 of them seabirds including **Storm Petrel, Manx Shearwater, Puffin, Gannet, Shag, Razorbill, Fulmar, Great** and **Lesser Black-backed Gulls, Kittiwake** and **Herring Gull**. This group of rocky islets has been a protected natural site since 1912. Thanks to the LPO, then only six months old, it became the first bird reserve in France, and was made a Nature Reserve in 1976. It is still managed by the LPO.

WHEN TO VISIT: The best time is spring to late July, although Gannets remain at their colony until early autumn and there are waders in winter. Birders and photographers will find morning boat trips better for good sightings and light.

ACCESS: Landing is only allowed on the Île aux Moines, where **Rock Pipit** and **Shelduck** breed but from the old fort birds on Île Plate can be scoped. The **Gannet** colony is on Île Rouzic and has over 15,000 pairs; Shags nest on Malban and most **Puffins** (some 250 pairs breed on the Reserve) can be seen around Rouzic, Malban and Bono. The only way to see the birds close up is to book a tour with the passenger boats that organise excursions around the archipelago. Commentaries are available in French, English and German. There are a variety of tours lasting from 1-11/2 to 3-31/2 hours from a variety of embarkation points. Not all the tours land. Departure times depend on daily tides.

The boat companies have a Joint Reservation Centre which is open all year round. Tel: 02 96 91 10 00. Telephone to make a reservation and then check-in 20 minutes before departure to pay for your trip. When you make a reservation ask for confirmation of your embarkation point as there are five. These are:

1) Gare Maritime de Trestraou, Perros-Guirec to the left of the beach, just beyond the sailing school.

2) Ploumanac'h to the right of the port at the end of the cul-de-sac.

3) Port de Perros-Guirec to the left of the port (red marking). Reception at 74 Rue Ernest Renan.

4) Trégastel to the right of the Forum de la Mer.

5) Port Blanc from the fishing slipway.

The boat company Les 7 Îles en Vedettes from Gare Maritime de Trestraou, Perros-Guirec are partners with the LPO and part of the boat fee goes to the local association. Tel: 02 96 91 29 60 or the Joint Reservation Centre as above.

Services run from March to November and in school holidays.

Group bookings are available throughout the year by booking in advance.

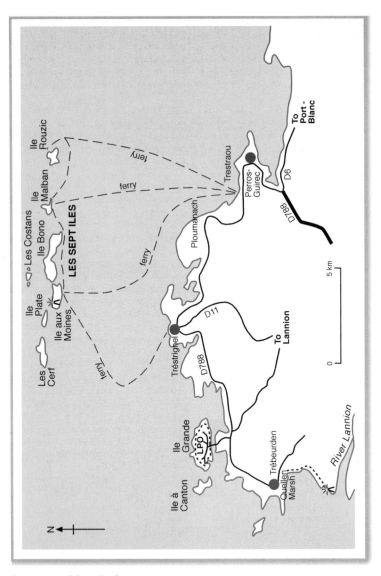

Brittany area 7 Sept- Iles Reserve

ÎLE GRANDE is an island linked by road to the D788 6 km south-west of TRÉGASTEL. It has a centre set up by the LPO to deal with oiled and injured birds, with a video link to the Réserve Naturelle des Sept Îles showing the Gannet colony. The modern centre is attractive and well laid-out with a display of model birds to be seen on Les Sept Îles, a touch board for birdcalls and information displays about bird migration. There is a small shop and bird leaflets but it is not a Nature Reserve.

Outside the centre there are seabirds off the rocks and on the mud flats including **Oystercatcher, Curlew, Turnstone, Redshank, Great Ringed Plover, Whimbrel, Sandwich** and **Common Terns, Shelduck, Gannet** and **Little Egret**, best seen from the bridge. Whitethroat, **Dartford Warbler, Sparrowhawk, Kestrel** may be seen on the heathland. The nearby CANTON ISLAND is reported to be good to visit at low tide, when it is possible to walk across to it. The same bird species are likely to be seen there.

Further south on the D788 is **QUELLEN MARSH**, which may be worth visiting when in the area. It lies some 15 km south-west of Perros-Guirec, on the outskirts of TRÉBEURDEN, behind Goaz-Trez beach (not marked on Michelin maps), where there are two car parks. The marsh has a map board and a waymarked circular 1.5 km trail around the edge of the marsh. There is an open decking style hide near the first car park, then the trail leads through woodland and on board walks with interesting plants and plenty of woodland birds. The area is grazed by Camargue horses to maintain its diversity. The trail emerges out to a road. Turn left and follow it back to the shore, passing a second screen hide overlooking the reed-filled marsh on the right, which has **Reed** and **Sedge Warblers** in summer, **Teal** in winter.

Other fauna: Grey and Common Seal may be seen throughout the year around the Sept Îles Reserve.

Accommodation: There is a variety of hotels and campsites around the Perros-Guirec and Trégastel areas.

Area 8. ST. MALO/ DINARD

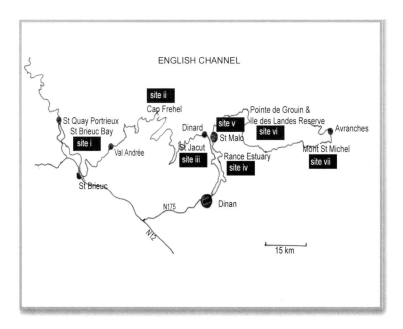

Brittany area 8 Sites i - vii

ST. BRIEUC BAY regularly holds 20,000 or more waterbirds in winter, including thousands of **Brent Geese, Oystercatchers** and **Dunlin** and hundreds of **Pintail** and **Bar-tailed Godwit** as well as **Curlew, Knot, Little Egret, Redshank** and many more species on passage.

WHEN TO VISIT: This is mainly of interest in winter but like other nearby sites can also be good during spring and autumn migration periods. The Information Centre just north of HILLION, is the *Maison de la Baie de Saint Brieuc, Site de l'étoile, 22120 Hillion.* Tel: 02 96 32 27 98, Fax 0296323028 maisondelabaie@wanadoo.fr which organises activities and birdwatching trips. There is parking and views over YFFINIAC COVE *(Anse d'Yffiniac) at all times.*

ACCESS: St. Brieuc Bay is huge and there is limited access although the coastal footpath GR 34 runs around most of the bay. The area extends from le Val-André in the east to St. Quay-Portrieux at the north-west. Starting on the east coast there are the following viewpoints:

POINT DE PLÉNEUF is a limestone headland at the north end of le VAL-ANDRÉ from where there are views across to the ÎLOT DU VERDELET, where there are breeding seabirds, including Cormorant which is rare on this coast. Access is from the coastal footpath GR34 or from the Parking in le Val-André.

Some 12 km south of le Val-André is the GOUESSANT ESTUARY and the MORIEUX CLIFFS. The narrow winding estuary of the River Gouessant is very attractive. **Shelduck** breed in the area and you can find crèches in season. There are wader roosts at ST. MAURICE and BÉLIARD at high tide. Access via local footpaths and the GR34. The D34 west from Morieux to Hillion crosses the river and a good footpath runs along the west bank from here to the rivermouth.

The POINTE DES GUETTES, North of Lermot, is a good seawatching viewpoint for **sea duck, auks, terns** and **skuas**. Best at incoming and high tides.

In the south of the bay, YFFINIAC COVE a nature reserve, is one of the top five bays in the world for extremes of tide and a very important wintering site for waterbirds. There are views over it from HILLION and from the GR34, especially walking south to Pisse-Oison. Best at high tide as the sea can go out for seven kilometres.

On the west side of the bay, north of St. Brieuc, the headland of POINTE DU ROSELIER lies north of the cove. This is an interesting vantage point over the northern end of St. Brieuc Bay. Follow signs on the D36 from the St. Brieuc bypass.

Further along the coast, which runs in a north-westerly direction north of the Roselier headland. At Les Rosaires is an important shingle bank with pebbles, dunes and dune plants, the ROSAIRES SHINGLE BANK *Cordon de Galets des Rosaires*. It can be good for passage migrants.

The next stretch of coast going north-west has the longest cliffs in Brittany, 104 km in all. At FALAISE DE PLOUHA these cliffs are sheltered from the westerly winds, permitting the growth of dense thickets of blackthorn which can be full of passerines on passage as well as breeding residents. Nesting seabirds include **Shag, Fulmar** and **Raven**.

Other fauna and flora: The dunes at *Bon-Abri*, on the coast of the Anse de Morieux between La Granville and Hillion, have very interesting flora, including Bee Orchid, Southern Marsh Orchid, Autumn Lady's Tresses. The marshy areas hold 8 species of cmphibian and there are otter in the River Gouessant.

Accommodation: Hotels and campsites at Val André, St. Brieuc, St. Quay-Portrieux, Plouha.

Site ii.

CAP FRÉHEL is Brittany's Land's End. Currently footpaths are wired off for the recolonisation programme to repair the cliff-top vegetation. There is a large car and coach park (charge 2€) and WC (charge 40 cents). It is nevertheless a Reserve managed by the SEPNB and an IBA for breeding seabirds, especially for hundreds of pairs of **Shag**. Other species likely to be seen include breeding **Herring** and **Great Black-backed Gulls, Kittiwake, Fulmar, Guillemot, Gannet, Razorbill, Rock Dove** (possibly genuine), **Oystercatcher, Linnet, Meadow and Rock Pipits, Black Redstart, Cetti's Warbler, Raven**.

ACCESS: The headland is reached from SABLES-D'OR-LES PINS by taking the coastal road, the D34A in a north-easterly direction. This is a scenic road running through open maritime heath with isolated willow scrub areas. Off-shore there are rock stacks and the cliffs are red sandstone. The seabirds can be seen best from the café area in the east at the TEIGNOUSE headland. The cliffs cannot be seen from the lighthouse. There is another viewing area to the west at the JAS headland. Offshore to the west are two rocky islets Amas du Cap and La Fauconnière which also hold breeding seabirds. There are walks and footpaths GR34 along the coast and all over the heathland.

WHEN TO VISIT: In late spring and summer for the breeding seabirds, which are close although the colonies are small. In autumn for the seawatching.

Other fauna and flora: Large Marsh Grasshopper, Sea Campion, Bluebell, Wall Pennywort, Thrift, Red Campion, Autumn Squill, Kerry Lily, Guernsey Centuary *Exaculum pusillum*, Solomon's Seal, *Dianthus* sp., *Ophioglossum azoricum* fern.

CAP D'ERQUY, the most westerly point of the headland lying between Sable-d'Or-les Pins and Erquy, is also of interest if you prefer a quieter spot. The pink sandstone cliffs run for 3.5 km along the coast and the area covers 170 ha. Long distance GR34 and local footpaths cross the headland. Take the road running north-west out of Erquy, signed to the headland.

There are several types of moorland with interesting heathland flora as well as good birdlife. Look for **Dartford Warbler, Black Redstart** and **Nightjar** on the heathland and seabirds as above offshore.

Other fauna and flora: Green Lizard. All four species of heather are here, and gentians including Marsh Gentian, Burnet Rose, Rockrose.

Accommodation: Hotels and camping nearby at les Pins and Erquy.

Site iii.

BEAUSSAIS and **LANCIEUX BAYS**, which are also good for passage waders and wintering waterbirds, can be accessed from St. JACUT-de-la-Mer, some 15 km south-west of Dinard. Species include **Bar-tailed Godwit, Great Ringed Plover, Little Egret, Brent Goose**, and **Shelduck**.

ACCESS: Turn off the D786 signed to St. Jacut. Almost immediately there is a lay-by with close views over the Baie de Lancieux. High tide and plus

Savis Warbler

or minus one hour are necessary for good views of birds. The east side of the bay has old polders and dykes around Lancieux and Ploubalay. The GR34 passes through.

North of St. Jacut is the POINTE DU CHEVET, sticking out into the bay. Follow the signs at the beginning of St. Jacut and park at the entrance to the one-way system on left or at the headland itself if it is quiet. There are views over the Île des Hébihens (Ebihens) and is probably best early morning or late in the afternoon. There will be disturbance in the holiday season. Rock Pipit and Cirl Bunting may be found on the headland and Common Tern out to sea.

Site iv.

RANCE ESTUARY Between the ports of Dinard and St. Malo lies the deep inlet of the Rance Estuary, which has a tidal power station. It stretches down to Dinan in the south and some of the best birdwatching areas are on the west and east banks deep in the estuary, which attracts wintering duck and grebes and waders on passage. These include **Goosander, Smew** and **Red-breasted Merganser**. Other species likely to be seen include **Pochard, Teal, Tufted Duck, Goldeneye, Great Crested, Little** and **Black-necked Grebes, Kingfisher, Cetti's Warbler**. In summer there are also **Reed** and **Sedge Warblers**.

Two viewpoints that are easily accessible, Taden in the extreme south-west of the estuary and the Souleac/Jouan inlet on the east shore, are described below. A telescope is very helpful.

WHEN TO VISIT: Taden is best in winter. The inlet is good both in winter and during passage.

ACCESS: In the far south of the estuary is TADEN, just north of DINAN. It is reached by taking the D766 or the D12 north from the centre of Dinan or by turning off the D176 dual-carriageway by-pass. Turn off at the Taden junction, confusingly signed in different places as either D766 or D166. Zero at the D12A junction and follow the signs to TADEN for 1.5 km. Go straight through the village and bear right signed to Plaine de Taden. At the next junction turn left and shortly afterwards bear right by the church down to the river the river (signed), where there is parking, picnic tables and WCs, 3 km from the D12A junction. The towpath runs in both directions and a 14 km round walk to Dinan is signed for the energetic. The river is wide here, with a belt of shallow fresh water, which is protected from shooting in winter and attracts wintering duck, and in cold spells may include many of the species listed above.

Some 7 km south of St. Malo on the east side of the estuary a minor road runs round an inlet from St. JOUAN-des-GUERETS south to St. SULIAC, parallel to the dual-carriageway N137. Driving north towards St. Malo turn off the D137 either at the Châteauneuf junction onto the D7 following signs to St. Suliac for 4.5 km or (easier) keep on the N137 for another 2 km and turn off onto the D117 keeping left at the junction signed to St. Souliac. In 1.5 km the D117 crosses the narrow south end of the inlet. Just before this on the right is a picnic spot under poplar trees, where you can park in a lay-by, beside a minor road to the right signed Vallée del la Rance. Explore this road later but first walk down to the bridge crossing the tributary running into the inlet. There are good views just before the bridge. There are also views over the main estuary from St. Suliac. Drive straight through the village down to the marina.

Return to the Vallée de la Rance road which runs alongside the inlet for some 2 km before joining the D117. It is intended for walkers and cyclists, so take care if driving. There are plenty of places to stop and scan and some footpaths lead down to the waters edge. Take the D117 north (left). There are good views over the estuary from the roadside near the ruined mill, Moulin du Beauchet and this area is also good for reedbed and scrub birds. Follow the D117 as far as St. Jouan-des-Guérets. North and west of

St. Jouan there are other roads leading to viewpoints over the estuary but the mill area is probably the best.

Driving south from St. Malo on the N137 take the turning signed Vallée de la Rance just south of St. Jouan, which loads to the ruined mill viewpoint and roadside views over the estuary. Follow the above directions in reverse order.

Site v.

In **ST MALO** itself, the intra-muros city is worth a walk round if you arrive at high tide. Park at St. Vio quay. Pass through the main gate and take the stairs up to the ramparts and walk round the walls clockwise. There can be wader roosts on the rocks and islets at high tide; at low tide there is a huge expanse of beach, mud-flats and islets.

Just north-east of St. Malo is the POINTE DE LA VARDE. From the port, follow signs to Paramé D301, then east to the Pointe, where there are 10 hectares of headlands of cliff, dunes and heath where **Dartford Warbler, Black Redstart, Stonechat, Rock Pipit** and **Serin** may all be found. The area around the ruined fort is fenced and attracts breeding birds as well as migrants due to the lack of disturbance. There are panoramic views back over the Rance estuary, St. Malo Bay and   the Côte d'Emeraude

There are interesting birding spots off the coastal road D201 all the way along the rocky coast from POINTE DE LA VARDE to the POINTE DU GROUIN

Site vi.

POINTE DU GROUIN and **ÎLES DES LANDES.** GROUIN HEADLAND is very dramatic with gorse-covered cliffs overlooking the 21 hectare islands of LES LANDES, which are one of the SEPNB's oldest bird sanctuaries. Breeding birds include **Cormorant, Shag, Herring and Great Black-backed Gulls, Shelduck, Oystercatcher, Dartford Warbler, Whitethroat, Linnet.**

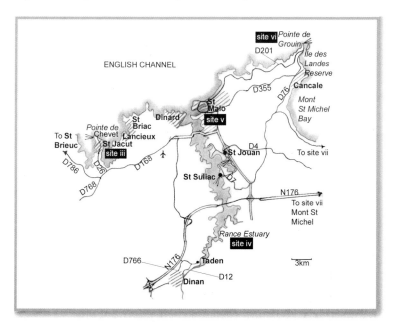

Brittany area 8 Enlargement of sites iii-vi   The Rance Estuary

ACCESS: Take the coastal road D201 north-east from ST. MALO or the same road north from CANCALE following signs to the Pointe du Grouin. The D201 from St. Malo is a very scenic road with many small headlands and a good beach at ANSE DU VERGER, where there is parking. Beyond the car park there is a marsh with reeds and clear water. It is probably best early in the morning before disturbance, or early evening when the beach visitors have departed. Birds include **Cetti's, Reed** and **Sedge Warblers** and the possibility of many more species during passage.

Site vii.

The polders and saltmarsh on the WEST SIDE OF THE BAY AT MONT ST. MICHEL stretch over the border into Brittany. The whole area is described in detail below (Normandy and the Channel Coast Area 1) but although the better birding sites are further east, the stretch of coastline around Ste. Anne's Chapel in Brittany can be interesting, especially during spring and autumn passage for waders, and in winter when there are **Scoters** on the sea, **Shelduck, White-fronted** and other **Geese, Short-eared Owl, Peregrine, Merlin, Marsh** and **Hen Harriers** hunting over the meadows where small flocks of **pipits** and **larks** (and sometimes a few **Lapland Longspur**) feed together with large numbers of **Lapwing** and **Golden Plover**. The coastal GR footpath 34 runs through the polders from Normandy and along the coast at St. Anne's and is worth walking especially in autumn and winter. As with all such coastal sites, it is important to time your visit for high or rising tides as at low tide all the birds in the bay are too far away to be observed, even with a telescope. It is very dangerous to walk out onto the mud-flats. They are treacherous and the tide comes in very fast.

ACCESS: From DOL-de-Bretagne or CANCALE, turn off the D155 at LE VIVIER-sur-Mer onto the D979. Check the pools and salt marsh along this short section. Turn of this road onto the D82 coast road in just under 4 km at CHERRUEIX, signed to Chapelle de Ste. Anne. There are two parking places. The first before the chapel enables you to get onto the embankment to scan the bay (only worth doing at high tide). Park beside the chapel to walk along the embankment and the GR34 for views over the saltmarshes and fields.

Accommodation: See under Normandy Area 1.

NORMANDY AND
THE CHANNEL COAST

Area 1   Mont St. Michel
Site i.   West side of Mont St. Michel bay
Site ii.   Mont St. Michel and east side of Bay *
Site iii.   East side of bay near Genêts *
Site iv.   Carolles cliffs *
Site v.   Pointe d'Argon and the Sienne estuary

Area 2   Cherbourg
Site i.   Vauville Reserve *
Site ii.   Cap de la Hague Seawatching Sites (S)

Area 3   St. Vaast-la-Hougue
Site i.   St Vaast Harbour *
Site ii.   Pointe de Saire *
Site iii.   Pointe de Barfleur (S)

Area 4   Cotentin Marshes Regional Nature Park
Site i.   Les Ponts d'Ouve Reserve *
Site ii.   Domaine de Beaugillot Ornithological
                   Reserve *
Site iii.   Pointe de Brévands, Veys Bay
Site iv.   Havre de St. Germain-sur-Ay
Site v.   The Mathon Peat Bog and Heathland
                   south of Lessay

Area 5   Pointe du Hoc *

Area 6.   Cerisy Forest, near Bayeux *

Area 7   Caen
Site i.   Orne Estuary Reserve *
Site ii.   Orne Estuary Dunes

Area 8   Le Havre
Site i.   Seine Estuary-Pont de Normandie *
Site ii.   Mannevilles Reserve *
Site iii.   Brotonne Forest *
Site iv.   Londe Forest *
Site v.   Seawatching sites north of Le Havre (S)

Area 9   Rouen
Site i.   Reserve de Grande Noë *
Site ii.   Les Andelys

Area 10 Dieppe to Somme Estuary

Site i.	Le Tréport and Ault (S)
Site ii.	Ponts-et-Marais Peat-bog in Bresle Valley
Site iii.	Hautebut Marsh and Hâble d'Ault Reserve*
Site iv.	Hourdel point
Site v.	Marquenterre Bird Park and Reserve *
Site vi.	Bay and marshes near Le Crotoy *
Site vii	Authie Bay *
Site viii	Crécy Forest *

Area 11 Le Touquet to Bologne

Site i.	Canche Bay Reserve *
Site ii	Hesdin Forest
Site ii.	Saint-Frieux and Hardelot
Site iv.	Portel beach
Site v.	Boulogne-sur-Mer Fishing Port
Site vi.	Boulogne Forest

Area 12 Cap Gris-Nez and Cap Blanc-Nez (S) *

Area 13 Calais

Site i.	Le Platier d'Oye Reserve *
Site ii.	Guînes Marsh

Area 14 Dunkerque (S)

Site i.	Clipon jetty (S) *
Site ii.	Digue du Braeck and Port - Est (S)
Site iii.	Avant-Port Ouest

Area 15 St. Omer   Romelaere Reserve *

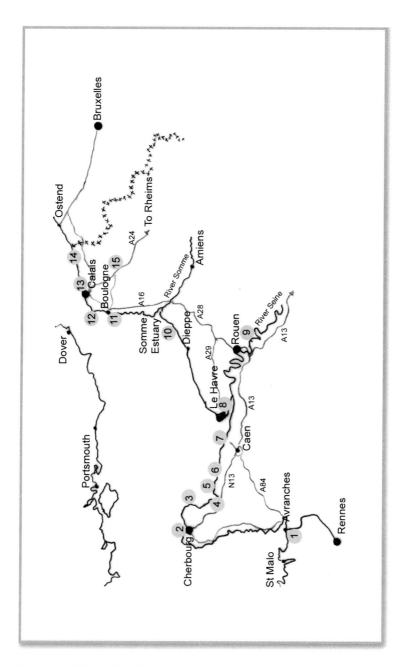

Normandy and ChannelCoast birding areas

NORMANDY, a beautiful, historic region of France and an understandably popular tourist destination, also has much to offer the visiting birdwatcher. Most of the sites described are coastal but they range from headlands for seawatching and cliffs with breeding seabird colonies to estuaries and river mouths with vast mud-flats as well as marshes, both salt and freshwater. Inland there are forest and heathland sites, lakes and river valleys to be explored.

The cliffs and estuaries continue north through Basse-Normandie into Picardie and Nord-Pas-de-Calais. For that reason the Channel coast sites of these last two regions are included in this section as, with very few exceptions, similar bird species will be seen on passage and wintering all along this coast, so the best months to visit applies to all of them and good seawatching conditions will also be common to all. The choice of site may depend mainly on your port of arrival or where you plan to stay in France.

The sites described below have easy access but most involve some walking. Very few French reserves consider the needs of the handicapped. Where a hide or nature trail is suitable for a wheelchair, this is stated in the description of that site. Most of the woodland sites and some of the cliff-top sites need a moderate amount of walking to find all the species listed but this is mainly on the level along good paths, though they may be muddy in spring and winter. Seawatching needs patience, water and wind-proof clothing and good eyesight - and can be addictive!

WHEN TO VISIT: Spring (March to May) and autumn (August to November) will certainly provide the longest species list as these are the best times for migrating waders and passerines, as well as being the months when an impressive passage of seabirds passes along the coast. There are still some waders, as well as plenty of duck and other wildfowl throughout the winter, and the breeding season has much of interest as several species that are not easy to see in southern Britain are all relatively easy to observe in Normandy.

For the best seawatching conditions see page 71, under The Hague area.

Maps: Blay-foldex Carte No. 2 Normandie 1cm=2.5 km. Michelin 59 and 54 1 cm = 2 km.

Area 1. **MONT ST. MICHEL**

Mont St. Michel Bay is a very large bay with islands (one the famous tourist site, another a private reserve) and extensive sand and mudflats. Surrounding the bay are saltmarshes, polders (water meadows, arable land) and some rocky cliffs. 20,000 or more waterbirds pass through on passage or winter here as well as it also being an important area for migrating passerines.

Although much of this bay is a Ramsar Site or a Special Protection Area, a great deal of shooting occurs throughout the autumn and winter, even in No-hunting areas, where the signs forbidding it are peppered with shot! Care should therefore be taken if walking on the saltmarsh during the hunting season.

Like all the sites along this coast, this is a high-tide site; it is important to arrive at the right times if large numbers of birds of different species are to be observed at reasonably close quarters. A rising tide pushes birds landwards and the hour or so just before and after high tide is best. Hotels and tourist offices should have tide tables. It can be very dangerous to walk out over the flats at low tide, as the sea comes in fast and there are dangerous currents. Birdwatching should be done from the land at the sites described below.

WHEN TO VISIT: Whilst this is primarily an autumn and winter site (late August to March), there is always plenty to see in spring as quite a few species breed in the marshes or on the islands, and of interest even in summer, although tourist numbers are very high, so there is a lot of disturbance, beaches are crowded and parking anywhere difficult.

In autumn and winter, as at most times of year, **Gulls** are the most numerous species encountered, with huge roosts of **Black-headed Gulls** as well as **Herring, Lesser** and **Greater Black-backed** but there are also huge numbers of waders, duck and geese. **Brent** and **Greylag Geese** are the commonest but search for other species. **Shelduck** are the most obvious wildfowl, (they also breed here) but there may also be tens of thousands of **Common Scoter** in the bay, as well as smaller numbers of **Teal** and **Wigeon** on passage or wintering. **Oystercatcher** are the most numerous wader, with up to 20,000 in winter, as well as large numbers of **Grey Plover, Knot, Dunlin, Black-tailed Godwit** (on passage) and **Bar-tailed Godwit** (in winter), **Curlew and Ringed Plover** on the mudflats. There are large flocks of **Golden Plover** and **Lapwing** in the nearby polders where raptors (**Merlin, Peregrine, Hen** and **Marsh Harriers, Short-eared Owl**) hunt. Among the flocks of pipits and larks feeding in the fields and on the saltmarsh, look for **Snow Bunting** and **Lapland Longspur**.

In spring the above wildfowl and waders will be seen on passage, as well as many other species. **Yellow Wagtails** can be numerous on passage, but they also breed on the saltmarsh, as do **Kentish** and **Little Ringed Plover, Quail, Skylark, Meadow Pipit**, and **Reed Bunting**. **Hobby** and **Hen Harrier** hunt there on passage.

May to July are the best months to watch breeding **Shelduck**. Wader post-nuptial migration begins in August. **Osprey** may stop off in September as well as some of the Dutch population of **Spoonbills**.

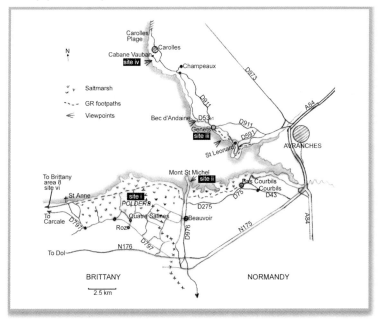

Normandy area I sites i - iv Mont St. Michel

Site i.

WEST SIDE OF MONT ST. MICHEL BAY The coast to the west of Mont St. Michel is mainly polders and saltmarsh stretching to the border with Brittany and beyond. There are footpaths along some of the dykes which give good views over the fields and saltmarsh, signed here as Les Herbus.

Beware; there is a lot of shooting on this side of the Bay, even in the dark.

ACCESS: To reach the polders north of ROZ-DE-COUESNON, leave the N175 before (if coming from the west) or (from the east) soon after the Mont St. Michel junction. Follow the Roz-de-Couesnon signs to the centre of the village, where you turn right down a narrow road signed Jardin Publique and Panorama. Go past the Public Garden and in 700 metres, after twisting down the hill from the village, this road meets the D797. Go straight across onto the C7 towards Quatre Salines. This road is signed Route de la Baie and there is a large plan of the polders at its start. In QUATRE SALINES continue straight on, following signs for Mont St. Michel par les polders. The fields here are often hunted over by harriers, Kestrel and Merlin. There can be large numbers of small birds in the fallow and stubble fields but they are difficult to spot except when they fly. Keep stopping and checking the pipit and lark flocks; there may be Lapland Longspur among them. The road finishes at the coastal footpath that runs along a dyke between the polders and the saltmarsh - Les Herbus. Short-eared Owls and Buzzards often use the bushes growing on the dyke as lookout posts, so scan along before climbing up. It also affords excellent observation over the saltmarsh for birdwatchers! Walk along the dyke towards Mont St. Michel for as long as you like.

Return to the car and retrace your route to the Y-junction before Quatre Salines. Turn east, signed Mont St. Michel. There can be large flocks of Lapwing and Golden Plover in the fields, and a few Grey Herons or Little Egrets. The polder roads can be very circuitous, or dead-end at a farm but eventually lead to the D478 and the bridge at BEAUVOIR. At the river, drive along the west bank, always towards the Mont, which is clearly visible. At 0.6 km from the bridge, at Bellevue St. Joseph, keep right. In another kilometre the road comes to a dead end, and the start of another stretch of the coastal footpath. It is possible to park here and walk in either direction for as long as you like. Mont St. Michel is 2.6 km by the footpath; St. Ann's Chapel in Brittany (see Area 8 vi.)13 km to the west marks the end of the polders.

Return to BEAUVOIR and cross the bridge, turning left (north) onto the D976 towards Mont St. Michel.

Site ii.

MONT ST. MICHEL AND THE EAST SIDE OF THE BAY The road to Mont St. Michel runs through all the hotels and restaurants and then along the causeway to the large car-park on its east side. There can be good birding from the causeway so you might prefer to walk along it, though there can be a lot of traffic in the tourist season. Alternatively, it may be worth paying for the car park, and birding from the end of it. The GR223 coastal footpath starts on the east of the causeway just after the hotel/restaurant complex and runs through an area of saltmarsh. It can be worth walking some way along it, especially at high tide. Otherwise, take the Route de la Baie marked by a schematic design of Mont and sea, the D275, which runs east from the D976 parallel to the footpath and turns into the D75. Zero at the start. In 6.2 km in the village of BAS COURTILS go straight on at the slightly staggered crossroads towards the Maison de la Baie on the D288. At the Maison (an information centre) take the C201 towards La Greve. At 7.4 km turn left to ROCHE TORIN. This is a dead-end road leading to the edge of the bay. There is a small parking place at 8.0 km and from here one can walk over the saltmarsh back towards the Mont

Site iii.

THE EAST SIDE OF THE BAY NEAR GENÊTS More extensive views over the saltmarsh and east side of the bay can be obtained from north of Avranches, between the headlands of Grouin du Sud and the Bec d'Andaine, north of Genêts village.

ACCESS: From the dual carriageway that bypasses Avranches to the west, linking the A84 motorway, leave on the first exit, the D973, signed to Cherbourg, Granville. Go straight over the roundabout and very shortly turn left (west) in the first village MARCEY-LES-GREVES onto the D911, signed Vains, Jullouville. Zero here. In 2.5 km turn left again onto the Baie road, D591, signed to ST. LEONARD. At 2.9 km turn left (signed Route de la Côte). The bay and saltmarsh can be glimpsed on the left between the houses. The footpath GR223 runs along the edge of the Bay here. Do not turn left towards St. Leonard's but continue left on the blue marked road. GROUIN DU SUD is some 7 km along this road. There is space to park and excellent views over the Bay. Continue on the Route de la Côte to GENÊTS at 11.7 km (one sign says Bacilli at one point but the next turning is again signed Genêts). There is parking beside Le Pont from where it is possible to walk out over the saltmarsh.

Having spent some time here, continue north on the D911 in the direction of JULLOUVILLE, turning left (west) at the end of Genêts onto the D35 E1 to the BEC D'ANDAINE, in 1.7 km. There is a large carpark here and footpaths lead onto the marsh in both directions. There is also a circular viewing platform on the dunes, ideal for scanning the bay with a telescope. All the birds listed for the Mont St. Michel site can be seen from here, notably very large numbers of Shelduck, Gulls, Oystercatchers and Curlews, as well as many other waders during migration periods. The grass, scrub and trees on the landward side mean that many passerine species can also be observed; there are flocks of finches, pipits and larks in winter.

Site iv.

CAROLLES CLIFFS North of Genêts the coastline becomes progressively higher and rockier. From the higher ground good views of the mudflats, as well as over the sea, can be obtained, and in addition the heathland vegetation on the cliff tops provides habitat for some different species.

WHEN TO VISIT: A site for all seasons and unusually one that is good during late summer. Breeding birds are always easiest in spring but can also be found throughout the summer. **Lesser Whitethroat, Melodious Warbler, Dartford Warbler, Stonechat** breed on the heath and the latter two species can be observed in winter as well. **Black Redstart** and **Raven** breed on the cliffs; **Hobby** hunts over the heath in summer; **Golden Oriole** and **Wood Warbler** breed in the woods.

In autumn the woods and bushes shelter migrating finches, pipits, larks and buntings, including **Ortolan**. **Common Scoter** can be numerous in the bay below (from June onwards) and are often very close to shore. There may also be **auks** on the water and in late summer, **shearwaters** can be observed flying past or on the sea.

ACCESS: From the Bec d'Andaine return to GENÊTS and the D911 and continue north along this coast road through ST. JEAN-LE-THOMAS where the road starts to climb up a wooded hill. Do not turn right into Champeaux on the D21 but continue on the D911 towards Parking de Falaises/Sol Roc. 700 metres after the D21 junction turn left to the Parking de Falaises. Take the right fork and drive down the narrow twisting steep road to the sea. **Scoters** and other waterbirds can often be very close inshore here. **Purple Sandpiper** (rare in Normandy) can be found on the rocks and there are good views of the mudflats to the south and the cliffs above.

Return to the D911 and continue north. In 3.8 km turn left towards CABAN VAUBAN just before the road sign marking the start of CAROLLES. There is a large car park 750 metres up the road. Caban Vauban (a small stone cabin) can be seen from the car park and reached in five minutes walking along the Sentier Littoral (marked). There are good views over the sea from the path and from the Caban while the gorse and scrub is habitat for warblers and other passerines, both breeding and on passage. During migration periods, also check the small oak wood beside the car park. You can continue walking past the cabin and follow the footpath north to the Lude Valley (which can also be reached from the centre of Carolles village) but the path down to Port du Lude is steep and not particularly productive.

Site v.

POINTE D'ARGON AND THE SIENNE ESTUARY Although someway north of Mont St. Michel Bay, this site can most conveniently be visited after the previous one. The mouth of the Sienne River at the Pointe d'Argon is an area of mudflats, saltmarshes, heathland, dunes and sandy beaches. It is a high-tide site, as the mudflats are so extensive that birds disperse over a huge area when the sea is out and only gulls (**Black-headed, Herring** and **Great Black backed**) and **Cormorants** will be seen. This is an important area for wintering seabirds and waders and the bird list is similar to Mont St. Michel.

ACCESS: From COUTANCES take the D20 to PONT-DE-LA-ROC, then the D650 and the D72 towards ARGON-COUTAINVILLE (the D44 also runs direct to Argon but the D650 follows the river and gives some good views over the estuary). In LA RUE D'ARGON turn left at the crossroads signed to the Pointe d'Argon. Follow the Pointe signs for 6.4 km to the headland, which is a Protected Natural Zone. There are several left turns but all are well signed. There is a view over the mussel beds but drive on for another 1.5 km past the lighthouse to the river mouth.

Accommodation: The whole area from the Brittany border up to the Sienne Estuary is a very popular tourist region and there are numerous hotels, large and small, around Avranches, Mont St. Michel, and up the coast to Coutances as well as in many small villages. There are also a great many Chambres d'hôte (B & B) at farms, especially around the Mont St. Michel area. You will see the signs while driving around

Area 2. **CHERBOURG**

Site i.

VAUVILLE RESERVE The Mare de Vauville Natural Reserve is a 2 km long freshwater lake with extensive reedbeds bounded by high dunes on the seaward side and heathland and low hills inland. The water level is variable and the lake may dry up entirely in hot summers. The Reserve protects not only birds but also an interesting dune flora and fauna. Seawatching from the dunes can be good but wind surfing causes considerable disturbance on the beach. There is a hide overlooking open water at the south end of the reserve. Although the Reserve is fenced, access is free and the gate is always open.

Contact Tierry Démerat, BP 102, 50441 Beaumont-Hague Cedex for further information about the reserve, guided walks or group bookings. The Groupe Ornithologique Normand at the Université de Caen, Dept. Biologie/Ecologie, 14032 Caen Cedex run the reserve. Tel: (0033) (0) 2 31 43 52 56

WHEN TO VISIT: Spring is best but late autumn/winter can be interesting. In winter various duck species can be observed on the lake: **Mallard, Tufted Duck, Shoveler, Pochard** have all bred here. Other migratory species to be seen in winter include

Teal, Pintail, Gadwall, Goldeneye, Snipe and **Curlew** (which breeds nearby). **Water Rail** may be spotted from the hide and **Black-necked Grebe** in spring. There are usually a few **Bearded Tit** in the reedbeds in winter and plenty of **pipits** on the dunes, where a few **Kentish Plover** breed. **Cetti's Warbler** can be heard all year round; **Grasshopper, Reed** and **Sedge Warblers** breed here, as do **Reed Bunting** and **Marsh Harrier**. The nearby heathland and gorse scrub provides habitat for species such as **shrikes, Dartford Warbler, Whitethroat** and **Stonechat,** while **Melodious Warbler** can be found in the taller bushes near the lake.

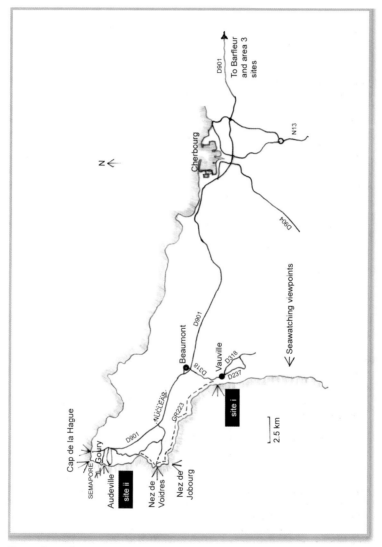

Normandy area2 sites i and ii

ACCESS: Turn off the D901 Cherbourg-Cap de la Hague road at BEAUMONT 18 km from the centre of Cherbourg. Go right (north) into BEAUMONT village and follow the signs for the D318 to VAUVILLE; it runs south back under the D901 and continues for 2 km to the start of Vauville, a long straggly village. In another kilometre turn right, following the signs to the Reserve and in another 200 metres turn right again. There is parking beside the beach on the edge of the fenced reserve and a footpath runs for the length of the lake to a hide at the south end. The reedbeds afford very few glimpses of open water and if you are only interested in observing birds from the hide, then it might be better not to turn off to the reserve in Vauville but to continue through that village and take the D237 coast road for 1.4 km to LE PETIT THROT. Park wherever it is possible in this hamlet and walk down the no-entry Sauf riverains lane. The entrance to the Reserve is the first footpath on the right in 100 metres; it is not signed. Walk down to the Reserve boundary where the hide is only another 100 metres from the gate.

The D237 road gives good, if distant views over the reedbeds and open water.

Other fauna and flora: There is an interesting freshwater as well as a dune flora, which includes Purple Loosestrife Lythrum salicaria, Small-flowered Buttercup Ranunculus parviflorus, Burnet Rose Rosa pimpinelifolia, Spiked Speedwell Veronica spicata, Portland Spurge Euphobia portlandica and Sea Thrift. As might be expected many amphibians can be found on the reserve: Marbled Newt Triturus marmoratus, Midwife Toad Alytes obstretican, Tree Frog Hyla arborea and at least nine dragon-/damselfly species as well as numerous aquatic invertebrates. The area is also good for butterflies.
<u>*Accommodation*</u>: There is no hotel or campsite very near but plenty around Cherbourg.

<u>Site ii.</u>
CAP DE LA HAGUE SEAWATCHING SITES The headlands at la Hague are some of the best seawatching sites in Normandy, given the right wind and weather conditions. In the north, around Goury, the coast is rocky but low and there are reefs and tide-races out to sea. In the south, around the Nez de Voidries and Nez de Jobourg, the granite cliffs are much higher and there are colonies of nesting seabirds. Inland, the gorse moorland, with low walls and small stone houses is bleakly picturesque. It differs from most of Normandy, resembling more a "land's end" peninsular in Brittany, Cornwall or Ireland.

Fulmar, Shag, Great Black-backed and **Herring Gulls, Jackdaw** and **Raven** nest on the cliffs and can be seen year round. In winter **Purple Sandpiper** may be found on the rocks, together with **Oystercatcher** (another breeding species) and sometimes **Lapland Longspur** and **Snow Buntings** on the heath. In autumn, especially when westerlies are blowing, but also in spring, **Gannets, Manx, Balearic, Yelkouan** and **Sooty Shearwaters, petrels, gulls** (including **Sabine's**), **terns, Great** and Arctic **Skuas** may be seen on passage, sometimes close inshore. At these seasons, migrant passerines (larks, thrushes, finches, buntings, wheatears) may be found on the heath behind the coast.

The normal autumn passage is from the North Sea with birds flying down the coast from a north-easterly direction but depressions and storms over the Atlantic and westerly winds can produce a good passage from the Atlantic; exactly the same conditions that make for good seawatching in south-west England.

ACCESS: Take the D901 from Cherbourg, past the nuclear plant to AUDERVILLE. To reach the first site, the signal station on the north coast, take the D401 on the right at the very end of the village (signed to Semaphore) and drive for 1.5 km. The road bends left towards the sea by the station building and just beyond it, on the coastal footpath, there is a lay-by surrounded by a semi-circular wall. This makes a reasonably sheltered spot from which to seawatch. This northern headland is the best spot for observing migration. GOURY lighthouse is a 25-minute walk from here left along the footpath. Alternatively, drive back to AUDERVILLE and continue on the D901 for 400 metres to the end of the road. There is a car park on the right (north) at the end of Goury village, from where it is a short walk to the memorial cross facing the offshore lighthouse and island reserve. The cross is another good seawatching spot. The rocks around the lighthouse and the inland pools may also contain some species.

To reach the NEZ DE JOUBOURG/NEZ DE VOIDRIES cliffs return to Auderville. At the start of the village (just before its sign) turn onto the D401 E1 signed to NEZ DE JOUBOURG/BAIE DE ENCALGRAIN. This 6 km long coastal road runs past the Baie de Encalgrain to DANNERY, where you must turn right onto the D201 and then right again (both turns are clearly signed to NEZ DE JOUBOURG. There are two large car parks 200 metres apart before the headland. Park in the furthest one and walk the short circuit that starts at the nearby building. There are good views of Joubourg cliff (**Shag, Great Black-backed Gull** etc) and several spots for seawatching from the northern headland Nez de Voidries. The coastal footpath from here leads back north to Goury lighthouse or southeast down the coast. The heathland around Dannery can be good in spring and summer for **Dartford Warbler, Whitethroat** and **Stonechat**.

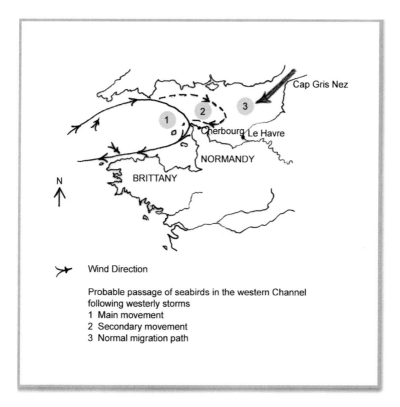

Seabird movements in the English Channel

Area 3. **ST. VAAST-LA-HOUGUE**

<u>Site i.</u>
ST. VAAST HARBOUR The port of St. Vaast lies some 30 km east of Cherbourg. It is situated on the boundary between the low, sandy coastline of the Cotentin (see next area) and the granite plateau that forms the tip of the peninsular. A long spit of land with old fortifications half encloses and protects the southern, shallow bay while the Saire headland to the north marks the limit of the northern one. There is an island and other fortifications in the harbour, all of which make good roosts for seabirds.
WHEN TO VISIT: St. Vaast is essentially an autumn and winter site when large numbers of waterbirds feed close inshore and can be easily watched from the harbour or fort. For this reason it provides some of the most interesting birdwatching in the region between September and March. But, like all coastal sites, it is best at high-tide
Grebes are very numerous and all five species can be seen (**Great Crested, Slavonian** and **Black-necked** are the most common), **Red-throated, Black-throated** and **Great Northern Divers** may be spotted among them and there can be quite large flocks of **Red-breasted Merganser;** Shelduck are very numerous in the inner harbour and flocks of **Common Scoter, Eider** and (fewer) **Velvet Scoter** can be seen out to sea, together with auks (**Razorbill, Guillemot**). Both **Shags** and **Cormorants** constantly fly by and perch on the rocks. Waders on the mud flats and small island include **Curlew, Ringed Plover, Grey Plover, Oystercatcher, Turnstone** and usually a few **Little Egrets**. Wintering passerines are numerous around the fort: both **Meadow** and **Rock Pipits, White Wagtail, Black Redstart**, and many **finch** species. Gulls are much in evidence around the boats in the harbour; amongst the **Herring, Black-backed** and **Black-headed**, there are sometimes a few **Mediterranean Gulls** and **Sandwich Terns**.
A few grebes and sawbills may be seen in late spring and summer but of more interest during these seasons are the **terns**, both **marsh** and sea, **Gannets, gulls**, breeding **Shelduck** and some waders, mainly **Oystercatcher**.
ACCESS: From CHERBOURG, take either the D901 to BARFLEUR, then the D902 south to QUETTEHOU or the N12 to VALONGES and then the D902 north-east to Quettehou. From this town take the D1 east for 2.5 km to ST. VAAST. Drive through the town to the sea front and park by the port. Having checked the gulls around the boats, walk right, past the Chantier naval building to the small chapel, signed Chapelle des Marins. There is an observation platform behind it that gives good views out to sea north and east. From the right of the chapel there is another viewpoint looking south towards the spit. There will be **divers, auks** and **grebes** on the sea. It is also worth walking to the end of the jetty on the left of the chapel, as there are good views from here looking towards the nearby island, Tatihou, as well as the rocks and fortifications in the harbour, which always have many **Cormorants, Shags** and often **waders.**
The best views, however, are from the spit with the fort at its end, La Hougue. From the chapel you can see the footpath that leads along the waters edge. It is best to walk along this and make a circuit of the fort; this will give good views over both the inner harbour and the sea. However, if the weather is bad, you can drive along the spit to the fort, using the car as a hide, park by the tennis courts and just walk the circuit, which is under a kilometre in length. If driving, return towards the centre of town and turn left at the roundabout with a piston/propeller, following all the signs to Le Hougue through the one-way system. Stop wherever you can pull onto the side and scan both sides of the spit. Park by the tennis courts/children's playground. This is a good area for passerines and a good spot for scanning out to sea; flocks of sawbills are often close inshore here. The footpath, signed, starts beyond the tennis courts.

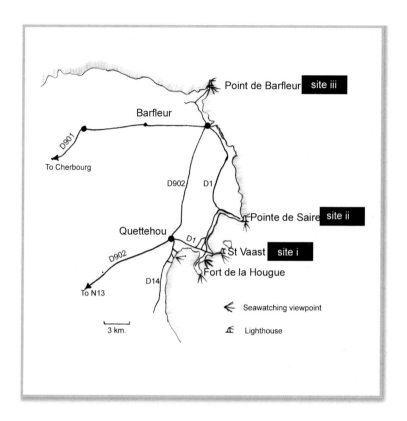

Normandy area3 sites i - iii

Site ii.

POINTE DE SAIRE The Saire headland by the lighthouse is another good birding spot. There are not normally so many birds on the sea, but it can be a better place to watch birds on passage and there are waders on the rocks or, at low tide, the beach below the lighthouse: **Oystercatcher, Grey Plover, Dunlin, Turnstone, Sanderling, Curlew, Purple Sandpiper** in winter, many more on passage. **Brent Geese** are usually here in winter. Serins have been seen in gardens at Réville, just inland.

ACCESS: From the port at St. Vaast drive north along the coast road, the D1. It may be worth stopping at intervals and climbing the sea wall to look out to sea. In 3 km the road crosses the river Saire. Stop and check the reeds here; there are usually fair numbers of passerines, certainly on passage and even in winter. **Fan-tailed Warbler (Zitting Cisticola)** has been found here in winter, also **Cetti's Warbler** and **Stonechat**. Turn right towards JONVILLE at the junction immediately after the river. Follow the signs through Jonville to the Phare where you can park. It is 2.5 km from the river to the lighthouse.

Site iii.

POINTE DE BARFLEUR If you are in the area during the spring or autumn migration and there is a good passage of birds out at sea, then it might be worth driving north to the lighthouse at Pointe de Barfleur as this headland juts well out to sea. Autumn seawatching from here can be very good indeed when northerly winds push birds down from the North Sea into the Baie de la Seine, and then close to the headland here as they head out into the Atlantic. Westerlies and Atlantic storms can also drive birds close to land (see map for the Cap de la Hague Normandy Area 2 site ii). **Shearwaters, petrels, Gannets, divers, grebes, auks, terns, gulls** and **skuas** have all be observed in good numbers.

ACCESS: Return to the river junction and go straight on along the D328 until it meets the D902. Turn right (north) for BARFLEUR and take the coast road, D116 out of town in the direction of GATTEVILLE. Follow the signs to the Phare at Raz de Barfleur 2 km.

The lighthouse at CAP LÉVY, 16 km nearer to CHERBOURG, is another sea-watching site. Continue on the D116 coast road to FERMANVILLE. Follow the signs to the lighthouse and headland. **Middle Spotted Woodpeckers** have been spotted near the church at Fermanville.

Accommodation: This is a tourist area, so there are hotels in all the towns mentioned. There should be no trouble finding rooms in autumn or winter.

Area 4. **COTENTIN MARSHES REGIONAL NATURE PARK**

THE MARAIS DU COTENTIN AND DU BESSIN is a huge (25,000 hectares) area of marshland in the centre of Normandy, straddling the borders of the Calvados and Manche departments and stretching from the west to the east coast. The Park is criss-crossed by rivers, canals and ditches and large stretches of the lower-lying areas will be flooded in winter. There are also peat bogs, dryer moorland on the low, rounded hills, a patchwork of small fields enclosed by hedgerows (bocage) and scattered woodland as well as two estuaries, one on each coast.

This variety of habitat makes for excellent birding, with several areas being of particular interest: the estuaries (Veys Bay on the east, Havre-de-St.-Germain-de-Hay on the west coast), the Marais de la Sangsurière Reserve in the northwest, the Mathon peat bog and heath areas near Lessay in the southwest and Les Ponts d'Ouve "discovery area" near Carentan.

Site i.

LES PONTS D'OUVE This site includes a Park reception house as well as a 100-hectare bird reserve with hides. The staff at the reception area are welcoming, extremely helpful and most speak English. There is a bird check list (with English names) showing the status of all species seen on the reserve and the staff will suggest other area of the Park worth visiting and tell you what birds are currently about. The free maps and booklets (on accommodation, places to visit, etc) have English editions. Within the Park Centre there is also an exhibition and video room, binoculars can be hired, as can motorboats to explore the river for a couple of hours. There are guided tours, which must be booked in advance. However, it is feasible to walk around the lake

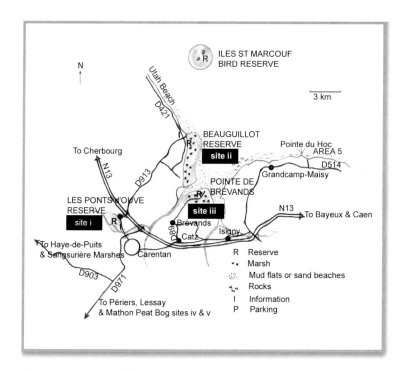

Normandy area4 sites i - iii Cotentin marshes

and hides on your own, and most visitors will prefer to do this; it takes two to three hours to walk the 5.5 km circuit, depending on how much there is to see from each hide or about an hour to visit just the large hide *Grand Observatoire,* which has wheelchair access. Guided visits are the only way to get the most from the Sangsurière and Lessay reserves. Ask at the Park reception house about these.

The Ponts d'Ouve is open every day 9.30 - 19 h from April to September and every day except Mondays 9.30-13 h and 14 - 17 h from October to March. The charge is €3 for adults or €4,50 for a guided visit. Groups and children at reduced rates. Boat trips (for 4/5 people) are €4,50 for an hour. The centre is closed for a fortnight at the beginning of October and for a month from mid-December. In winter, wellington boots may be necessary. Les Ponts d'Ouve, 50500 Saint Côme du Mont. Tel: 02 33 71 65 30 Fax: 02 33 71 65 31 e-mail: ponts-douve@wanadoo.fr web site: http://www.parcs-naturels-regionaux.tm.fr/lesparcs/cobeb-en.html

WHEN TO VISIT: Mid-April to the beginning of May is the best time but autumn passage (August-October) is also excellent. This is a good site throughout the year.

In winter, count on seeing a good variety of duck and gull species, including **Common Gull, Bittern** (quite common in winter), **waders (including Curlew, Golden** and **Grey Plovers, Snipe, Jack Snipe), Water Rail, Kingfisher, Redwing, Reed Bunting, Rock** and **Meadow Pipits, Stonechat** and **Cetti's Warbler**. In spring there may be **Bluethroat** on passage as well as **Garganey** and more wader species, while breeding birds include **Common Sandpiper, Sand Martin, Yellow Wagtail, Whinchat, Grasshopper, Reed** and **Sedge Warblers** and **White Stork**.

There are now 25 pairs of breeding storks in the Park, and some should always be seen at Ponts d'Ouve. Ask at the reception centre about other sites. **Marsh, Hen** and **Montagu's Harriers** all breed in the Park and **Marsh Harrier** is quite common at the Ponts d'Ouve, while the other two are seen there occasionally. **Quail** and **Corncrake** are rare breeders but can be heard in the spring.

ACCESS: Leave the N13 motorway from Bayeux to Cherbourg at the exit north of CARENTAN onto the D 971 that bypasses Carentan on the north. Turn first right (north) onto the D913 signed Utah Beach/ St.Côme-du-Mont. The Reserve is on the left (west) in just over half a kilometre. If coming from Cherbourg and the north, you can turn off at the D913 exit further north. Follow the signs to St.Côme-du-Mont and turn south.

There are regular bus services from Cherbourg and trains from Caen and Cherbourg to Carentan

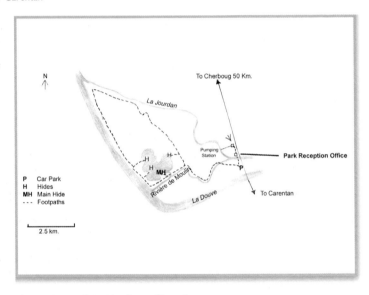

Normandy area 4 site i Les Ponts d'Ouve Reserve

Site ii.

DOMAINE de BEAUGUILLOT ORNITHOLOGICAL RESERVE This is a large (500 ha), 3 km long protected area on the north coast of Veys Bay. Composed of polders, flooded meadows, saltmarsh and beach, much of it is inaccessible to visitors but there are three well positioned hides, views over a large expanse of polders and a dyke giving good views over the marsh. In winter the pools and flooded fields attract all the commoner **duck** species in good numbers (**Pintail, Teal, Gadwall, Shoveler, Shelduck, Wigeon, Pochard, Mallard**) with a few **Greylag Geese** and hundreds of **Lapwing** and **Golden Plover**; other common waders include **Snipe** and **Black-tailed Godwit** (with many more species during migration), **Buzzard, Marsh Harrier, Peregrine, Merlin** and **Stock Dove**. On the beach there will be **Oystercatcher, Dunlin** and **Curlew**. Check the lark and finch flocks in the polders for **Twite, Reed** and **Snow Bunting**; **Short-eared Owl** hunts over the fields and there are also many passerines in the trees and bushes and reed-filled ditches.

WHEN TO VISIT: The bird list is similar to the Pont d'Ouve's, so there should be interesting species throughout the year, but this reserve is definitely best from September to March.

ACCESS: Continue on the D913 northeast from the Ponts d'Ouve and Carentan, cross over the N13 following the signs for Utah Beach. In 14 km at the Utah Beach Museum, turn right, signed to the Reserve. This road runs alongside the Reserve for just under 3 km, then turns left into a car park at the D329 junction. There is a plan of the Reserve and information boards along the footpath. Walk along the gravel track towards the sea. The hides overlooking pools and wet meadows are on the left, polders on the right. In about a kilometre the track meets a dyke, along which it is possible to walk southwards. From here there are good views over the saltmarsh.

Site iii.

POINTE DE BRÉVANDS, VEYS BAY Veys Bay is an IBA for the huge numbers of duck, gulls and waders that occur there on passage and in winter. 5000 hectares of mudflats are exposed at low tide in the Bay. Unfortunately, much of the surrounding marshland is also heavily shot over, so the safest birding is in the Reserve (see site above) as it can be quite unpleasant trying to watch birds with so many hunters around. There are good views over the polders and saltmarsh at the Pointe de Brévands in the south, so it may be worth ignoring the hunters and visiting this point.

WHEN TO VISIT: Autumn and winter are best. Wintering birds include up to 20 thousand **Brent Geese**, thousands of **Pintail, Shoveler, Oystercatchers, Dunlin** and **Curlew. Common** and **Velvet Scoters** and **Eider** winter out at sea. On passage there are thousands of **Sandwich, Black** and **Common Tern**, fewer **Little Tern** and up to a couple of hundred **Spoonbill. Redshank, Knot, Ringed Plover** are the commonest waders on passage but surprising species often turn up. **Marsh Harrier** can be seen all year round and a few pairs of **Montagu's Harrier. Corncrake** and **White Stork** breed nearby

ACCESS: Leave the N13 at the junction south of CARENTAN and turn towards CATZ on the road running parallel with the N13. Zero. In 2 km turn left (north) onto the D89 for CATZ and BRÉVLANDS. At 5 km fork right and continue along an increasingly narrow dyke road towards the marsh. There are views from a dyke at 8.4 km and the dyke road ends near the sea in about 9 km. Turning and parking can be difficult. There are gun butts and decoy ducks on the left-hand marshes but not so much disturbance on the right side. Look out for **Short-eared Owl** and hunting raptors there.

Site iv.

HAVRE DE ST. GERMAIN-SUR-AY The estuary on the west coast of the Cotentin Park is especially good for waders on passage, but most of the species listed for the two sites above can also be found there. Access is less easy but there is a good coastal footpath through the dunes around the point.

ACCESS: The D650 coast road running north from Granville skirts the Ay river mouth and there are good views over the east side of the bay from this road. (If coming from the west, the D72 from LESSAY joins the coast road just before the viewpoint). To reach the footpaths and for views over the north and west sides, continue on the D650 to ST. GERMAIN-SUR-AY and take the D306 west, through la Gaverie, crossing another river mouth to ST. GERMAIN PLAGE. The coastal footpath GR223 starts from here and circuits the headland leading back to the D306. There is also a short stretch of footpath leading east from ST. GERMAIN-SUR-AY.

Site v.

THE MATHON PEAT BOG AND HEATHLAND SOUTH OF LESSAY

The Mathon peat bog is primarily of interest to botanists, but there are also breeding **Nightjar** there as well as on the Landes heathland that lies south and east of Lessay, where **Hoopoe** can also be found. **Black Woodpecker** and **Crested Tit** can be found in the conifer plantations. Parts of these habitats can be seen by driving south from LESSAY on the D2 and exploring the minor roads D394 and D94. Or go east on the D900 for about 5 km. It is worth listening in suitable habitat (see notes under Special Species at end of book) at dusk in spring and early summer for Nightjar. Visits to the Reserve area (and to the Sangsurière Nature reserve in the north) can only be arranged through the Park. Phone 0033(0) 2 33 46 37 06 or ask at the Park reception house at Les Ponts d'Ouve.

Other fauna and flora: 10 or 12 Harbour Seals live in Veys Bay and can often be seen near the Beauguillot Reserve. Muskrats are often near the hides in Beauguillot. Many areas, including Beauguillot Reserve, have interesting dune, marsh or peatbog flora and insect populations; ask at Les Ponts d'Ouve for directions and more information. Sundews, Sea Holly *Eryngium maritimum*, Common Rest-harrow *Ononis repens*, Yarrow Broomrape *Orobanche purpurea*, Yellow Bartsia *Parentucelia vicosa*, orchids including Bee *Ophrys apifera*, Loose-flowered *Orchis laxiflora*, Southern Marsh *Dactylorhiza praetermissa*, Marsh Helleborine *Epipactis palustris* can all be found in appropriate habitats.

Accommodation: There are hotels in almost all the towns and larger villages within the Park, as well as many campsites, gîtes and chambres d'hôtes. The Park publishes a booklet *Hébergement & Restauration* listing all these with full details (addresses, telephone numbers, prices, etc) as well as restaurants and country inns within the Park. It is obtainable from Les Ponts d'Ouve reception (address above).

Area 5. **POINTE DU HOC**

The cliffs at the Pointe du Hoc lie between Veys Bay and Omaha Beach, just outside the Cotentin Park. They are nevertheless an IBA, being at the western end of the Bessin cliffs, which are the most important site in France for breeding **Fulmars** and **Kittiwakes**. Both these species can be seen from the Pointe du Hoc in spring and summer as well as many others: **Lesser Black-backed** and **Herring Gulls, Cormorants, Jackdaws** and **Black Redstart** all breed on the cliffs. **Dartford Warbler** can be found on the heathland on the cliff tops. In autumn and winter, the clifftop can provide some excellent sea-watching: **Red-throated Diver, Shag, auks, Red-breasted Merganser, sea terns, skuas** and many more **gull** species can be found on the sea or flying past.

ACCESS: Take the coast road D514 from GRANDCAMP-MAISY eastwards. Turn left (north) onto the D514A signed to the Pointe and park in the large carpark in 600m. The Pointe du Hoc is a WWII battle site. Walk to the monument on the point for a seawatch before taking the footpath to the right (east). Very soon you will see another headland in front of you with seabird colonies on the cliffs. Where the mown grass of the battle site finishes, the gorse and scrub are better for small passerines such as Dartford Warbler, although the footpath is uneven and often muddy. You can walk to the next headland or scan the cliffs and sea wherever there is a viewpoint.

Area 6. **CERISY FOREST** near **BAYEUX**

Cerisy Forest, known 1000 years ago as the Grand Fôret, was given by William the Conqueror to the monks of Cerisy Abbey. 80% of the trees are beeches, many over 100 years old. Well managed since WWII, Cerisy has been made a Reserve mainly to protect a rare, endemic sub-species of *Onrysocarabus auronitens cupreoniten* - the *scarab à reflects cuivres* or coppery scarab beetle! However, with so many mature trees, it is also a good spot for forest birds and **Middle Spotted Woodpecker** is especially easy to see here. **Black Woodpecker**, a more recent arrival, is more elusive. Both these species are easiest to find between November and March, when **Woodcock** winter here. Breeding birds include **Buzzard, Honey Buzzard** and **Long-eared Owl. Short-toed Treecreeper, Nuthatch** and **tit** species are common and **Hawfinch** may be found among the wintering feeding flocks of **finches** and **tits**.

ACCESS: Cerisy is 16 km southwest of BAYEUX on the D572. Coming from Bayeux, zero when you reach the large roundabout at the entrance to the forest. In 2.7 km take the C2 tarmac road on the left, signed to Montfiquet. In 300 metres park on the right by the entrance to a footpath *Sentier de découverte de la Nature*. Walk a short distance down the footpath; the trees are young but good for warblers. On the opposite side of the road there are mature beeches. Try for woodpeckers, especially **Middle Spotted,** here. A little further on, at 3.4 km by the T-junction with the Route Forestière de la Belle Epine there are again some suitable trees on the left. Walk a little way into the wood.

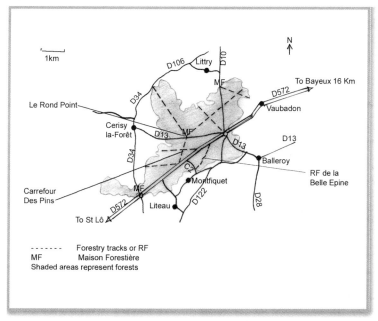

Normandy area 6 Normandy area 6 Cerisy Forest

Retrace your way back to the D572. In another 300 metres there is a forest road on the right leading to a *Maison Forestière* with a large car park with notice boards beside it. Park here. A marked footpath into the forest starts from the parking and can be productive if there are not too many people about. **Middle Spotted Woodpeckers** often seem to be around car parks and clearings. They are extremely noisy small birds and some of their calls closely resemble those of Nuthatches, so do not be fooled! They are usually found in the top branches of large deciduous trees. Another site for **Middle Spotted** is 500 metres up the road towards the *Maison Forestière* where a forest track crosses the road and a car can pull off near a more open area. Further on again, at the *Carrefour des Pins* there is a parking area beside a forest crossroads; these are also good walking tracks. At the *Maison Forestière de Rond Point*, at the end of this road, there is another parking area with a map of the forest.

If you turn right (east) here on the D13 you will arrive back at the roundabout on the D572. Before you get there, stop off about half way along at a parking place in an area with quite a few dead trees. This triangle of roads, and the paths leading from them, contains some of the biggest trees in the forest and seems to be the best area for woodpeckers.

Other fauna and flora: Besides the scarab beetle, there is a great diversity of insects in Cerisy and some trees have been specially planted to encourage insect life. Butterflies and moths include White-letter Hairstreak, Camberwell Beauty, Lesser Purple Emperor *Apatura ilia,* Cliften Nonpareil *Catocala fraxini* and Broad-bordered Bee Hawkmoth *Hemaris fuciformis.* Among larger animals, Red and Roe Deer, Beech Marten, Badger, Fox and Wild Boar are found here. Amphibians include Fire Salamander *Salamandra salamandra* and Agile Frog *Rana dalmatina.*

(For other forests further inland in Normandy look under South Central region, Area 1.)

Area 7. **CAEN**

Site i.

ORNE ESTUARY RESERVE On the right bank of the Orne River mouth, the opposite side to the ferry port, is a Reserve where marked trails and hides provide some good birdwatching over part of the estuary, which is an IBA for passage waterbirds, especially **Spoonbills**. The Reserve is therefore best in spring and autumn but there are plenty of birds to see in winter and even late summer. As at any estuary site, the Reserve is best at high tide when the birds are pushed off the mudflats into the river mouth. Species that may be seen between August and April include **Guillemot, Grey Heron, Little Egret,** duck species (**Wigeon, Teal, Shoveler), Golden** and **Grey Plovers, Snipe, Redshank, Black-tailed Godwit, Avocet, Curlew, Oystercatcher, Reed Bunting, Black Redstart, pipits, Skylark, Linnet, Goldfinch**. In summer breeding species include **Nightingale, Sedge Warbler, Swift** and **Sand Martins. Barn Owl** and **Short-eared Owl** hunt over the Merville dunes.

ACCESS: Leave the CAEN ring road at exit 3 and take the road to OUISTREHAM and the car ferries. Just after the large cement works on the right, turn off onto the D514 signed to MERVILLE (If you are coming from the car ferries, it is the first main junction to the left). Cross both canals and turn left, still on the D514, direction MERVILLE/CAROURG. It is also signed to the *Maison de la Nature de l'Estuaire.* This Information Centre (14121 Sallenelles. Tel: 31 78 71 06) is on the left 3.2 km from the junction. It is open every day between 15/6 - 3/9, otherwise Sunday afternoons only. There is a car park and you can either walk or continue driving past the Maison, turning right (there is a lot of shooting over the marshes on the left) and then parking in 300 metres opposite the bar in the village of SALLENELLES. There is a wooden signpost by the parking place pointing to the *Reserve de Gros Banc* and the footpath is marked red and white. There is a raised path on a high bank that gives good views over the mudflats on the far side of the river as well as over the stream and scrub to the right of the bank. There can be good numbers of waders on the mudflats at high tide but only gulls, **Grey Heron** and **Little Egret** at low.

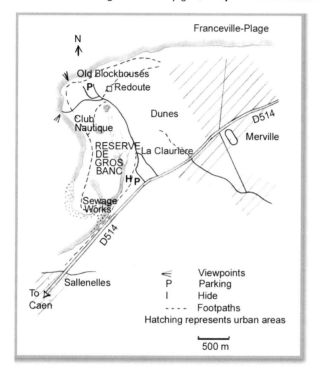

Normandy area7 sites i and ii Orne Estuary and Dunes

Kingfisher can be seen along the stream and **Reed Bunting** and **Cetti's Warbler** in the scrub all year round.

Walk along the raised path, then over sand for 1.5 km towards 2 small houses. There are grassy footpaths cut through the scrub and woodland on the right and it may be worth exploring these in spring (alternatively they can be reached from the end of Sallenelles village beyond the car park). Just beyond the two houses is the start of a 3.5 km circular walk around the *Boucle de Gros Banc par Pointe de Merville* with hides overlooking open water.

If you do not want to walk along the river, then drive on 800 metres from the end of SALLENELLES and park, either by the two houses or better, continue for another 500 metres past the sewage works and park beside the tower hide and map of the Reserve. This is just 2 km from the Maison Information Centre and if you do not wish to walk the whole circuit, good views can be obtained from the tower hide.

Site ii.

ORNE ESTUARY DUNES Roughly 100 metres past the tower-hide entrance, the first road on the left is signed to le Port/Base nautique. This narrow road runs along the edge of the Reserve and leads to a large car park on the dunes by some WWII blockhouses, one of which serves as a raised observation platform. Look for **Black Redstart** and pipits around the buildings. **Eiders** and **Scoters** can sometimes be seen out at sea. There is a path through the dunes towards the sea. The road ends beyond the blockhouses at the sailing base, which can sometimes be worth a quick visit. (If you would like to get nearer birds on the opposite (left) bank of the river or use the hide on the dunes that can be seen from the Reserve, then retrace your steps on the D514 to where it crosses the first canal. Between the two canals a minor road signed to the "pleasure port" runs towards the sea).

Area 8. **LE HAVRE**

Site i.

SEINE ESTUARY - PONT DE NORMANDIE Whilst not an outstanding site, the 3,700 hectare reserve (protected since 1997) on the north bank of the Seine estuary close to the industrial port of Le Havre provides good birding at any time of the year except perhaps during the height of summer, and can be useful to fill in a couple of hours or so while waiting for a ferry. In spring, it may even be worth a special visit to see the large number of **Bluethroats** (most are on passage but some breed). Ideally, high tide is the best time for close views of waders on the mudflats but even at low tide birds can be 'scoped from the raised embankment or the footpath by the Normandy Bridge.

There is a good variety of wader species, with **Godwits**, **'shanks**, **Ruff**, **Lapwing** and **Sandpipers** in spring and autumn; **Oystercatcher**, **Curlew**, **Dunlin** and **Avocet** in winter; a few **Bittern** breed and **Spoonbills** can be seen on passage, together with **Bluethroats**, in March and September. In winter there are often **divers**, **Great**, **Crested**, **Little** and **Slavonian Grebes** and many **duck** species **(Mallard, Pintail, Pochard, Shelduck, Wigeon, Gadwall, Tufted Duck, Goldeneye, Mergansers, Velvet Scoter)** with Garganey occasionally on passage in spring. Various **gull** species can be seen, especially at the river mouth, as well as **Common** and **Sandwich Terns** in spring and autumn as well as the occasional **Skua** species in autumn. **Marsh Harrier** can be seen over the reedbeds and grassland throughout the year, with Hen **Harrier**, **Peregrine** and **Merlin** in **winter**, and occasionally **Short-eared Owl**. The reedbeds and riverside bushes hold Reed **Bunting, Bearded Tit** and **Cetti's Warbler** throughout the year and **Sedge, Reed, Grasshopper** and **Savi's Warblers** in the breeding season. **Snow Bunting** and **Twite** sometimes turn up during hard winters. *ACCESS:* If coming from Paris: Zero at the Tancarville tollbooths, on the Le Havre side of the bridge. Take the N182, then the A1317 in the direction of LE HAVRE for 7 km before turning off at the first major intersection towards the industrial zone, signed *ZI Portuaire, Centre Routier, Pont de Normandie, Port du Havre.* Bear left again, following the same signs, cross the canal and take the first road on the left at 9.6 km from the bridge, signed *Port Sud* and *Route de l'Estuaire.* This is the estuary road that runs south of the Canal du Havre through rough (sometimes flooded) meadowland and reedbeds. Immediately pull in to the lay-by on the right and scan the rough fields on both sides for raptors. At 10.2 km it is possible to cross the railway line on the right and take a gravel track running along the edge of the fields. Scan the numerous posts, a favourite perching place for raptors. Continue along the road, pulling off into any lay-by (most are on the left so watch out for lorries leaving the port) to scan for raptors and warblers. The fields are normally waterlogged in winter with productive small pools and patches of reeds. Nearer the bridge it is worth walking along the verge from one of the parking places to the double roundabout before the tollbooths.

If coming from the Le Havre ferries: Either drive to the Tancarville bridge and follow the above itinerary or follow the signs to Pont de Normandie, bird around the bridge (see below) and then follow the above route in reverse.

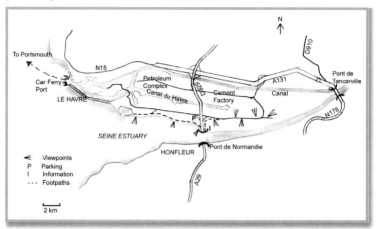

Normandy area 8 site i Le Havre

If coming from Caen: cross the bridge and park on the right after the tolls.

It is approximately 19 km from the Tancarville Bridge to the D929 and the new Pont de Normandie bridge over the Seine. The walkway from the toll/restaurant area to the bottom of the bridge provides excellent views over reedbeds and mudflats at low tide. Do not go through the tolls but park on the Le Havre side of the river. Finding the car park can be a little confusing. Go right at the roundabout, as if driving towards the tollbooths but keep to the right, go slowly and take the slipway leading right to *Aire de la Baie de Seine,* parking and bar. In 200 metres at the "give-way" lines, cross the line and turn immediately right into the car park. From here walk towards the bar/restaurant area and take the stairs to the footbridge from where you can walk along the footpaths that lead to the bridge on both sides of the road. It is possible to walk along one side and back along the other (this takes about 45 mins to 1 hour) or carry on walking right over the bridge to the left bank of the Seine.

There are good views over the marshes and mudflats from the foot of the bridge. There is a large gull roost on the river here and other species likely to be seen include **Marsh Harrier, Curlew, Avocet, Shelduck, waders, herons** and **egrets** with **Reed Bunting, Stonechat, Bearded Tit** and other passerines in the reeds. If you are very lucky a **Bittern** may fly over. Return to the parking and bar. For lazy birding there is even a sitting area outside the bar that overlooks the marsh, from where **Bearded Tits** can often be seen.

The reserve's Avocet Centre also has a viewing area overlooking the reedbeds. The Centre is next to the bar and toilets in the restaurant building. Current opening hours are Friday, Saturday and Sunday from 14.00 - 18.00 but in winter, if it is quiet, it may close early. Information is available on the reserve, current species and where they may be found.

An alternative walk from this area can be taken along the footpath that runs parallel to the estuary road on the riverside. It will give different views over the reedbeds. To reach the parking place for this walk take the estuary road in the direction of Port Sud, turning off left after 200 metres following the "Parking" sign. The path starts from the parking area. Note that you cannot get into this parking from the bridge roundabout and you cannot drive along this path.

The old way to reach the riverbank and gull roost was some 5 km nearer to Le Havre, 24 km from zeroing at Tancarville, still off the estuary road. About 30 metres before the traffic lights by the turning to *Terminal d'Ocean,* almost opposite a large Information board, a potholed, rough and muddy track leads (left) for some 200 metres towards the embankment running along the north bank of the Seine estuary. It now seems to be marked "*Access interdit*" and if lorries are working on the site it may be impossible to walk down here. If you can walk or drive it, then go to the old embankment road alongside the Seine and walk along this in the direction of the Normandy Bridge, searching the bushes for **Bluethroat** in spring and scanning the mudflats. It is even possible to get down to the river's edge but not usually worthwhile; the height of the embankment is preferable. There are usually more birds near the Normandy Bridge but there is a large gull roost towards the river mouth.

Site ii.

MANNEVILLES RESERVE The Reserve was created to preserve a small part of the lower valley of the Seine and one of the most important peat bogs in northern France. The 93 hectares of the Reserve lie within the Natural Regional Park of Brotonne, on the left bank of the River Seine. It comprises lakes, water meadows (grazed by Camargue horses and Highland Cattle), reed-beds and woodland. The largest stretch of water, *La Grand-Mare,* is a hunting reserve (not included in the Reserve) and the local hunters' association have built a tower hide overlooking the lake. This unspoilt piece of countryside, with its low, black-and-white-timbered, thatched houses and barns, must be one of the better-kept secrets of the port area; it seems centuries away from the industrial complexes and oil refineries only a few kilometres to the west. There are marked footpaths and cycle tracks around the Reserve.

The lake is of most interest from autumn to spring, when hundreds of ducks can be found there (**Mallard, Shoveler, Teal, Wigeon, Shelduck** are the most numerous but cold spells in the north bring in more species), together with **Coot** and **Moorhen**. It is an important migratory stop, not only for wildfowl but also waders in September and March-April. **Black Stork, Osprey, Spoonbill** and even the occasional immature **White-tailed Eagle** are among the other species that frequently turn up on passage. **Marsh Harriers** can be seen over the reedbeds and **Cetti's Warblers** heard throughout the year. In summer **Reed** and **Sedge Warblers** also breed as well as **Corncrake** and **Curlew** nearby. There are good areas for **Water Rail** observable from the hide. **Short-eared Owl, Merlin, Hen Harrier** and **Twite** are winter visitors, while **herons** and **egrets** also turn up. **White Storks** started to breed here again in the 1990s and there are now several pairs and up to 20 young each year. Platform nests have been erected for them. **Little Owls** are quite numerous on the periphery of the marsh.

ACCESS: Zero at the tollbooths on Tancarville bridge. In just over 7 km turn onto the D810 in the direction of PONT-AUDEMER. In the village of ST.OPPORTUNE LA MARE (11.2 km from tolls) turn right, following signs to *Reserve de la Faune de la Grande Mare.* The lane leads first through woods, then opens to give a view of the lake. At 13 km the road forks. To reach the lake, go left, still following the signs to the

Reserve. At 13.8 km there is space to park, a picnic area and access to the tower hide. You will need a telescope as the ducks are on the far side of the lake.

To visit other parts of the Reserve, return to the road fork and take the right-hand lane. Signed *Circuit de marais Vernier*. In 250 metres you will come to a large hide which gives good scope views over the northern part of the Grand Mare. There is also some riverside woodland here, good for passerines in summer. A cycle/walking track continues on from here and makes a circuit through woodland, or parts of the woods can be explored from the entrance road.

Other fauna and flora: Interesting marsh vegetation includes Pale Butterwort *Pinguicula lusitanica,* rare in Normandy, *Rhynchospora alba* and Long-leaved Sundew *Drosera intermedia.* There are four species of newts, three of frogs and two of toads as well as Fire Salamander *Salamandra salamandra.* The moth *Mamestra splendens* occurs and several dragonfly species.

<u>Accommodation</u>: There are some Gîtes and bed-and-breakfast (*Chambres d'hôtes*) within the Reserve close to the lake. There is a small bar and restaurant in St. Opportune and plenty of accommodation in nearby Le Havre.

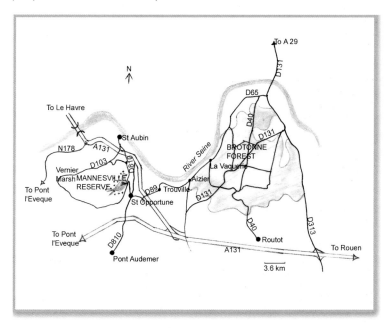

Normandy area 8 sites ii and iii Mannevilles Reserve and Brotonne Forest

<u>Site iii.</u>

BROTONNE FOREST The forest is a mixed beech/oak woodland with conifer plantations, forming most of the Regional Park, which was created to form a "green lung" between the two agglomerations of Le Havre and Rouen. It holds the usual woodland breeding birds to be found in northern France: **Buzzard, Honey Buzzard, Sparrowhawk, Woodpeckers (Green, Black, Great, Middle** and **Lesser Spotted), Common Nightjar, Wood Warblers, Nuthatch** and both **Common** and **Short-toed Treecreeper** among others. However it covers a vast area and is much used by the public. One of the better areas with plenty of large, mature trees for woodpecker species is the south-west corner, which can be easily reached by car from ST. OPPORTUNE and birded after visiting the site above.

ACCESS: From the D810 in the centre of ST. OPPORTUNE take the D95. In a couple of kilometres fork left, cross the motorway, then the D89 in TROUVILLE-LA-HAULE and follow the signs for Vieux Port, on the Seine. The road runs alongside the river with the forest starting on the right. Go through the village of AIZIER and on to hamlet of LA VAQUERIE, some 10 km from St. Opportune. There is a walking track to the forestry house Maison de la Vaquerie 300 metres after the end of the hamlet. About 200 metres further on take the Route Forestière de la Mare de Chèvre on the right. In 2 km there is a parking area, the Aire de la Vaquerie with footpaths leading off both sides of the road. Take the left-hand forestry road which crosses the D131 (which runs north-south through the forest) and continue until it meets the D40. Any areas with large old trees, well spaced out, are good for **Black Woodpecker,** and there are a few in this area. Recently cut areas attract **Common Nightjar** and give an open space for watching raptors above the trees. It is possible to make a circuit on the D40-D131, stopping to look and listen in any promising areas and walking along forestry tracks for as far as you wish. The Route Forestière au Loup is another good woodpecker area.

If continuing on to the next site, the Londe Forest, take the D131 northwards to its junction with the D490. Turn south and join the A13 motorway at junction 25.

Site iv.

LONDE FOREST This is another large public forest, though not as big as Brotonne. It has a very similar bird population: **Buzzard, Honey Buzzard, Nightjar, Green, Black, Great, Lesser** and **Middle Spotted Woodpeckers, Grasshopper** and **Wood Warblers** and **Hawfinch.** However it is heavily hunted over from the end of October to the end of February, (unfortunately the best time of year to find woodpecker species) and should be avoided on hunting days - check the notices.

ACCESS. Turn off the A13 motorway at junction 24 and take the N138 in the direction of BRIONNE. This road runs through the centre of the forest. 4 km from the motorway exit; a Route Forestière crosses the N138 with a large parking area on the right-hand side (west) of the road. It is possible to drive down this forestry track but better to walk, taking some of the smaller footpaths that lead off it into the forest. If you wish to explore the eastern side of Londes Forest, take the forestry road opposite the parking area and at its junction with another broad forestry road, turn left down the R.F. de la Valleé des Joncs. Keep along this track for several kilometres before turning right following the signs for the Château Robert le Diable (or left if you wish to return directly to the N138). Again, the best strategy is to drive (or cycle) stopping in suitable habitat for the species you wish to see and then walking a short way into the forest. See notes at back of book under "Special species" for more detailed suggestions for finding woodpeckers, etc.

Site v.

SEA-WATCHING SITES NORTH OF LE HAVRE There is excellent sea-watching from the cliffs north of Le Havre right up to the Belgian frontier, and although Cap Gris Nez and Dunkerque are the best known, similar species should be seen from any of the sites listed below, given the appropriate weather conditions. **Kittiwakes** and **Fulmars** breed on the Normandy cliffs.

The English Channel is, as most British birders know, an important seabird migration route and the French coast is better for observing the southwards autumn migration than the English side because the prevailing north-east winds funnel the birds from the North Sea through the Channel into the Baie de la Seine before they turn west into the Atlantic. They are normally much closer to the French coast than the English side and follow the coastline for long stretches.

Seawatching starts in August when **shearwaters** and **terns** fly past in large numbers, often accompanied by skuas. **Sooty** and **Manx Shearwaters** are the most numerous, although a few **Balearic** and **Cory's** may occur (these two latter are more likely to be seen from sites further south down the Atlantic coast). **Arctic** are the commonest **Skua** but quite large numbers of **Great** and **Pomarine** have been counted. Skua and shearwater numbers peak in September, when the first divers and auks appear. **Leach's** (and other species of) **Petrels** arrive with northerly or north-westerly gales. Thousands of **Gannets** pass from August to December. October is possibly the best month for a variety of species **(Gannets, geese, Kittiwakes, gulls)** while November is good for divers and auks. A clear day in September or October with a force 3-5 north-east wind offer the best conditions for watching passerines on passage from further north (thrushes, larks, finches, starlings, buntings) although a westerly (or the days following gales from the west) will be best for American vagrants. Any on-shore wind at this period is likely to bring shearwaters and petrels closer inshore, especially just after gales in the Atlantic or depressions to the north-west or west, and in winter sea ducks **(Scoters, Eiders)**, divers and auks **(Razorbills**, etc.) can often be seen in flocks quite close to land.

A series of depression in the south-west Atlantic will also push birds (terns, auks, petrels, shearwaters, Gannets and Kittiwakes) east towards the French coast but rarely further north than Normandy before the prevailing winds from the north turn them round to fly back west into the Atlantic. In these conditions birds are often seen close inshore at the Hague (Area 2. Sites ii and iii) and along the north Brittany coast.

See map of seabird movements in the English Channel on page 71 (Normandy area 2)

The nearest seawatching point to Le Havre is ENTRETAT, where there are cliffs south (Falaise d'Aval) and north (Falaise d'Amont) of the town. A coastal footpath, the GR 21, runs along the top of the cliffs here before turning inland at the Valleuse d'Antifer south of the Aval cliffs. Take the D940 north from Le Havre for some 25 km, turning off west (left) when you reach Entretat.

Other possibilities continuing north up the coast are:

North of FECAMP off the D79 by the chapel of N.D. de Salud or the lighthouse.

The cliffs of Falaise d'Aval at ST VALERY EN CAUX

The lighthouse PHARE D'AILLY off the D75 near Varengeville-sur-Mer some dozen kilometres west of Dieppe.

None of these sites, however, are as good as Cap Gris-Nez (Area 12) or Dunkerque (Area 14)

Area 9. **ROUEN**

Site i.

RESERVE DE GRANDE NOË   Southeast of Rouen, the Seine forms a series of meanders (*boucles* in French). At the Boucle de Poses there are chalk cliffs on the right bank and many gravel quarries on the low, left bank; some are still worked, others have been flooded and are now used for leisure activities. The Grande Noë, a private reserve of some 70 hectares, is one of these lakes. It has a web site: http://seb.kepka.free.fr/noe.htm which will give maps and a bird list for the area as well as up-to-date sightings.

WHEN TO VISIT: The whole stretch of the Seine and the surrounding areas here form an Important Bird Area, especially for wintering birds. There is a large **Cormorant** roost and a heronry; **Coot, Moorhen, Great Crested Grebe**, hundreds of duck in winter (mainly **Pochard, Mallard, Gadwall, Tufted Duck, Teal, Wigeon, Shoveler**); **Smew** and **Goosander** may turn up in cold spells and **Red-crested Pochard** has occurred in September.

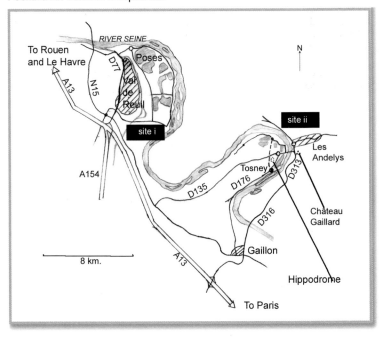

Normandy area 9 sites i and ii Rouen

In winter also hundreds of **Lapwing** and **Golden Plover** are found in the fields nearby, together with **pipits, larks** and **finches**.

During migration periods in spring and autumn **Spoonbills** from Holland use the lake as a stopover as do many species of **wader** (March and September are the best months for these); **terns** and **gulls** use the reserve in summer and early autumn. **Kingfisher** can always be seen from the hides at any season.

Cetti's, Reed and **Sedge Warblers, Reed Bunting** breed in the reserve and can be heard from April onwards; in spring and early summer **Nightingale** and **Golden Oriole** can be heard in the surrounding woodland.

ACCESS: The Reserve is less than 20 km from the centre of ROUEN and it takes about I hour in a car to reach it from the north of Paris. Leave the A13 motorway at exit 20 in the direction of PONT DE L'ARCHE. Go through this town and just before LES DAMPS (the two towns join) zero at the N15 crossroads. Continue straight over and on to the D77. At 5.1 km is the start of VAL-DE-REUIL. At 6.1 km turn left towards Gare (station). Cross the River Eure and the railway line and at 7.8 km turn right at the T-junction, signed to *Reserve Ornithologique*. Go straight over the next crossroads at the junction with the N147, still following the Reserve sign. The lake is on the left. In 300 metres there is a signed Parking on the right with a hide opposite overlooking the heronry. This hide displays lists of recent sightings. Organised walks start from here on Sundays in October, November and December. A footpath leads from the hide towards the north end of the lake. 500 metres south of the car park, beside a Neolithic cemetery (shown by a large notice board) there is another hide, a short distance off the road. This one gives good views of the southern end of the lake. Just beyond this hide is a crossroads. Turn left (east) here, as the minor road which runs along the southern boundary of the reserve towards the D110 is worth exploring. The next lake often holds different species of birds to the reserve and can be quite easily scoped from the road. Search the fields opposite for large flocks of Lapwings and passerine species in winter.

There are also birds to be found on the other lakes in this area. Check the large ones further north by turning left at the T-junction after the railway line.

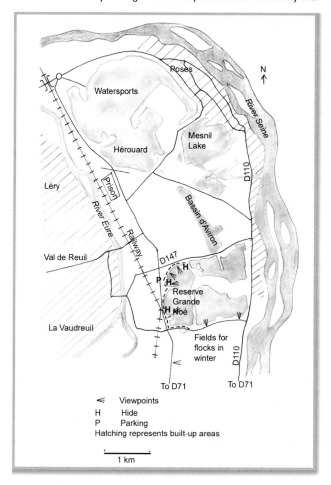

Normandy area 9 site I Reserve de Grande Noë

LES ANDELYS South of the previous site, enclosed within another meander west of the town of Les Andelys, is an area known as the Normandy steppes, dry and warm alluvial terraces dotted with old quarries, where a few pairs of **Stone Curlew** still remain, as well as **Red-backed Shrike, Stonechat, Honey Buzzard** and **Hobby**.

ACCESS: Leave the A13 (exit 17 Gaillon-Les Andelys) or the N14 and at the southern outskirts of Les Andelys, directly opposite the old castle, cross the Seine on the D135 in the direction of TOSNY. At the roundabout at the place called Les Carrières, go straight on (not left towards Tosny) for just under one kilometre to where a wide gravel track crosses the road by an old sign "Hippodrome". The track is drivable but it is likely to be more productive to park here and walk north towards La Garenne and then south past the west side of the Hippodrome, a cross-country course with fairly short grass. By the end of the summer the grass is very long elsewhere and most of the surrounding land is private and /or fenced, so it is necessary to stay on the track.

If you drive past the hippodrome the track meets the D176 near Tosny. Turn left and you arrive back at the roundabout on the D135.

WHEN TO VISIT: end-April to September. Early morning or dusk are the best times to see and hear Stone Curlew. To be sure of seeing them, go on one of the LPO Haute-Normandie (see introduction) organised walks, especially in the autumn when many Stone Curlew are forming post-nuptial flocks.

Other fauna and flora: The area has an interesting dry-grassland flora and orchids in spring. Green Lizard is found here at the limit of its range in the north-west; Natterjack and Parsley Frog occur and some grasshoppers and crickets normally considered as "Mediterranean" species.

Area 10. **DIEPPE to the SOMME ESTUARY**

The coast from the mouth of the River Bresle up to the estuary of the Somme has some reasonably good bird-watching sites. There are cliffs with breeding colonies and seawatching points, as well as marshland, small lakes and the mudflats of the Somme bay.

ACCESS: To reach this coastal area, leave the A28 motorway at exit 5 and take the D1015 towards EU and le TRÉPORT. On the road between GAMACHES and BEAUCHAMPS check the old flooded gravel pits on the left (south) side of the road. They can often be good for birds in winter or during migration. A kilometre after EU, turn right (north) at the roundabout onto the D940.

Site i.

Seawatching between **LE TRÉPORT and AULT** The lighthouse at le TRÉPORT, on the left bank of the canal, can be good for gulls but a better seawatching site is the **BOIS DE CISE CLIFFS**. The Bois (wood) is one of the few remaining natural woodlands on the Channel coast. Of botanical interest, it also contains typical woodland birds: **Great Spotted Woodpecker, Nuthatch, Short-toed Treecreeper, tits** and **warblers. Black Redstart** can always be found around the houses or cliffs at the Bois de Cise.

ACCESS: Some 2 km after the EU roundabout, turn left (north) off the D940 onto the minor road signed to le Bois-de-Cise. In 500 metres fork left towards *"Vue panorama sur Baie de Somme"*. It is difficult to park on the side of the road here except out of season and it may perhaps be better to take the right fork and park lower down. Follow the "Panorama" signs that lead past some houses to a small grassy area on the cliff top beside a plough and anchor. From here there are good views north as far as the Somme bay.

Cormorants, Jackdaws, Starlings can be seen on the cliffs, which in summer also hold **Fulmars**. Breeding starts in May and the young birds can be seen in the nests during July and August. At low tide there are plenty of **gulls** on the rocky beach below and good seawatching (see notes page xx). There are steps down to the beach below the cliffs from the lowest point of the village if you want to search the beach for waders, but this is really a seawatch site.

Other fauna and flora: Red Squirrel may be found in the wood. Bluebells, Lily-of-the Valley and Wood Anemones are attractive in spring.

AULT (which can be seen from the Bois-de-Cise) is perched on cliffs that are also good for a seawatch. Going northwards on the D940, take the D19 towards Ault and the sea. In the town, where the road turns right to run parallel with the coast along the cliff top, there are seats with a sea view.

Site ii.

PONTS-ET-MARAIS PEAT-BOG IN BRESLE VALLEY The peat-bog vegetation and reedbeds near the estuary of the River Bresle are a breeding site for **Bluethroat, Savi's Warbler, Reed** and **Sedge Warblers** in the reedbeds, **Cetti's Warbler** (resident), **Melodious Warbler** and **Red-backed Shrike** in the shrubby areas. In the surrounding fields **Yellow Wagtail, Meadow Pipit, Skylark, Corn Bunting, Grey Partridge** and possibly **Hen Harrier** may be seen.

WHEN TO VISIT: Mid-April to June is the best period. In winter much of the area will be flooded and inaccessible except to some duck species, such as **Teal**.

ACCESS: The D1015 runs from BLANGY-SUR-BRESLE to EU-LE TRÉPORT alongside the River Bresle. 2Kms before the junction with the D925 in EU, a very minor road leads left off the D1015 and crosses the river into PONTS-ET-MARAIS. Park beside the church, go right (towards Eu and the sea), skirting around a factory on an asphalted road that soon becomes a dirt track. The river is on your right and in about 500 metres there is a reedbed this side and rank vegetation on the left. This is good habitat for the above species but considerable patience is needed to see Bluethroat, which is a very skulking species. April-May, when it is singing, is the best time, as it is for most of the above species.

Farther on the path leads through hay meadows belonging to the Ferme de L'ÎLE, skirts around the farm and a track leads back to the D1015. The land on the opposite side of the road is higher and mainly agricultural.

Site iii.

HAUTEBUT MARSH AND HÂBLE D'AULT RESERVE The large Hâble d'Ault Reserve, marked on maps as a *Réserve Ornithologique* and on the ground signed as a *Réserve de Chasse* (no-hunting reserve) is, in fact, heavily shot over, there are hundreds of decoy ducks on the pools and the whole marsh is covered with gun butts. Unfortunately this is basically a winter site, best for birds from September to March, which coincides with the hunting season. It is probably dangerous to walk around the reserve on weekends but there will be people shooting there at almost any time, any day.

The Reserve (in the north of the marsh) covers the site of an old coastal lagoon, now separated from the sea by a sand and pebble bank. The marsh consists of numerous flooded gravel pits, of varying sizes, grassland, wet hollows, mud banks and reedbeds. The areas is criss-crossed by gravel and dirt tracks, making access and views of the ponds relatively easy. The high pebble dyke gives good views over the sea, where Scoters and Eider may be seen in winter, terns, Gannets and gulls on migration (notably Little Gull in spring). Many **duck** species, including **diving duck** and **sawbills** in winter, should be found here but many will be shot. **Grey Heron, Little Egret, Mute Swan** and **Coot** are the commonest species. **Snow Bunting** and **Horned Lark** can sometimes be found near the beach in winter; **Kentish, Ringed** and **Little Ringed Plover** all breed here. Look for **Kentish Plover** among the bare pebble areas near the sea south and north of Cayeux-sur-Mer. **Northern Wheatear** may also be seen here in summer. **Lapwing** occur all year round in the inland meadows and many migrating **waders** can be found around the muddy edges of the ponds. **Bluethroat** can be heard singing in the reedbeds in April and May. **Aquatic Warbler** is a regular August visitor and many Nearctic duck species turn up here but whether they are true vagrants or escapes poses the same problem as in Britain. In all, 270 species of birds have been noted in the Hâble d'Ault reserve.

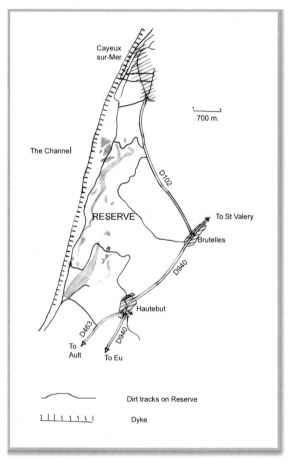

Channel Coast area 10 site iii Hautebut Marsh and Hable d'Ault Reserve

WHEN TO VISIT: March and April are the best months for duck on passage, April and May for waders, August and September for terns. The winter is perhaps of most interest, especially during really cold spells when many northern birds move south, but hunting is a problem.

ACCESS: The D463 from Ault and the D940 meet at HAUTEBUT, which is the starting point for the marsh and Hâble d'Ault Reserve. In the centre of HAUTEBUT village, which is very small, take the lane signed to the Marais. (If coming from the south, this is on the left just after the roundabout at the entrance to the village). Roughly 250 metres down the lane, by a duck weathervane, there is a raised viewpoint with a map of the area giving extensive views over the marsh to the seawall. After scanning, turn left here; the tarmac soon deteriorates into a dirt track and leads among deep pools, full of decoy ducks and surrounded by shooting butts. Make a circuit through the ponds if you wish but take care! It might be safest to remain in your car during the hunting season, but if the tracks are very muddy do not attempt to drive them. Take the track leading left towards the pebble bank and drive north below it. **Linnets** and **Pipits** (**Meadow** and **Rock**) are numerous here in winter and in most winters there are also small flocks of **Snow Buntings, Lapland Longspurs** and **Horned Larks**. These latter species often feed in the salt marsh around the salicornia bushes. Climb onto the top of the dyke where possible to scan the sea and search for **Kentish Plover**. Just before CAYEUX village there are usually large flocks of gulls on the beach, most of them to the north towards the mouth of the Somme.

Site iv.

HOURDEL POINT For closer looks at more gull flocks, continue on through CAYEUX village and take the coast road D102 north towards the HOURDEL lighthouse on a point sticking out into the mouth of the Somme. There will be thousands of gulls on the mud and sand banks at low tide, mainly **Herring Gulls** with a few **Great Black-backed** among them but most species occur here and American vagrants often turn up. Check through the flocks of **Black-headed Gulls** for **Mediterranean Gull**.

Continue on the D102 which loops back along the canal and through marshland (called *"mollières"* here) to join the D 3. Take the D3, which also runs through similar habitat, to the roundabout with the D940 outside ST VALERY-SUR-SOMME.

The *Maison de l'Oiseau,* prominently signed off the D3, is a bird museum with a display of free-flying raptors. However it does also have a small marsh area with a nature trail and hide

Accommodation: There are three hotels in St. Valery, including the recommended *Logis de France* Guillaume de Normandy overlooking the Somme. As this is a holiday area, there are campsites all along the coast.

Site v.

MARQUENTERRE BIRD PARK AND RESERVE which covers 250 hectares, is the southern part of a larger Maritime Reserve stretching from the Somme Estuary up to Authie Bay. The Bird Park, apart from the section nearest the entrance which has wildfowl enclosures with pinioned birds, is an excellent reserve with a variety of habitats: fresh and brackish lagoons, sand-dunes, water-meadows, marsh, reedbeds and pinewoods. 315 bird species have been recorded here since 1973. It is managed by the *Conservatoire du Littoral* (see introduction), the LPO and various regional conservations bodies and twinned with the Danube Delta and Zwin in Belgium. Well-marked trails with 12 hides at strategic points give good views over the water and can be spectacular on an incoming tide when thousands of waders fly in from the bay.

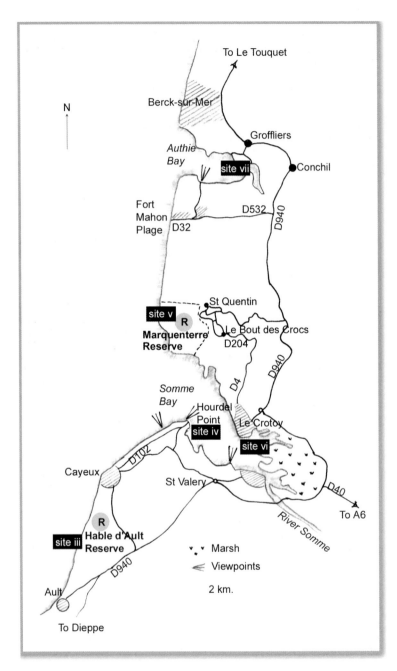

To Le Touquet

Berck-sur-Mer

Groffliers

Authie Bay

site vii

Conchil

Fort Mahon Plage

D32

D532

D940

St Quentin

site v

R

Marquenterre Reserve

Le Bout des Crocs

D204

D4

D940

Somme Bay

Hourdel Point

site iv

Le Crotoy

site vi

Cayeux

D102

St Valery

D40

To A6

River Somme

R

Hable d'Ault Reserve

site iii

Ault

D940

Marsh

Viewpoints

2 km.

To Dieppe

Channel Coast area 10 sites iii - vii

British birders may find the hides inconvenient, as the "windows" are just small holes cut at varying heights, difficult to scope through. They are probably impossible for wheelchair users, even if a chair could be pushed along the tracks between them, which are often muddy. The only trail recommended for those with "limited mobility" is the short parcours d'initiation around the wildfowl enclosures. There are wardens with telescopes in the hides during spring and autumn weekends.

It takes at least two to three hours to walk around the trails plus however long you wish to spend in the hides.

The entrance fee is currently €9.15 for adults, (€6.86 for students, the unemployed or members of the RSPB, LPO or other Conservation Societies), well worth the cost as far more bird species are likely to be seen here than at the other viewpoints over the Somme Bay. There is a restaurant, shop and picnic area at the entrance and binoculars can be hired. Tide times are displayed near the entrance as well as a list of bird species currently on the reserve.

The Park is open every day from 15/03 to 11/11. In summer (1/04 to 30/09) from 9.30 to 19.00 - ticket office closes 17.00. In spring and autumn it opens between 10.00 - 18.00 - ticket office closes at 16.00. In winter (12/11 - 14/03) there are guided visits at weekends only, on Saturdays at 14.00 and Sundays at 10.00 and 14.00, as well as at 14.00 in the school holidays. The walks start from the restaurant La Fôret in the nearby holiday village.

For more information you can telephone 33 (0) 836 68 80 21 or 03 22 25 03 06, fax 03 22 25 08 79 or check web site www.marcanterra.fr

WHEN TO VISIT: Late August, September and October are probably the best months to visit this area. 222 species have been counted during the autumn migration. Always try and time your visit to arrive at the hides nearest the sea (hides 4-7) just before high tide if you wish to see spectacular numbers of waders and wildfowl. There will be large numbers of passage waders (**Black-winged Stilt, Black** and **Bar-tailed Godwits, Ringed Plover, Dunlin, Curlew, Whimbrel, Redshank, Spotted Redshank, Greenshank, Snipe, Jack Snipe, Knot**) as well as resident breeders such as **Oystercatcher, Avocet** (small numbers), **Lapwing** and usually a few American vagrants. These are the best months for **Spoonbill** numbers; they start arriving in August, though a few can usually be seen in the park every month of the year. **White Storks** and a few **Black Storks** can be seen on passage during these months. There are good numbers of **terns** (**Arctic, Common, Sandwich, Little** and a few **Roseate), gulls** and a few **Arctic Skuas**. Many raptors, including **Kites, Merlin** and Osprey, pass through in these months. The first **Rough-legged Buzzard** may turn up in October. Flocks of migrant passerines (finches, larks, hirundines) peak in October. Small numbers of **Great White Egrets** can usually be seen in autumn and winter, often staying until late spring.

Towards the end of autumn duck numbers start increasing and a cold spell further north brings **Goldeneye, Smew, Goosander, Red-breasted Merganser, divers** and **sea-ducks, Eider, Scoter**, the occasional **phalarope** and sometimes **Whooper** and **Bewick Swans. Kingfisher** can often be seen from hide 11.

Winter is the season for large numbers of dabbling duck and geese (**Greylag** are most numerous on passage, **Bean** in winter with lesser numbers of **White-fronted, Barnacle, Brent**) and **Cormorants** as well as continuing huge roots of waders (**Oystercatcher, Dunlin, Curlew, Bar-tailed Godwit**), wintering passerines (**pipits, larks, Siskin, Twite, Fieldfare** and often **Snow Bunting** and **Horned Lark**) and **raptors** (**Buzzard, Rough-legged Buzzard, Merlin, Peregrine**). Wintering thrushes love the Sea Buckthorn bushes that are abundant along the paths.

The spring passage is not as large as the autumn one (185 species counted) but is notable for returning **sawbills, Garganey, White Storks** and **Spoonbills** in March-April as well as small numbers of **Bluethroat** on passage.

There is a large heronry in the Park, easily observed, so from February onwards **Grey Herons** and **Little Egrets** (some 20 pairs) will be active here. Since 1992 a few pairs of Cattle Egrets have joined the colony, the most northerly breeding site in France of the two latter species. If you do not find Cattle Egrets in the meadows within the Park, then they can sometimes be seen from the D4 in flooded fields north of Le Crotoy. There is currently an attempt to breed **Night Herons** in captivity (see them and other species in the large, netted enclosure nearby) so they too may soon be breeding freely. The heronry is of interest until mid-July, when it is deserted. Seven pairs of **White Storks** now breed on the Reserve.

Other resident breeders include **Avocet, Oystercatcher, Little Ringed Plover, Shelduck**, a few **Kentish Plover** in the dunes and many passerines: **Golden Oriole, Serin, Nightingale, Fan-tailed Warbler, Lesser Whitethroat, Willow Warbler** in the trees, scrub and **Sea Buckthorn** bushes and **Reed, Sedge** and **Savi's Warblers** in the reeds. **Firecrest, Crested, Long-tailed** and **Coal Tits** as well as a few Crossbill can be found in the pines (more of the last species after an irruption year).

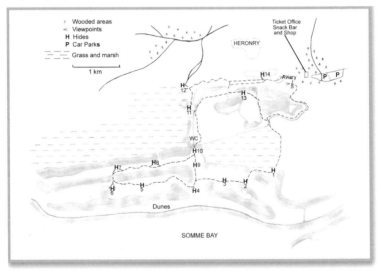

Chanel Coast area 10 site v Marquenterre Bird Park and Reserve

ACCESS: Whether arriving from the north or the south, leave the D940 at the roundabout outside LE CROTOY (zero here) and take the D4 in the direction of ST. QUENTIN, which is signed to Parc Ornithologique du Marquenterre. In 1.5 km turn right at the T-junction, again following the signs. At 1.7 km from the roundabout there are flooded meadows on the left and a canal on the right; although the species here are mainly Coot and Mute Swan, check for Cattle Egret. Continue along this road which bends right at 4.4 km (signed to Parc) still with the river on the right. At 5.9 km turn left onto the D204 (again signed). Bend right again at 6.5 km, still keeping on the D204 and at 7.3 bend left at another sign. At 8.4 km turn left, leaving the D204, then turn right in 50 metres. At 9.2 km you will see the entrance to the Parc. The car parking and ticket office is 800 metres up a gravel track on the left. (The restaurant "La Fôret" is to the right).

Shortly after the ticket office and at the start of all the trails there is an excellent viewpoint overlooking most of the reserve. This is possible the best place from where to watch migration in the autumn, or raptors in winter.

Site vi.

BAY AND MARSHES NEAR LE CROTOY If for any reason you cannot visit the Park, there is access to the Somme Bay from BOUT DE CROC village and a little further south another part of the Bay and the Crotoy marshes between le CROTOY and la MAYE can be visited.

ACCESS: At the roundabout on the D204 (700 metres from the Park entrance) turn down the *Chemin de Bergers,* which is signed *Accès à Baie.* Follow this sandy track for 1.2 km until it is barred beside a map showing footpaths. Then there is a short (300 m) walk to the sea and along the dunes edging the bay. Follow the trail for at least a kilometre or for as long as you like. This is part of a longer (15 km) circular walk along the coast, through dunes, pinewoods and marshland. Most of the species listed under Marquenterre Park will be seen if all or part of this walk is followed.

Alternatively follow the D204, then the D4 in the direction of LE CROTOY. In the town fork right to the signed *Plage de la Maye* and in 300 metres turn right again at T-junction, following signs to the camp site. In 1.5 km there is parking beside the beach, with distant views over the bay. Unfortunately hunters use this beach. Both these sites are best on an incoming tide, but never walk out into the estuary.

Other fauna and flora: There is an interesting dune and marsh flora, with 380 plant species recorded, including Grass of Parnassus, Sea Spurge, Yellow Horned Poppy, Sea Bindweed, Fragrant Evening Primrose and eight species of orchid, including Early Marsh Orchid *Dactylorhiza incarnata* and Marsh Helleborine *Epipactis palustris*. Amphibians include Natterjack Toad *Bufo calamita* and Viviparous Lizard *Lacerta vivipara*. 27 Dragonfly species have been recorded, including *Libellula quadrimaculata,* and 37 mammals. Those most likely to be seen in winter are Roe Deer, Wild Boar, Fox, Muskrat, Polecat, Weasel and Rabbit. Mouflon (wild sheep) and Henson horses graze the meadows. Common or Harbour Seals *Phoca vitulina* and the much rarer Grey Seals *Halichoerus grypus* can sometimes be seen in the bay. There are about 50 of the former but only 4 or so of the latter. The dunes at Marquenterre are one of the best places to observe Grey Seals while Hourdel point is good for Common Seals.

<u>Accommodation</u>: There are hotels in St. Valery (see site above) and a Logis, L'Auberge de la Dune, 3 km from the Reserve in Saint-Firmin-les-Crotoy. Gîtes and holiday cottages are available in Marquenterre itself for a weekend or longer stay. Phone for details. There are campsites near Le Crotoy and la Maye.

Site vii.

The dunes at **AUTHIE BAY**, some 12 km north of Marquenterre, are a likely place to spot **Crested Lark,** if you have not already found this species. Many of the birds listed under Marquenterre can also be seen in the bay and on the saltmarsh: **gulls, Shelduck** and **waders**; the latter especially in spring on the south (Somme) side of the bay. The pines, deciduous trees and Sea Buckthorn shrubs on the inland side of the dunes are good for passerines in spring and summer: **Nightingale, Whitethroat, Lesser Whitethroat, Willow Warbler, Chiffchaff, Serin** and many other finches can be found here and **Common Nightjar** may be heard at dusk from May to July. In winter, Short-eared owl and Hen Harrier may be observed hunting here.

WHEN TO VISIT: the inland area is best visited in spring and early summer; spring and autumn are best for waders.

ACCESS: Take the D940 north from LE CROTOY in the direction of BERCK-SUR-MER. In 22 km, at the village of GROFFLIERS, follow the signs for *base nautique* from the roundabout in the centre of the village, past the campsites to the wind-surfing - *base de voile* STERNES car park. **Crested Larks** can often be seen around the carpark or by the footpath that starts on the left near the entrance to the car park. The footpath, which makes a 2.5 km loop, is suitable for wheelchairs.

The south shore of the bay can be reached from FORT-MAHON-PLAGE. Leave the D940 3.5 km south of CONCHIL-LE-TEMPLE turning west (right if coming from the north) onto the D532 for 7 km to FORT-MAHON. At the main crossroads in town take the Rue de l'Authie right (north) towards the bay. There are water meadows on the east and dunes with vegetation on the seaward side. Park at the carpark on the edge of the bay and take a footpath, the *Sentier des Pêcheurs*, which starts from here.
Other flora and fauna: A good area for amphibians: Warty, Smooth and Alpine Newts, Natterjack Toad, Common Tree Frog, Common and Edible Frogs.

Site viii.

CRÉCY FOREST covering over 4000 hectares, composed mainly of beeches and oaks with some conifer plantations, lies some 15 km north of ABBEVILLE and about the same distance east of LE CROTOY and the coast. It can therefore easily be visited from the Somme Bay if you fancy a spot of forest birding for a change. **Buzzard, Honey Buzzard** and **Sparrowhawk** breed there. Breeding passerines include **Nuthatch, Short-toed Treecreeper, Redstart, Hawfinch** and **Wood Warbler** in mature woodland with **Melodious** and **Grasshopper Warblers** in the cleared, scrubby areas. Check all "yellow" warblers carefully as some **Icterine** may also breed here. **Hen Harrier** and **Common Nightjar** may also be found in the more open areas. **Woodpeckers** include **Green, Great** and **Lesser Spotted** as well as a few **Black** (difficult to find). There are **Woodcock** and finch **flocks**, which include **Brambling**, in winter.

ACCESS: From LE CROTOY take the D940 north to its junction with the D32 and follow this road eastwards for some 7 km until it meets the N1. Do not get onto the A16 motorway here but go south on the N1 towards NOUVION-EN-PONTHIEU. Just before this village (opposite a lay-by) there is a forestry road leading left (north) into the woods. Take this to the first crossroad within the forest and turn right towards the D 111 along the *Route Forestière de Forest-Montiers*. Park in one of the parking spaces alongside this forest road and walk towards the central crossroads *(Carrefour du Point Central)* or continue straight on towards another crossroads, the *Hutte des Grands Hêtres* and walk south-east from here.

Alternatively, take the D111 north from the centre of NOUVION village in the direction of CRÉCY-en-Ponthieu. Park in the forest at the crossroads with the *Route Forestière de Forest-Montiers at the Hutte des Vieux-Chênes*. Walk towards the central crossroads formed by the intersection of the R.F. du Millieu and the Allée Marcotte, marked by some venerable Spruce trees. North of the central crossroads is the Grands-Hêtres zone, Walk northwest towards to the *Sommière des Grands Hêtres* footpath. This is perhaps the best place for **Black Woodpecker** but as there are only some 4 or 5 pairs in over 500 hectares of suitable woodland they can be hard to find. It is easiest in very early spring when they are calling and drumming. A grid of roads and forestry tracks criss-cross the forest and it is worth exploring as many as possible. Some can be driven, others only walked along. Other good tracks for woodpeckers are *Derny, Domblast,* and the *Route de Silence de les Grandes Chênes*, all ones with large, mature trees nearby.

Other fauna and flora: Where there are seasonal ponds, look for the yellow and black Fire Salamander and newt species (Palmate, Smooth and Alpine). Wild Boar and Roe Deer are also attracted to these water holes. Red Squirrels are quite common. There is an attractive woodland flora and interesting beech wood fungi in autumn: *Russula cyanoxantha* The Charcoal Burner, *Lactarius blennius* Slimy Milkcap, *Lactarius pallidus, Marasmius alliaceus*

Area 11.**LE TOUQUET to BOULOGNE**

Site i.

The Nature Reserve of **CANCHE BAY** is situated on the northern shore of the Canche estuary, the most northern of the three Picardie estuaries. It is owned by the *Conservatoire du littoral* and is unfortunately smaller than intended, due to intense pressure from local hunters. There are three main habitats: dunes (both moving and stabilised with vegetation), the estuary and, where the two meet, marshes of varying degrees of salinity, depending on the amount of freshwater present. Botanists pressurised for the Reserve to be created (480 plant species have been recorded) but it is also important for many species of migrating and wintering birds, especially **Shelduck** and **waders**, notably **Golden Plover, Curlew, Ringed Plovers,** with many more species on passage. The Bay is also an important roost for *Larus* **gulls** (with up to 50,000 individuals, including thousands of **Great Black-backed** and often vagrants such as **Glaucous Gull** among them). A few pairs of **Shelduck** breed in rabbit holes on the marshes but there are otherwise fewer duck species in this estuary than some other sites. In summer the dune vegetation shelters numerous passerines such as **Nightingale**, *Phylloscopus* and *Sylvia* warblers, especially **Lesser Whitethroat,** as well as Woodlark, Common Nightjar and Northern Wheatear (the last three quite rare in the north). In winter there may be a few raptors, including the occasional **Rough-legged Buzzard.**

ACCESS: From le TOUQUET (or further south), take the D940 from ETAPLES, following signs for the *Baie de Canche*, north towards CAMIERS for 2 km to the British cemetery, where there is a car park and notice board. The *sentier du Tadorne* footpath is signed from the cemetery. There are hides and viewpoints along the length of the 2-hour walk. The *sentier des Mollières* is shorter (about I hour).

Site ii.

HESDIN FOREST with several good areas of mature beeches, lies along the Canche valley. It has the woodland species one would expect, including **Short-toed Treecreeper** and is a good site for **Reeve's Pheasant**, especially at the end of summer when numbers are swelled by the season's young birds. **Black Woodpecker** has been reported but not confirmed.

ACCESS: Hesdin is 24 km east of the A 16 opposite Berck-Plage. Leave the motorway at exit 25 and take the D303 for 4 km to the NI/N39 junction and the N39 eastwards to the Hesdin turning. The D928 runs north from Hesdin through the forest, with forestry roads running off it. A more attractive road is the D349 that turns off the NI, 4 km further north. After I6 .5 km at AUBIN-St. Vaast take the DI54 left (north) towards CAVRON. Where it runs along the western side of the forest, park at the barriers by the forestry road leading east into the forest and walk down to the picnic area and explore some of the side trails. This is the best area for pheasants.

Pine woodland sites: **SAINT-FRIEUX** and **HARDELOT**. A short walk through the pine woods, dunes and fields on the slopes of SAINT-FRIEUX (152 m) should enable you to find some woodland species, including as **Green, Great Spotted** and **Black Woodpeckers** (a recent arrival), **Coal, Long-tailed** and **Crested Tits, Honey Buzzard, Goshawk, Sparrowhawk, Hobby, Nightjar, Tree Pipit, Willow Warbler, Chiffchaff, Whitethroat, Lesser Whitethroat, Song Thrush, Nuthatch, Crossbill**. On the dunes several pairs of **Woodlark** breed, the highest density in the region, due in part to the warm microclimate here. The other local woods hold similar species.

WHEN TO VISIT: Whilst the woodpeckers are easier to hear and locate early in the year, May-June are the best months for most of the other species.

ACCESS: From BOULOGNE or ETAPLES take the D940 south or north respectively towards DANNES. At the crossroads to this village, turn right (west) towards the sea, following the signs *dunes du Mont Saint-Frieux*, in under 300 metres you will find the main car-park for the site. The signed sentier de la Palme d'Or leads off from here. **Crested Tit** can be found in the rather thin pines on the left. At the crossroads signed *Pomme d'Or/Chablis*, take the left track towards *Chablis/Mont St.* Frieux. There is older, unmanaged **woodland** here with many dead trees, so this is a good area for woodpeckers. In about 500 metres you will come out of the woods into pastures and further along onto an area of dunes, where **Woodlark** and **Tree Pipit** may be found. Do not leave the path, the dunes are very fragile. Keep right at the next crossroads in the direction of *Mont Saint-Frieux*. The large pines on the slopes of the hill are another place to look again for **Crested** and **Coal Tits**, as well as **Nightjar** if you are here at dusk. **Crossbills** have been seen here more and more frequently in recent years. From the top of Saint-Frieux the English coast can be seen on a clear day. It is also a good raptor viewpoint, where with luck **Honey Buzzard, Buzzard, Sparrowhawk** and **Hobby** may be seen.

On the return walk, turn right at the first crossroads on the way down in the direction signed retour P (parking). The walk is about 5.5 km in length and will take between 2 and 3 hours (or longer if you stop to raptor watch).

It is also worth exploring the HARDELOT woods, a northward continuation of St. Frieux. Take the D119 from NEUFCHATEL-HARDELOT towards BOULOGNE, stopping at any of the parking places where tracks lead off into the woods.

Other fauna and flora: Red Squirrels are likely to be seen in the woods but Wild Boar and Roe Deer, though present, are shyer and most likely to be seen at dusk.

PORTEL beach, just south of **BOULOGNE**, is an important roost for Mediterranean Gulls between August and March. There will be **Kittiwakes** and other gull species there too and a few **waders**, especially in autumn.

Gulls are also attracted to the freshwater pools in the 27 hectare **PARC DE LA FALAISE**, where many species, including **Mediterranean**, roost regularly, and **Sabine, Ring-billed, Iceland** and **Glaucous** have been noted among them. Part has been set aside for wildlife and the mixture of trees, bushes, brambles and wetland is proving very attractive to birds with over 190 species recorded. Bittern can be heard in the reeds. **Reed Bunting, Reed, Marsh, Sedge** and **Grasshopper Warblers, Whitethroat** and **Lesser Whitethroat** all breed; **Fan-tailed Warbler** has attempted to; many more passerines and waders stop off during autumn passage including recently Pallas Warbler and Red-breasted Flycatcher. In winter there are **Redwing, Fieldfare, Redpoll** and **Siskin** in the trees.

ACCESS: From the south, take the D119 (coast road) to PORTEL. Follow signs to the *Plage* and Parking and *Camping du Phare*. Park on the sea wall and check the beach south of the harbour.

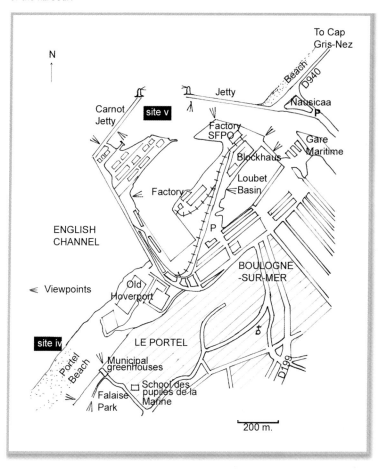

Channel Coast area 11 sites iv and v Portel and Boulogne

Site v.
BOULOGNE-SUR-MER FISHING PORT is, like Portel above, essentially a gull-watching site. From autumn to spring there are thousands of gulls around the harbour: **Great** and **Lesser Black-backed**, **Herring** and **Yellow-legged**, **Common, Black-headed** and **Mediterranean.** In autumn Little Gull may be among them as well as skuas. Glaucous Gull turns up regularly. Kittiwakes nest on the dock buildings. In cold spells look for sea duck and Red-necked Grebe among the Great Crested Grebe which are more common; five grebe species have been recorded here. Snow Bunting has been seen around the docks. The two long jetties make this a very sheltered harbour.

WHEN TO VISIT: Essentially a winter site: November to February.

ACCESS: Entering the town from the south on the D119, follow the signs *ZI Portuaire* and turn left at the roundabout with the seagulls. Follow the signs *Port du Peche* along the railway lines and through the industrial area, down the *Rue du Petit Peche* towards the *Capitainerie* for the southern side of the harbour and south jetty.

To reach the north jetty, follow signs through the town to *Nausicaa/la Plage* and park on the sea front. Walk along the jetty with the red light and check the beach near Nausicaa for gulls.

Other fauna: Nausicaa is a superb sea-life centre

Site vi.

BOULOGNE FOREST, damp woodland with Oak and Ash predominant, lies some five kilometres east of Boulogne, between the N42 and the D341. It is also crossed by the D254 between la Culbutte and la Capelle-les-Boulogne. This last road is one of the best from which to explore it. There is also a forestry road leading north from the village of Hesdin, on the N1 south of the forest. Stop wherever there are areas of mature trees for woodpeckers and finches. Search for **Melodious Warbler** around clearings and on the edges.

Area 12. **CAP GRIS-NEZ**

CAP GRIS-NEZ some 20 km south of Calais and a similar distance north of Boulogne, is the closest point of France to England; the Straits of Dover being only 40 km wide here. It also marks the limit between the Channel and the North Sea as well as a change of direction in the coastline, which runs almost due north-south from the Somme estuary to Gris-Nez but then turns to run south-west to north-east up to Denmark. The cliffs at the Cap are some 50m high, overlooking the Bay of Wissant. **Gannets, auks, divers, skuas, shearwaters, gulls, terns, geese** and **duck** all pass in their thousands between mid-August to November. Spring passage takes place from mid-February to the end of May with numbers peaking in April, but is never as impressive or easily viewed as the post-nuptial migration in the autumn. Besides the cliff-top site, there is a variety of habitat nearby: dunes, marsh, wet meadows, heath, sand and shingle beaches, so that many thousands of waterbirds and passerines regularly stop off here. These include both **Little** and **Red-necked Grebe, Spoonbill, Brent Geese, Shelduck, Pintail, Shoveler, Ferruginous Duck, Oystercatcher, Ringed, Kentish** and **Grey Plovers**, thousands of other waders (**Curlew, Dunlin, Bar-tailed Godwit**, etc) **gulls** and **terns** (**Roseate** the rarest, **Sandwich** and **Common** the most numerous). There will regularly be 20,000 or more waterbirds on passage and many also winter here, notably **gulls, Dunlin** and **Oystercatchers**. Large flocks of passerines (**larks, wagtails, thrushes, finches, buntings**) can be observed migrating south or feeding on the cliff tops, while in winter **Horned Lark, Twite, Snow Bunting** and even the occasional **Lapland Longspur** can be found here.

For fuller and more detailed information on conditions for seawatching and species likely to be seen, read the notes under Le Havre site v or the articles listed in the Bibliography. Best conditions at the Cap are north or north-westerly winds above gale force 3 to 4, ideally the days following a storm. If the wind is very strong and the sea rough, then Gris-Nez is a better site than Dunkerque harbour (area 13) as neither observer nor equipment will get so wet but its disadvantage is the height of the cliff, which means that birds are further away and smaller species can be hard to identify.

WHEN TO VISIT: Mid-August to November, preferably when a north-west wind is blowing. October and November are the best months for the greatest numbers of birds but August and-September are best for **Fulmars, Gannets, Skuas, gulls** and **terns; Gannets** are numerous from August to November, as are **shearwaters**, especially **Sooty Shearwater** with smaller numbers of **Manx; Eiders** are always present, **Common Scoters** can be seen every autumn month but **Velvet Scoters** are more common end-October/ November, when **sawbills, Razorbill** and **Guillemot** numbers also increase, as do **Red** and **Black-throated Divers**. A few **Sabine's Gulls** are recorded every autumn, especially after westerly gales, and other rarities recorded a few times include **Black-browed Albatross**, a **Frigatebird** sp., **Bulwer's** and **Fea's Petrels**. In winter there are usually **Brent Geese** and some waders (**Curlew, Oystercatcher**, etc) on the rocky shore with many more wader species during autumn and spring passage. Outside migration periods, early morning and late afternoon are the best times for birds.

ACCESS: Take the coast road D940 from either Calais or Bologne (or turn off the A16 at exit 7 onto the D191), following the signs *site des Caps*. Leave it at the roundabout just south of AUDINGHEN and take the D191 for three kilometres through FRAMZELLE, bearing left towards the lighthouse, where there is a car park. Walk to the coastal footpath that runs around the headland in front of the lighthouse. The best seawatching site is on the clifftop by the lighthouse beyond the *Centre Régional d'Observation et de Sauvetage Maritime* (CROSMA - the buildings you can see by the carpark) looking north. Some old wartime bunkers, visible from the carpark, give shelter from the wind, except when it is from the north or northwest, but may be occupied weekends in September and October. An umbrella and a folding stool can be useful and warm, waterproof clothes and gloves are essential. The bushes near the lighthouse parking area and near the Hotel and bar *du cap Gris-Nez* can be good for watching migrant passerines, as can the grassy areas around the lighthouse, the cliff path going east and the cliff between the Sirène restaurant and the Court Dune headland.

Alternatively, keep right in FRAMZELLE towards the car park for the beach - *plage du Cap Gris-Nez*. Park here by the information board and take the coastal footpath *GR du Littoral* eastwards. From the cliff top there are good views over the bay to the north, looking towards the English coast and some 500 metres further along the footpath there is a lookout from the *Pointe de Courte Dune* and beyond this some scrubby vegetation that may hold passerines.

The fields east of Framzelle are crossed by minor roads or tracks and dotted with patches of thin woodland which may shelter passerines in the autumn: **Black** and **Common Redstarts, Ring Ouzel, Spotted** and **Pied Flycatchers, warblers** and **buntings**. **Yellow-browed Warbler** has quite frequently been seen here. Turn east in Framzelle village or take one of the tracks leading off the D191 south of the village. **Short-eared Owl** hunts over the fields west of Framzelle, south of the lighthouse in winter. The cereal fields along the D191 and the D940 are worth searching for **Dotterel** (between mid-August and September) or **Lapland Longspur** (October on) among the flocks of larks found here. From TARDINGHAM footpaths lead towards the marshes. Also in winter **Snow Bunting** and **Twite** are often observed from the dunes along Wissant beach (see Access below).

CAP BLANC-NEZ is a chalk headland at the east end of Wissant Bay. Though not as good a sea-watching site as Cap Gris-Nez, in autumn and winter **divers, Eider** and other **sea-ducks** can be observed from the cliffs where colonies of **Fulmar, Kittiwake, Herring Gull** and **Jackdaw** breed. In winter **Short-eared Owl** may be observed hunting over the rough grassland below and around the radio mast and the passerines listed above can also be seen around Cap Blanc-Nez. A few years ago,

Common Rosefinch was starting to breed on the grassy slopes here but its expected range expansion seems to have contracted. It may return.

WHEN TO VISIT: unlike Cap Gris-Nez, which is a winter site, Blanc-Nez is best at the end of spring when **Grasshopper Warbler** and **Corn Bunting** may be heard, and seabirds are breeding on the cliffs, although it can still be interesting in winter for divers, etc. on the sea.

ACCESS: Return to the D940 and head north towards Calais following the signs to Cap Blanc-Nez, go through ESCALLES and take the first road left, signed to the Cap (opposite the hill of Mont. St. Hubert with a radio mast on the right) and drive to the monument where you can park. The coastal footpath back towards Cap Gris-Nez and north-east to Calais can be clearly seen from the grassy slopes below the monument. It is worth walking along both ways for some distance. The footpath can also be reached by turning off the N940 at the south end of ESCALLES and taking the road seawards towards the church.

To reach the beaches and dunes, leave the D940 at WISSANT, halfway between the two headlands. Leave the Centre Ville following *Plage* signs towards the beach. There is a beach carpark to the right of the small square with a dolphin statue. Early morning visits are best. The beach becomes very busy at weekends, even in winter.

Other fauna: Harbour Seals are regularly observed on the rocks below Cap Gris Nez.

Area 13. CALAIS

Site i.

LE PLATIER D'OYE RESERVE has unfortunately become notorious in recent years for confrontations between birders and hunters. Although it is a protected Reserve, hunters flouted all signs and warnings and regularly shot over it, arguing that their hunting butts had been in place before the area was created a reserve in 1987. Hopefully new legal action may force hunters to respect the law; the situation in winter 2002 seemed hopeful.

WHEN TO VISIT: This site is best in autumn and winter, which is, of course, the hunting season. It is probably best to avoid weekends if local hunters are feeling confrontational. It is also excellent in early spring. There is a hide with identification charts overlooking a scrape near the carpark which is always full of birds. Beyond it a signed path with hides leads through Buckthorn bushes, flooded meadows and dunes, some 13 metres high (look for **Crested Lark**) to the beach. This site is the first French stopover for migrating birds passing south down the coast in the autumn and is especially good for **waders** and **duck** from August to November and for duck and geese in February/March. Migrating **thrushes** and **finch** flocks pass through in October. Breeding species include **Shoveler, Tufted Duck, Avocet, Little** and **Kentish Plover, Snipe**, large numbers of **Lapwing** and a breeding colony of **Sandwich Tern** (395 pairs in 1999). A few **Black-winged Stilt** bred in the 1990s. **Avocets** can be seen from autumn to spring. In winter this reserve is a good place to find **Horned Lark, Snow Bunting** and **Lapland Longspur**.

ACCESS: From Calais take the D940/N1 north-east (direction Gravelines) for 12 km to OYE-PLAGE (or turn off the A16 at exit 20 onto the D219 for 5 km north to the cross-roads in OYE-PLAGE). In the town turn left (north) towards the sea at the traffic lights at the main crossroads, following the signs to *Réserve Naturelle*. After a kilometre turn right and in 100 metres left. Bear right in another 1.2 km. The carpark at the entrance to the reserve is on the left in another kilometre. It is signed all the way.

There is a WC and facilities for the disabled. LEAVE NOTHING VALUABLE IN YOUR CAR. Follow the footpath signed *circuit du Platier d'Oye* that starts from just beyond the car park. It takes about 2 hours to walk the loop. Alternatively stay in the excellent hide overlooking the scrape situated at the beginning of the circuit. It is suitable for wheelchairs. A telescope is useful.

There are guided tours of the reserve between 9.30 - 12.00 on the first Saturday of every month. Groups can book a visit. Tel: 03 21 32 13 74

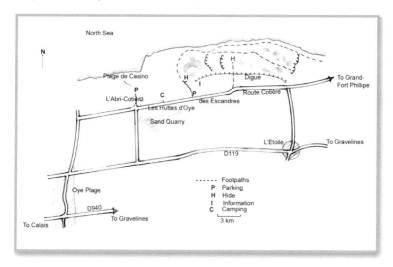

Channel Coast area 13 site i La Platier d'Oye Reserve

Site ii.

GUÎNES MARSH lies some 10 km south of Calais car terminal, 2 km north of GUÎNES. Formed from an old peat bog that is now reedbeds, marsh and small lakes, all the usual water birds are likely to be found there. Besides **herons, Mallard, Coot, Moorhen** and **Little Grebe**, you are likely to see **Kingfisher, Water Rail, Marsh Harrier, Reed Bunting** and in spring and summer, it is an excellent reserve for **warblers**. Nine species have been recorded here: all the *Sylvia* and *Acrocephalus* warblers of the region, including **Marsh,** in addition to **Savi's** and **Cetti's**. **Bluethroat** turns up in spring. **Golden Oriole** may be found in the poplars near the start of the walk and **Little Owl** in the pollarded willows.

WHEN TO VISIT: April, May and June are the best months.

ACCESS: From Calais take the D127 in the direction of GUINES, turning left onto the D248 E before reaching Guines, 4.8 km from where the D127 passes under the A16 motorway. The marsh lies to the right (south) of the D248 E and you can park on the edge of the road. The entrance to the footpath is 500 metres past a track on the right and 750 metres before the T-junction with the D248. A sign *sentier des Têtards* marks the start of the footpath, which is a loop of about 3 km.

Other fauna and flora: Guînes has an interesting marsh and aquatic flora, best from April to June, which are also the best months for birds. Amphibians are numerous: Common Toad *Bufo bufo,* Common Frog *Rana temporaria,* and Great Crested Newt *Triturus cristatus.* Muskrat is among the mammals found here.

<u>Accommodation</u>: There are hotels, *Chambres d'Hôte* (bed and breakfast) and campsites the length of this coast but they will be very full in summer and autumn. Most are open in winter and do not need booking in advance, though they may be full at weekends. Berck-Plage, Hardelot-Plage, Wimereux, Wissant and Escalles are small seaside towns with reasonably priced *Logis de France* hotels, conveniently situated for the sites above. In addition, **Serin** and **Black Redstart** are likely to be found around these resorts. There are hotels belonging to various chains just off the motorways outside the large ports.

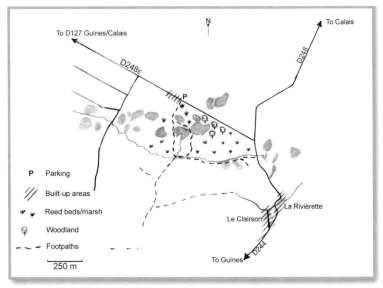

Channel Coast area 13 site ii Guines Marsh

Area 14. **DUNKERQUE**

<u>Site i</u>.
Dunkerque has been recognised as one of the best sea-watching sites in northern Europe and for some years regular counts of seabirds have been undertaken there. The **CLIPON JETTY** by the Avant-Port Ouest in Dunkerque harbour is a favoured sea-watch spot as it projects almost 3 km out to sea and is near sea level, thus giving the observer very close views of many different species during favourable weather conditions. Its one drawback is that in rough weather with onshore winds of gale force 4 or 5 (the best conditions for seabird passage), waves breaking over the jetty will soak both birders and their equipment and it is positively dangerous in storm conditions.

Shipping forecasts are broadcast on *France Inter* (162 kHz) at 20.03 every evening and give wind strength, current weather conditions and a forecast for the next 24 hours area by area. Pas-de-Calais is the local area. The same equipment and clothing are needed here as for Cap Gris-Nez.

Clipon has a good website, in French and English, listing the latest sightings with photos and including practical information on the site. http://users.skynet.be/digibirds/Clipon.htm
WHEN TO VISIT: Bird species recorded here are approximately the same as for Cap Gris-Nez (above) and the season is the same: August to December with numbers of most species peaking end September/October.

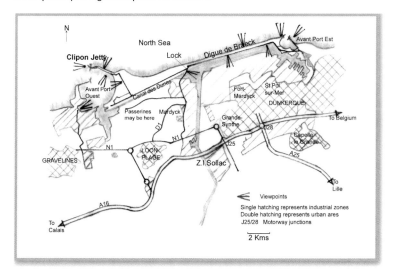

Channel Coast area 14 Dunkerque sites

ACCESS: The Clipon jetty is in the Loon-Plage (Nord) section of Dunkerque, some 12 km west of the town centre, part of a huge unfinished industrial area. Leave the A16 motorway at exit 25 and zero at the roundabout. Take the *Centre Commercial/Port Mardych* direction (*Sollac* is the building on the right) and drive for 1.3 km to the second roundabout (with traffic lights), turn left onto the N1 in the direction of *Port Ouest/Loon Plage* and continue for 2.3 km to a set of traffic lights. Turn right here onto the small road signed to *Port Mardych/Le Clipon/ZIP de Mardyck*. Follow this road for 5 km (it is signed Le Clipon) to the lock on the Canal des Dunes. Cross to the north bank of the canal and turn left, running alongside the canal, past the windmills. Stop where possible and check the canal for **divers, grebes** (all 5 species), **sawbills** and even **Long-tailed Duck** in winter. On the sea side hundreds of **scoters** and **Eider** may be found in winter. In about 4 km from the lock take the first turning right, signed *Route de la Jetée du Clipon*. Keep straight on through the dunes (watch out for **Crested Lark**) until you reach the jetty, turn left and drive to the end where you can park. There may be up to 50 sea-watchers here in suitable conditions and the best viewing sites, in the shelter of any large concrete blocks which do not restrict the view, will be taken early. Warning: hunters are numerous in the dock area, and though they are not allowed to shoot from the jetty itself, may be found around the entrance to it; they can be quite aggressive. There will also be fishermen on the jetty.

The entry to the Clipon jetty gives excellent views over the *Avant-Port Ouest* harbour and beaches. **Divers, grebes, cormorants, sea ducks, Long-tailed Duck, terns** and **gulls** can all be observed here in autumn and winter. There may be passage waders on the beach and **Crested Lark** can usually be found on the waste ground.

Site ii.
DIGUE DU BRAECK AND PORT-EST Return to the canal lock. A continuation of the Canal des Dunes road runs northeast towards the Avant-Port-Est. This 5 km stretch gives excellent views over the sea and the inland waterway. Just after the road crosses the canal the waterway widens out to form the *bassin de Mardyck*, where there are often **grebes**. Drive up onto the Digue du Braeck and stop anywhere along it to scan the sea and the basin for **divers, grebes** and **auks**. **Great Northern Diver** is a regular winter visitor and Little Auks sometimes seek shelter here after autumn storms. At low tide, the beach is good for flocks of **waders** and **gulls; Iceland, Glaucous** and **American gulls** have been spotted here. **Snow Bunting** are regular. At the end of the Digue, seawatching from the jetty of the old port can be an alternative to the Clipon jetty and is also a good spot for views of sea duck, etc.

Site iii.
AVANT-PORT OUEST To reach the west side of this harbour, it is necessary to retrace your route back to the N1 and take it westwards in the direction of LOON PLAGE/GRAVELINES for almost 7 km. At the big crossroads with traffic lights just before Gravelines, turn right following signs to *ZIP des Huttes/Port petrolier*. At the roundabout in 300 metres follow the signs *Institut Pasteur* for 2.7 km. Park by the round, blue-striped storage tank where there is a view over the west side of the harbour, the most sheltered and the best for close views of divers, grebes and sea ducks.
Other fauna: Seals, Grey and Common, can sometimes be seen from the harbour or nearby beaches.
<u>Accommodation</u>: There are numerous hotels, in all price ranges, in Dunkerque but if you do not want to go into the town-centre, there are also several hotels belonging to the cheaper chains such as Formule 1 on the outskirts of Dunkerque, just off the motorway. The Formule 1 at Saint-Pol-sur-Mer (1 rue Francois Arago, 03 28 64 69 00) has been recommended by birders.

Area 15. **ST. OMER**

ROMELAERE RESERVE is situated in the heart of an old peat bog. It is an area of marshland, water meadows, reed-beds and small patches of woodland, separated by earth dykes. Where the peat was extracted during the 19th century lakes have formed. There are board-walks leading through the reedbeds, which cover about a quarter of the reserve, to the lake at its centre. It is a 5 km return walk to the lake and hide (count on at least two hours; longer in spring if you are waiting for Little Bittern to fly over the reeds) or it is possible to make a shorter 2-3 km loop around the nature trail (this is the only part accessible in winter, when it is not very interesting). There is a Visitors' Centre, La Grange Nature by the entrance to the reserve in Clairmarais, and recent sightings are written up outside it. Entry to the reserve is free. The boardwalks are suitable for wheelchairs and those with limited mobility.
There are signs in Braille. 200 bird species have been counted in Romelaere of which about 60 breed there. These include **Little Bittern** (only 2-6 pairs), **Marsh Harrier** (1-3 pairs), **Little Owl** (check the pollarded willows), **Kingfisher, Bluethroat, Reed Bunting,** and **Water Rail**. The Reserve is especially good for *Locustella* and *Acrocephalus* warblers: **Reed, Great Reed, Marsh, Sedge, Grasshopper, Savi's** and **Cetti's Warblers**, as it is one of the few remaining places with large reedbeds.

Its colony of **Cormorants** has been growing since 1992. **Black Tern** may be seen hawking over the lake in May and **Ospreys** regularly stop off here for quite long periods in spring and autumn. There are many **duck** species in winter and more on passage (mainly **Shoveler, Gadwall, Wigeon, Teal**) together with some waders. One or two **Bittern** winter there.

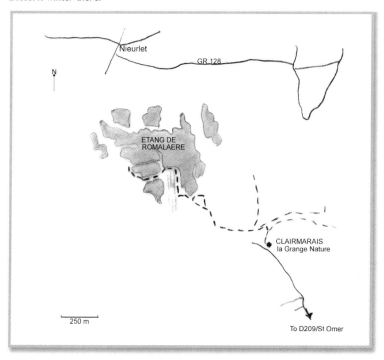

Channel Coast area 15 Romalaere Reserve

WHEN TO VISIT: Good all year around, though most of the reserve is closed from 15 December to 15 March. April, May and June are the best months but September-October can also be productive.

ACCESS: Leave ST. OMER following the signs for the station - *gare SNCF*. Cross the canal and zero in front of the station Turn right in the direction of CLAIRMARAIS and take the D209 turning left at the next junction. It is 3 km from the station to CLAIRMARAIS. In the village, turn left by the church, following the sign to Grange Nature and continue straight on for 700 metres. Park in the Grange Nature car park on the right. The entry is on the right of the visitors' centre. Follow the signs to Romelaere Reserve and then take the boardwalk. (The GR 128 (marked red/white) goes past the reserve and another footpath *du bocage au marais* is marked in yellow. They could be quite interesting to walk along, time permitting).

The Reserve is open from 8.00-20.00 from March to September and from 8.00-17.30 October to December. It is shut from 15 December to 15 March but it is possible to walk the short nature trail or the footpaths described above. The visitors' centre, with videos and suggestions for other walks, is open at weekends 1/03 - 15/11 from 14.30 - 17.30 plus Sunday mornings in April, May, June and September and every day during the Easter and summer holidays. Call 03 21 87 90 90 for further information or fax: 03 21 87 90 87. e-mail: infos@parc-opale.fr

Other fauna and flora: 27 mammals have been counted on the reserve, of which Muskrat may be the most obvious. Edible Frog *Rana* **esculenta** and Common Toad *Bufo bufo* are common amphibians. There are 18 fish species and many dragonflies among the 400 insects counted on the Reserve. The impressive marsh flora (230 plants, 20 protected species) includes Bladderworts and Water Soldier *Stratiotes aloides*.

Blacknecked Grebe

PARIS REGION

Area 1   **Trilbardou** sand quarries

Area 2   **St. Germain Forest** *

Area 3   **Central Paris**
Site i.	Bois de Bologne
Site ii.	Bois de Vincennes
Site iii.	Montsouris Park
Site iv.	Butte-Chaumont Park
Site v.	Père Lachaise Cemetery and other parks.
Site vi.	The River Seine

Area 4 Rambouillet area
Site i.	The forest *
Site ii.	St. Hubert and Hollande Lakes
Site iii.	Saclay Lake Nature Reserve
Site iv.	St. Quentin-en-Yvelines Reserve *

Area 5 Sénart Forest *

Area 6 Fontainebleau *
Sites i/vii.	The forest
Site viii.	Chanfroy Plain/Trois Pignons Forest
Sites ix/xi.	Wetland sites

This region covers approximately that of the historic Île de-France, from Beauvais and Compiègne in the north, down to south of Fontainebleau, west to Dreux and east to Montmirail and Esternay, a rough square of 16,186 square kilometres centring on the capital and extending for 60 to 80 km all around. This is the area covered by the Centre Ornithologique Île-de-France. It includes some large forest areas (Chantilly, Rambouillet, Fontainebleau, not forgetting the Paris woods of Boulogne and Vincennes), major rivers, several lakes or reservoirs, farmland, airports, as well as a huge urban and industrial area.

To date 221 bird species have been counted in the Paris region (73 breeding and 83 occasional) many of them in the forests and woods surrounding Paris.

MAPS: The Recta-foldex *Region Parisienne 60 km autour de Paris* Scale 1 cm= 1 km 250 covers the whole of this area and the same firm's Île-de-France 1/150 000 covers a good part of it. CORIF (see address below under Central Paris) has published a map showing 50 birding sites in the Île-de-France. Entitled *"Oiseaux et forets en Île-de-France"* scale 1/250,000, it gives a list of species seen in every site and access details.

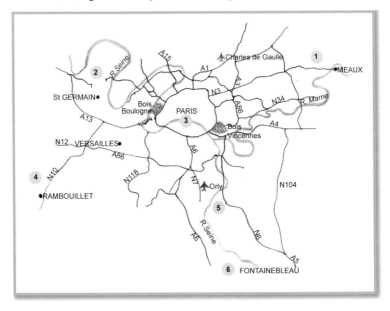

Paris Birding Areas

Area 1. **TRILBARDOU and JABLINES GRAVEL QUARRIES**

TRILBARDOU and JABLINES GRAVEL QUARRIES are situated some 40 km east of Paris, close to MEAUX, and have been studied by birders for more than 15 years.

More than 212 species, including rarities such as **White-headed** and **Ring-necked Duck, Iceland Gull**, etc., have been noted on the site, in spite of there being considerable disturbance from quarrying and shooting. Large numbers of **Pochard** and **Tufted Duck** winter there and there is a large gull roost. **Black Tern** and **Osprey** occur on passage and breeding birds include **Stone Curlew, Garganey** and **Marsh Warbler**. It is hoped that the site will soon be recognised and given some protection. JABLINES is a water-sports centre but still attracts numerous duck, both **dabbling** and **diving, grebes** and **herons** in winter.

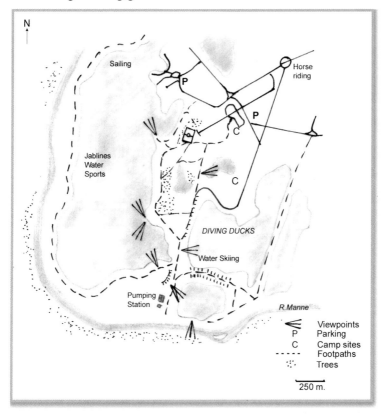

Paris area 1 Jablines gravel quarries

WHEN TO VISIT: Between October and March (Entry to Jablines is free during this period) and best in the morning (late afternoon for gull roost) and during very cold spells.

ACCESS: Some 10 km west of MEAUX, (or 20 km east of Charles de Gaulle airport) just south of the N3, the River Marne forms a large loop. The village of TRILBARDOU is at the north but within the meander there are large lakes (Jablines, Îles-les-Villenoy, marshes (Lesches). Leave the N3 for the D27 through TRILBARDOU (2 km from the junction) and then the D89 over the river towards the quarries. Afterwards continue south on the D89 to ESBLEY, and then take the D45A to JABLINES, continuing on the D45 towards ANNET, taking the left fork towards the lake, which is signed.

Park in the large P2 carpark and walk south to the first bay on the lake, behind the football fields, about 500 m. Continue south down the sandy bank of the lake. There are a couple of mounds which give good viewpoints, cross over the footpath to scan the second lake, which is good for diving duck. The footpath continues south past the pumping station to the banks of the River Marne. Turn left around the small lake and back to the carpark by the centre path between the two larger lakes. Keep an eye open for birders with 'scopes - it may mean that a rarity has turned up!

Area 2. **SAINT-GERMAIN-EN-LAYE FOREST**

Mixed, but predominantly Oak woodland west of Paris in a loop of the River Seine between St. Germain and Poissy, the forest offers a good selection of woodland species: **Black, Great** and **Lesser Spotted Woodpeckers, Short-toed Treecreeper,** seven Tit species including **Crested, Coal** and **Marsh Tits, Goldcrest, Redstart, Hawfinch,** and in summer **Golden Oriole, Nightingale** and several **warbler** species (including **Melodious, Wood, Whitethroat, Garden, Blackcap, Chiffchaff).**

The centre of the forest has the greatest concentration of Beeches, so look for **Black Woodpecker** here; most of the pines (for **Crested** and **Coal Tits, Goldcrest,** etc) are around the outskirts, where the soil is poorer.

ACCESS: From Paris take the A86 in the direction La Défense and Colombes, leave at exit 2a then take the N308 towards Sartrouville. Turn left in front of the Maisons-Lafitte château to the Park entrance and go straight on down the la Muette road to the swimming pool (signed *piscine).* Park at the car park for the swimming pool and enter the forest through the *Porte des Pétrons,* on the left after the *maison forestière.* (If coming by train, take the *J-Mermoz* and *P.Kreusscher* roads from MAISONS-LAFFITTE station to *rue de la Muette).* There is a *sentier botanique* (botanical footpath) marked on the trees by a green leaf inside an orange rectangle, which starts from the information board here. Take the "aller" circuit, checking the pines as you walk through them, keeping right. Keep on the botanical footpath to the clearing and parking area by the *Etoile des Pétrons* crossroads. Then leave the "aller" route and cross the route des Pavillons and take the *route d'Artois,* on the right of the *route de la Vente Frileuse,* to the path leading from the crossroads *étoile de Lamballe* to the *étoile de Provence.* The Scots pines on the left are good for tits, especially **Crested Tit,** and **Golden Oriole** can be heard on the right in spring and early summer. Go to the *étoile d'Artois;* turn left onto the *route de Monteclar,* and then right onto the *route d'Artois.* In a few metres, on the left, a path leads to a small clearing with low vegetation, good for warblers.

Return to the *route de Monteclar* and continue to the *étoile du Roi.* This is the best place for **Black Woodpecker;** look for trees where they have obviously been feeding and listen for their calls in early spring. Go left towards the *étoile du Bout du Monde,* marked by a large orientation cross. Listen for **Nightingale.** The section of the forest that is regenerating can be good for warblers. Follow the *route de la Vente Frileuse* to the left; it leads to the étoile des Pétrons. There cross the route des Pavillons and return to the starting point by taking the "retour" circuit of the *sentier botanique* back to the *porte des Pétrons* and the *maison forestière.* This walk will take about 3 hours. (Thanks to Jean-Pierre Lair and CORIF's web site for instructions).

Area 3. **CENTRAL PARIS**

Whilst few people would go to Paris purely for a birding holiday, some good, if relatively common, birds can be found in the city centre and the numerous parks and gardens in almost every arrondissement provide good walks. A little further out, the Bois de Bologne on the west and the Bois de Vincennes in the south-east offer even better birding, as do the reservoirs near Versailles (area 4). Further still from the centre, Fontainebleau has for many years been one of the best forest sites in northern France (see area 6 below). It should be noted that the December 1999 storms did considerable damage to the woods in the Paris region, as elsewhere in the north, and though great efforts have been made to clear the worst affected parts, the devastation is still apparent. Anyone working in Paris or wanting a break from the popular tourist sites will find much of interest, bird-wise, around the capital.

Two raptors will be found in central Paris; **Kestrel** and **Tawny Owl**. There are over 30 pairs of the former nesting in the city centre and birds can be seen perched on some of the city's famous buildings: Notre Dame, the Eiffel Tower, Arc de Triumph, Sacré-Coeur. **Tawny Owls** can be found in many of the city parks, such as Montsouris and Père-Lachaise. **Swifts** nest in high-rise buildings near the Louvre and can be seen screaming overhead during the summer together with **House Martins**. Another town bird is the **Black Redstart**. Look for them on roofs and chimneys. More surprising species to be found near a capital city are **Crested Tit** and **Firecrest**, nearly always in conifers (Montsouris, Bois de Bologne); **Short-toed Treecreeper** (not for nothing is it called in French the "Garden Creeper"); **Grey** and **White Wagtails** by the River Seine, reservoirs and park lakes; **Serin** breed in Pere-Lachaise Cemetery and Georges-Brassens Park, **Siskin** winter in the Bois de Bologne and Vincennes, **Jackdaws** can be seen around the Eiffel Tower, Notre-Dame and Sacré-Coeur and there are always plenty of gulls (mostly Black-headed) on the river. While these are common species, rarities do turn up in Paris from time to time, especially in the wooded areas.

(Paris is divided into 20 arrondissements or districts, so a number in brackets after a site e.g. (4th) refers to the arrondissement in which it is situated).

USEFUL ADDRESSES AND FURTHER READING: CORIF (Centre Ornithologique Île-de-France) 18, rue Alexis-Lepère, 93100 Montreuil-sous-Bois. Tel: 01 48 51 92 00 e-mail: corif@club-internet.fr Web site: http://perso.club-internet.fr/corif/
The Centre organises surveys in and around Paris as well as numerous bird walks for all levels of interest. Worth joining if you are staying in Paris for any time.

Fontainebleau has its own naturalist association ANVL at Route de la Tour-Denecourt, 77300 Fontainebleau. Tel: 01 64 22 61 17. e-mail: anv@club-internet.fr Web site: http://perso.club-internet.fr/anvl/ and runs bird walks free for members.

Balades Nature à Paris by Georges Feterman. Dakota Editions describes 14 walks in almost every arrondissement of Paris with excellent maps as well as a wealth of information about the birds, plants and trees of the city. He gives the addresses of many more local natural history societies in the area. Available from the LPO

For the serious student of Paris' birds Les Oiseaux d'Île-de-France by Pierre Le Maréchal and Guilhem Lesaffre. Delachaux et Niestlé is useful as it gives the status (historic and current) of all species noted in the area and where the rarer ones have been sighted.

MAPS: Tourist plans of Paris can be found at any kiosk or newsagent. Recta-foldex publish the Banlieue de Paris 1/50 000 with a Plan de Paris at 1/16 500 on the reverse as well as a Plan de Paris at 1/13 500. The annual Michelin Atlas Routier has a good plan of central Paris in the index but is rather too large to carry around.

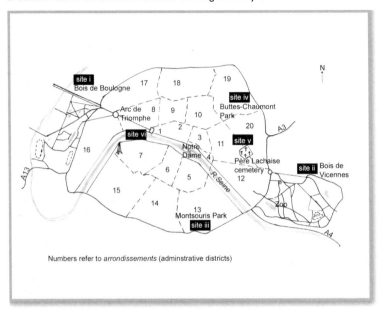

Paris area 3 Central Paris sites

Site i.

The **BOIS DE BOULOGNE**, on the west side, has a bird reserve covering about 3 hectares near the *Route de la Grande Cascade* footpath (between the *Allée de Longchamp* and the *Route de Suresnes*). This section of the Bois de Boulogne is right by the Porte Dauphine at the west end of Avenue Foch or off the Periphérique Extérieur. It is open every day. The best time to visit the Bois is early morning, before the crowds arrive.

Some of the species that might be encountered there include **Kingfisher, Redstart, Pied** and **Spotted Flycatchers, Golden Oriole** (best in May), **Nightingale, Crested Tit** (one of 7 tit species), **Firecrest, Short-toed Treecreeper, Black Redstart** (often around buildings) as well as many commoner species. In winter, **Pochard** and **Tufted Duck** can often be found on the Inférieur lake, together with **Mallard, Moorhen, Coot** and in spring, **Swifts** and **House Martins** hunt over the water.

The storms of December 1999 caused considerable damage and it may be some time before the longer-term effects on birds can be assessed.

ACCESS: Bus 244 or leave the metro at the *Porte Dauphine* or *Av. Foch* stations. Cross the Boulevard and enter the park by the Pavilion Dauphine, turning left onto the *Route de Suresnes,* which will bring you to the north end of the Lac Inférieur by the Royal Pavilion. It is possibly worth walking all around the lake before taking some of the tracks that lead though the reserve towards the *Allée de Longchamp.*

Alternatively, take the Metro no 1 line and get off at *Porte Maillot* station, *Av. Charles-de-Gaulle* exit and enter the northern sector of the Bois from *Boulevard André-Maurois*. There is a small pinewood before the Carrefour des Sablons, which can be good for woodpeckers. From the *Carrefour des Sablons,* walk left towards *Porte Dauphine.*

Site ii.

The **BOIS DE VINCENNES**, east of the 12th arrondissement, is the largest Parisian park. It covers over 995 hectares, of which 365 are wooded. 210 hectares were destroyed in the 1999 storms and a few areas are still dangerous but clearing and replanting should be completed by 2004. The clearings are likely to attract new species. There are also four lakes (Daumesnil (12 hectares) and Minimes (8 hectares) are likely to be the best for birds), many streams, as well as a zoo, the Paris Floral Park (30 hectares), an arboretum, Hippodrome, lawns, buildings, many restaurants, foot- and cycle paths, all providing plenty of varied habitats for birds. No wonder that in ten years 144 species have been observed here, of which 40 are widespread and common and 79 are rare or occasional visitors. Some of the more interesting resident and breeding species include a few **Middle Spotted Woodpeckers,** while **Great** and **Lesser Spotted** are more common; the couple of pairs of **Black Woodpeckers** have not been seen recently. About 50 pairs of **Short-toed Treecreeper** breed. **Kingfisher** can be seen around the lakes in winter. **Tawny Owl** also breeds; **Redstart** and **Black Redstart** (common) are both likely to be seen in spring and summer, as is **Stonechat**, several *Sylvia* and *Phylloscopus* warblers, both **Goldcrest** and **Firecrest** and **Pied Flycatcher.** Six Tit species, including **Crested Tit**, may be found as well as **Serin** and **Cirl Bunting**. An early morning walk should ensure 30 to 40 species. In addition Vincennes has a visitors' centre, the Maison Paris-Nature inside the Floral Park by the Chateau. The Floral Park is open 9.30 - 20.00 in summer but closes earlier in winter; entry is €1.50. There are maps and information on wildlife here; much not relevant to birders and not all the attendants are very knowledgeable. The Floral Park itself is too popular and crowded to be good for birds, except perhaps early morning and in winter. The Lac des Minimes, on its west side, is also best visited in winter.

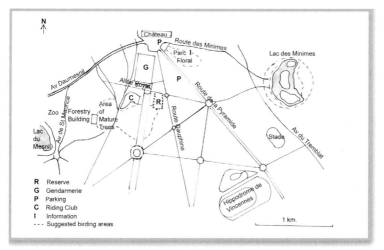

Central Paris site ii Bois de Vincennes

ACCESS: Vincennes is easily reached by car from the A86 or the eastern *périphérique*, *Porte de Vincennes* exit. Alternatively, take buses 112 or 46 or the metro to *Chateau de Vincennes*. From the large square in front of the château walk south down the route Dauphine to its junction with the Allée Royale. The Reserve, with a hide (always open) is situated south of the Floral Park, just south of the *Allée Royale*. The trees here are small and to find more mature trees it is worth walking westwards from the Reserve to the other side of the *Tourelle* road.

Site iii.
MONTSOURIS PARK lies in the 14th arrondissement at its eastern boundary, between the Porte d'Orléans and the Porte de Gentilly by the metro station *Cité universaire*. Walk north towards the Avenue Reille and then turn right towards the lake. There are many introduced species (Canada Geese, Red-crested Pochard, Ruddy Shelduck, etc) but the lake also holds wild birds, especially in winter. The many conifers in the park attract **Firecrest, Coal** and **Crested Tit** and it is one of the few places where **Lesser Spotted Woodpecker** may be observed. Listen for **Serin** singing in the spring.

Site iv.
BUTTES-CHAUMONT PARK northeast of the Seine, in the 19th arrondissement, is another good park for birds. It can be reached from either *Buttes-Chaumont* or *Botzaris* metro stations, both on its south boundary. It is well wooded and again, has a lake, which attracts a lot of wild birds in winter, especially **Black-headed Gulls.** In spring and summer, **Swifts** and **Martins hawk** over the water. Almost all the commoner species on the Paris list can be found here: woodland birds such as **Great, Blue, Long-tailed** and **Marsh Tits, Short-toed Treecreeper, Nuthatch, Robin, Wren, Dunnock, Jay, Tawny Owl;** finches **(Greenfinch, Serin),** warblers **(Chiffchaff** and **Blackcap).**

Site v.
PÈRE LACHAISE CEMETERY is in the 20th arrondissement, south of the last site. The nearest metro station, of the same name, is at the northwest of the cemetery. Take the paths that lead towards the southern part. All the bird species listed above under Buttes-Chaumont should also be seen here. Look for **Black Redstart** on the tombs and listen out for **Serin**, which breeds here.

Other sites in central Paris. Many of the larger parks and gardens will contain most or all of the species listed above for other sites. Some of the best are the JARDIN DU LUXEMBOURG in the 6th, les JARDINS DES TUILERIES in 1st, the JARDIN DES PLANTS in the 5th, where **Tawny Owl** breeds.

Site vi.
The **RIVER SEINE,** even in the heart of Paris, provides some opportunities for bird watching. Species that may be seen (depending on the season) include **Little Grebe, Cormorant, Grey Heron, Mallard, Tufted Duck, Common Sandpiper, Black-headed, Herring, Yellow-legged** and **Common Gulls, Grey, White** and **Pied Wagtails.**

Some of the best viewing points are the Statue of Liberty, opposite the Radio France building (16th), the Arts Bridge (6th), Barye Square, at the extreme south-east of l'Île St.Louis (4th).

Area 4. **RAMBOUILLET**

Site i.

RAMBOUILLET FOREST, although not as well-known as Fontainebleau (Area 6), is probably as interesting for birders and has a similar species list. Five Woodpecker species are found there, including **Black Woodpecker** (quite widespread) and (since 1991) **Middle Spotted**; the highest density of this latter species is in the north-west, especially near the Hollande lakes -see Site ii.. **Buzzard** and **Honey Buzzard** both breed, as do **Short-toed Treecreeper**, **Bonelli's Warbler** and **Redstart** and in the felled areas both **Nightjar** and **Woodcock** may be heard on spring evenings at dusk. Many of these species may be seen walking along the footpaths around the lakes (see site below)

Site ii.

ST. HUBERT AND HOLLANDE LAKES are a possible site for **Little Bittern** near Paris. The village of ST. HUBERT lies some 8 km north of Rambouillet town and east of the forest surrounding ST. LEGER-EN-YVELINES. Although all the lakes are very popular with fishermen and the Hollande lakes are used for water sports, there are still reedbeds where **Great Reed** (a few), **Reed** and **Sedge Warblers**, **Reed Bunting** and even a couple of pairs of **Little Bittern** still breed. **Melodious Warbler** can be found in scrubby thickets near the water. **Black** and **Whiskered Terns** are seen regularly during the spring migration and **Night Heron** could be spotted at this time. **Osprey** and **Great White Egret** are regularly sighted. The former usually during autumn migration, the later in December and January. **Cormorants**, **Grey Heron**, **Great Crested** and **Little Grebes**, **Coot**, **Black-headed Gulls** and the commoner duck species (**Mallard**, **Pochard** and **Tufted Duck**) are found there in winter.

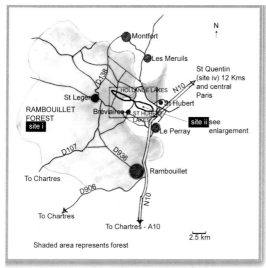

Paris area 4 sites i and ii Rambouillet and nearby lakes

The best viewpoints are from the embankments between the lakes, especially the one between the Pourras and Corbet lakes. **Little Bittern** are most likely to be seen from here, especially early in the morning or at dusk. Raptors flying over the forest are also likely to be spotted from here. Waders on passage are most likely to be seen around Bourgneuf lake where the reed beds are not so dense.

WHEN TO VISIT: Spring and early summer. There is little of interest in winter.

ACCESS: Zero at the roundabout as you turn off the N10 and take the D191 towards ST. HUBERT. In 900 metres turn left at the sign Lac St. Hubert. In 200 metres you can park on the side of the road and scan the lake. There is another parking space at the end of the embankment beyond the canal. Return to the D191.

700 metres from the junction fork left, by a stone gateway, down a pot-holed forestry road. Check the woods as the road bends left after about 400 metres (a walking track continues straight on). In another 200 metres there is a parking place by the woods (another area to check for **woodpeckers**) and one can walk to the lake and on to the embankment but there is much disturbance here from fishermen. It is best early in the morning in spring. Return to the walking track and follow it for about 1 kilometre until it turns left to another embankment about 500 metres away.

Return to the D191 and drive on for another 2 km, then turn left following the signs to the ÉTANGS DE HOLLANDE. There is a complicated one-way system but it is clearly signed. The lakes themselves are not very productive, too much water-sports, but the woodland around is good for woodpeckers, especially Middle Spotted, and other woodland species. There are finch and tit flocks in winter.

Other fauna: Muskrats make their winter lodges in the reeds. Roe and Red Deer and Wild Boar occur in the forest.

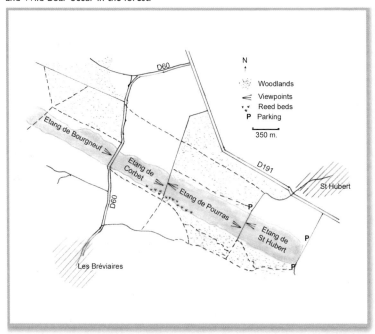

Paris area 4 site ii Enlargement of St. Hubert lakes

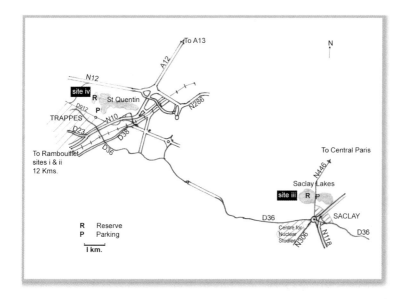

Paris area 4 sites iii and iv Saclay and St. Quentin

Site iii.

SACLAY LAKE NATURE RESERVE The two Saclay lakes lie each side of the N446; only the west one, (the Étang-vieux) is a reserve, the east lake (Étang Neuf) is hunted over but still holds some birds. **Great Crested Grebe, Grey Heron, cormorants,** common **duck** species and **gulls** are found in quite large numbers in winter and occasionally rarer species turn up. Saclay has often been a "twitching hot-spot" for Parisians. For an area so close to Paris, the surroundings are surprisingly rural and flocks of **Golden Plover** and **Lapwing** can be seen in the nearby fields in winter, as well as **Fieldfare.**

ACCESS: Access is very limited and consists of scanning the lakes from the roadside verges. However it is quite easy to park, as the verges are wide on the east side. From the D36 roundabout it is just 1 km north on the N446 to a good viewpoint betweens the lakes.

Saclay is very easy to reach from the A10 and A86 motorways. (See map above for this and the next site).

Site iv.

ST. QUENTIN-EN-YVELINES RESERVE St. Quentin-en-Yvelines lake near TRAPPES is a large lake and leisure area, of which the shallower, reed fringed western end is a Nature Reserve covering 90 hectares; 230 bird species have been recorded there. Members of the public are only allowed into the reserve on a few open days each year, which is probably why there are so many waterbirds there in winter and waders on passage, far more than on any other lake near Paris. Ring 01 30 62 20 12 to discover the open days (usually a Sunday) or to arrange a group visit. There are paths around the lake but much of the reserve is hidden by woodland. However, provided you have a telescope, there are a couple of reasonable viewpoints from where you can scan the lake when the Reserve is closed.

WHEN TO VISIT; From October to March there are large numbers of **Mallard,
Shoveler, Teal, Pochard, Great Crested Grebe, Black-headed Gull, Grey
Heron, Cormorant** and also some species otherwise rare in the Paris region:
Greylag, Shelduck, Gadwall and **Goosander**. In autumn many species of wader
turn up and exceptionally such rarities as **Spoonbill** and **Great White Egret**. In
spring a few **Black Terns** may be seen among the numerous swifts and hirundines on
passage. A few **Great Reed Warblers** and **Grasshopper Warblers** may breed in
the reedbeds, along with the commoner **Reed** and **Sedge Warblers**; **Cetti's** and
Melodious Warbler, Nightingale and **Red-backed Shrike** may be found in the
lakeside brambles and scrub. The trees surrounding the lake are good for woodland
species and finch flocks in winter.

ACCESS: Approximately 10 km south of the A13/A12 junction, on the outskirts of
TRAPPES, turn off the A12/N10 onto the D912 following the sign *Trappes Base de Loisirs*.
In 700 metres at a roundabout, turn right into the *Base de Loisirs*. Alternatively, by train
use Paris-Montparnasse station or RER line C for Rambouillet; get off at either Gare de
St-Quentin or Trappes. It is a 10 minutes walk after crossing the N10. Entry fee to the
Base de Loisirs is 1.50 euros and you will be given a plan of the lake and its activities and
a card to open the barrier when leaving.

Park in the space opposite the Reserve Office. A footpath (*Chemin de tour de
l'étang*) starts from just behind this carpark. At its start here is a map showing the
footpath in red, which is clearer than the entrance plan. Walk right to a hide and view
over the larger lake, used for water sports, and the east side of the reserve. The left-
hand path leads towards the golf course. Just past the club-house parking area a
hexagonal wooden platform with a central pole built on top of a slight rise gives scope
views of the *Bassin Intermediare* of the Reserve, though it is still quite a way off. The
path continues north along the boundary of the reserve but trees block any view of the
water, though the areas is good for passerines. It is quite a long walk to the next
viewpoint over the northern side of the reserve.

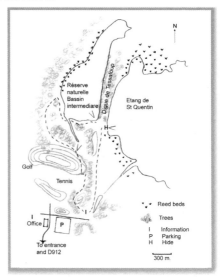

**Paris area 4 site iv.
Enlargement of St. Quentin Reserve**

Area 5. **SÉNART FOREST**

25 km from Paris, south of Orly airport and wedged between the busy N6 and N7 roads, Sénart Forest boasts some very old oaks, heathery heaths and damp areas with ponds. Besides the commoner forest birds there are **Honey Buzzard**, both **Black** and **Middle Spotted Woodpeckers, Wryneck, Redstart, Spotted Flycatcher, Melodious Warbler, Nightingale** and **Nightjar**.

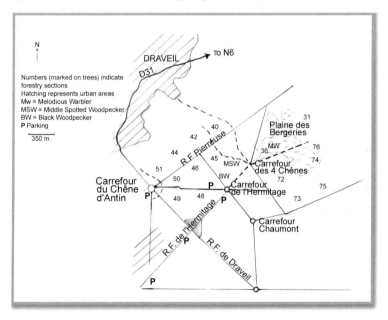

Paris area 5 Sénart Forest

ACCESS: Leave the N6 at the Montgeron-Glacière/Draveil exit. At the bottom of the sliproad, turn right (west) onto the D31 in the direction of Draveil. In 4 km turn left at the crossroads where there is a wooden cross. Take the *rue du chêne d'Antin* to the crossroads of the same name. Park here and take the forest road leading off between parcels 50 and 51 (painted black on white on trees). Follow this track for about 750 metres and then turn right between parcels 45 and 41 and take the path to the *Carrefour des Quatre Chênes*. This area, with some very old trees, can be good for both **Middle Spotted** and **Black Woodpeckers**. Take the path between parcels 36 and 72 which leads into an area of more open heathland with heather, young birches, conifers, and bushes. Among the many birds found in such a habitat are **Melodious** and **Grasshopper Warblers, Whitethroat, Stonechat**, occasionally **Wryneck** and even **Nightjar,** only likely to be heard at dusk. The next crossroads with a picnic area is also a good spot for many species, including the possibility of **Honey Buzzard.** From here you can retrace your steps or turn left and left again back to the starting point.

The forest of **NOTRE-DAME**, north-east of Sénart, is another urban site for **Black Woodpecker** as well as most of the species listed above.

ACCESS: NOTRE-DAME is best reached from the N4 from Paris or by leaving the N104 motorway at exit 16 and taking the N4 towards Paris. Either way, leave the N4 just east of LA QUEUE EN BRIE at traffic lights and take a very minor road south into the forest towards the Château des Marmosets, where there is a parking area. Walk east with the château on the right and a large lawn on the left. Take the discovery trail (sentier de découverte) into the forest and walk around parcel 116 (right and right again) back towards the château. This is where **Black Woodpeckers** have been seen. To look for **Grey-headed Woodpecker** continue south down the Chemin des Quatre Chênes, crossing the wide Route Royale, to the Étoile Sixtine. Just south of this crossroads is parcel 124 where Grey-headed can sometimes be seen on dead trees.

Area 6. FONTAINEBLEAU

The 170 square kilometres of Fontainebleau forest, some 60 km southeast of Paris, together with nearby heathland, lakes and marshes are classified as an IBA. The forest is mainly composed of Beech, Oak and Hornbeam with Scots Pine and other conifer plantations. There are rocky sandstone ridges and limestone outcrops within the forest, clearings of sandy heathland and bogs and pools in the depressions.

The forest is managed by the Office National des Forêts and several areas are protected reserves. There are information boards by the parking areas showing which parts are reserves. Note that the areas designated as Integral reserves, and this covers most of the Biological ones, are completely unmanaged. This means that nothing is planted and when a tree falls, it is left. The December 1999 storms caused considerable damage to Fontainebleau Forest and while great efforts have been made to clear the parts open to the public, some reserve areas are still dangerous and are currently out of bounds to the general public, although it is possible to walk around the perimeter - see sites below. It is obvious that so much dead wood is going to be attractive to woodpeckers and other hole-nesting species and these reserves are likely to be the best places to search for them. Luckily birds are often around the edges and so visible.

In the past Fontainebleau was well-known to British birders as a reliable site for **Black Woodpecker.** It still is but nowadays there are sites for this species closer to the Channel. Fontainebleau remains, however, an excellent site for many species. Some of the more important breeding birds are **Honey Buzzard, Nightjar, Grey-headed, Middle Spotted** and **Black Woodpeckers, Dartford Warbler** and **Red-backed Shrike.** Additionally there are **Buzzard, Hobby, Green, Great** and **Lesser Spotted Woodpeckers, Wryneck, Golden Oriole, Pied Flycatcher, Wood Lark, Tree Pipit, Redstart, Black Redstart, Crested Tit, Melodious, Bonelli's** and **Wood Warblers** and **Firecrest. Short-toed Treecreeper** is common but there may also be **Common Treecreeper. Night Heron** seem to have stopped breeding in the Larchant marshes but may be seen there on passage. One or two pairs of **Little Bittern** breed but in addition there are **Kingfisher, Grey Heron** and many commoner water birds, especially during migration periods.

Maps: IGN 1:25,000 no. 2417 OT covers the forest and nearby areas. It is essential if walking for any distance. It is available in local newsagents. A paperback "La Forêt de Fontainebleau" published by the Office National des Forêts, also available locally, describes 33 walks with clear maps.

WHEN TO VISIT: A spring visit (April-June) will produce the longest species list. The woodpeckers are easier to hear and see earlier in the year when the trees are not in full leaf. February is not too early; March is ideal.

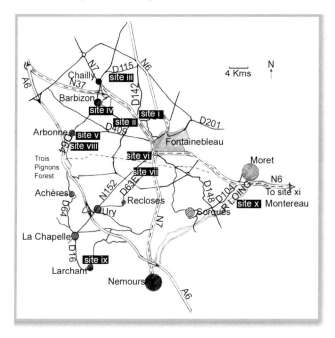

Paris area 6 Fontainebleau birding sites

Forest sites i-vii.
Faced with a huge forest like Fontainebleau, either a lot of luck or a lot time is needed to find all the more interesting species. However the roads around the reserve area of Gros Fouteau is one of the best for finding all the **woodpecker** species, notably **Black** and **Grey-headed** as well as many of the other woodland birds listed above. The reserve of la Tillaie is also a good area and there are often **Firecrest** and **Hawfinch** there. A third area in the north around the Carrefour de l'Epigne is easily reached and fairly quiet. **Middle Spotted Woodpecker** can be heard here. **Black Woodpecker** and most of the other woodpecker species have been seen around the aqueduct south of Fontainebleau town, but this is a noisier and busier area. Readers will find other sites; always look for areas with mature trees. These are often the parts designated as *Réserves Biologiques.* Early morning is the best time to find woodpeckers.

Site i.
AROUND THE RÉSERVE BIOLOGIQUE
NORTH OF FONTAINEBLEAU TOWN
ACCESS: From the N6 turn west onto the minor *Route des Hauteurs de la Solle* south of the Hippodrome. It is a difficult turning as the *Hauteurs* road is easy to miss and turns back sharply on itself. It is the first turning off after the Hippodrome entrance, so slow down after the Hippodrome if coming from the north.

Some 300 metres along this minor road there is an area of dead and damaged beeches on the south side, which is a good spot for **Grey-headed Woodpecker**. In fact, several species, including **Lesser Spotted** can be found around here and **Short-toed Treecreeper** are common. **Crested Tit** can be found in any of the strands of old Scots Pine that are along this road, as can **Bonelli's Warbler** in spring and summer The road continues along the rocky ridge overlooking the Hippodrome and wherever there is a viewpoint, look over the forest below for raptors displaying in spring or even for **Black Woodpecker** flying. This species is often near the road a little further on, just past the small "auberge" restaurant "Le Mont Chauvet" some 2.6 km from the turning. There are old, dead trees on the north overlooking the forest, opposite a ride on the left, by parcel 261. Just beyond this there is a large parking area and it can be productive to walk along any tracks that are not barred and explore the clearings around. The drivable road swings south and comes out on the outskirts of Fontainebleau just east of the N7.

Site ii.
THE RÉSERVE BIOLOGIQUE DE LA TILLAIE is a square south of the N7. It is possible to reach it by turning off the N7 onto the D301 the *Route Ronde* and parking in 1 km just opposite the turning signed to the Gorges d'Apremont. Although closed to the public, it is possible to walk around the outside of la Tillaie by taking the *Bouquet de Roi* path and turning north up *la Tillaie* back to the N7. Check for **Hawfinch, Firecrest, warblers** and **woodpeckers.**

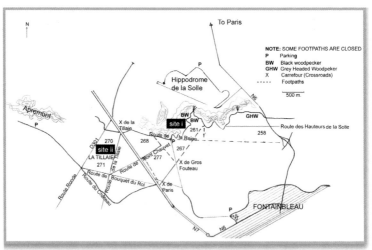

Paris area 6 Fontainebleau sites i and ii

Site iii.
A good area for **Middle Spotted Woodpecker**, if you have not found it in the sites above, is off the D115 in the north of the forest. Halfway along, 1.3 km from its junctions with the N 6 and the D64 is a forestry crossroads, *Carrefour de l'Epine Foreuse*, with a large parking area and numerous tracks branching off north and south. **Grey-headed Woodpecker** is only a short way down the *Route de l'Epine Foreus*e and **Middle Spotted** down the *Route du Nord*, going south, in parcel 833. Woodpeckers are highly mobile so the whole area is worth exploring. **Short-toed Treecreepers** are also quite numerous here.

Site iv.
Nightjars are found in the open areas of heath within the forest. One such area is described under the Chanfroy Plain site below. Another is the heathland around the *Gorges et Platières d'Aprement* on the west side of the forest towards Barbizon. Park at any of the parking areas along the signed Gorges d'Aprement road leading west from the D301 and walk towards the open areas just before dusk.

Site v.
A walk around the Gorges de Franchard, parts of which are also a *Réserve biologique* is another good area with a variety of habitat (rocky areas, pond) along a short walk. Turn off the D301 1.7 km south of the Gorges d'Aprement turning and park at the *emitage de Franchard* crossroads. You can walk along part of the GR11 or follow the blue-marked footpath.

Site vi.
The areas around the aqueduct de Vanne that runs east-west south of Fontainebleau town can be productive especially where it crosses the N152 and the N7 some 2 km south of the Obelisk roundabout.

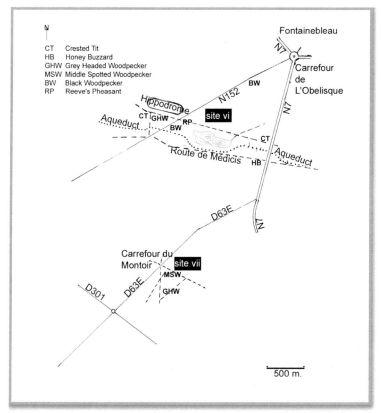

Paris area 6 Fontainebleau sites vi and vii

There is another Hippodrome west of the N152. The area between it and the aqueduct can be productive especially for **warblers** and **Crested Tit**. **Grey-headed Woodpecker** has been found here too. The woods between the N152 and the N7 south of the aqueduct should also be explored. They can be good for **woodpeckers, Honey Buzzard** and **Reeves' Pheasant** has been seen here. Unfortunately there is nowhere easy to park on either of these busy roads, so it may be necessary to walk from town.

Site vii.
The D63E leads west off the N7 about 650 metres south of the aqueduct. 1.5 km down it and about 1 km from the roundabout, the clearing on the east of the *Carrefour du Montoir* has been found good for **Grey-headed** and **Middle Spotted Woodpeckers, Hawfinch** and **warblers.**

Site viii.
CHANFROY PLAIN/TROIS PIGNONS FOREST On the western edge of Fontainebleau, abutting the adjoining forest of Trois Pignons, is an open area of Scots Pines and sandy heathland, heather covered, with marshy and rocky areas, very different from the denser woodland to the east. The variety of such different habitats allows one to observe several species rare in this part of the Île de France and not to be found elsewhere in Fontainebleau. They include **Hoopoe, Cuckoo, Nightjar, Red-backed Shrike, Wood Lark, Redstart, Black Redstart, Meadow** and **Tree Pipits, Stonechat, Melodious, Dartford** and **Bonelli's Warblers, Whitethroat, Yellowhammer** as well as **woodland** species such as **Buzzard, Pheasant, Green Woodpecker, Nightingale, Firecrest, tits.** In winter there are **Redpoll** and **Siskin.**
WHEN TO VISIT: As for sites above. Late spring is the best period. This area is very popular with walkers, so avoid weekends, and go early in the morning or evening. Dusk is the time for Nightjars, and also for Wild Boar.
ACCESS: Leave the A 6 motorway at exit 13 direction Fontainebleau. From Barbizon, on the west of the forest, take the D64 south through ARBONNE-LA-FORÊT (or take the D 409 from Fontainebleau town). At the roundabout at the end of ARBONNE follow the sign to ACHÈRES and in 1 km turn left at the signs "*Forêt domaniale des Trois-Pignons/ Carrière des Fusillés*". There is a large carpark in 400 metres. LEAVE NOTHING VALUABLE IN THE CAR. The following walk describes a rectangle; two main parallel paths, with minor ones running between the two at right angles. One route is given below but obviously any part of it can be omitted.
    Continue on foot past the barrier along the *Chemin de la Plain de Chanfroy*. The first part leads through pines; Check for **Firecrest, Crested Tit** and four *Phylloscopus* warblers **Bonelli's, Wood, Willow** and **Chiffchaff.** Take the second turning on the right, opposite a seat beside a large Scots Pine numbered 74. This leads through a sandy, heather-covered area good for **Dartford Warbler, Whitethroat** and **Wood Lark.** When you reach a footpath running at right angles, turn left, **Nightingale** is often singing here. In about 500 metres, turn left again on to the footpath, *le Chemin des Mares*, which runs through the old quarry area with water-filled ponds, where there may be **Reed Warbler. Wood Lark** can be heard here too, and **Ring Ouzel** turns up on passage in April. Cross the *Allée des Fusillés* back to the main *Chemin de la Plain de Chanfroy* and keep straight on, taking a sandy path up the slope to a little hill crowned by a solitary oak. The bushes in this area are very good for birds: **Red-backed Shrike, Stonechat, Black Redstart** and **Melodious Warbler. Nightjar** may be heard here at dusk or near the *Rocher de la Reine* rocky area south of the aqueduct. This sandy path curves back to the main footpath in about 300 metres,

cross it and continue straight on to the *Allée des Fusillés*. Turn left along this path to its junction with the *Route du Liteau*. Both **Buzzard** and **Honey Buzzard** may be seen over the open areas. Either continue straight on for as far as you wish before turning back, or turn right (south) towards the *Rocher de la Reine* footpath.

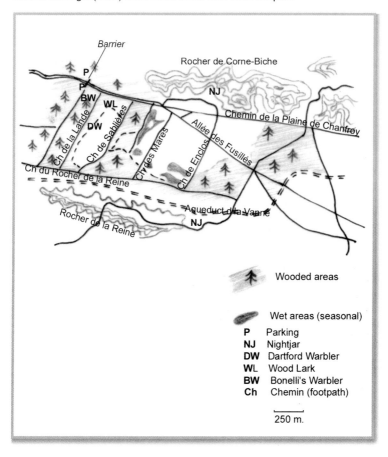

Paris area 6 Fontainebleau site viii Chanfroy Plain

Site ix.
For water birds, there are marshes near **LARCHANT,** south of the Trois-Pignons Forest but this is a private reserve and so access is limited. For information on visits, etc. call le Marais, 77132 Larchant. Tel: 01.64.28.16.03
ACCESS: From LA CHAPELLE-LA-REINE, south of Achères, take the D16 south to its junction with the D4 and turn left into LARCHANT. A footpath, leading off from the GR13 runs north-east from the church past the north side of the marshes or the same path, *le Chemin de Larchant,* can be picked up just beyond the cemetery off the road leading to Larchant Forest, near L'Éléphant parking area.

Site x.

It is also possible to walk along the **LOING VALLEY** where there are several large flooded sand quarries with reedbeds and sandy islands suitable for **Common Tern.**

ACCESS: From the Obelisque roundabout south of Fontainebleau, take the D148 eastwards to SORQUES and turn left onto the D104. It runs past some reedbeds and water that may be worth looking at. In 2.5 km park by the Maison Forestière where the GR 13b crosses the road and walk south (right) along it. It leads past several stretches of water.

The lakes near Gretz-sur-Loing may also be worth visiting. Take the D40d, leading south off the D104, towards the camping site at Gretz and then follow any of the paths leading left (north-east) towards the lakes.

Site xi.

Slightly further east, the **CANNES-ÉCLUSE** lakes in the Seine valley east of Montereau can be good in winter for **duck** and **grebe** species. Upriver the flooded sand quarries are used by gulls and breeding **Common Tern.** Waders will be present on passage.

ACCESS: Cannes-Écluse is 23 km east of Fontainebleau just off the N6. It can also be reached from the A5, exit 18 and the D411. The D124 runs north from the town past some lakes before joining up with the D411.

Other fauna and flora: Red Squirrel, Wild Boar, Roe and Red Deer are among the mammals likely to be observed in Fontainebleau. Green Lizard may be seen on Chanfroy Plain. Butterflies are abundant in late summer; both woodland and heathland species. Fontainebleau is equally a botanical site. Oak and Beech woodland, rocky sandstone ridges, limestone outcrops and boggy areas make for a very rich flora. Woodland plants include Red Helleborine, Military, Lady and Bird's Nest Orchids, Wintergreen and Angular Solomon's Seal. Other orchids to be found include Lizard and Monkey.

<u>Accommodation</u>: Fontainebleau is a very popular area, as much for Parisians as for foreign tourists. There are plenty of hotels, mainly expensive, in and around the area. Barbizon, the "painters village" on the western edge of the forest, has several hotels and restaurants, is quieter and conveniently situated for all the sites above. The large A6 motorway service area near Nemours, south of exit 16, has several of the cheaper hotels.

NORTH CENTRAL REGION

ALONG THE BELGIUM BORDER
Area 1. Scarpe - Escaut Regional Nature Park

Site i.	Goriaux Lake *
Site ii.	Flines-Lès-Mortagne Forest
Site iii.	Blue Lake
Site iv.	Vred peat bog

Area 2. Ardennes Plateau

Site i.	Trélon Forest
Site ii.	The High Ardennes

NORTH OF PARIS
Area 3. Compiègne Forest and The Oise Valley

Site i.	Compiègne Forest
Site ii.	The River Oise and Sacy Marsh

THE CHAMPAGNE LAKES
Area 4. Argonne Lakes

Area 5. Lake du Der-Chantecoq

Site i.	Itinerary around the Lake du Der *
Site ii.	Itinerary around The Side Lakes And Maison de l'Oiseau
Site iii.	Horre Lake

Area 6. The Forêt d'Orient Regional Nature Park

Site i.	Itinerary around Orient Lake *
Site ii.	Itinerary around Amance and Temple Lakes *
Site iii.	Forest areas *
Site iv.	Ramerupt Lake

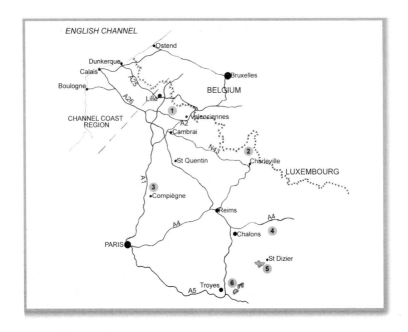

North Central Birding areas

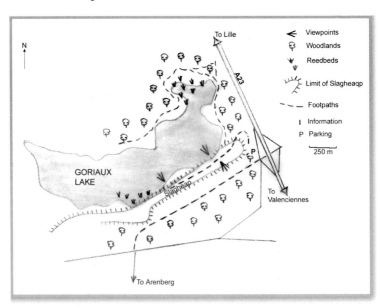

North Central area 1 site i Goriaux Lake Reserve

ALONG THE BELGIAN FRONTIER

Situated in one of the most densely populated parts of France (376 inhabitants per square kilometre - four times the national average), near the frontier with Belgium, in an old mining area, the valleys of the Scarpe and the Escaut still remain an IBA. Named after these two rivers which run through its centre, the Scarpe - Escaut Regional Nature Park covers a variety of habitats: river valleys, peat bogs, woodland and lakes. Very few of the forests are old, most have been replanted since World War II.

An important site for wintering waterbirds, with hundreds of **Shovelers** and **Teal** on passage, the area also has a few pairs of breeding **Little Bittern** and several hundred pairs of **Bluethroat** as well as **Grasshopper** and **Savi's Warblers, Reed, Sedge** and **Marsh Warblers, Reed Bunting.** The park includes the forest of Saint-Armand-Raismes with its Ornithological Reserve of Goriaux Lake, and several other wooded areas where **Honey Buzzard, Black Woodpecker, Golden Oriole** and **Hawfinch** breed. Visiting the sites below the number of people living in this region is not obvious except at weekends, when they become very crowded.

Further west along the frontier, the Avesnois Regional Nature Park, which contains some huge forests, reaches to the Ardennes plateau and so allows the circulation of birds and animals between France, Belgium and Germany. Trélon Forest in the east of this Park, on the lower, western edge of the Ardennes, is surrounded by a chain of small étangs, but some are privately owned, others too much used for water sports to be good for birds. The Ardennes are another IBA and though the bird list looks impressive, with species such as **Black Grouse, Hazel Grouse** and **Nutcracker,** on the ground it is a very difficult area to work. The forests are huge, access is limited and the relatively few footpaths are very popular with walkers. There are only a very few pairs of **Tengmalm's Owls** and **Black Grouse,** so forget seeing them. There are many more **Hazel Grouse** but this very difficult species is easier to locate in Belgium and both **Black** and **Grey-headed Woodpeckers** can be found more easily in smaller woods in the region.

Area 1. SCARPE - ESCAUT REGIONAL NATURE PARK

Site i.

GORIAUX LAKE *(Mare à Goriaux)* Ornithological Reserve is a large lake (over 90 hectares in a 270 hectare reserve) surrounded by Raismes-St. Armand forest. The lake was formed by mining subsidence and the flat top of the remaining slagheap makes an excellent viewing point over both the lake and the forest. More than 300 species of birds have been recorded there and up to 2000 duck may be counted in autumn; **Teal** is the most numerous but most species occur, including sawbills during cold spells. It is also a very good site for **Black Woodpecker**

In spring, the reedbeds hold singing **Bluethroat** as well as *Acrocephalus* and *Locustella* warblers. **Willow Warbler** and **Nightingale** are common in the wet woodland. There are **Honey Buzzard, Buzzard** and **Black Woodpecker** in the surrounding woods as well as **Short-toed Treecreeper** and many commoner woodland species. **Hobby** may be seen hawking over the lake in summer and **Osprey** is regular on passage. **Geese, duck, Lapwings** and **Brambling** flocks pass through in autumn, often in large numbers and **Siskin, Twite, Redpoll** and **Snow Bunting** have been seen among the young birches on the slopes of the slag heap in winter or early spring and from the top Woodcock may be seen flying at dusk. Recently **Great White Egret** has wintered with the **Grey Herons** and **Cormorants**.

WHEN TO VISIT: March to June is best but autumn (September-November) can also be good for movements of wildfowl, waders and finch flocks. There are always duck in winter as well as feeding flocks of finches, tits and other woodland birds. It is best to visit early in the morning, especially at weekends, even in winter

ACCESS: North-west of VALENCIENNES turn off the A23 (direction Lille) at exit 6 and turn left underneath the motorway in the direction of WALLERS. You will see signs for the *Forêt Domaniale Raismes-St. Armand* immediately ahead of you and the entrance to the car park for the Reserve. Before you start walking, try for **Black Woodpecker** in the trees behind the car park. Early in the morning it can often be heard and seen from the parking area.

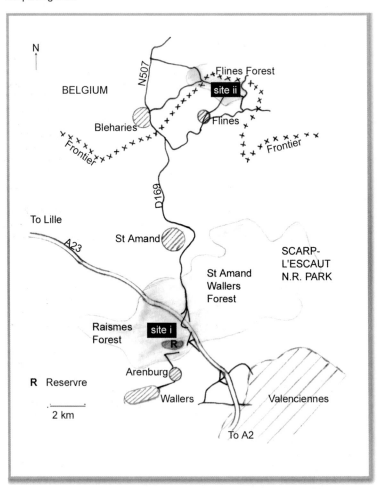

North Central Birding area 1 sites i and ii Raismes and Flines Forest

Walk through the barrier towards the map and information boards. Check these for latest sightings, etc. Also look in the trees between the car park and the boards for **Short-toed Treecreeper**. Climb up the slagheap, looking out for finches in the birches on the way up. From the flat top there is a good general view of the lake, though a telescope is advisable. It is also a good viewpoint for raptors flying over the forest. Look behind, away from the lake, for **Black Woodpecker;** it can often be seen flying towards the heap.

After some time on top, climb down and walk up the east side of the lake through the damp woodland to the reeds at the far end. Get as close to the reedbeds as possible. If the path is open, one can walk for 6,5 km all around the lake, but just this first part can be quite productive.

Other fauna and flora: Beware of mosquitoes, which can be a nuisance in summer! Dragonflies are plentiful, including *Libellula depressa*. Roe Deer may be seen in the forest.

Site ii.

FLINES-LÈS-MORTAGNE FOREST is a comparatively small public forest north of the above site, running along the Belgian frontier. Within it is a small reserve, Breux. Parts of the forest are damp and it is one of the few woods in this region with centuries-old Beeches. This makes it attractive to **Black Woodpecker,** which is always easier to find in a small area of forest. In addition there are **Hawfinch** here, **Golden Oriole** in summer and most of the other woodland species that can be found at Goriaux above. *ACCESS:* Immediately after exit 6 on the A23 (Lille) motorway is the D169 junction to ST. ARMAND-les-Eaux and Bléharies in Belgium. Take this road past St. Armand and turn off at MAULDE to the village of Flines. The forest is signed from here but it is along, roundabout route through country lanes. You can also follow the blue signs to Maubray airfield, which brings you to the forest. Alternatively, cross the frontier into Belgium at Maulde, turn right at the crossroads in Bléharies to Laplaigne and there follow the blue signs to the airfield.

The main forest roads form a cross east-west/north-south. Listen for **Black Woodpecker** at the crossroads in the centre, by another blue airfield sign, where there are some old beeches. A little further south there is a large open, parking area which is also a good spot both for woodpeckers and finches.

Site iii.

THE BLUE LAKE, the site of an old chalk pit in the Scarp valley east of Arras, can provide a pleasant, undemanding walk around it and through the marshes alongside the River Scarp. **Kingfisher, Great Crested** and **Little Grebe, Coot** and **Moorhen** will be found in the water. **Reed Bunting** and **Reed Warbler** breed in the **reedbeds. Turtle Dove** and **Golden Oriole** are among the woodland species.

WHEN TO VISIT: A 2 hour walk should give you a good list of the commoner species in the area spring to autumn. In winter, although there may be a few duck on the lake, it is unremarkable. Good numbers of duck and geese pass through on passage, however. Avoid weekends, when it can be very crowded, even in winter.

ACCESS: Leave the A1 (Paris-Lille) motorway at exit 16 (direction VITRY) to FRESNES-le-Mountabon. In the village take the first road right towards BIACHE-SAINT-VAAST, then turn off onto the D46 towards PLOUVAIN and ROEUX. From here follow the signs *Lac Bleu*. Park at the small car park by the restaurant and take the footpath which leads you around the lake clockwise. At the end of the long straight stretch, turn left towards the narrow tarred road that runs under the A26 motorway. Turn right immediately after the motorway bridge and in 50 metres, take the footpath than runs through the Plouvain marshes. You will see a campsite on your left. It leads alongside some étangs and in about 500 metres at the crossroads with the D42 turns right until in another 500 metres, you reach the river bank. Turn right again and follow the Scarp, which has been canalised. Go under the A26 again and in about 750 metres, when you arrive at the old loading area, now a boating stop, turn right back towards the lake. Continue the circuit by turning left back to the starting point.

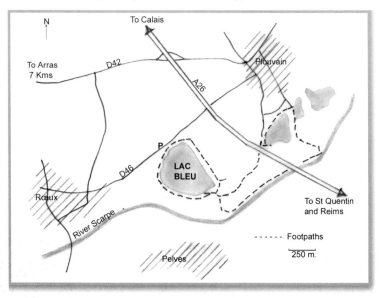

North Central area 1 site iii Lac Bleu

Site iv.
VRED PEAT BOG, some 16 km west of Goriaux, together with Faux wood to its north boasts an impressive list of species: **Grasshopper** and **Savi's Warblers, Reed** and **Marsh Warblers, Bluethroat, Reed Bunting, Teal, Coot, Golden Oriole, Water Rail, Marsh Harrier, Honey Buzzard.** Unfortunately it can only be visited by appointment. Contact the Mairie 03 27 90 51 33 or the Regional Park office on 03 27 19 19 70 for details of guided visits.

Area 2.   THE ARDENNES

The Ardennes plateau, rocky and heavily wooded, extends into France roughly halfway along the northern frontier, around the point where the frontier forms a "finger" pointing up into Belgium. An isolated mountain range, thickly forested, the Ardennes hold a number of "special" birds, not otherwise found outside the Alps, Vosges and Jura. **Nutcracker, Hazel Grouse. Black Grouse** and **Tengmalm's Owl** are some of these, although except for **Hazel Grouse,** they only occur in very small numbers and Hazel Grouse are very elusive. Other breeding birds in the Ardennes are **Honey Buzzard, Black** and **Red Kites, Hen Harrier, Black, Middle Spotted** and

BRITTANY

Breeding seabirds on La Fauconnière on Cap Fréhel looking east to Fort La Latte. Both headlands are good seabird and sea mammal watching spots.

BRITTANY

Europe's most Southerly Northern Gannet breeding colony on Les Sept Iles Reserve is most impressive in the spring. Many other seabirds also nest here.

BRITTANY
The Penhir headline and the Taz de Pois islands on the Crozon Peninsular.
Red-billed Chough and Northern Wheatear breed on the cliffs of this western promonotory.

BRITTANY
Breeding seabird colonies off Cap Fréhel on the north coast.

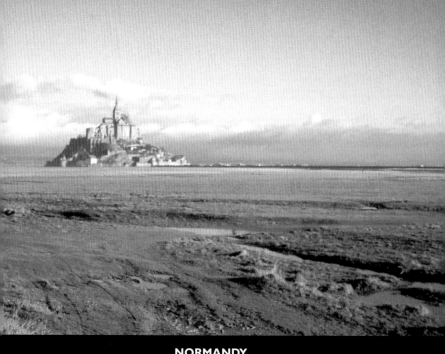

NORMANDY
The mudflats,saltmarshes, polders and rocky shores around Mont St. Michel Bay attract thousands of gulls, wildfowl and waders on passage and in winter.

NORMANDY
The reedbeds, marked trails and hides at the Orne Estuary Reserve near Caen provide good birdwatching from August to May.

THE CHANNEL COAST
Cap Gris-Nez, here seen from Cap Blanc-Nez, provides some of the best
seawatching along the Channel coast, especially in autumn.

THE CHANNEL COAST
Romelaere Reserve, near St. Omer, is an area of marshland, lakes and water meadows with
boardwalks leading through the reedbeds. Spring is the best time to look for breeding
Acrocephalus and Locustella warblers, Black Tern, Little Bittern and Marsh Harrier.

PARIS REGION
Fontainebleau, like most large beech and oak forests in northern France, is home to Black, Grey-headed and Middle Spotted Woodpeckers as well as Honey Buzzard and numerous woodland passerines.

SOUTH CENTRAL REGION
The flooded water meadows of Normandy and the lower Loire Valley near Angers attract thousands of waders in spring and are important sites for Corncrake.

NORTHERN CENTRAL REGION
Goriaux Ornithological Reserve, near the Belgium frontier, is a large lake formed by mining subsidence in the Scarpe-Escaut Natural Regional Park. The flat top of the slagheap in the foreground makes an excellent viewpoint over the lake and surrounding forest, which is a good site for Black Woodpecker.

CHAMPAGNE
Der-Chantecoq is the northernmost pf the two large Champagne lakes that are one of the best winter sites in Northern France for waterbirds, cranes and the chance of White-tailed Sea Eagle.

LORRAINE
Lindre and nearby lakes form one of the best sites in the north-east, especially from autumn to spring. The surrounding forests also provide good birding including breeding Collared Flycatcher.

ALSACE
The River Rhine at Plobsheim Lake where tens of thousands of waterbirds winter. Birds are normally close to the French bank in the morning.

ALSACE
The River Rhine at Rhinau-Kappel. An important site for passage and wintering waterbirds. The riverside forest holds six species of woodpecker, Black Woodpecker, Black Kite, Honey Buzzard and Golden Oriole.

ALSACE
The lower slopes of the southern Voges mountains. Black Woodpecker, Nutcracker, Hazel Grouse, Crested Grouse, Crested Tit and Crossbill may be found in the conifer forests.

Grey-headed Woodpeckers, Wood Lark, Red-backed Shrike and **Crossbill.**
It is a good area for woodland birds in general, particularly breeding raptors, but
very difficult to work.

Site i.

TRÉLON FOREST lies on the western edge of the Ardennes, at a lower altitude, very
close to the Belgian frontier and within Avesnois N.R. Park. Surrounded as it is by a
chain of small lakes, it is a good area for raptors, wetland birds on passage and woodland
passerines. Raptors include **Buzzard, Honey Buzzard** and **Goshawk; Black
Woodpecker** is difficult, **Middle Spotted** fairly common. **Hawfinch** can be found in
mature woodland, **Crested Tit, Firecrest** and **Goldcrest** in the conifer plantations.
Grasshopper and **Wood Warblers, Lesser Whitethroat, Northern Grey** and
Red-backed Shrike all breed. **Melodious Warbler** is found in bushes outside the
forest, often near water. **Woodcock** is easier to flush in winter but a few breed. The
lakes are too popular with tourists in summer to hold many birds but are worth
exploring in late autumn or winter.

WHEN TO VISIT: spring is best, as early as February-March for woodpeckers and
displaying raptors, though Honey Buzzard will not be back until April-May. Autumn can
also be quite a good season, especially for water birds.

ACCESS: Trélon is a long way from anywhere! Roughly 25 km south of MONS and
CHARLEROI. From VALENCIENNES (see sites above) take the D 934 and D962 (or
the N49 to Maubeuge, then N2) to AVESNES. From here take the D951 for 16 km to
Trélon.

From Trélon take the D963 north out of the town. In 2 km there is a junction,
with a restaurant beside a small lake on the right. Depending on the season, check
the lake for duck or the bushes and trees for **warblers,** from the restaurant car park.
The forest can be explored either by continuing left along the D963 to where a forestry
track crosses it or better, by going right past the lake and taking the D119 through
the forest. **Middle Spotted Woodpecker** are quite numerous along this stretch
of road, though it is difficult to park. To get further into the forest, in just under 4 km
turn left (west) down the St. Hubert turning by an old brick house. Turn left again in
900 metres by a wooden seat (when you can see a cleared area ahead). Park here or
at the end of this track and walk on down the grassy ride. Check areas of mature
trees for **woodpeckers** and **Hawfinch.** Return to the "seat" turning and continue to
the large cleared area for **Grasshopper Warbler** and **shrikes**.

The Val-Joly lake can be reached by continuing down the D119, which runs past
an arm (often dry but good damp woodland) and turning left (west) at Eppe-Sauvage.
Beyond the lake, at Liessies crossroads, it is possible to take the D963 back through
the forest to Trélon.

Another walk, through slightly different habitat, can be taken from the village of
WALLERS-TRÉLON, 5.5 km west. From the village take the D 83 towards MOUSTIER.
There are good views over the woods along this road, so look out for **raptors** flying
and for **warblers** and **shrikes** along the hedgerows. In just over 2 km turn right at
the junction with the D283 towards BAIVES village. Turn right on the outskirts to
climb the mont, both for the view and for **warblers,** and continue along the lane
back to the starting point of Wallers-Trélon.

Site ii.

THE HIGH ARDENNES is a site for anyone who likes a challenge! The only way
into them is by taking the D13 north-east from Charleville-Meziers to the Belgian
frontier or the D1 to Montherme and then continuing north on the D 989 through
Hargnies to Vireux-Wallerand/Vireux-Molhain (either side of the river) and on up the

N51 to Givet. Stop where it is quiet and explore any minor and forestry roads leading off. This should certainly give you woodpeckers and with some luck, **Nutcracker,** early and late in the year. The D989a to les Vieux Moulins has some fairly good walking tracks from its end, but they are very busy at weekends. Early morning is the best time to hear **woodpeckers** and game birds calling but the whole route cannot be covered in one morning. There is a Reserve at *Vireux-Molhain*, on the D47 near the Belgium frontier south of Givet but it is there to protect the fossils! However, **Eagle Owl** has been heard near here, so it is worth trying the D47 or suitable habitat around Givet.

 Hazel Grouse, Tengmalm's Owl and **Nutcracker** are all supposedly easier to find in Belgium.

Area 3. **COMPIÈGNE FOREST AND THE OISE VALLEY**

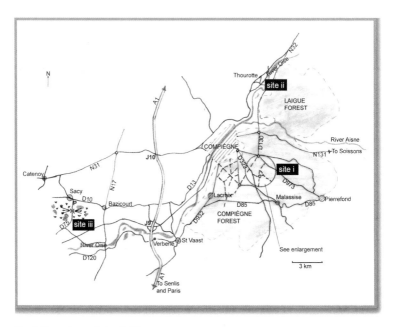

North Central area 3 sites i - iii

<u>Site i.</u>

COMPIÈGNE is the largest forest in Picardie; 14,458 hectares composed mainly of mixed deciduous trees (oaks, beech, hornbeam) with some conifer plantations. It is managed by the Office National des Forêts (see introduction) and has many strands of mature trees, good for woodpeckers. Several minor D (departmental) roads cross it and forestry tracks lead off from them. Some of these are drivable, others only for walkers. The forest is popular with the public and hunting takes place on certain days throughout the autumn and winter - check notices. In spring parts of the forest are carpeted with Bluebells, Wood Anemones and Lily-of-the valley.

Woodpeckers include **Black, Middle Spotted** and **Wryneck. Buzzard** and **Honey Buzzard** both breed here. Other summer breeders include both **Spotted** and **Pied Flycatchers, Grasshopper, Melodious** and **Wood Warblers;** there may be a few **Icterine Warblers,** so check all "yellow" warblers carefully. **Hawfinch** can be found year round as can **Crossbill, Goldcrest, Crested** and **Coal Tits** in the Scots Pine plantations. In winter there are often **Redwing** and flocks of finches **(Chaffinch, Brambling, Siskin).** Both **Common** and **Short-toed Treecreeper** breed.

ACCESS: Leave the A1 motorway at exit 9 (from the south) or 10 (from the north or west). When you get on to the dual-carriageway ring road around COMPIÈGNE, zero. At the large crossroads south of the town, follow the signs for SOISSONS for |2.6 km. At the next roundabout go straight on in the direction of PIERREFONDS. In another 1.2 km (at 3.8 km) turn right onto a hard-surfaced forestry road. At 5 km from zeroing you will come to a signed crossroads *(Carrefour des Nymphes)*

This is a good place to start listening for woodpeckers and searching the newish regrowth and sapling trees for warblers. Woodpeckers may be heard in the mature oaks here. Take the *Grand Octagon* dirt road to *Hamadryads* crossroads where there are more mature trees a little distance in from the road. At *Puits des Chasseurs* there are good, large trees and the conifers around *Puits de Berne* are good for Crested Tit. Some of the better parts of this forest are the areas nearest to town, just off the D130 and D332. Around the hamlet of MALLASSISE **Black Woodpeckers** can sometime be heard in the old, stag-headed Oaks near the junction of the D85/D85E.

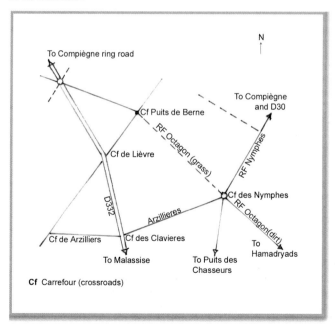

Enlargement of part of Compiègne Forest showing forestry tracks

Site ii.

The RIVER OISE runs through the town of Compiègne from northeast to southwest. The section north of Compiègne between THOUROTTE and VENDEUIL is an IBA, being one of the more important breeding sites for **Corncrake** in France, with some 20-25 pairs. (See notes on "Special species" at end). There is some marshland along the river, notably south of TERGNIER and VENDEUIL. Other habitats include water meadows, Poplar plantations and some riparian woodland. South of the town there is a series of flooded gravel pits.

ACCESS: There is access to parts of the river (from north to south) at Vendeuil where the D421 cross the canal and tracks lead off; at Travecy, where the D643 cross the river; at Frette where there is some open water off the D424 and the D1132 runs alongside the river and at Thourotte where the D66 runs from le Plessis-Brion north to Ribecourt alongside the river.

South of Compiègne there are some old or active gravel pits west of Verberie around Moru and Pontpoint along the D120 and D123. Leave the motorway at exit 9 and take the D155 into Verberie then drive east on the D123, leaving it and turning right (north) at Moru to follow the river.

WHEN TO VISIT: Winter or migration periods are the best times to visit, when there are many waders **(Dunlin, Lapwing, 'shanks, Snipe, Black-tailed Godwit, Green, Wood** and **Common Sandpipers). Black Tern** may be seen over the lakes in spring with many hirundines, including **Sand Martin,** and this also the best time to listen out for **Corncrake** and **Golden Oriole,** find **Blue-headed Wagtail** and many warbler species, including **Melodious.**

Site iii.

West of Compiègne, north of the river, **SACY MARSH** is easy to reach and has some good birds: **Bittern** and **Little Bittern** have been seen here, **Marsh Harrier, Hobby, Honey Buzzard** in summer and **Osprey** on passage. **Bluethroat** can also be found on passage but **Reed, Sedge, Cetti's** (and possibly **Savi's) Warblers** breed. **Nightingale** and **Reed Bunting** are quite common.

ACCESS: To reach SACY MARSH take the D10 from BAZICOURT west through St. Martin-Longueau for 4 km to SACY-le-Grand. The marsh can be observed from the D75, which runs south from the D10 at SACY-le Grand. Turn south onto it and stop wherever possible along the first two kilometres, especially at the small bridge in the centre. This is where **Bittern** has been heard and **Little Bittern** may be seen flying in May.

WHEN TO VISIT: As for site ii above but March is the likeliest time to hear **Bittern** and May-June is best for **Little Bittern, raptors** and **warblers.**

Area 4-6. **THE CHAMPAGNE LAKES**

Geographically Champagne is divided into "dry" and "wet" regions: dry Champagne comprises the chalk hills in the north covered with the vinyards that produce the famous "bubbly"; wet Champagne to the south is a land of forests and large lakes, many man-made. LPO Champagne-Ardenne have a useful website at www.lpochampagneardenne.com which gives itineraries and maps for sites and walks in the whole area, not just around the famous lakes but also in the valley of the Marne and even between Reims and Châlons in the intensively cultivated north. Additionally they keep up-to-date lists of sightings, mainly for the Lac du Der region but also noting any interesting birds observed elsewhere as well as running birding weekends at the lakes in the autumn and winter. LPO Champagne-Ardenne, 4 place du Marechal Joffre, BP 27, 51301 Vitry-le-Francois, Cedex Tel: 03 26 72 54 47 Fax: 03 26 72 54 30 email: lpochamp@club-internet.fr

Maps: Michelin 241 1 1 cm=2 km covers areas 3, 4 and 5. Series bleu maps 1 cm=250 m can be obtained from local newsagents and the visitors' centres at Sites 4 and 5.

Area 4. **ARGONNE LAKES**

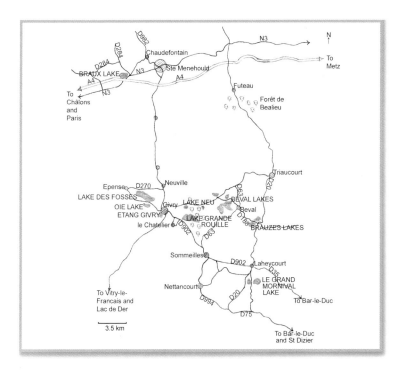

North Central area 4 Argonne Lakes

The **ARGONNE LAKES,** marshes and reedbeds, some 40 km north (more by road) of the more-famous Lac du Der (Area 5) are mainly natural. They are surrounded by wet meadows, grassland and forest, and access to many of them is difficult. They are an IBA for birds breeding in reedbeds and forests and part of the 235,000 hectare Ramsar Site "*Étangs de la Champagne Humide*".

Buzzard, Honey Buzzard, Black and **Red Kites, Goshawk, Black, Middle Spotted** and **Grey-headed Woodpecker** breed in the **woodland, Marsh Harrier, Bittern** and **Little Bittern** (a few) and **Great Reed, Reed** and **Sedge Warblers** in the reedbeds and **Hen Harrier** and **Corncrake** in the fields. **Red-backed Shrike** can be found everywhere in suitable habitat. **Golden Oriole** are also quite numerous; May and June are the best months to hear them singing and so track them down. In fact, spring and autumn are good seasons to visit these lakes, although in winter there are always reasonable concentrations of **Teal, Pochard, Tufted Duck** and **Wigeon** on most lakes, as well as a few **Smew, Goosanders** and **Goldeneye** (more numerous during really hard spells) as well as **Pintail** and **Shoveler** (many more of these latter species on passage). In good "eagle" years **White-tailed Eagle** can sometimes be observed around the more wooded lakes; Great White Egrets are increasing in number each winter. **Kingfishers** can be found al through the year and **Coot, Grey Heron** and **Cormorant** are common. At the end of summer and beginning of autumn, when water levels are low, passage waders include **Snipe, Redshank, Spotted Redshank, Greenshank, Curlew** and **sandpipers. Ferruginous Duck** and **Garganey** can occur on passage. **Osprey** also use the lakes as a stop-off during post-nuptial migration and both **Black** and **Red Kites** pass through, often in quite large numbers.

ACCESS: The Argonne can be quickly reached from the Channel ports via the A26 motorway to REIMS, then the A4, leaving it at the STE-MENEHOULD exit, 29. If coming from the south, and Lac du Der, take the D982 north from VITRY. Some of the most interesting and accessible lakes are BRAUX, near STE-MENEHOULD and GRAND MORINVAL, BRAUZES, BELVAL, FOSSES and D'OIE, which are all fairly close to the town of GIVRY-SUR-ARGONNE, a good starting point.

GIVRY is at the junction of the D982/D902 16 km due south of STE-MENEHOULD and the A4 motorway and 35 km north-east of VITRY.

To visit the D'OIE and FOSSES LAKES, both within a triangle of roads north-west of GIVRY, take the D70 west from the centre of town through REMICOURT towards EPENSE. 1.5 km from Remicourt you will see OIE lake on the left close to the road. Good views can be had from the roadside but watch when parking, the verge can be soft.

A little further along the D70 there is a dirt track leading off right towards another stretch of water. This is the southern tip of FOSSE lake. It is possible to walk along this track. Alternatively, for good views of the north end, drive into EPENSE and turn right onto the D270, signed to la NEUVILLE. In a couple of kilometres Fosse lake can be seen on the right. It can be scanned with a scope from the raised bank of the verge; however, in a few years the trees planted around the edge of the lake will limit the view.

Continue into NEUVILLE, turn right (south) onto the D982 and in 2.5 km you will arrive back in Givry.

To visit the BELVAL and BRAUZES lakes, east of the town, take the D54 towards LES CHARMONTOIS and BELVAL. In just over two kilometres there is a small lake on the right, among trees, that is worth checking. In 7 km you will come to the junction with the D354, signed to BELVAL. One of the larger Belval lakes lies immediately south of this road. 1 km from the junction there is a gap giving a view of part of the lake. The D354 then swings right and in another 700 metres the old sluice gate (100 metres before the signed picnic area) provides a good viewpoint. This lake has a good surround of reeds and is good for warblers in spring. **Kingfisher** can usually be seen here and it is popular with herons (including **Great White Egret** in winter).

Continue along the D354 through the village of Belval and in 5.5 km from the junction with the D54 you will see the BRAUX lakes on both sides of the road. These are normally some of the most productive, especially in winter when a few **Smew** and **Goosander** join the **Shovelers, Pochard** and **Tufted Duck.** It is also good for **herons** and **Great White Egrets.** Park just before or after the lakes and walk back between them.

A few hundred metres beyond the lakes is a staggered crossroads with the D20. Turn right (south) onto it and drive 5 km into LAHEYCOURT, the starting point for GRAND MORINVAL lake. Continue on the D20 south of its junction with the D902 in the centre of town and in 400 metres from the sign showing the end of Laheycourt, turn left onto a minor road just before an isolated farm. In 1 km from this turning you will see the lakes on both sides of the road. Park on the verge. You have to look through a wire fence but as these lakes (especially the eastern one) can be good for birds, they are usually worth visiting.

The final lake, BRAUX, is 4 km west of Ste-Menehould along the N3. Access is from the slip road (part of the old road) just after the D384 turning, signed to Braux Château. There are good views over the lake from the slip road and it is possible to walk a short way around the west side of the lake. In winter most of the birds listed above for this season can be seen there and it is also good in spring (marsh terns on passage) and during the breeding season.

South-east of STE-MENEHOULD is the Beaulieu Forest, good for **woodpeckers,** especially **Middle Spotted** and **Black** and woodland birds in general. Take the D2 north from TRIAUCOURT, or south from LES ISLETTES, 9 km east of Ste-Menehould. The forest lies between the villages of Futeau and Beaulieu-en-Argonne and has good strands of mature trees. There are several forestry tracks to walk along and places to park on the verge beside the D2.

Accommodation: There is a Logis, excellent but expensive, in Futeau and another in Ste-Menehould.

Area 5. LE LAC DU DER-CHANTECOQ

LE LAC DU DER-CHANTECOQ is the northernmost of the two large Champagne lakes that have become a "mecca" for European birders in winter. Together with the Forêt d'Orient lakes (Area 6) it is possibly the best-known birdwatching site in northern France. They, and the Argonne Lakes to the north, are all part of the huge Ramsar site "Étangs de la Champagne Humide". Der-Chantecoq is the largest artificial lake in Europe. It covers 4,800 hectares and was created to regulate the flow of the Marne and so ensure a constant water supply to Paris.

Its attraction for birds lies in the variety of habitats it offers: numerous wooded inlets, several islands, a regular variation in water level, ensuring large areas of mudflats and wet meadows in autumn and winter.

WHEN TO VISIT: this is generally considered a winter site but October-November and March are the months with both the largest number of species as well as the greatest number of birds. Late spring is best for breeding birds. The weather is often better early or late because there are frequent foggy days in winter when it can also be very wet and cold. Although normally the colder the weather the better the birds! Water sports cause a lot of disturbance in summer and the water levels are also very low, so July and August are best avoided, although waders are starting to return and birds are concentrated into the few "quiet zones".

The star attractions of Der-Chantecoq are the **Cranes** and the regular presence of wintering **White-tailed Eagle;** between two to five birds have been found here between November and March every winter for at least the past decade. More than 20,000 Cranes regularly use the lake on passage (the greatest numbers in November and March) and each year several thousands overwinter here: In mid-November 2000 over 76,000 Cranes were counted and there were still 11,000 in January 2001 and 14,000 in February.

Other wintering species include all three **divers** in small numbers; thousands of **Great Crested Grebe** with usually some **Red-necked, Black-necked, Slavonian** and **Little** among them; a few **Bewick's** and **Whooper Swans;** thousands of geese of which **Greylag** are the most numerous, followed by several hundred **Bean,** a few dozen **White-fronts** and often a few **Red-breasted, Lesser White-fronted** or even a **Snow Goose.** All the ducks on the French list have been observed here at some time; on passage and in winter: **Wigeon, Teal, Shoveler, Pochard** and **Tufted Duck** are the most numerous, but **Shelduck, Goosander, Smew, Goldeneye, Eider, Scoter, Velvet Scoter** and **Long-tailed Duck** are all regular in small numbers. A few **Great White Egrets** turn up every year and their numbers are increasing.

Besides the **White-tailed Eagles,** a few **Peregrines** also winter here and there are sometimes **Rough-legged** among the numerous wintering **Buzzards.** (Be warned - many of the Common Buzzards here are exceptionally pale - check their tails). When there is a **Waxwing** eruption into western Europe, then the mistletoe-covered trees around the village-port of GIFFAUMONT, in the south, is a good site, as it is for wintering thrushes and finches, including **Redpoll.**

In autumn, when water levels are lowest and mud flats exposed, there are large numbers of waders, often including hundreds of **Spotted Redshank** and a few **Great Snipe** among the **Dunlin, Lapwing, Curlew** and **Snipe.** Some waders spend the winter round the lake, notably thousands of **Lapwing. Black Stork** are regularly seen on passage, especially in September and March.

Although most birders will visit Der in winter, spring passage is also impressive. Besides duck, gulls and waders, it includes **Black Tern** and **Blue-headed Wagtail,** whilst breeding birds include a few **Bittern, Little Bittern** and **Purple Herons, Corncrake** and **Marsh Harrier.** In spring, the nearby HORRE lake, 20 km to the south-west, (site iii. below) may be better for these species because the difficulty is finding them in a lake of this size. From March to July **Red** and **Black Kites** and **Honey Buzzard** breed in nearby woodland and can be seen around the lakeside; more pass through on migration. The same woods hold six **woodpecker** species **(Black, Great, Middle** and **Lesser Spotted, Green** and **Grey-headed)** and **Crossbills.** February-March is probably the best period to find woodpeckers, when they are at their most vocal and the northern promontory of Cornée du Der one of the best places.

At all seasons a good number of rarities turn up (Snow and Lesser White-fronted Geese, Black Stork and White-billed Diver in winter 2001) but the lake is so vast that a considerable amount of luck is needed to discover them. However, the web-site provides reasonably up-to-date information as does the list in the Maison de l'Oiseau, near Chantecoq port and there are always plenty of birders around to share information.

ACCESS: Lac de Der can be reached quickly from the Channel ports via the A26 motorway to Reims and then the N44 to VITRY-LE-FRANCOIS, which is the northern apex of a triangle of roads surrounding the lake: the N4 to St. Dizier to the north, the D384 that runs down the east side of the lake and the D396 on the west; these two meet at BRIENNE -LE-CHATEAU. Branching off these roads the minor D12, D13 and D57 run close to the lake. From them it is possible to reach the lake at 11 points, some better than others. The map shows the numbered viewpoints and the text describes a day's itinerary by car, starting and finishing at GIFFAUMONT. Unless you hear of a rarity somewhere, then it is a good plan to follow this itinerary on your first morning, later returning to the best sites. Obviously it is as easy to start from Eclaron or elsewhere, as it is a circular tour. Many parts (or all) of the itinerary could well be cycled, though obviously this will take longer than a day. Cycles can be hired at Giffaumont (see information on accommodation below).

Site i.
ITINERARY AROUND LAC DU DER
From the D13/D55 junction just outside GIFFAUMONT village, take the D13 westwards, signed to *Site de Chantecoq/Maison de l'Oiseau,* ARRIGNY/VITRY. Zero here. Check the trees along the road for **thrushes** and **finches,** and the fields for flock of feeding **cranes** and **geese.** In 4.8 km turn right just before the roundabout to the car-park of Site de Chantecoq/Observatoire, (**1**). There are good views from this small port as well as a hide a short distance to the left. Look for **Black Redstart** around the port buildings. This is one of the best places to look for **White-tailed Eagle,** especially if it is sitting on the island. In autumn and winter, there are always plenty of **swans**, **geese, duck, cranes** and **waders** to be observed from the hide and in spring, **terns** and **warblers. Common Tern** have been breeding on the specially erected floats or small artificial "islands" since 1990. This site is especially good early morning and evening, above all in winter when the cranes are arriving or leaving their roosts and **Cormorants** are flying to theirs on the island. Also it is usually the first stop for many local birders, who may be able to tell you the latest sightings and where to find any rarities.

From the port you can walk north along the tarmacked *digue* road for several kilometres, which brings you closer to some of the bays and also the island, where a **White-tailed Eagle** or **Peregrine** may be perched. However, in bad weather, or if pressed for time, you can drive along two stretches of the digue (one-way only), stopping wherever you like to scan. To drive the digue, return to the roundabout and zero again. (The left turning off the roundabout leads to the Maison de l'Oiseau. It, and the nearby lakes, are covered as a separate site below but you may like to check the recent sighting list in the shop, ask for directions or just have a coffee and browse if the weather is really bad!)

From the roundabout drive for 1.4 km along the D13 to the parking and turning for the *Route de Digue.* (**2**). Park on the left side of the road if you wish to walk and scan from the digue, otherwise turn right onto the digue to drive back (one-way) towards the hide and roundabout. At 3.6 km from the roundabout there is another stretch of drivable digue (**3**), but visibility from this part is limited, although it is always worth checking out.

The next viewpoint (**4**) is from the *Presqu'île de Lazicourt* signed from the roundabout another kilometre up the D13. There can be good views of **Bewick** and **Whooper Swans** from here, as well as **sawbills** and **geese** but equally there may be nothing. There is some shallow water in the bay on the left and a view over the lake from beyond the turning circle. The road with a barrier leads to a campsite. Do not drive down it in winter as you may be trapped!

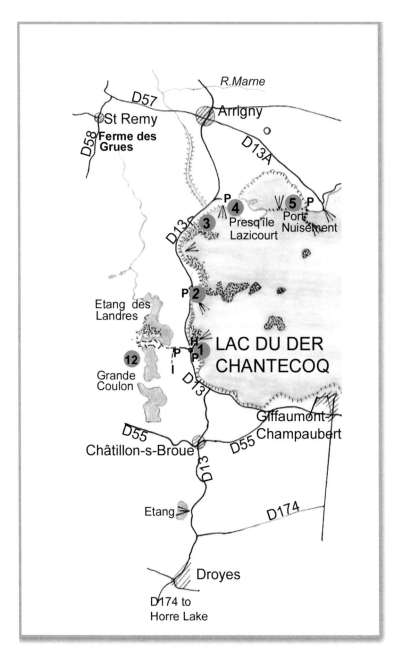

North Central area 5 Lac du Der West

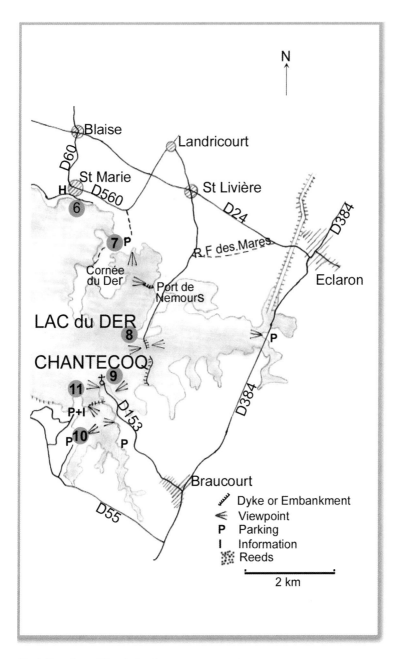

North Central area 5 Lac du Der East

Viewpoint (**5**), *Port de Nuisement* gives better views over the *Bassin Nord* and is often a good site for rarities. It is the main site for diving ducks; so anything from dozens to hundreds of **Tufted Duck** and **Common Pochard** will be found here, and **Golden Eye, Velvet Scoter, Ferruginous Duck** and **Scaup** often turn up in small numbers as well as **divers, grebes** and **sawbills. (White-billed Diver** was here in 2001). To reach the port take the D13a from the centre of ARRIGNY village towards Ecollemont. At the Y junction in 1 km keep right towards NUISEMENT. There is a view of part of the bay from the embankment beside the turning to the *Base Nautique de Ecollemont* (worth checking) but better views are obtained by continuing to the small port at the end of the road, 4.4 km from Arrigny. From the road-end there is a view of the lake and some small islands, otherwise inaccessible, but many birds shelter in the basin behind the dam. To view the north side of the dam you have to go through the sailing school complex on the right. It is possible to walk along the jetty to view any birds tucked under the south side.

Driving back towards ARRIGNY, check the ploughed fields each side of the road for **Hen Harriers** and **Cranes.** The fields alongside the D57 running north-west from Arrigny to ST. REMY are also good for these two species. A farm is specially managed for Cranes in this commune, so there are always plenty of them in this area (*Ferme aux Grues,* Hameau d'Isson, 51290 Saint Remy en Bouzemont. Tel: 03 26 72 54 10 or 03 24 30 06 20) is off the D58 a kilometre south of St. Remy)

Whether or not you have made a detour towards St. Remy, to reach the next viewpoint over Lac du Der, take the D57 east from ARRIGNY for 5.5 km to ST. BLAISE and turn right (south) onto the D60 leading to ST. MARIE-DU-LAC (**6**). The old water tower on the edge of the village has been turned into an observatory with stunning views over the lake (especially good from late afternoon when the Cranes are flying in to roost as most spend the night in the northern part of the lake).

La Cornée du Der, (**7**), a long wooded peninsular with numerous small bays is the next area to visit. Go through St. Mairie on the D560, past the campsite and turn right in a kilometre towards the *Plage de Cornée.* You are now in woodland good for **Goshawk, Sparrowhawk** and both **Middle Spotted** and **Black Woodpecker** (perhaps the easiest site to find them around Lac du Der) but you will notice the damage caused by the December 1999 storm. You will see a track leading straight ahead (explore this later) but for now keep left on the one-way system towards the beach area. The parking/picnic area is good for **Middle Spotted, tits, Goldcrest, Hawfinch** and sometimes **Crossbills** in the conifers. Take note of **treecreepers,** both species are here. In the winter there is little disturbance, at other seasons try it early in the morning. Walk through the trees for a view over the bay; although this is not normally the best site for waterbirds, it can spring surprises. If the sun makes scanning difficult, the next viewpoint looks over the bay from the opposite direction.

Make the circuit around the one-way system until you return to the road leading south; this time take the road through the woods that you did not take before. There are various places where you can catch a glimpse of the lake. The track ends in small turning circle with some mature trees nearby. Try here for **Black Woodpecker** (and Middle if it was not by the beach area).

Return to the beach junction but there turn right towards the D24 and right again in about a kilometre when you reach it. In just under 2 km you will reach STE. LIVIERE. The turning to the right is clearly signed to the *Port* and *Presque'île de Nemours/La Brèche* (**8**). It is 4.4 km to the Brèche (the breach made in the old digue of the smaller reservoir of Champaubert when Der was created) but on the way check out the Port/sailing club on the right; it looks west across to the Cornée du Der and can be useful in the morning. The best view into the northeast corner of the lake (sometime called Vieux Der) is from the digue of the old reservoir (you can walk to the breach). **White-**

tailed Eagle is sometimes found in this section where there is a heronry.

Half way back to Ste. Liviere you may prefer to take the forestry road *R.F. des Mares* that leads off to the right (east). It loops back to the D24 just before ECLARON. The woods here should also be good for woodland species though they seem emptier of bird life - it possibly depends on the amount of forestry work and therefore disturbance.

Take the D24 into ECLARON and the D384 south out of the town. In 2 km there are another couple of viewpoints over Vieux Der from the right (west) side of the road with parking nearby. Continue into BRAUCOURT, 7.4 km from Eclaron and turn right on the D153 towards the *Presque'île de Champaubert* (**9**). Drive to the end of the road, about 3.7 km. There is an excellent view in front of the church (the only building left when the old village was flooded). On the right (east) is a bay which is a "quiet zone", so often full of birds. Though it is gated, there seems no obstacle to walking to the hide overlooking it. When water levels are low in the autumn there are large numbers of waders on the mud banks and in winter this is the place to find good numbers of **geese.** It is possible to walk over the dam/bridge to the *Station nautique de Giffaumont* (**11**) from here and this can give good views in both directions, especially into the south basin. There are often large concentrations of **grebes** and **sawbills** in this part of the lake.

On the return to BRAUCOURT, stop at the beach (signed *Plage*) beside the sailing school (*Ecole de voile*) to look over the enclosed southern bay and check for **Goosander** and **Smew.** Whatever the weather conditions, there are likely to be a few here in winter.

In Braucourt, zero at the junction and take the D384 for a kilometre before turning off right (west) onto the D55 signed to GIFFAUMONT. In 4.6 km there is a turning right to *Stade Nautique*. Drive to the end of this road, another 2.6 km, (**10**). The view from the picnic table looks across to the old church. In winter the quiet backwater on the right of the road could be the best place for close views of **Smew** and **Goosander, Tufted Duck** and **Pochard.**

The final stopping point of the tour is at the Port de Giffaumont (**11**). Return to the D55 and turn right towards Giffaumont. There is another water tower here, which has also been turned into an observatory but is not so good for birds. Turn right into the port/ *Station Nautique.* There will be plenty of **gulls** and **grebes** (mainly **Great Crested**) around the boats to check. Drive on and park beside the sailing school building and the causeway leading back towards the church. This viewpoint gives more good views of the southern part of the lake.

It is less than 2 km from the port to the village of Giffaumont.

Site ii.

ITINERARY AROUND THE SIDE LAKES and Maison de l'Oiseau (full name: *La Maison de l'Oiseaux et du Poisson*) is signed to the left (west) at the roundabout on the D13 by the Site de Chantecoq Port and hide (the first stop on the itinerary above). It is an education centre (videos, exhibitions, whole or half day guided tours) as well as a shop and snack bar. Binoculars can be hired. Most usefully, a list of current sightings is chalked up above the counter and the staff are helpful and knowledgeable. In short, it is a good place for a break at any time, but especially if the weather is foggy or wet. It is open 9-12.00 and 13.00-17-00 all year. Tel: 03 26 74 00 00 Fax: 03 26 74 73 74 and a 24 hour "twitch line" 03 26 72 51 39

Three smaller side lakes or *étangs,* Landres, Grand Coulon and le Forêt can be reached from the car park. These reed-fringed lakes are possibly better in spring or autumn when Der Lake is low; nevertheless, in winter there is chance of some birds not to be found on the main lake. The side lakes (**12**) can be good for **swans, diving** and dabbling ducks, **Kingfisher, Great White Egret** and there is a good chance of finding **Bearded Tit.** In spring, **Bittern** and **Great Reed Warbler** breed in the reeds and **Red-backed Shrike** in the brambles and hedges. The marked trail around the lakes leads through woodland, where the commoner woodland species can be found.

The Maison sells a booklet with sketch map giving details of the species likely to be seen along this nature trail (*sentier de découverte nature*).

ACCESS: From the first car park walk down the wide, muddy, grassy track leading straight on (the drive to the Maison is on the left). The path is not signed at this entry point. It can be very wet indeed in winter and Wellington boots are advisable. After some 500 metres a sign leads to the first hide on the right, overlooking Landres. Return to the main path and continue through the wood; the trail is now marked with paint. Turn left at the bend to reach the hide overlooking Grand Coulon and continue round the circuit to reach a third hide on the west arm of Landres. It is about 800 metres from here back to the edge of the wood.

Site iii.
HORRE LAKE is situated some 20 km (by road) southwest of Giffaumont and 10 km west of MONTIER-EN-DER. It is quite a large lake (330 hectares) surrounded by private woodland and can be viewed from only one point. Nevertheless, it is worth visiting if you have time, especially in spring and summer, as it is very attractive.

In winter there is always a good number of all the diving and dabbling ducks found in the region, including **Smew,** and **Great White Egret** is regular. In spring migrants often include **Garganey, Osprey,** and marsh terns while breeding birds include **herons, duck, grebes, Bittern, Great Reed Warbler** and other passerines. Raptors breeding in the surrounding woodland include **Black** and **Red Kites** and **Honey Buzzard.** Nearby farmland can be good for **Hen Harrier** in winter and **Red-backed Shrike** in summer. Autumn migration is noted for **Black Storks** as well as many waders.

ACCESS: The only feasible viewpoint is from the D173 between the villages of PUELLEMONTIER and LENTILLES. From either Lac de Der or Montier, get to DROYES on the D13 from Montier. Zero at the D13/D174 crossroads in Droyes. Take the D174 to PUELLEMONTIER, where it changes to become the D173. Go straight on (bearing right) in the direction of LENTILLES and there is a place to view the lake in 8 km, just before a white house with wooden barns

Accommodation: There are small Logis de France hotels at Giffaumont-Champaubert (recommended) and at Eclaron, two good bases. Both are heavily booked in autumn and winter, especially at week-ends, and both also close for some weeks during this period. **Booking in advance is essential.** If you turn up on the off-chance you may have to sleep in the car! Otherwise the nearest hotels are in St. Dizier or Vitry, not nearly so convenient for early-morning birding. There are plenty of gîtes in this area (not so many available in winter), and some chambres d'hôtes (B & B). Contact the Tourist Office for addresses and more information: Office de Tourisme, Lac de Der Chantecoq, and Station Nautique. Maison du Lac, 51290 Giffaumont-Champaubert. Tel: 03 26 72 62 80 Fax: 03 26 72 64 69 e-mail: LAC-DE-DER@wanadoo.fr

Cycle hire is available from the Brochet du Lac, St. Remy, Le Cycloder, St. Marie and (quadricycles only) Boutique Vert Marine at the Station Nautique, Giffaumont, which is only open Sunday afternoons except during July and August. Check opening hours, telephone numbers, etc. with the Tourist Office.

Other fauna and flora: In addition to the 270 bird species recorded, 40 mammal, 45 dragonflies and over 200 wetland plant species are found around Der. Amphibians include Alpine Newt. Both Coypu and Muskrat can be seen around the lake. See also fauna listed under the Forêt d'Orient site below.

LAKE AND REGIONAL NATURE PARK OF THE FORÊT D'ORIENT

Some 40 km south of Lac du Der and 20 km east of Troyes, three large man-made lakes lie within the Regional Nature Park of the Forêt d'Orient, which was created in 1970 and covers some 70,000 hectares. The best-known and largest lake is the most southerly LAC D'ORIENT (2500 hectares), constructed in 1966 to control the flow of the Seine but lakes AMANCE (500 hectares) and TEMPLE (1800 hectares), both built in 1990, also offer good birding, especially Amance which has gained quite a reputation for rarities. Like Lac du Der (Area 5), these lakes experience pronounced changes in water-levels; the mud-flats exposed in autumn attracting large numbers of waders. All the lakes are surrounded by forest and the northern part of d'Orient is a reserve, where hunting and water-sports are not allowed. This attracts large numbers of duck, geese, and cormorants. Nearly all the species listed under Lac du Der will also be found on d'Orient, including **Cranes** and **White-tailed Eagle,** but in smaller numbers. Perhaps because of a run of milder winters or growing numbers of tourists, Orient does not seem as good for birds as it did some years ago. However, in very cold spells more birds can be found here than on Der as it is perhaps more sheltered. Several thousand **Cranes** use the three lakes on passage and several hundred may overwinter there but they are never as visible as at Der. A thousand or so **Mallard,** and almost as many **Teal** winter there together with smaller numbers of **Tufted Duck, Common Pochard, Gadwall, Goldeneye** and **sawbills. White-headed Duck** has been spotted twice and **Ruddy Duck** are being noted more and more frequently (both may be escapes). Orient is becoming one of the best wintering sites in inland France for **Bean Geese,** often accompanied by **White-fronts** though their numbers seem to be decreasing as **Greylag** numbers increase. Seven heron species have been counted, including **Great White Egret** regularly every winter while both **Bittern** and **Little Bittern** breed in the reedbeds, though both are becoming rare. **Black Storks** have been seen regularly since 1986, and it is possible a few pairs may breed nearby; one or two may overwinter. **Osprey** use the lake on passage and **Booted Eagle, Honey Buzzard, Goshawk** and **Sparrowhawk** breed in the Park's woodland. In the more open areas, both **Black** and **Red Kite, Hen Harrier, Short-toed Eagle** and **Hobby** may be sighted in spring, while both **Merlin** and **Peregrine** are regular in winter. 31 wader species have been counted on passage; numbers depend on water levels and exposed mud-flats. All the five **grebe** species found in France have been seen on the lakes, though **Great Crested Grebe** is by far the most common.

In the woodland, all six woodpecker species may be found, including **Black, Grey-headed** and **Middle Spotted. Northern Grey Shrike** can be found year round, **Red-backed** in summer and **Tawny Pipit** (very rare in the north of France) in dry areas in May and September.

WHEN TO VISIT: As for the Lac du Der. There is a lot of disturbance at this lake in summer and on winter weekends.

ACCESS: As at Lac du Der, there are various observation points all around the lakes. A good base and starting point is MESNIL ST.PÈRE, basically a lakeside holiday resort, almost deserted in winter except at weekends, where there is bird-watching from the jetty in the harbour unless wind-surfing is taking place. Mesnil is some 20 km from

TROYES along the N 19, turning left into the village 5 km after LUSIGNY-sur-Barse. Scan the dam on the left; grebes, divers, sawbills and Shelduck may be here. There are always plenty of gulls in the harbour, mainly from the large Black-headed Gull roost. The following itineraries need a car, or possibly a bicycle for the energetic, and are the only feasible ways of seeing all the sites around the lakes, as public transport is almost non-existent. It is, of course, possible to walk along any stretch of the suggested itineraries, especially the embankments.

Site i.
ITINERARY AROUND ORIENT LAKE

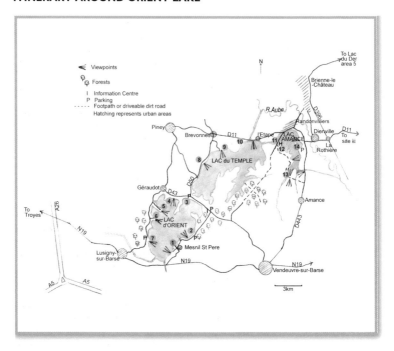

North Central area 6 Forêt d'Orient Lakes

From MESNIL (**1**) a minor road, the D43, leads north-east along the east shore of the lake for 6 km, with various viewpoints over the water, and places to park beside the road, until it joins the D79 by the Maison du Parc. The first viewpoint from where it is possible to walk over the grass towards the lake is 1 km from town. Stop at the viewpoint (**2**) in 1.9 km just before the PINEY Forest (3 km from the jetty), as **Grey-headed Woodpecker** has been seen here. A third view of the lake occurs in 2.7 km. At the D79 junction, visit the *Maison du Parc* if you need booklets, maps, etc or a picnic stop. It no longer seems to have an up-to-date sightings list (courtesy of the LPO), but may do so again; the staff should know what birds are about. Turn left onto the D79 km in the direction of GÉRAUDOT. In 2.6 km there is parking for the tower hide overlooking the north of the lake (**3**). The short walk through the wood can be a good spot for woodpeckers, tits and other forest species, especially in the early morning before there is too much disturbance. The hide is especially interesting in autumn for **Cranes** and on winter mornings as it is one of the possible sites for sighting **White-tailed Eagle** in winter and **Osprey** on passage. In summer **Great Reed, Reed, Sedge Warblers** and **Reed Bunting** can be seen and heard from the hide. In another 0.4 km the road forks and you must decide on whether to keep left to Géraudot on the D43 and then circle the lake back to Mesnil or whether to turn right onto the D50 and follow the west shore of Temple Lake. Your decision will be influenced by any information obtained at the *Maison du parc* and on the amount of time you have to spend.

If making a circuit of Lake Orient, zero at the junction. The next stop is at 2.3 km for GÉRAUDOT beach/picnic area (**4**), where there are often Bean Geese in winter, and good views over the lake. After GÉRAUDOT village turn south onto the D1 towards LUSIGNY. Keep left when the road forks and turn left at the sign for the Presque'île de la Picardie. By the picnic area (in about 350 metres) there is a good view of the cove if you walk through the trees (**5**). There are also footpaths through the woods but the 1999 storms caused extensive damage and they were still closed in 2001. Return to the road, continue south and take the next left turn signed to the Ecole Française de Voile; turn left again and go to the end of the track about half a kilometre from the road. This viewpoint (**6**) gives even better views over Bourgetterie cove than the previous one. There are often flocks of diving ducks in the bay.

From now on the D1 runs very close to the lakeside for several kilometres through LANVOUR forest, although there is not very much visibility until you get to the car park on the right-hand side of the road (west) (**7**). On the right side there is a good view over the lake (best in afternoon) and footpaths in both directions.

Go through LUSIGNY and turn left onto the N19 to return to MESNIL.

Site ii.
This itinerary takes you along the north shores of **AMANCE AND TEMPLE LAKES.** Start from the D43/D50 junction, some 3 km east of GÉRAUDOT. At the junction turn north up the D50. After a kilometre the road runs alongside the dyke of LAKE TEMPLE for several kilometres. Stop wherever you can park and climb the embankment (**8**) As you are looking east, this is better in the afternoon. Temple can however be disappointing; there never seems to be as many birds on it as on the other lakes. Just as you reach BRÉVONNES (7 km from the junction) turn right down the road signed *Bois 2000 menuiseries;* this industrial estate leads down to a furniture factory right beside the dyke where you can park. Climb to the top of the dyke to look over this corner of the lake (**9**). It is possible to walk along the footpath on top of the embankment. You can walk all the way to L'ETAPE but if there are not many birds then one or two stops to scan are probably sufficient. There is another access track to this dike path after BRÉVONNES village from the D11 which runs east to RANDONVILLIERS. It is the only track on the right (south) running through farmland just over 2 km from the end of Brévonnes. The track turns right below the dike and runs along to the furniture factory. The final stop for Temple Lake is by the canal leading into the lake just before L'ETAPE. Again it is possible to climb the embankment and walk along the digue wall (**10**). In L'ETAPE the *Rue de Caron* on the right leads to the lake.

LAKE AMANCE, though smaller and with lower water levels, is a far more interesting lake ornithologically. To make a circuit go into RANDONVILLIERS and take the first right signed to CARON/*Lac de Temple. Zero.* In 1.4 km the road crosses the canal linking Temple and Amance lakes (**11**). Turn left immediately after the canal onto a dirt track. In 300 metres there is a hide on the left, excellent for viewing waders on the mud flats in autumn when the water level is low (**12**). In winter there are **duck,** geese, **Bewick Swan, Curlew, Avocet, Shelduck,** thousands of **Lapwings** and sometimes a **Peregrine. White-tailed Eagle** turns up here fairly frequently. **Cranes** fly over at dusk. During spring passage **Black** and **Whiskered Terns** and **Little Gull** say be seen. To continue the circuit, keep on the dirt track between the lake and the (fenced) wood; there are various places to park and scan the lake. In 4.6 turn right (left is a dead-end to the lake) and in 5.4 turn left towards the lake. At 5.7 km a dyke road crosses the lake (**13**). There is always water on the right-hand (south) side, which is good for **Goosander, Smew, Tufted Duck, Pochard,** and **Osprey** on passage. In the shallow water and mudbanks on the left there are usually waders, even in winter: **Curlew, Dunlin,** a few **Redshank** or **Spotted Redshank, Golden Plover, Snipe.** In autumn there are also **sandpipers, Ruff** and a selection of other **waders.**

Cross the dyke and enter the forest (try for **woodpeckers** here). At 7.3 km the track meets the D443. Turn to the left towards PORT-DIENVILLE, which is sometimes worth visiting in winter. At the roundabout with the DI I, turn into the *Station Nautique* and turn left towards the beach, following the parking signs (**14**). There is a very large carpark extending to the lakeside (free outside the high season). To check the port area turn right. There may be **Golden-eye, sawbills, Kingfisher** and wintering **waders.** It is possible to walk around Lake Amance; it is about 17 km and the footpaths are signed.

Little Bittern

<u>Woodpecker sites</u> **Grey-headed, Black** and **Middle Spotted Woodpeckers**
(as well as **Great Spotted** and **Green**) should all be found fairly easily in the Park.
One good spot for the first three is in the Forêt de Temple on the east bank of that
lake. Take the D79 right (east) from the *Maison du Parc* and turn left (north) in 2.5 km
onto the Route Forestière de Temple. In 1.75 you will come to a picnic area just
before a roundabout (**15**). Middle Spotted can easily be seen and heard here. In fact
the density must be quite high for they can be heard almost anywhere along the forestry
road, from the D79 turning to the picnic area. They are noisy and very territorial
and the forestry road seems to be the border between territories. Grey-headed is much
shyer, quieter and altogether more elusive but they can be heard and seen flying among
the trees on the north side of the picnic area. (Read the notes in *Special Species*
at the end of this book before searching for any woodpecker). The drivable road is
barred beyond the roundabout but there are several marked footpaths and nature
trails starting from here which may be worth walking when there are not too
many people around.

Other sites for woodpeckers have been mentioned in the text for the Orient circuit;
try near the tower hide and also the opposite side of the road from the Maison where
there are mature trees. Black has been seen here though they seem more difficult to
find since the 1999 storms which destroyed many mature trees.

<u>Site iii</u>.

LAKE RAMERUPT A small lake some 12 km east of Lake Amance and Dienville is
worth visiting in spring or summer as both **Bittern** and **Little Bittern** breed there and
the reedbeds are good for **warblers.** There is also an interesting flora. It is less
interesting in winter, although there are **duck** and **Grey Heron.**

ACCESS: From DIENVILLE go east to LA ROTHIERE on the D396. The lake is 6.7 km
from here. Go straight over and through the village towards Petit-Mesnil/la Giberie, a
very long village. At the D11c/D2 crossroads go straight on, then fork left in 150
metres. The lake is 1.25 km down a dirt track. There are two hides and a footpath
leading off on the right from near the information board. It takes about 45 minutes to
walk to the hides and back.

Other fauna and flora: Wild Boar can be seen in the forests and around the lakes in
winter, when they often sleep piled one on top of another for warmth. Since the Park
was created, their numbers have grown from several dozen to several thousand. Roe
Deer are also numerous. Both these species can be seen in semi-freedom at the
Parc animalier on a wooded peninsular jutting out into the eastern side of the lake from
D43. Usually open the first Sunday in each month but check at the gates or at the
Maison du Parc. Wild Cat and Pine Marten are regularly observed. Reptiles include six
snake and five lizard species. Amphibians include Natterjack, Midwife Toad, Yellow-
bellied Toad, 5 newt species and Fire Salamander. 19 butterfly species have been
recorded; one that is both spectacular and relatively common is the Purple Emperor.
The caves, quarries and hollow trees in the Park are important sites for hibernating bats,
including some large colonies of Greater Horseshoe and several species, quite rare for
the north of France, can also be seen in summer: Natterer's, Nathusius' Pipistrelle,
Whiskered Bat among them

<u>Accommodation</u>: There are Logis de France in Mesnil-St. Père, Lusigny and Montieramy,
all near the southern end of Orient Lake and Brévonnes and la Rothière in the north.
All are very convenient for birding the lake but the advice given above under Lac du Der
also applies here. Winter weekends can be fully booked. Mesnil has a campsite. The
Maison du Parc, 10220 Piney. Tel: 03 2543 81 90 has lists of gîtes and chambres d'hôtes
or contact Sud Champagne Tourisme, 10500 La Rothière Tel: 03 25 92 21 79 Fax: 03
25 92 26 16 email: sud.champagne.tourism@wanadoo.fr.

SOUTH CENTRAL REGION

Area 1. Normandy-Maine Forests
    Site i.   Perche Forest
    Site ii.   Écouves Forest
    Site iii.   Perseigne Forest
    Site iv.   Bercé Forest

Area 2. Rille Lake *

Area 3 Nantes
    Site i.   Gâvre Forest
    Site ii.   Grand-Lieu *
    Site iii.   Greé Marshes.

Area 4. Angers
    Site i.   North of Angers *
    Site ii.   South of Angers

Area 5 Saumur
    Site I.   Fontevraud Abbey *
    Site ii.   Little Bustard plains near Montreuil-Bellay

Area 6 The River Loire (sites going upriver from west to east)
    Site i.   Angers
    Site ii.   Saumur
    Site iii.   Villandry
    Site iv.   Tours
    Site v.   Orléans
    Site vi.   Châteauneuf
    Site vii.   Île de Cuissy Reserve
    Site viii.   Cosne-sur-Loire (or La Charité-sur-Loire) Reserve *

Area 7 Orléans Forest *

Area 8. The Sologne
    Site i.   Marcilly Lakes *
    Site ii.   Étang de l'Arche
    Site iii.   Forêt de Bruadan
    Site iv.   Ligny-le-Ribault
    Site v.   Allogny Forest

Area 9. The River Allier
    Site i.   The Val d'Allier Nature Reserve *
    Site ii.   Mars-sur Allier, near Nevers

Area 10. Burgundy Forests

Site i. Auberive Forest
Site ii. Châtillon Forest
Site iii. Citeaux Forest

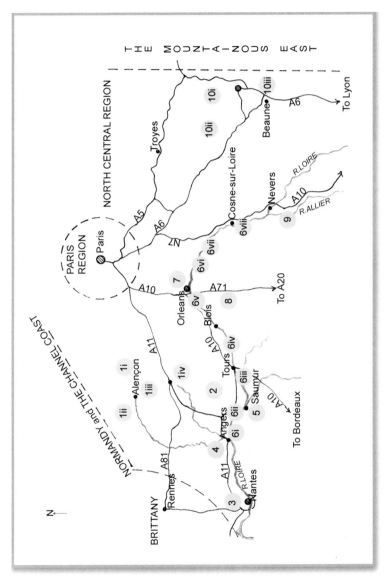

South Central region birding areas

Large parts of these forests lie within Normandy but they are right on the south-eastern border, extending into other Departments, and a long way from the Normandy coastal sites, so they have been placed in the South Central Region.

The Perche is a region famous for its hills, forests, lakes, rivers, and beautiful countryside and its famous heavy horses, Percherons. Perche Natural Regional Park contains Perche, Réno-Valdieu and Bellême Forests, while Écouves and Perseigne Forests lies within the Normandie-Maine Regional Park. Although each forest has a character of its own, they are all classified as Important Bird Areas and similar species will be found in them all, including good populations of **Honey Buzzard, Nightjar, Black** and **Grey-headed Woodpeckers** and **Woodlark,** besides of course many other species, including **Middle Spotted Woodpecker, Hen Harrier,** all the **tit species,** both **Common** and **Short-toed Treecreeper, Redstart, Wryneck** and several **warblers** (**Grasshopper** and four *Phylloscopus* species, **Wood, Chiffchaff, Willow, Bonelli's**). They are predominantly Beech and/or Oak forests, with some conifer plantations; all are managed for forestry and can be explored via a network of forestry roads and tracks but a great deal of shooting takes place in all of them in winter. If you are there between mid-October and the end of January, check the notices and avoid hunting days. Be especially careful when boars are being hunted with hounds.

Site i.
PERCHE FOREST, some 35 km northeast of Alençon, is criss-crossed by forest roads and has several accessible forest lakes (many are private), clearings and some heathland. The variety of habitat here makes for a good bird list

South and east of Perche Forest, forming a triangle with several small lakes in the centre, are RÉNO-VALDIEU FOREST, 9 km east of Mortagne, and SENONCHES, 35 km east. All these forests have reasonably high densities of **Grey-headed Woodpecker,** often found in the clearings around the lakes or where there is dead wood, as well as good numbers of **Middle Spotted** and **Black Woodpeckers, Golden Oriole** and **Honey Buzzard. Black Kite** can often be seen in summer. **Melodious Warbler** may be found in Senonches, where there are both **Common** and **Short-toed Treecreepers. Teal, Pochard** and **Mallard** winter on the lakes; **Golden Plover** and Lapwing in the fields. During migration **Black Stork, Crane, Osprey** and **Marsh Harrier** have all been observed, together with large numbers of waders, around the lakes.

ACCESS: The D930 from MORTAGNE-au-Perche runs north along the western boundary of PERCHE FOREST. At the junction with the D251, roughly 15 km from the centre of Mortagne, there are some mature beeches where **Middle Spotted Woodpecker, Treecreepers** and with luck, **Black Woodpecker** can be found. This area by some lakes is a good birding spot but very popular at weekends. Other likely areas can be reached by taking the forest road east to BRESOLETTES and on to the Étoile crossroads, from where forest tracks radiate out.

RÉNO-VALDIEU FOREST is reached by taking the D8 east from MORTAGNE-au-Perche. After 8 km the D8 runs through the centre of the forest, with forestry roads leading off it north and south.

SENONCHES FOREST is best accessed from the D941 between Senonches town and la FERTÉ-VIDAME. 3 km north-west of Senonches go through the village of TARDAIS and in 1 km turn left (south) onto the forestry road D155. Park by the

Sauveloup roundabout and explore parcels 80,81 and 107 to the north-west, looking for areas of mature beeches for **Black Woodpecker**. **Middle Spotted Woodpecker, Melodious Warbler** and **Common Treecreeper** can usually be found near the Sauveloup roundabout. **Grey-headed Woodpecker** is often where there is dead wood around parcels 111, 112 and 113, south of the forest track leading back towards Tardais. There is a small lake just south of Tardais and another further west along the D941 which may be worth checking out when there are few people around.

Other fauna and flora: The usual forest animals occur here: Roe Deer, Wild Boar, Beech Marten, and Badger. 12 bat species have also been recorded (including Greater and Lesser Horseshoe Bats, Bechstein's and Barbastelle), 14 amphibians and 10 reptiles as well as numerous insects. The Perche forests are noted for their fungi and there is also a notable flora, including about a dozen orchid species, in the woods, wet meadows and especially on the limestone heaths around Bellême (including Marsh Helleborine *Epipactis palustris,* Monkey *Orchis simia,* Burnt *Orchis ustulata,* Man *Aceras anthropophorum*). There is a small reserve, mainly for the flora, west of Bellême at les Houlles Blanches by Saint-Martin-du-Vieux-Bellême.

Site ii.
ÉCOUVES FOREST some 10 km north of Alençon, together with Andaines, Perseigne and Sillé-le-Guillaume forests, form a quarter of the Natural Regional Park of Normandie-Maine, which covers 234,000 hectares. Écouves alone is a huge forest (over 8000 hectares) and although the forest holds plenty of bird species, including all those listed for the site above, finding them is never easy. Six woodpecker species (**Black, Green, Grey-headed, Great, Middle** and **Lesser-spotted**) occur in the Park, both **Treecreepers** as well as both **Goldcrest** and **Firecrest**. **Honey Buzzard, Goshawk** and **Sparrowhawk** nest in the forest. **Red-backed Shrike** can be found on the outskirts but prefers hedgerows around fields, as does **Little Owl**. **Wood, Grasshopper** and **Bonelli's Warblers** all breed in Écouves.
ACCESS: The D26 north from ALENÇON runs through the middle of the forest. The Croix de Medavy, 14.5 km from the city centre, a crossroads marked by a WWII tank, is an excellent spot for **Middle Spotted Woodpecker,** as are any of the forestry tracks leading off from this junction.

Site iii.
PERSEIGNE FOREST, some 10 km south-east of Alençon is a mainly Oak forest covering one of the Normandy hills. It also has six woodpecker species; in addition to Goshawk, Buzzard and Honey Buzzard, as well as Grasshopper, Wood, Melodious and Bonelli's Warbler and all the commoner woodland species, including Firecrest.
Some 10 km (more by road) further east, BELLÊME FOREST has similar species as has SILLÉ FOREST, west of the N138 between Le Mans and Alençon.
ACCESS: Take the D311 east from ALENÇON, turn left onto the D236 on entering the forest. In just under 4 km, a forestry road runs back south-west. It links with other forestry roads, some drivable, others that can be walked. The D234 meets the D236 in the north and this also has forestry roads running off it. As before, stop and explore any strands of mature oaks and look for raptors above cleared areas. There is a Maison *Forestière* near Neuchâtel.
To reach BELLÊME you can either continue along the D311 from Alençon through Perseigne Forest to MAMERS and north of this town turn off onto the D931. In 3 km fork right onto the D210 towards LA PERRIÈRE. At this village turn right at the main square towards PERVENCHERES. In 500 m and just before the château of Montimer, turn right again. This forestry road leads to the Montimer crossroads, the *rond-point*

de Montimer where you can park. Listen for **Golden Oriole.** Walk south on the *Moulin Butin à Hôtel Moisy* footpath in the direction of the *Chêne de l'Ecole*, an impressively large oak. This is a good area for woodpeckers. Forestry tracks are arranged on a grid system, so by turning left and left again twice more when you have seen enough you will complete a square and return to the Montimer crossroads.

To explore the eastern side of the forest, return to Mamers and pick up the D955 to Bellême where you turn north onto the D938 that runs due north to MORTAGNE, cutting through the eastern part of BELLÊME FOREST for the first 5 kilometres. Walk along any forestry track leading off the road to explore this side

Site iv.

Further south, 20 km south-east of Le Mans and north of Tours, **BERCÉ FOREST** is another large old Oak, Beech and Chestnut forest. It has a similar bird list to the forests above, also with all six woodpecker species, Buzzard, Honey Buzzard, Nightjar, both Short-toed and Common Treecreepers, Goldcrest and Firecrest and Phylloscopus warblers.

ACCESS: The N138 from TOURS to LE MANS and the A28 runs through the west side of the forest. Take the D13 east from St. Hubert for 2 km to the *Rond des Forges* crossroads with a *Maison Forestière* nearby. There are tracks to explore from here or else take the forestry road north to the *Rond-de-la* Lune junction and try some of the roads leading off into this north side of the forest.

Area 2. **RILLÉ**
(or PINCEMAILLE) LAKE

40 km north-west of Tours, is a 250 hectare reservoir created in 1977 for agricultural irrigation. Part of it is used for water-sports and here the water-level remains constant. The rest of the lake is subject to fluctuations in level, flooding fields in winter and creating mud-flats at the end of summer. The waterside vegetation has had time to mature and there are also some reed-beds, the largest in the northern Channay arm. The lake is surrounded by tracks from which it is easy to scan the lake and there are two hides. The mainly coniferous woodland on the south shore can also be of interest, notably for **Black Kite, Black Woodpecker** and **Goshawk. Honey Buzzard** and **Hobby** may be seen in late spring, **Peregrine** in winter. The whole area is considered an IBA and over 200 bird species have been recorded.

Further information can be obtained from: Groupe Ornithologique de Touraine, 148 rue Louis Blot, 37540 St. Cye-sur-Loire. Tel/fax: 02 47 51 81 84

WHEN TO VISIT: The autumn migration period (August - November) is always lively, and there are good numbers of duck in winter. The spring passage is normally less interesting but rarities like **Black Stork** have turned up and may even breed nearby. There are duck until March and **Osprey** may use it as a stopover. April to June are the best months for the largest number of species over the whole area. **Reed Warbler, Sedge Warbler** and **Reed Bunting** breed in the reed beds.

In autumn you could see three *Grebe* species, **Spoonbill,** most common **duck** species, many **waders** (sandpipers, Snipe, 'shanks, Curlew, Lapwing), **Common** and **Whiskered Tern. Tufted Duck** and **Goldeneye** join the **Pochards** and **Teal** in winter, **Water** and **Meadow Pipits** flock on the fields to the north, **Siskin** and **Brambling** can be found around the lake. **Cormorants** are common. **Marsh Harrier** are often see hunting over the lake.

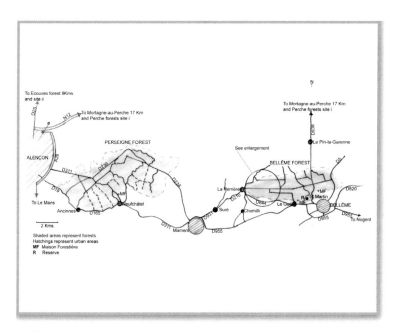

South Central area I site iii Perseigne and Bellême Forests

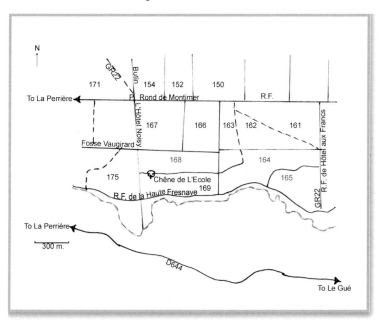

South Central area I site iii Enlargement of part of Bellême Forest

ACCESS: From Tours or Saumur take the D57 north for 20 km from LANGEAIS, on the north bank of the Loire to RILLÉ. At the crossroads, take the D49 direction Mouliherne and in just over 2 km, after the campsite, you will see the entrance to the lake on the right. If coming from the west and ANGERS or LE MANS, leave the A11 at exit 12 and take the D766 eastwards through Baugé to NOYANT. 500 metres from the D766 in Noyant, turn left at the small roundabout onto the D141 to BREIL (careful, there are two left turns very close together) and 2 km after this village, turn left (east) at the crossroads, signed to Rillé.

In 4 km turn left where it is signed *Planches à Voile*. In 600 metres there is a picnic and parking area with a view over the Rillé arm of the lake. You can walk from here but it is also possible, outside holiday periods and busy weekends, to drive around the lake stopping at the hides and wherever there is a view over the lake.

Cross the embankment which gives good views over the Rillé arm and the main lake, which can also be watched from the hide on the left just after the embankment. Continue on the main track, turning left 1 km from the carpark signed to *Grande Maison* and in another kilometre go straight on at the junction past the bird information board. In 800 metres there is a T-junction. Walk left to the hide on the lakeside, parking on the wide grass verge. Retrace your steps to the information board junction and this time turn left. In 600 metres turn left again and where the road crosses the Channay arm (there is another Information board) check the reeds and bushes. Continue along the road for just over 2 km until you see a left turning signed *Point de embarcadère*. 100 metres down here is another view over the west side of the lake. Return to the road and continue on to the next left turning, in just over 1 km, which leads to the dam. The gate may be locked but there are some views through it.

Either return the way you have come or get onto the D62/49 from the village of Guémorin.

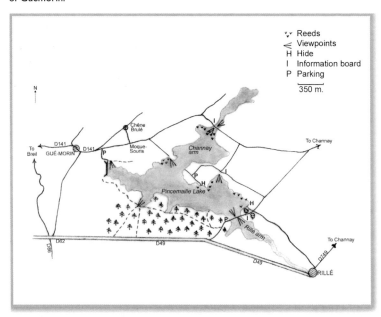

South Central area 2 Rillé Lake

The woods around the picnic area can be quite good early in the morning but another area to search for woodland birds is by taking one of the forestry tracks from the D62/49 which leads to the south of the lake. This is a good area for raptors and woodpeckers.

Area 3. **NANTES**

Site i.
GÂVRE FOREST is a large, predominantly beech wood some 45 km north of Nantes, holding a good selection of woodland species and raptors: **Buzzard, Goshawk, Sparrowhawk, Black Kite, Hobby** and **Hen Harrier** breed there and all six species of **woodpecker** can be found, although **Black** and **Grey-headed** are elusive, but **Middle Spotted** is relatively common. **Woodcock** may be flushed in winter, **Golden Oriole** and **Nightjar** heard in summer (the latter at dusk in the clearings). Among the passerines there are **Marsh** and **Crested Tits, Wood** and **Bonelli's Warblers, Redstart, Pied Flycatcher.** In the cleared patches, **Whitethroat, Yellowhammer** and **Cirl Bunting** may be found and **Dartford Warbler** where gorse is growing.
ACCESS: From Nantes take the dual-carriageway N137 for 24 km to the Nort/Blain junction, turn west onto the D164 for 9 km to BLAIN. The D15 north out of the town enters the forest in about 3 km and in another 2 km comes to the central crossroads, the *Carrefour de la Belle Etoile.*
Gâvre is also easy to reach from the Brière marshes (Brittany area 1) by taking the D2 from GILDAS to the D164 crossroads and turning right. You will reach the outskirts of the forest in about 6 km.
From the *Belle Etoile* crossroads, where there is space to park and a plan of the forest, explore the roads leading off in turn. Start with the *R.F. de Caheils.* 800 metres from the main road is a good spot for **Middle Spotted Woodpecker.** There are also plantations of Scots Pine for **Crested Tit** and **Bonelli's Warbler** and some open areas with gorse for **Dartford Warbler, Nightjar** and **Hen Harrier.** The *Allées Forestiéres de Vieilles Bauches* and *Ville au Duc* are worth exploring, so is the *Rond-pont de la Menardière.* Try the A.F. *de la Petite Coutée du Nord* north up the D15 and the *R.F. de les Epine de Haies* for **Black** and **Middle Spotted Woodpeckers.**
There is a *Maison Forestière* in the centre of Le Gâvre.
<u>Accommodation</u>: The *Logis Auberge de la Forêt* in la Maillardais is comfortable and has an excellent restaurant.

Site ii.
GRAND-LIEU Lake is some 12 km south of Nantes and the River Loire but included in this guide as it is such an important site for many breeding birds otherwise scarce in the north. It certainly is a "big place" and its size, the surrounding vegetation and lack of access make it good for birds but difficult to bird.   The lake covers about 1000 hectares in summer but may flood to over 6000 hectares in winter, forming the largest lake in France. That is not all that is big about Grand-Lieu; it attracts superlatives. It has the largest **Grey Heron** colony in the world, the biggest colony of Cormorants in France and the largest Starling roost. It has a number of breeding "firsts" for France and is the most important site in France for **Great White Egret** and **Spoonbill.** Even African Spoonbill bred here recently. Other regular breeders include **Purple Heron, Night Heron, Little** and **Cattle Egrets** and **Sacred Ibis, Honey Buzzard, Black Kite** and **Marsh Harrier.** Thousands of duck winter here and quite a lot of them,

including **Garganey,** breed, as do small numbers of **Black Tern, Bluethroat** and **Bearded Tit. Marsh terns** are numerous on passage.

On the downside, although it is classified as a Ramsar site, there is hunting in winter, pollution both from lead shot and agricultural effluents leading to eutrophication and even outbreaks of botulism.

Web site www.ac-nantes.fr/peda/disc/svt/granlieu/default/html gives a tour of the lake and details of threats to the environment, etc.

WHEN TO VISIT: Can be interesting in winter though flooding makes access difficult. Spring is the best time for heron species. Both migration periods are good.

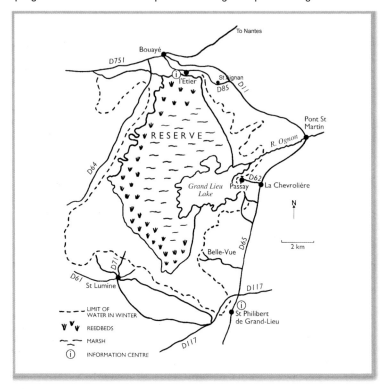

South Central area 3 site ii Grand-Lieu Lake

ACCESS: On the north side of the lake, the *Maison de la Réserve, 15 rue de la Châtaigneraie, 44830 Bouaye.* Tel: 02 40000 32 62 81 has an exhibition on the lake and can arrange guided tours, currently from Wednesday to Saturday between 14.00 - 18.00. They will also suggest viewpoints. Otherwise the best access point is from ST. AIGNAN Grandlieu, on the D85. A short walk from the signed car park give good views over the lake, though a 'scope is necessary.

A longish walk starts at PONT ST. MARTIN on the D11. Park by the bridge over the river and follow the river towards the lake, if possible. The walk leads through a variety of wetland habitats.

On the east side, lanes radiating from the villages of BELLE-VUE and PASSEY, both on minor roads north-west of the D65, seem to lead towards the lake but then end at remote farm houses or circle back without getting anywhere near the water. It is worth driving around some of these lanes and scoping the lake, especially in winter and during migration periods.

In the south, the village of ST. LUMINE-de-Coutais has made a tower hide from its bell tower. Tel: 02 40 02 90 25.

Other fauna and flora: Otter, Genet, Coypu and European Mink are among the mammals found here and 37 species (some very abundant) of dragonflies have been identified. There is also a rich marsh flora with over 550 plant species including the protected Common Sundew *Drosera rotundifolia* and Great Spearwort *Ranunculus lingua*.

Site iii.

THE GREÉ MARSHES north of ANCENIS, on the River Loire some 30 km east of Nantes, are another area of flooded meadows with some permanent marshland, not as important or impressive as the ones north of Angers (see area 4 below), and very close to busy roads and industrial areas but of interest in late winter and spring when duck and waders on passage may stop off there. As at Angers, **Pintail, Shoveler, Gadwall** and **Garganey, Black-tailed Godwit** and **Ruff** are the main migrants. **Garganey** and **Little Grebe** also breed and among the breeding passerines are **Blue-headed Wagtail and Whinchat.** In winter there will be **Lapwing, Wigeon, Shoveler, Teal, Pochard** and **Tufted Duck.**

ACCESS: The wetland lies between the D923 and the D19 south of the A11 motorway. Turn off the A11 at exit 20 and zero at the roundabout. After 1.1 km turn left off the D923 just north of the industrial area. After a further 700 metres turn left again and then turn right following signs to *Le Marais*. This is in fact a house but there are view of the marshes and flooded fields from just beyond it. It is possible to drive all around the flooded area by continuing to the D19, turning south to the N23 and then back north along the D923, stopping wherever there are views of the water.

Area 4. ANGERS

North of Angers the rivers Sarthe, Loir and Mayenne join to form the Maine, which flows through the town to join the Loire. The French name, *les Basses Vallées Angevines* (BVA) refers to the vast, low-lying areas that are periodically flooded. Most of the BVA are water meadows, traditionally farmed for hay and grazing, separated by hedgerows and drainage ditches bordered by ash and willows, poplar plantations, ponds or small lakes. This rich habitat makes for a great diversity of both plant and animal species and is especially important for **Corncrake** (this is the best site in France for this species) and **Spotted Crake,** as well as **geese, Shoveler, Pintail, Garganey, Black-tailed Godwit** and other waders **(Lapwing, Golden Plover, Ruff, shanks and sandpipers)** on passage. Breeding birds include **Quail, Lapwing, Kingfisher, Whinchat, Blue-headed Wagtail, Reed** and **Sedge Warblers, Reed** and **Corn Buntings.** The BVA are both an IBA and a Ramsar site.

To preserve this traditional landscape, the LPO, working with LIFE, the local and government departments and partly funded by the EU, has run for over a decade a programme to acquire and manage these water meadows and educate local people as to their value. Currently the LPO owns 330 hectares and farmers are discouraged from cutting hay before July 25th, and advised to cut from the centre outwards, so giving young **Corncrakes** a chance to escape. This policy is clearly working as the number of singing male Corncrakes has increased from 330 in 1994 to 470 in 1997, well over one third of the total French population

LPO Anjou has a good web site with excellent maps of the area to enlarge and download: www.lpo-amjou.org

WHEN TO VISIT: Best from late February to June. From mid-February, returning geese spend some time here. **Pintail, Wigeon** and **Common Pochard** are the most numerous duck at the end of winter. Thousands of **Black-tailed Godwits** (15% of the European population) pass through with numbers peaking in March. The end of spring is the time to look for **marsh terns, Garganey, Corncrake** and **Spotted Crake** (listen for their calls at dusk along overgrown ditches) and the best time for breeding species. **Corncrake** can be heard calling from evening through the night. They are easy to hear, very difficult to see. Usually only movement in the grasses gives away their presence. There can be very little to see in this area during summer and autumn.

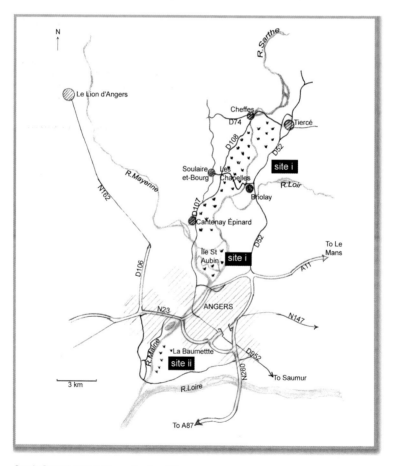

South Central area 4 Angers sites i and ii

<u>Site i</u>.
The flooded meadows **NORTH OF ANGERS** can be explored by leaving the A11 at exit 14 and heading north on the D52 for 14.5 km to TIERCE.
1. Take the D74 left (west) off the by-pass direction CHEFFES. Stop along the D74 in 1.3 km. There is a picnic site on the right of the road by the River Sarthe for views north across the river. On the opposite side of the road a walking track (jump the ditch and go past the gate) leads through flooded meadows for as far as you can, or wish, to walk. This is a good area for birds. A little further up the D74 is a bridge with a lay-by just before it, another good viewpoint but if you reach the bridge you have gone too far for the footpath.
2. A second good area is around BRIOLLAY, 6.5 km south of Tierce on the D52. Take the D109 west from Briollay crossing the river (good viewpoint soon after the bridge) towards SOULAIRE-ET-BOURG, although the road may be flooded after heavy rainfall in spring. Good views right (north) along this stretch of road, especially after 2.5 km just before the road bends left towards les Chapelles. This is a good site for **Quail, Corncrake** and **Spotted Crake.**
3. At LES CHAPELLES, before Soulaire-et-Bourg turn left (south) towards NOYANT (signed to Angers par Cantenay-Epinard). At the end of the village, 1.7 after the junction, take the track on the left leading out into the water meadows.
4. Continue south on the D107 towards Cantenay-Epinard and at the minor crossroads just north of the village take the left track to LE VIEUX CANTENAY. Another minor road leads to this hamlet from the centre of Cantenay-Epinard and off this road, signed to the Château and Châtillon, is a hide and a raised platform overlooking the *pré de l'Abesse*.

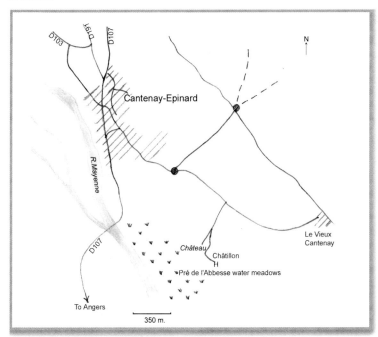

South Central area 4 site i Enlargement of Cantenay-Epinard area

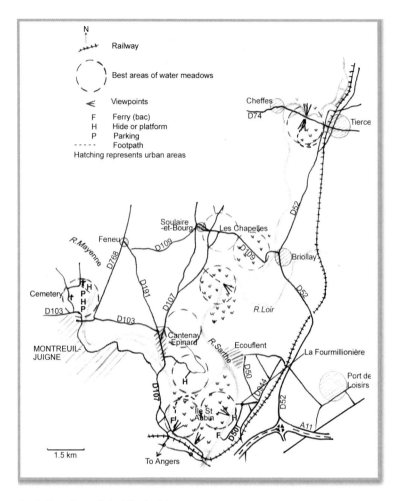

South Central area 4 site i North of Angers

5. Another good wetland area with hides is the Juigné marshes just north of MONTREUIL-JUIGNÉ. Take the D103 east from Cantenay-Epinard. Turn left at its junction with the D768 and immediately after the road crosses the River Mayenne, turn right back onto the D103 signed to the *Chateaux/ Tibeaudière/Plessis-Macé*. There are two parking area on the right within a few hundred metres, one almost opposite the Château entrance near the hide. From the first one walk along the path by the marsh, through the wooden barriers to the hide.

A second hide has been erected on the north side of the marsh. From the D103 turn right after the cemetery (1 km from the bridge junction and just north of the hide). In 500 metres where signed to Pruille/Vauleard turn right again and in 120 metres a dirt track leads on by a small iron cross. Walk down some 100 metres to the raised hide.

6. The area known as the Île St. Aubin is enclosed by rivers. It is close to Angers and just north of the A11. It can be observed from various viewpoints off the lanes leading east from the D107 between Cantenay-Epinard and Angers, though these minor roads may be flooded in wet springs. There is also a hide on the east side, beside the River Sarthe, near ECOUFLANT. To reach this, get onto the D50 leading to Ecouflant. Turn off the D50 opposite Ecouflant station and in 400 metres turn left by *la Fourmillonière*. 500 metres from *la Fourmillonière* is a grassy track with a wooden barrier leading to a raised platform. It can also be reached by turning off the D50 by the railway bridge south of the station. In 300 metres at the T-junction turn right towards. The hide is roughly halfway between this junction and *la Fourmillonière*. It too can be flooded in spring.

Site ii.
SOUTH OF ANGERS and still in the built up area, there is another good water meadow site, **LA BAUMETTE** just south of the large LAC DE MAINE.

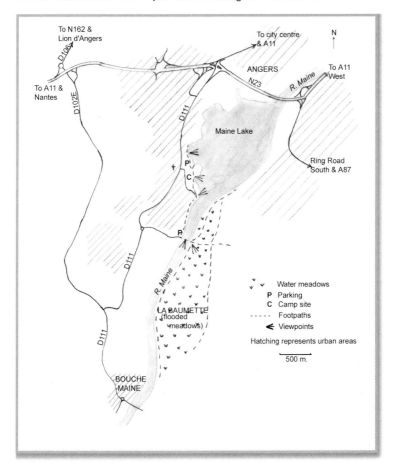

South Central area 2 site ii La Baumette water meadows south of Angers

ACCESS: Drive through Angers southwards following the "All directions" signs until you see *Lac de Maine camping /Bouchemaine* signs. Follow these through shopping and residential areas on the D111 to the campsite where there is a large car park from where to walk to the lake (opposite a rocky hill topped with a cross). By the lakeside is a *Maison de l'Environment*. Walk to it for information and a view of this side of the lake.   The lake can be very empty in winter and summer but could be interesting in spring. It is possible to walk from the lake to the water meadows on a way-marked path. Ask for directions at the Maison.

To drive, continue south on the D111 and at the next roundabout turn left, signed to *Pont de Pruniers*. The road runs past houses to the riverside, where there is parking space and information boards. The footbridge is a good viewpoint from where to scope the fields. The footpaths on the Pruniers bank of the river lead back to the lake. Cross the bridge for footpaths leading around the meadows but they will be still be underwater in early spring.

Other fauna and flora: This is a good area for dragon and damselflies. Some 250 plant species have been noted in the water meadows, including some rare and protected species such as Gratinole *Gratiola officinalis, Inula britannica,. Stellaria uliginosa, Cardamine parviflora*. The most spectacular flowers in April are Snakeshead Lily *Fritillaria meleagris* called locally "gogane" or "chaudron". At the end of May, on the slightly higher ground grow colonies of Narrow-leaved Water-dropwort *Oenanthe silaifolia* and Marsh Ragwort *Senecio aquaticus* and in the lowest areas Gratiole and Tubular Water-dropwort *Oenanthe fistulosa*.

Area 5. **SAUMUR**

Site i.

FONTEVRAUD ABBEY, the most northerly site for **Rock Sparrow,** lies just off the D947 4 km after it turns due south at MONTSOREAU. At Fontevraud, bear left at the roundabout for the town centre and Abbey (signed).   Park at the next small roundabout by the *Mairie* (if this is possible). From spring to autumn, when you are likely to find Rock Sparrow, this is a very busy tourist site and there are large carparks on the outskirts of the town. It may be best to use these and walk to the town centre. The entrance to the Abbey is through the large green gates opposite the *Mairie*. It is open from 9-18.00 (21.00 in summer). No tickets are issued half an hour before closing time. Currently a long-term restoration programme is in progress and this may cause some disturbance to the sparrows. It is best to visit as soon as the site opens in the morning or in the evening to avoid disturbance by visitors. Listen for the sparrows' distinctive call and look for them perched on roofs and walls. Even if the Abbey is closed, look for them around the entrance courtyard. (See notes on this species at end of book for other breeding sites in the area).

Accommodation: There is a *Logis*, La Croise Blanche, just opposite the Abbey entrance

Site ii.

The fields between **MONTREUIL-BELLAY** and **LOUDUN** are the last site in Maine-et-Loire where **Little Bustard** breed. In 1999 some 18 males and 15 females were observed there and there were at least 13 nests. A count at the beginning of September when birds flock before migrating, found 56 birds here. However this species is in frightening decline (see notes under Special Species at end of guide) and should not be disturbed during the breeding season. When they arrive back in March and start calling or during September are the best times to observe them. Their preferred habitat is lucerne fields.

This is also a good area for **Montagu's Harrier** and other raptors, **Stone Curlew** and **Crested Lark.**

ACCESS: Take the N147 south from Saumur for 30 km to where it loops around MONTREUIL-BELLAY and turns south-east. Drive slowly along the 16 km between here and the LOUDUN by-pass, turning off onto the many minor roads, looking out for Lucerne fields and any farm tracks leading off that you can take without trespassing. The best area is close to Montreuil.

Area 6. **THE RIVER LOIRE**

The River Loire is one of France's most important waterways and the last unaltered and free-flowing large river in western Europe, although there are several nuclear power stations along its banks. Rising in the southern Massif Central, it flows almost due north for some hundreds of kilometres, meets the River Allier near Nevers, continues north-west to Orléans where it turns to flow west into the Atlantic by St-Nazaire. The famous "chateaux of the Loire" lie along the stretch west of Orléans. Climate, architecture and history suggest that southern France starts south of the River Loire. Its mouth forms the southern limit for the half of France covered in this book, and all its upper stages lie in the south, but as it loops north at Orléans much of the east-west middle section of the river lies within this book's definition of the northern half of France.

A mature, wide river in this section, wooded along many stretches, the face of the Loire has been changed by gravel extraction, dredging, nuclear power stations and the growth of the towns spanning it but there are still sandy islets, marshes and water meadows along its banks. Some of the flooded gravel-pits make good habitat for birds. Dredging has created conditions that suit wintering **duck** and **grebes; Sand Martins** and **Kingfishers** nest in the sand-banks; the gravel and sand islands are breeding sites for **Common** and **Little Terns, Stone Curlews** and **Little Ringed Plovers** as well as attracting numerous waders and marsh terns on passage; gulls also roost there in winter with some remaining in summer (mainly **Black-headed** but also **Yellow-legged, Common, Herring, Lesser Black-backed** and **Mediterranean**). In summer, **Hobby** hunt **Sand Martin** and other hirundines over the water and **Black Kite** scavenge for food; many **warblers, Grasshopper, Melodious, Garden, Cetti's, Whitethroat** and **Blackcap** nest in the scrub and trees on the banks. In winter large numbers of **Cormorants** and **Grey Heron** roost. Almost any stretch of the Loire where there is reasonable access and views over the water will offer something of interest to birders.

WHEN TO VISIT: April to June is the best time for both breeding birds and migrants. The autumn migration period (July/August to November) can be good if the river is low and there are plenty of mudbanks for waders. Though there may be duck in winter, especially during cold spells, the river is often too high and running too fast for them.

Site i.

ANGERS AREA   The best views of the Loire are from the D952 where it runs along the embankment on the north bank between la DAGUIENIÈRE and ST. MATHURIN. There are sandbanks and islands but unfortunately few parking places outside the villages; large gull roosts in winter.

Site ii.
Up-river from **SAUMUR** the D947 runs along the south bank of the Loire between SAUMUR and MONTSOREAU and there are large islands opposite the villages of SOUZAY and PARHAY. There is a large car park in Souzay looking across to one island. Park in Parnay or just outside and take any of the tracks leading down to the river. Parnay Island is protected and has a large breeding colony of **Black-headed Gulls,** as well as plenty of **Little Ringed Plovers, Common** and **Little Terns. Kingfisher** and **Sand Martin** are other riverside birds quite common along this stretch.

Site iii.
VILLANDRY Down-river from Tours some minor roads run close to the river along the embankment on the south bank. Down-river from VILLANDRY, there are some good spots to view the wooded islands and gravel banks. Zero at the château. In under 200 metres, opposite the *Cheval Rouge* hotel, turn right (north). Ignore the first turn left but at the embankment turn left down river. In 2.3 km bear right onto the cobbles and follow the river for as long as you wish. It runs along the bank, sometimes very close to the river for almost 16 km.

Site iv.
Up-river from **TOURS** there are large sand bars with breeding tern colonies and wooded banks where many other species typical of the Loire region can be found. The best viewpoints are off the D751 which runs along the south bank.
Leave the A10 at exit 21 and zero. Head east towards ST. PIERRE centre. At the second roundabout in 1.3 km turn left (unsigned but in the opposite direction to town centre) onto the embankment road. At 6 km there is a roundabout signed to la Ville aux Dames with a car park just off the roundabout for the *Île de Rochecorbon Espace Naturelle*, which is open 10.00-17.30 in winter, to 19.00 in spring and 21.00 in summer. This semi-reserve, although very popular with families and with picnic and play areas, is worth walking through. **Black Woodpecker** has been seen around the parking area and in spring there are always plenty of species both on the river and the banks. It is best to visit early in the morning if possible and avoid weekends.

Continue up-river towards MONTLOUIS, where you can park and walk along the river. Between Montlouis and Lussault (some 12 km from Île de Rochecorbon) there are a few parking spaces beside the road where you can leave the car and walk. It is not worth following this road up-river any further than Lussault.
Accommodation: There are hotels of all categories in all the towns mentioned, as well as plenty of campsites in summer. This is however a very popular area and pre-booking may be necessary, especially at weekends, at any time of the year.

Site v.
East of ORLÉANS as far upriver as Sully, is a typical stretch of the middle section of the River Loire. The numerous sand islands and gravel-pits form good habitat for birds. All the species listed above are likely to be found during the course of the year. Of special interest to the west of the town is a small (20 hectares) island reserve, SAINT-PRYVÉ-SAINT-MARTIN, right beside the bridge that carries the A71 motorway over the river.

Up to 60,000 passerines have been counted roosting in the reeds on autumn passage; mainly **Swallows** and **Sand Martins** but also numerous **Grey** and **Yellow Wagtails** and hundreds of **Reed** and **Sedge Warblers.** More than a quarter of a million birds have been ringed here over the years; most frequently **Reed Bunting, Blackcap, Swift, Chiffchaff** but also **Bluethroat,** (both sub-species), **Penduline Tit** and such rarities as **Little Bunting** and **Barred Warbler.** The commonest wader is **Common Sandpiper** and there are thousands of **Cormorants** in winter. Further upstream, check the roosts of **Black-headed Gulls** for Mediterranean; some have bred here in recent years.

The reserve is managed by the Association des Naturalistes Orléanais, *Maison de la Nature*, 64 route d'Olivet, 45100 Tel: 0238566984 and access to the island is only possible by joining one of their organised visits. However the island and the neighbouring stretch of river can be easily seen from the south bank.

Besides the island reserve, the river just east of Orléans can be good in spring (though access is not particularly easy) but the best site is some is some 20 km upriver, east of CHATEAUNEUF

ACCESS: To observe the SAINT-PRYVÉ reserve, leave the A71 at Exit 01. Zero at the tollbooths. Take the second right at first roundabout. At the first lights in half a kilometre, turn left onto the N152, direction *Centre*. At the third set of lights, at a major crossroads, turn right direction ST. PYRE and turn right again at the next lights. Cross the new bridge back to the south bank of the Loire. At the roundabout turn right, following the direction Pointe de Corpin. Drive under the motorway and park on the verge. Walk down the road on the right, which is signed as a dead-end with no access except for residents (*sauf riverains*). Walk down this road for views across to the island.

To observe more stretches of the Loire east of Orléans, go back to the roundabout and take the road signed to the centre off St. Pyre. At the crossroads turn left onto the D951 through eight sets of traffic lights to ST.JEAN de Blanc. In St. Jean leave the D951 and take the river road, signed to the left, through ST. DENIS-EN-VAL. Take the Rue Jehan du Lys if you can find it. Otherwise there are several dead-end roads leading down to the river (follow any signs to kayak centres) and a cycle track running along the embankment. Walk along this. There is also some old gravel pits and scrub on the left, between the road and the river, which are worth checking.

Site vi.
A less confusing, and more productive site is some 20 km upriver, east of **CHATEAUNEUF.** Take the D60 out of CHATEAUNEUF. On this road between GERMIGNY (3 km from the end of Chateauneuf) and ST. BENOIT there is a parking area with information boards right beside the Loire. It is easy to miss, start looking some 2 km from GERMIGNY. Turn back right onto a sandy track (private but with access) where you can park and walk down river, back to Chateauneuf if you wish but the first kilometre or so is probably the best. **Little** and **Common Tern, Mediterranean** and **Black-headed Gull** all breed around the island here and **Black Tern** can be seen on passage. Other breeding species are **Little Ringed Plover, Kingfisher, Common Sandpiper** and **Grey Wagtail.** In winter **Grey Herons, Cormorants** and **duck** (mainly Mallard) are common. It is also possible to walk along the river bank in ST. BENOIT or to continue through the town on the D60 and take the first turning on the left leading down to les Prouteaux from where another riverside footpath leads back towards St. Benoir.

Other fauna: Beavers have bred on the St. Pyre reserve (probably the offspring of animals released in the Reserve further upstream) and both Muskrat and Coypu (both escapes) occur.

Accommodation: There are a number of hotels (all categories) in and around Orléans as well as in most of the other towns mentioned in the text. Camping is possible in summer. Contact the Tourist Information Offices in Orléans for details of gîtes or *chambres d'hôtes*.

Site vii.
The **ÎLE DE CUISSY RESERVE** between Sully-sur-Loire and Gien, is another large sand island attracting breeding **Common Tern, Little Ringed Plover** and the species listed above for the previous Loire site in summer. Where it differs is that the **Ospreys** breeding in nearby Orléans Forest regularly visit this area to feed; most days they can be seen towards noon! Migratory Ospreys and large numbers of different **wader species** can be observed on passage, especially in autumn when the gulls also include **Mediterranean**. There is also a large gull roost in spring. In winter numbers of duck, often including **sawbills** and **Eider** may be attracted to the site because of the warm water from the nearby nuclear power station.

ACCESS: From SULLY on the south bank of the river take the embankment road upriver through CUISSY towards LION-EN-SOULIAS. All this stretch of the river can be good. The Île de Cuissy is signed.

Site viii.
COSNE-SUR-LOIRE (or LA CHARITÉ-SUR-LOIRE) RESERVE
Further upriver from Orléans, the Loire has turned to run north-south. The stretch south of COSNE is wide and shallow with sandy islets and mud banks. Riverine forest, marshes and water meadows can be found along its banks. The terraces above the river produce some of the best-known Loire wines: Sancerre in the north and Pouilly in the centre are famous wine centres. **Stone Curlew, Little Ringed Plover, Common and Little Tern** and **Common Sandpiper** breed on the alluvial islets and can be seen from the banks in spring. **Warblers** (including **Melodious**) **Golden Oriole** and **Nightingale** can be heard in the riverside scrub and trees. **Kingfisher** and **Sand Martin** breed along the banks. During the autumn passage, **Osprey** can often be seen and well as several species of waders. In winter **Cormorants** are the most common species but **Bean** and **Greylag Geese** roost on the sandbanks. This area has been a Reserve since 1995. 360 species of birds and animals have been recorded here and 480 plant species.

WHEN TO VISIT: May-June are the best months or August-September.

ACCESS: As this is a reserve, access is not always easy along much of its length but there are stretches of minor roads mostly on the east bank that run close to the river. The northern limit of the Reserve is south of Sancerre.

1. Leave the N7 2 km south of the Sancerre junction to the village of BOIS-GIBAULT and from there take the D243 towards POUILLY-sur-Loire (11 km north of LA CHARITÉ-sur-Loire and about 16 south of COSNE). After 1.5 km, just after the level-crossing, there is a parking space beside the river with a bench and a Reserve notice. A stop here gives good views across to a sand island, where there are normally **Stone Curlew** from the second week in March. The terns arrive later. A GR footpath, marked in red and white, runs back towards Bois-Girault and continues along the D243 to Pouilly.

2. Near POUILLY there are several good views of the river from the D243 which runs along the east bank north to les GISARMES and south down to MESVES, a GR footpath following it along all this stretch. On the southern outskirts of MESVES take the road towards the river signed to the *Étang Communal* from where you can walk south along the riverbank.

3. To view the west bank, cross the bridge at POUILLY and take the first turning right (north) in les Vallées. After 2 km it comes close to the river. Park where it turns sharply inland again and continue walking along the riverbank.

4. Return to Pouilly bridge and staying on the west bank, continue further upriver on the D187 towards HERRY. After some 7 km look for any tracks leading to the river at *la Cafarderie*. 3 km south of Herry, take the dead-end road off the D7 leading to the

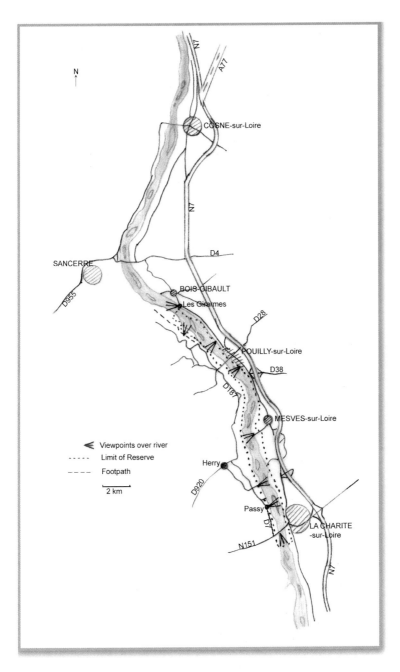

South Central area 6 River Loire site viii Cosne-sur-Loire Reserve

175

hamlets PASSY on the riverbank. If you turn left, it is possible to drive for 600 metres north along the embankment *la levee de Napoléon*, which is then blocked but it is possible to walk on north with good views over the sandbanks and river. Turn right in Passy to join the D7 which runs close to the river for a couple of kilometres to LA CHARITÉ-sur-Loire, where you can cross the bridge back. To the west bank and the N7 motorway. The Reserve finishes just south of la Charité and there are good views of the sandbanks and islands from the bridge.

Other fauna: Both Otter and European Beaver can be found along this stretch of the river and Red Deer sometimes come to drink. Beavers can normally only be seen at dusk.

Accommodation: This is a popular tourist area and there are hotels in all the towns mentioned and campsites at Pouilly and Charité-sur-Loire.

Area 7. **ORLÉANS FOREST**

The Forêt d'Orléans covers a vast area to the north of the town of Orléans, continuing east along the north bank of the River Loire. It is managed for forestry, hunted over and criss-crossed with forestry roads. It holds all the breeding species that one would expect to find in woodland in the northern part of France, including **Buzzard, Honey Buzzard,** one or two pairs of **Booted Eagle, Goshawk, Sparrowhawk, Black** and **Middle Spotted Woodpecker, Nightjar,** as well as many **warblers** and **finches** but its main claim to fame is that a few pairs of **Osprey** have returned to breed there after an absence of more than 40 years. They are carefully wardened, the forest is managed to protect them and a hide has been set up by the *Étang de Ravoir* to allow easy and safe observation of a nest through telescopes. Each year between April and August, some 4000 visitors come to watch the Ospreys.

WHEN TO VISIT: The Ospreys arrive back in March and start re-furbishing their nest. The young will have flown by mid-July.

ACCESS: From the northeast of ORLÉANS take the dual carriageway N60 in an easterly direction to north of CHATEAUNEUF-SUR-LOIRE and join the D952 at the large junction. (If you have been to the Loire site vi. near Chateauneuf, just return to that town and get straight on the D952). Continue east for 15 km to LES BORDES. 4.2 km from the lights at the D961 crossroads in les Bordes, turn left (north) onto the gravel forestry road running north towards the central forest crossroads. There are brown signs to *Observatoire* with a picture of an Osprey at the entrance. Keep on this main track; the hide is well signed. In 2.3 km there is place to park on the right and signs pointing to the Étang de Ravoir and the hide (*observatoire*). The lake is within the Ravoir Biological Reserve, so the path is well signed with details of trees, plants, etc. It takes about 5 minutes to walk through the woods to the hide.

The position of the **Ospreys'** nest is shown in the hide and the best views are from the left-hand side. Goshawk, **Black Kite** and **Booted Eagle** are some of the other raptors that could be seen from here. **Little Tern** and **Common Tern** may feed over the lake in spring while on the water there will be **Great Crested Grebe, Grey Heron, ducks** and **cormorants.** You could find **Crested** and **Coal Tits** in the conifers on the way to the lake, as well as **Great, Blue** and **Marsh.** Try for **Middle Spotted** and **Black Woodpeckers** around the car park or go further towards the central crossroads for **Black.** Look for strands of mature trees.

Nightjars can be heard at dusk in open, felled areas, which vary from year to year as trees grow and others are cut.

Other fauna and flora: There are several pools on the way to the lake (ancient sand extraction) good for dragon and damselflies (including some rare species), as well as orchids and other marsh and forest plants. The information boards are helpful.

North of this site, around Pithiviers, is an area of cereal crops and grassland, known as the Beauce. It is a traditional site for **Short-toed Lark,** though they are now very difficult to find. There are also **Bee-eaters, Ortolan Bunting** and **waders** on passage in the pools around the sugar-beet plants. (If you wish to explore this area look under entries for Short-toed Lark and Bee-eater in "Special Species" at the end of the book).

Area 8. THE SOLOGNE

The Sologne, an area of over 37,500 hectares of medieval man-made lakes, reedbeds, wet meadows, scrub and woodland, is an important site for wintering and passage waterbirds: **grebes, Cormorant, Grey Heron,** many diving and dabbling duck species, sawbills as well as **Hen Harrier, Merlin, Osprey** (on passage) and **Cranes** (in the autumn). Some interesting species also breed there: **Night Heron, Purple Heron, Honey Buzzard, Short-toed Eagle, Marsh Harrier, Whiskered Tern,** a few **Black Tern,** and in the woods **Black** and **Grey-headed Woodpeckers.**

Unfortunately, the lakes are on private land and fenced off, there are few public footpaths and access is restricted to a limited number of viewpoints from lay-bys alongside public roads. Additionally, the whole area is much hunted over in autumn and winter. This makes it a much less interesting site for birders than the BRENNE, further south. However, it is easily reached from either the A10 or A71 motorways and can be worth a quick detour, if passing through the area, to look at some of the best lakes.

(Anyone having driven this far south, may like to continue for another 100 km south down the A20 to the BRENNE (described in detail in "A Birdwatching Guide to France south of the Loire), which is similar but better. Without this guide, go first to the Maison du Parc, at le Bouchet northwest of Rosnay (open 10 -18) for a map and information on walks, reserves and hides in the area.)

ACCESS: The Sologne lies south of Orléans and east of Tours, in a triangle formed by the A10 and A71 motorways and bounded on the south by the D765 from Blois to Romorantin Lanthenay and the D724 from there to the A71 motorway. Some of the easiest lakes to view lie in the area around St. VIATRE. Leave the A71 or the N20 at LAMOTTE-BEUVON (exit 3) and take the D923 westwards. A kilometre from the motorway slip-road turn south onto the D49 towards ST. VIATRE. Zero here for an itinerary around MARCILLY-en-Gault.

Site i.
MARCILLY LAKES In St Viatre turn left, then right past the information centre, *Maison du Parc,* which is open from 15/05 to 15/09 10-12 and 14-18 h. There is a large plan of the area nearby. Keep on the D49 in the direction of MARCILLY. (If coming from the south, leave the motorway at the Salbris exit 4, go into Salbris, out on the N20 and take the first turning left (west) onto the D121 towards MARCILLY). At 9.2 km the Chemin de Brosses footpath on the right leads past the Étang of the same name. Another lake, the Étang d'Omblin, can be viewed on the left from the road here. It is

worth walking some distance along the Brosses footpath to get views of the reed beds around the lake, as these can be good for **Sedge, Reed** and **Savi's Warblers.** **Marsh Harrier** is often seen over the reeds.

Continue to MARCILLY village and turn right (north) at the crossroads onto the D121 towards Neung. Take the first right turning onto a very minor road, the C6, a kilometre or so beyond Marcilly. This road leads to la FERTE-BEAUHARNAIS and passes between some of the more viewable lakes where it is worth stopping wherever it is possible to pull off the road and scan the lakes. There is also some good woodland here with mature trees, worth checking for **woodpeckers.** One of the best lakes in the region, the Étang de Marcilly, is on the right where the D63 crosses the C6. There are always plenty of duck species here in winter, predominantly **Shoveler,** and it is the best site for wintering **Great White Egrets.** It can most easily be viewed from the corner of the C6 by the crossroads.

When you have finished watched Marcilly Lake, go straight over the cross-roads, still keeping on the C6 and continue for some 200 metres. There is a lake, the Étang de Marguilliers, on the left. When you have watched this lake, return to the crossroad, turn left (east) towards St. Viatre, passing the Étangs de Marcilly and Favelle (some of the larger lakes) on your right to return to St. Viatre. In spring, look for **Black** and **Whiskered Tern** especially over Marguilliers lake, where **Great Crested, Black-necked** and **Little Grebes** can also be found. **Shoveler, Gadwall, Teal, Pochard** and **Mallard** can be seen all year round and in hard winters **Merlin, Goldeneye** and **sawbills** may turn up. Of the migrants, **Cranes** and **Greylag Geese** can sometimes be found in late autumn and **Garganey** and occasionally **Ferruginous Duck** can be seen on Marcilly Lake in spring. At this season too **Bittern** can sometimes be heard on Marcilly Lake but very few pairs (between 2-10) breed in the Sologne. **Reed Warbler** and **Reed Bunting** can be found in most reedbeds.

Site ii.

Another IBA in the area is the **ÉTANG DE L'ARCHE,** where a few pairs of **Black** and **Whiskered Tern** breed and many duck species winter. **White-tailed Eagle** has over wintered in the past.

ACCESS: It lies some distance from the St.Viatre-Marcilly triangle described above, being 15 km west of ROMORANTIN and can be reached by taking the D59 from this town to ROUGEOU. Turn north onto the D119 and almost immediately west onto the D63. In 3 km at a crossroads, the minor road south (left) leads to the lake.

Other fauna and flora: Amphibians, as one might expect, are numerous and include four newt species, Common Tree, Edible, Common and Agile Frogs, Spadefoot and Midwife Toads as well as several reptiles: Green Lizard, Wall Lizard and Whip Snake. About 35 species of Dragonfly and Damselfly have been counted in the Sologne; they include Orthetrum brunneum, Onychogomphus uncatus, and Anax parthenope. The European Pond Terrapin can be found in some of the Marcilly lakes.

WOODLAND SITES: The woods in this area have breeding **Grey-headed, Middle Spotted** and **Black Woodpeckers, Woodlark, Redstart, Buzzard** and **Honey Buzzard.** A good time to find the **woodpeckers** is late February or early March, when they are calling and drumming and the trees are not yet in leaf. The woods along the C6 have several good places to stop and listen. Look for **Black Woodpecker** in the woods with the largest trees; **Middle Spotted** may be in the same area but often seems to prefer smaller copses with younger trees, provided there are some mature ones amongst them; they are nearly always found high in the canopy.

Site iii.
The **FORÊT DE BRUADAN,** southwest of MARCILLY, is a good site. Take the D49
south from the village and turn right (west) after about 4 km onto a minor road that
cuts through the centre of the wood. The D60 from LOREUX to MILLANCAY also
crosses it further south.

Site iv.
Further north, the woods west of the D15 some 3 km south of **LIGNY-LE-RIBAULT**
are another site for **Black Woodpecker.** A GR footpath goes through this wood,
starting from the D15 beside the cemetery soon after its junction with the D19 south
of Ligny. If walking from Ligny, take the D15 direction Villeny, cross the two bridges,
turn right and leave the D15 in about 500 metres by the cemetery. Fork left where the
footpath branches for woodpeckers. It is also possible to walk a 3-4 hour circuit
through the woods back to Ligny following the GR. It leads past several small lakes.
Map IGN no. 2121 E 1/25,000 useful.

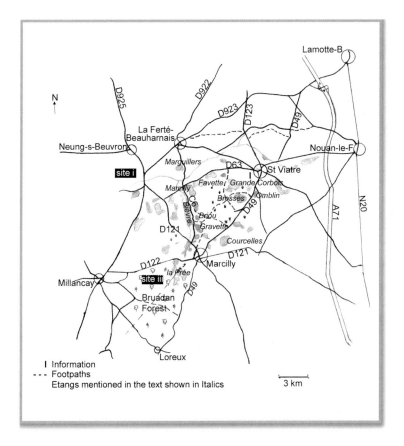

South Central area 8 sites i and iii

179

Site v.
ALLOGNY FOREST, 30 km north of Bourges and 52 west of SANCERRE (see River Loire site viii above) is on the south-east boundary of the Sologne. It is a mature oak wood and being one of the smaller state forests in the Vierzon area is easier to bird. **Black, Grey-headed** and **Middle Spotted Woodpeckers** are here as well as **Buzzard, Goshawk** and **Hen Harrier. Redstart** and **Pied Flycatcher** are among the smaller woodland passerines.

ACCESS: The D944 runs along its western edge and the D50 from Allogny to St. Martin cuts through its centre with forestry roads leading off from it. As always, look for parcels of mature oaks where you can park and walk the tracks leading north and south if searching for **woodpeckers** and **flycatchers.** Views of raptors can often be had from the clearings. Warblers often prefer younger woodland.

Other fauna: There are Wild Boar, Roe and Red Deer in the Sologne forests.

Area 9. **THE RIVER ALLIER**

The River Allier is almost as important as the River Loire as both a migration route and a site for breeding and wintering birds. There are several heronries along the central stretch of the river where **Grey Heron, Little Egret** and **Night Heron** are quite numerous. **Purple Heron** and **Bittern** are very much rarer breeders in the reedbeds

Site i.
THE VAL D'ALLIER NATURE RESERVE.
South of Moulins (and slightly south of the limits of this guide) some 20 kilometres of the river have been made into a reserve. As in the River Loire sites, **Little** and **Common Tern, Little Ringed Plover** and **Stone Curlew** breed on the gravel islets. **Cetti's Warbler** can be heard calling in the thick vegetation on the riverbank. **Grasshopper Warbler, Willow Tit** and **Wood Lark** are other breeding passerines. **Black Kite** is seen regularly during the summer and on passage. **Osprey** and large flocks of **Crane** are common on passage.

ACCESS: Access to the river is very limited. Views over part of the river in the south of the Reserve can be had from the D32 which crosses the river between CHÂTEL-de-Neuvre and LA FERTÉ-HAUTERIVE and 2 km further south from the village of MONÉTAY-sur-Allier. The Maison des Oiseaux at Bressolles on the N9 4 km south of Moulins arranges visits and will suggest areas to visit or contact LPO-Auvergne, 9 rue de Montilly, 03000 Moulins. Tel: 04 70 20 07 31.

Site ii.
MARS-SUR-ALLIER near **NEVERS** Further north at MARS-SUR-ALLIER near NEVERS, a stretch of the river, though not a nature reserve, is an IBA for its heron colonies where about 100 pairs of **Night Heron** nest. Most of the other species listed above can also be seen.

ACCESS: Unfortunately access to this stretch of river is very limited, which is probably why there are heronries. The land bordering the river is private and there are no public roads. From NEVERS take the N7 south for 12 km from exit 37 of the A77 to MOIRY. Turn west for 4.5 km to the small village of Mars-sur-Allier, which straggles along this road and ends at the river. Just before the church take the lane running right which also ends on the riverbank a little further north. From here you may be able to see **Night Herons** flying up and down river, especially at dusk.

Area 10. **BURGUNDY FORESTS**

Site i.
AUBERIVE FOREST is, by French standards, quite small but it is accessible, beautiful and contains some interesting species. Situated some 50 km north of Dijon, 20 km south-west of Langres, it is right beside the A31 motorway, so anyone driving south might like to make a quick birding stop. It is not too far south of the Forêt d'Orient area and is, in fact, still just in Champagne.

Like Clairvaux Forest, to the north (but which is larger and much harder to work) breeding birds include **Black, Middle Spotted** and **Grey-headed Woodpeckers, Honey Buzzard, Hazel Grouse** and **Tengmalm's Owl** (these last two near impossible to find) and woodland warblers and finches. On the outskirts **Woodlark** and **Song Thrush** are numerous, **Northern Grey** and **Red-backed Shrike** quite common.

ACCESS: Leave the A31 motorway 15 km south of the A5/A31 junction at exit 6 and turn west towards CHÂTILLON on the D428. In 4.1 km at a forest crossroads, turn right and listen for woodpeckers along this forestry road. A footpath, the GR7 starts on this corner and leads off to the left, running more of less parallel to the road for a while before climbing north. Walk this for a while or explore the next forestry road leading off to the right, the *RF Montavoir*, also crossed by the GR footpath.

Site ii.
CHÂTILLON FOREST is another large beech and oak forest, with pine plantations, some 30 km west of Auberive, in Burgundy. It is an IBA with the same species as listed under Auberive, but of special interest for **woodpeckers,** with six species breeding there. 10 years ago a few pairs of **Black Storks** started to breed there but more recently disturbance has affected them; the situation my improve again.

ACCESS: From AUBERIVE village continue on the twisty but scenic D428/D928 through RECEY to VOULAINES. In this village turn left and left again in 3 km, taking the minor (forestry) road towards the old Abbey. Châtillon is criss-crossed with drivable forestry tracks and many footpaths. One forestry road bisects the forest running northwest towards Châtillon, with others leading off it, but usually the east side of the forest south of Voulaines is the most productive. Always search for woodpeckers in strands of old, mature trees (see notes under Special Species at the end). There is a lot of hunting in both Châtillon and Auberive forests in autumn and winter. Never ignore hunting signs, especially when hounds are being used, but go further on, find an area that is not being hunted and stay near main tracks.

Site iii.
CITEAUX FOREST, yet another Burgundian beech and oak forest, equally heavily hunted over from June to January, is also an IBA with six **woodpecker** species. **Middle Spotted** is especially common and there is a reasonably density of **Grey-headed**. It is also close to the A31 motorway; access is easy and woodpecker species can be seen from the roadsides without the need for long walks into the interior, which can be dangerous (and prohibited) during the hunting season.

ACCESS: Leave the A31 at the NUITS-ST.GEORGES exit (south of DIJON) and go east on the D8 through AGENCOURT towards ST.NICHOLAS-LES-CITEAUX, 7 km. In St. Nicholas turn right onto the C2 towards ARGILLY. Zero here. The forest starts in 700 metres. There are bigger trees among the smaller ones on the right after 2 km. Listen for **Black Woodpecker** here. **Middle Spotted** should be heard and seen anywhere you stop. In 2.8 km at the RF de Phillipon, on the right, stop and bird around this corner. Both **Grey-headed** and **Middle Spotted** have been seen here. At 3.5 km the *RF de Gaty* is good for **Middle Spotted.** When you reach the crossroads with the D35 turn left and left again at the next crossroads in just over 1 km. At 6.4 km you will reach the crossroads of *RF de Berrault* and *Gaty* (1.3 km from the D35. This is a good area for **Middle Spotted** and **Black Woodpeckers, Buzzard** and **Goshawk,** as there are quite a number of large trees. There are some "woodpecker" trees around here, visible from the road. Check the holes.

As with any forest site, an area that is good one year may have been felled the next. It is usually necessary to drive/walk around searching for suitable habitat.

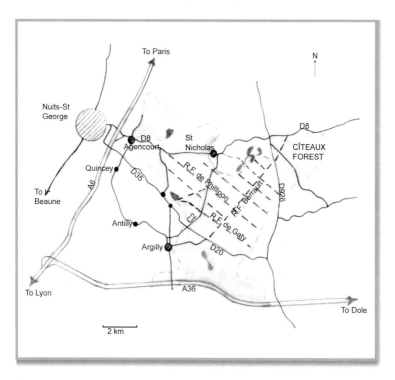

South Central area 10 site iii Citeaux Forest

THE MOUNTAINOUS EAST

Area 1. Nancy area

Site i.	Madine and Lachaussée lakes
Site ii.	Reine Forest and lakes
	(Lorraine Natural Regional Park)
Site iii.	Parroy Lake and Forest *
Site iv.	Lindre, nearby lakes
	and Romersberg Forest *

Area 2. The Northern Vosges

Site i.	Château de Falkenstein
	and Lakes Baerenthal and Hanau
Site ii.	Haguenau Forest
Site iii.	Donon pass

Area 3. Strasbourg/ Rhine Valley area

Site i.	Offendorf
Site ii.	Rohrschollen Island
Site iii.	Plobsheim/Krafft lake *
Site iv.	Erstein Nature Reserve
Site v.	Bruch de l'Andlau

Area 4. Colmar area

Site i.	Rhinau-Kappel Lake
Site ii.	Illwald Forest/Ried De Sélestat *
Site iii.	Sigolsheim
Site iv.	Stork sites

Area 5. The southern Vosges /
Ballons des Vosges Natural Regional Park/
Hautes Vosges

Site i.	The Route des Crêtes
Site ii.	The Hohneck *

Area 6. Mulhouse area

Site i.	Rhine island Reserve
Site ii.	La Harth Forest
Site iii.	Petit Camargue Alsacienne Reserve *
Site iv.	Michelbach Lake *

Area 7. The Jura - Besançon-Dole area.

Site i.	Île du Girard Reserve *
Site ii.	Petit-noir
Site iii.	Chaux Forest
Site iv.	The Serre Massif
Site v.	Baume-les-Messieurs *

Area 8. The Jura - Pontarlier area

Site i.   Mont d'Or. *

Site ii.   Lac Remoray Reserve *

Site iii.   Frasne Nature Reserve *

Site iv.   Joux Forest

Area 9. The Haut-Jura area

Site i.   Risoux Forest

Site ii.   Massacre Forest

Site iii.   The Reserve Naturelle de
la Haut Chaîne du Jura *

The mountainous east birding areas

INTRODUCTION

This region covers the eastern part of Lorraine, Alsace and Franche-Compté. This section is entitled "The Mountainous East" as both the Vosges and the Jura ranges run down the centre of the area, but they are flanked by the well-watered plains of Lorraine on the west and the broad, fertile and now highly-developed Rhine valley to the east. In spite of being heavily industrialised, there are several reserves along the River Rhine, which is still an important habitat, especially for wintering water birds. The remaining riparian woodland, so hung with climbers and ivies that it appears almost tropical, is another important habitat, especially for woodpeckers.

The mountains are largely covered with beech, oak or coniferous (fir, spruce, pine) forest, with scattered small lakes and peat-bogs. All the forests, especially in Lorraine, suffered appalling damage in the storms of December 1999. Millions of trees were blown down and there are very large areas of the forest sites described below that were destroyed and are still, two years on, being cleared. The damage and subsequence disturbance has obviously affected the bird populations quite considerably. Capercaillie were already in serious decline before the storms and the long-term effects on all forest bird populations cannot yet be assessed.

There are three large Natural Regional Parks in the region: Lorraine, the Vosges du Nord and the Ballons des Vosges, which covers the Vosges du Sud mountains. The two parts of the Vosges are very different in altitude, climate and geology, the north being lower and gentler but even the southern Vosges mountains have been gently eroded; their rounded tops being very different from the jagged peaks and ridges of the younger Alps.

The east goes in for extremes of climate, with cold winters and hot summers. Lorraine and the western slopes of the Vosges receive more rain than the eastern side, which is drier and sunnier and is where the famous Alsace vinyards are sited. Wildenstein on the western slope of the Vosges is the wettest place in France, while Colmar, only 32 km away, is the driest!

Further south, the Jura mountains, also heavily forested, are the source of other important rivers, notably the Doubs, which has stretches of good bird habitat. The highest peaks of the Jura stop clouds from the west and so the region is wet; the area around Mont-Fier receiving about 2 metres of precipitation a year. The northern and continental influences ensure that it is also one of the coldest areas of France, where winter temperatures can fall to -35° C with an average temperature of only + 5°C. This is why the sub-alpine stage starts at the relatively low altitude of 1300-1400 m. and snow lies well into spring. The alpine influence means that the southern Haute-Jura is the only site in northern France, as defined by this guide, where some more "alpine" species can be found, while its latitude also enable more southerly ones such as Crag Martin and Eagle Owl to occur.

Alsace has been described as the place where the difference between France and Germany blurs. Certainly a glance at the place-names on a map, or a visit to a winstub or a bierstub where the German-speaking locals are drinking Gewurztraminer, Edelzwicker or the locally brewed lager, makes it seem more German than French. There are also legal differences between Alsace and the rest of France, arising from the years of German annexation between 1871 and 1918. However, what on hears spoken is not German as spoken in Germany but Elsasserdeutsch, a dialect, and naturally everyone also speaks French.

The sites in this region fall into three categories: wetland, forest and mountain sites. For the first, the lakes are very large and a telescope is essential to get the best from your birdwatching, most of which is done standing in one spot and scanning the lake. Quite a large number of species should be seen. Forest sites demand more walking, but much of this is on the level along reasonable paths, though they may be muddy in winter and spring. Keen hearing to locate birds by their calls is helpful but a reasonable number of species should be easily identifiable. The mountain sites are much more demanding; the walking is often strenuous, distances longer, there are fewer birds around and a great deal of luck is needed to locate some mountain species, such as Capercaillie, Hazel Grouse, Citril Finch, Alpine Accentor, etc.

All three regions have active LPO branches.

LPO Alsace has some 1800 members and 13 salaried staff. It is affiliated to the regional federation: Alsace Nature. Its administrative office for the Bas-Rhin is 18, rue du 22 November, 67000 Strasbourg. Tel: 03 88 22 07 35 Fax: 03 88 22 81 28 email: Alsace@lpo-birdlife.asso.fr. The Haut-Rhin office is at 4, rue du Cerf, 68190 Ensisheim. Tel: 03 89 81 15 82 Fax: 03 89 26 43 59 email: haut-rhin@lpo-birdlife.asso.fr. Its web site gives some of the best sites in the region, with brief instruction how to get there, some taken straight from the entries in the LPO book (see Bibliography) but others are new and updated.

LPO Alsace has run a Birdline since 1996. Its telephone number is 03 89 81 05 34. It is not updated daily but gives some idea of the location of current rarities, provided that you can follow rapid French. It lists a dozen sites as the best for rarities; that is, those that produce the greatest number of sightings. Krafft-Plobsheim (Area 3) comes top, followed by Michelbach Lake (Area 6), the Rhine at Rohrschollen and Gambsheim (Area 3), the Petit Camargue Alsacienne (Area 6) and the Rhinau-Kappel lake (Area 4). Recent rarities include White-tailed Eagle, Sabine's Gull, White-winged Black Tern, Sociable Plover, Booted Eagle, and Broad-billed Sandpiper.

LPO Lorraine's telephone number for up-to-the-minute sightings is: 03 83 23 45 83 and Franche-Comté (GNFC): 03 81 61 00 81

Area 1. NANCY AREA

Site i.
MADINE AND LACHAUSSÉE LAKES LAKE MADINE is another very large lake, the largest in Lorraine, some 120 km by road northeast of Lac du Der. It is an important site for water birds, even if it does not compare with Lac du Der; it lacks the numbers of wintering **Cranes, White-tailed Eagle** is only an occasional rather than a regular winter visitor and there are fewer birds, though most of the same species occur. In spite of the above, Madine is worth visiting if you are in the region as it is easily accessible. Another IBA, LAKE LACHAUSSÉE, 10 km north of Madine, is better for breeding birds but access is limited.

WHEN TO VISIT: Like the Champagne lakes, Madine is essentially an autumn and winter site (October to March); although there are some good breeding birds, there is even more disturbance (sailing, fishing) during the summer. Lachaussée is probably best in late spring.

Many diving and dabbling ducks can be seen in winter: **Pochard, Tufted Duck, Shoveler, Gadwall, Teal;** both **Smew** and **Goosander** arrive during cold spells when the numerous **Great Crested Grebes** may be joined by **Slavonian** or **Red-necked.** There is a **Grey Heron** colony and large **Cormorant** and **Black-headed Gull** roosts in winter. When the water levels are low in early autumn, many species of wader arrive. **Ferruginous Duck** has been regularly observed on passage. **Cranes** stop off at this lake or Lachaussée (see below) in spring and autumn, when **Osprey** too is often seen, **Hen Harrier** may be spotted in the nearby fields in winter and **Black** and **Red Kites** and **Hobby** in the spring and summer. Woodland birds include **Golden Oriole, Middle Spotted Woodpecker, Short-toed Treecreeper, Fieldfare** and **Collared Flycatcher** (only likely to be found May/June and difficult at this site. Sites ii -iv are better for this species).

ACCESS: If driving from Paris eastwards, leave the A4 motorway at junction 32 (zero at the tolls) and take the D908 south to FRESNES, *Lac de Madine* is clearly signed at every junction from FRESNES down to VIGNEULLES. Here take the D179. 4.5 km from Vigneulles (25.6 from motorway toll) turn right (west) onto the D133 signed to HEUDICOURT. At 27.6 turn left (signed Madine 2-3) and follow 3 for a view over the lake at 28.1 km.

Return to the D133 and turn left onto the D908 into HEUDICOURT (32.1 km). Near the beginning of the village turn left towards the lake down the *Rue du Lac*. This street turns into a dirt track signed *Tour de Lac* which soon branches: take the left path to one viewpoint and the right to a dead end by a board with a map of the lake and footpaths. From here walk left to the end of the point and then right past a small lake. These three viewpoints give the best views of the northern end of the lake. The right path continues south for some way; it is possible to walk all around the lake.

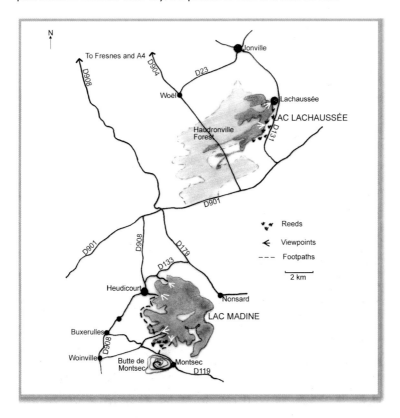

East area 1 site i. Madine and Lachaussée lakes

If you have neither the inclination nor time to walk around the lake, drive to the woods and viewpoints at the south end. Return to HEUDICOURT and continue south down the D908 to WOINVILLE (5.5 km). Turn east onto the D119, signed to *Butte de Monsec* and you will reach the southwest arm of the lake in about 3 km. A sign *Tour de Lac* leads left through an old oak wood (check for **Middle Spotted Woodpecker** and **Collared Flycatcher** in spring). When the track forks keep right on the most used one which leads to a turning circle and parking for *barque* as well as a good view of this arm of the lake. The next track signed *Tour de Lac* off the D119 leads down to another reed-fringed arm some 300 metres from the road. This could be good for warblers in spring. The D119 runs away from the lake after Monsec. (The much-signed *Butte* is a hill with a war memorial and views over the lake).

The east side of the lake is only accessible from footpaths.

The ÉTANG DE LACHAUSSE, north of Madine and just east of the D904 is an IBA with breeding **Bittern, Purple Heron.** and **Marsh Harrier** in the reedbeds; **Black Kite** breed in the woods to the west and can often be seen over the water and **Cranes** regularly roost here on passage. It could be visited on the way back to the motorway by taking the D901 east from Vigneulles for 8.5 km and then the D131 north to LACHAUSSÉE village. The D131 runs close to the lake but reeds may limit views. However there are places from where the reeds can be watched for herons flying, and there is access to and views of the northern part of the lake from the village of Lachaussée, where there is a hide level with the digue in the enclosure of the property belonging to the *Association des Paralysés de France* where there is a restaurant. It is normally open to the public although it is on private property. Obviously it is suitable for the handicapped.

Site ii.
REINE FOREST and lakes cover a large area to the south of Madine Lake. Forming part of Lorraine Regional Park, is a mixed deciduous forest with Oak predominating. It is dotted with smallish lakes, many with reedbeds, which are used for fish-farming, and has both dry and wet meadows on the outskirts; so is a good area for raptors, woodland, water and meadow birds both during the breeding season and on passage.

Among the forest species, six woodpeckers breed in Reine Forest, including **Black, Grey-headed** and **Middle Spotted,** as well as **Wryneck.** Other breeding species include **Black Kite, Buzzard** and **Honey Buzzard, Collared Flycatcher, Wood Warbler** and **Hawfinch.** In the reedbeds there are several pairs of **Bitterns** and **Marsh Harriers** (the Étang de la Mosée is probably the best lake), **Reed** and **Great Reed Warblers.**

Osprey, marsh terns, even a few **Black Stork** may stop over during migration. Marsh terns are best in spring, **Osprey** and **Black Stork** in August-September.

WHEN TO VISIT: May and June are good months, especially for **Honey Buzzard** and **Collared Flycatcher** but February-March are the easiest for **woodpeckers.**

ACCESS: Reine Forest lies inside an inverted triangle of roads with TOUL as the apex in the south: the D908 runs down the southwest side to TOUL, the D904 runs up the east from Toul and the D958 joins the two on the north side. Coming either from Toul or Lake Madine 10 km north of the forest, take the D908 towards BOUCQ. 2.8 km northwest of Boucq, turn right onto the D147, which runs straight through the Rangéval section of the forest for over two kilometres. You will notice forestry tracks leading to small lakes left and right, which you can see through the trees. At the end of the straight stretch, there is a Y-junction where you can park and walk right along the forestry road (RF) towards Mosée lake. (The D147 swings left and leaves the park after the junction).

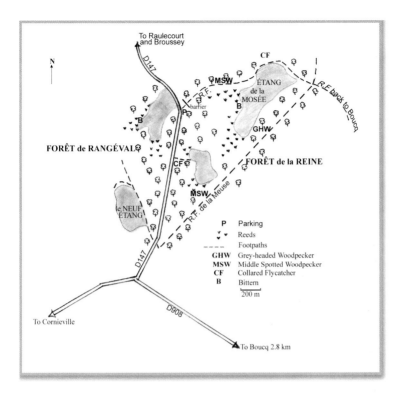

East area I site ii Reine Forest

A second way into the forest is to take the D10 from the centre of BOUCQ in the direction of SANZEY. At first it runs through open fields (good for finch flocks and raptors). When the road enters Reine Forest turn left onto the Sentier des Grands Arbres. There is a parking area some 200 metres before the Maison de la Forêt de Boucq (now a refuge for bats) and the next 4 to 5 kilometres can be walked or driven. Continue on for almost 2 km to a road junction and turn left. This road leads towards the boundary of the Rangeville/Reine forests, 1.8 km further on. There are some bigger oaks, good habitat for **Black Woodpecker** and **Collared Flycatcher,** at parcel 38. To reach the picnic area turn right at the junction. Several footpaths are signed, with walks taking about 2 hours there and back but they tend to lead out of the forest. For birding, it is probably best to walk or drive along the main forestry road for as long as necessary, stopping and listening frequently wherever the habitat seems suitable.

Other fauna: Reine Forest is good habitat for bats, including Great Horseshoe, Whiskered and Long-eared. As in most French forests, Roe Deer and Wild Boar are common.

<u>Accommodation</u>: There are very few hotels in this area, although there is a Logis de France at Heudicourt (see Lake Madine above). Most of the accommodation around Madine is in holiday homes or campsites. There are more hotels around Nancy and Lunéville (but see below) and from there it does not take long by car to reach Lake Madine and Reine Forest.

PARROY LAKE AND FOREST lie 25 km east of NANCY and 10 km north-east of LUNEVILLE. The lake (covering 68.5 hectares) was created at the end of the 19th century to feed the Marne-Rhine Canal and the water levels are sometimes very low at the end of summer, exposing mud-banks which are attractive to waders on passage. The extensive reedbeds which cover the northern part of the lake have breeding **Little Bittern, Purple Heron, Marsh Harrier, Savi's** (now extremely rare), **Sedge** and **Great Reed Warblers. Water Rail** and **Spotted Crake** have been seen at the end of summer in the marshy area below the hide. **Marsh Harrier** hunt over the reedbeds spring to autumn and **Hen Harrier** in winter. Other interesting species that have been noted here at different times of year include **Great White Egret, Night Heron, Black Stork, Eider, Short-toed Eagle, Temminck's Stint, Sabine's Gull, Caspian Tern, Bluethroat, Penduline** and **Bearded Tits.**

Osprey, Hobby, Black Tern, waders and many passerines occur on passage, especially in autumn.

In winter, **Goldeneye, Smew** and **Goosander,** as well as **grebes** and **divers,** may be observed among the commoner duck species **(Mallard, Shoveler, Teal, Tufted Duck and Common Pochard)** in the deeper water below the southern embankment if the lake is not frozen over.

Goshawk, Black, Grey-headed and **Middle Spotted Woodpeckers** as well as both **Common** and **Short-toed Treecreepers** may be found throughout the year in PARROY FOREST, a large mature oakwood south of the canal. In the breeding season they are joined by **Black and Red Kites** and **Collared Flycatcher.**

WHEN TO VISIT: spring and early autumn are the best seasons but Parroy is of interest all year round.

ACCESS: To reach the lake from LUNÉVILLE take the D914 north for 9 km, turning right (east) onto the D2 1 km after crossing the River Marne at EINVILLE. The turning to BURES is in 7.5 km.

To visit the forest beforehand take the N4 east from LUNÉVILLE to MARAINVILLER. Zero as you turn left onto the D161 towards LANEUVEVILLE. In 5.4 km in the centre of this village turn left at the crossroads onto the C5. The C5 runs north through the centre of Parroy Forest. There is a crossroads at 9.1 km. Park here and walk some way down the forestry roads that lead off into the forest.

Continue on the C5 north to MOUACOURT and just after the village turn left (west) onto the D2 towards PARROY village. If you wish to explore the forest further, turn left again just before the bridge crossing the river and follow the forestry road back into the forest towards the area called Le Puits. Stop anywhere along here where there are mature trees.

To reach the lake from the forest continue along the D2 through PARROY village. In just over 1 km there is a parking area with a view north over the lake and south over the canal, very wide at this point. Climb the bank from the car park to scan the lake. **Diving duck, sawbills** and **divers** may often be found here in winter. The embankment also provides enough height to allow you to scan the canal on the opposite side of the road. It is possible to walk around the lake from the embankment. However the reedbeds in the north of the lake are better viewed from the hide situated near the sailing school. To reach this continue west on the D2 for some 800 metres and then turn right (north) onto the D2L to BURES In 400 metres there is a view over reedbeds and just beyond this a footpath, signed Circuit de l'Étang, leads off right around the lakeside to the sailing base. This walk can be good for passerines in spring and autumn and also gives views over the lake and reeds.

To continue by road go on to Bures and turn right onto the road leading to the *Base de Voile*. In 800 metres there is a car park by the club building. Walk down the road to the left of the building, following the wire fence, towards the lake where there is a footpath leading to the hide, 300 metres away. The path between the reeds and a hedge can be productive and the hide gives excellent views over the distant woods (for **kites** and other raptors), the reedbeds for **harriers, bitterns** and **herons** and the northern part of the lake for **duck** in winter. Do not forget to check the muddy edges just below the hide. Recent sightings are written up in a book.

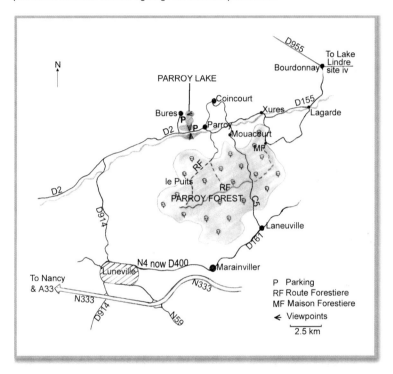

East area I site iii Parroy Lake and Forest

Site iv.

LAKE LINDRE used to be almost as popular with Continental birders as the Champagne lakes further west, partly because it was another site where Cranes and White-tailed Eagle could almost be guaranteed every winter and rarities turned up regularly. Recently it seems to have lost out a little in popularity, both birds and birders preferring other lakes but it remains the best site in the east of Lorraine and one of the best sites in northern France for wintering birds.

Lindre is an artificial lake, covering 630 hectares, created early in the middle-ages and used for fish-farming   This activity means that fishing and hunting are banned and water sports discouraged, which has prevented the growth of "holiday homes" that have sprung up around other lakes in the region.   Furthermore, the farming ensures a plentiful food supply throughout the year for fish-eating birds so recently the General

Council of the Moselle has recognised its ornithological interest and encouraged nature tourism. Furthermore, ROMERBERG FOREST to the north-east and other nearby woodlands are as good for woodpeckers and other forest species as the woods surrounding the Champagne lakes. **Black, Grey-headed** and **Middle Spotted Woodpeckers** are resident, as are both **Treecreeper** species while **Collared Flycatcher** is a summer breeder. It arrives at the end of April and is rarely seen after mid-June.

Lindre is emptied in the autumn, to refill during the winter and spring, so the varying water levels ensure mud flats for waters in autumn and deeper water for diving birds in winter.

WHEN TO VISIT: Lindre is of interest throughout the year, though autumn and winter are usually considered the best seasons.

In autumn, after the lake has been emptied in September, vast mud-flats appear which remain until December, providing food for **Great White Egrets** (up to 80 individuals some years), thousands of **Lapwings** accompanied by **Golden** and **Grey Plovers, Ruff, Curlew, 'shanks, Dunlin** and **Snipe. Cormorants** and **ducks** start arriving, notably **Teal** (up to 30,000) and **Shoveler** (some 20,000). **Cranes** may spend some time here in October-November and a few dozen remain here all winter, returning to their roost on the Tarquimpol peninsular every night. One or two **White-tailed Eagles** usually arrive in November as well as the odd **Rough-legged Buzzard;** local raptors include **Peregrine** and **Goshawk.** (A Spotted Eagle wintered regularly from 1989 to 1998 but has not returned since. Other recent autumn rarities have included Sociable Plover, Pectoral Sandpiper, Grey and Red-necked Phalaropes).

In winter as the lake begins to fill up, duck species from further north: **Goldeneye, Smew** and **Goosander** start arriving, especially during very cold spells. A few **Bewick's** and **Whooper Swans** turn up each winter and from December, **Greylags** start to appear, followed in mid-January by **Bean Geese,** whose numbers peak to about 100 in February. In some years another 100 or so **White-fronted Geese** arrive here in December-January. **Long-tailed Duck, Eider** and **Scoters** turn up from time to time. If the water is deep enough, divers and **Slavonian** and **Red-throated Grebes** may be found near the Lindre-Basse embankment.

Spring comes late to Lorraine but by the beginning of March, when **Red Kite** and **Cranes** are passing through, **White Storks** and **Black Redstarts** return to nearby houses and by mid-April **Marsh Harriers, Black Kite** and **Black-necked Grebe** should be back and **Bitterns** may be heard booming from the reedbeds. A few **Little Bittern** and **Purple Heron** breed most years and one of the best places to see them fly over the reedbeds is from the parking west of Tarquimpol village. Another good area at this season is the easterly arm of the lake near Guermange village. About a hundred pairs of **Great Reed Warbler** breed on Lindre and nearby lakes. Breeding ducks species include **Red-crested** and **Common Pochards, Tufted Duck** and **Gadwall.** Platforms have been erected for **Ospreys,** in the hopes that they may stay and nest. They are easily observed between mid-March and the end of April.

April and May are the best months for both breeding species and spring migrants. There is often a strong passage of **Black Terns** and **Little Gulls** at the end of April-beginning May, often accompanied by a few **White-winged Black** and **Whiskered Terns.**

Summer is the quietest season, but all the breeding species can be observed busily feeding young, especially early in the morning. If water levels are low enough in August, the first passage waders stop by on their way south and **Black Stork** and **Osprey** are seen regularly.

Lindre is surrounded by several smaller lakes, the best around GÉLUCOURT and ZOMMANGE which are worth visiting when making a circuit around the lake. Two other large lakes, Stock and Gondrexange, are nearby. Stock is surrounded by too many holiday homes and is too disturbed to be good for birds but in winter GONDREXANGE has good numbers of **Smew, Goldeneye** and **Goosander** and sometimes **Red- and Black-throated Divers** in November-December. **Osprey** turn up here regularly on passage and **Collared Flycatcher** breeds in the surrounding woods.

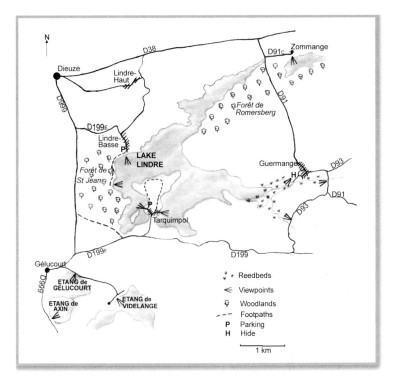

East area I site iv Lindre Lake

Two or three days, at least, are needed to cover the whole area thoroughly, especially if you include Parroy Lake. With more time, it might be worth exploring more of the smaller lakes, especially those around Morhange, 20 km north of Lindre (Bischwalk, Vallerange, Morhange, la Mutche). These, however, are private, so do not trespass and watch out for hunters.

ACCESS: Lindre is a 45 minutes drive north-east of NANCY, via the N74 for 32 km to MOYENVIC, then the D38 for 12 km to DIEUZE where you turn right (south) onto the D999.

Lindre is also easily reached from Parroy Lake (site iii above). From Parroy take the D2, then the D155 to BOURDONNAY and turn right (east) onto the D955 to MAIZIÈRES-les-Vic. Turn left (northeast) onto the D999. The village of GÉLUCOURT is 7 km away and as you approach it, several lakes are visible from the road and can be scanned from the verges. To reach the larger lakes of GÉLUCOURT and VIDELANGE, take the lane signed to the *Chapelle des Templiers* on the right (west) near the Lindre end of the village. Do not go down to the chapel but take the lane running left along the lakeside. Parts of Gélucourt lake can be seen well from here. **Red-crested Pochard** is among the ducks nesting here and **Purple Heron** and **Little Bittern** can often be seen in spring-summer. Gélucourt is excellent for waders at the end of summer, when the water levels are very low. Look over the distant woods for raptors **(buzzards, Osprey, Peregrine)** and **Cranes** (on passage and in winter). The lane continues to a junction leading to a farm, from where Videlange lake can be scoped. It is good for **Smew** and **Shoveler,** among other ducks, in winter and **Osprey** and **Great White Egret** in autumn.

After checking the lakes at GÉLUCOURT, continue towards LINDRE by turning right after some 600 metres onto the D199F towards TARQUIMPOL, signed to the *Étang de Lindre.* The GR5 footpath, which joins the road at a bend after 1.3 km leads towards the west side of the lake through woodland and may be worth walking along for a short distance. The best views over the southern arms of the lake, however, are at TARQUIMPOL from either end of the village street. At the entrance to the village, you will notice that there is a stork platform by the lake where a pair is in residence all year round. In the village turn left down the *Rue de l'Étang* to a small parking/picnic area by the lakeside that gives good scope views over the south-western arm of the lake. A footpath, which leads out onto Tarquimpol peninsular, is signed from the carpark but you will probably not see much more than you would by scanning from the village, though it may be good for passerines. Walk through the village to the storks' nest for views over the east side of the lake. In winter **Whooper Swans** and **Goldeneye** are often among the species here.

Continue the circuit around Lindre by returning to the D999 and heading north towards DIEUZE The woodland to the west of the road, St. Jean forest, is worth exploring in May-June for **Collared Flycatcher** or **Middle Spotted Woodpecker** at any time. Turn off right in 4 km onto the D199E to LINDRE-BASSE. Follow signs to the Étang de Lindre through the village to the carpark and walk down the Sauf riverains road to the lakeside. There is a centre for captive-bred storks on the right and they are always accompanied by numerous Grey Herons in winter. There are good views over the lake from the pump house, where recent duck counts and notices are displayed. A footpath leads around part of the lake past the stork centre; check for **Kingfisher.**

To reach ROMERSBERG FOREST, GUERMANGE and the smaller lakes on the east side of the lake, follow the signs for LINDRE-HAUTE and at the junction leading to this village, go straight on to the D38 and then right (east). In 3 km turn right off the D38 onto the D91 towards ZOMMANGE and GUERMANGE. In 1 km from the junction turn left onto the D91C for 500 metres to ZOMMANGE, from where you can view the lake of the same name, which can be good for water birds in winter **(grebes, Great White Egret, Peregrine, Smew, Goosander, Goldeneye, Cormorants, Coot, gulls), Cranes** and **Osprey** in spring and autumn.

Return to the D91 and head south. As you enter ROMERSBERG FOREST, you will notice a picture of a Collared Flycatcher! The strand of mature oaks on the right just after this sign is a good place to start looking for woodland species. In a kilometre from the Zommange turning, a forestry road runs west towards Lindre lake. It is worth walking along this for some way. ROMERSBERG has both **Common** and **Short-toed Treecreepers, Black, Grey-headed** and **Middle Spotted Woodpeckers,** which can be heard calling from February. **Collared Flycatcher** arrives at the end of April but is very difficult to see after mid-June. Other woodland species include **Black** and **Red Kite** and **Goshawk.**

Emerging from the forest, continue along the D91 to GUERMANGE. There is a hide at the lake-end of the village, in need of repair and closed in February 2002. A new one is scheduled for later in 2002. It is still possible to watch the reedbeds from near the hide. Take the road past the school sign towards the church. It ends at a farm by the hide.

Another viewpoint over the reeds is by the river beyond the village. Turn right onto the D91 in the direction of TARQUIMPOL and stop by the blue bridge where there is a view along the river to the reeds. This could be a good place to listen for Crakes in spring and to watch for **Purple Heron, Bittern** and **Little Bittern flying.** In winter **Hen Harrier** hunts over the reeds and fields and duck, such as **Goosander,** may be seen on the river.

To complete the circuit of Lindre Lake, keep following the signs for TARQUIMPOL, turning onto the D93 and then the D199.

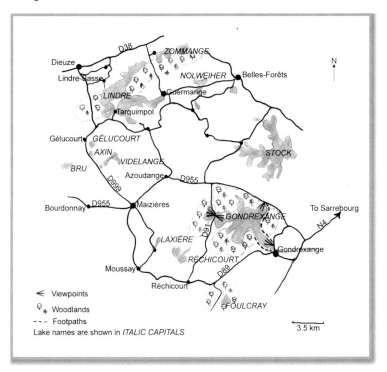

East area I site iv Lindre and surrounding lakes

The other large lake in the vicinity that is worth visiting, especially in winter, is GONDREXANGE, 16 km to the south-east of Lindre (more by road). There are often more **Smew, Goosander, Goldeneye, divers** and other wintering birds here than at Lindre and they can be easy to see from the D91 (also good for **Great White Egret** and woodland birds) and the dam and embankment at Gondrexange village.

Gondrexange serves as a reservoir for the Marne au Rhin canal, which crosses it and though it is much used by fisherman there is relatively little disturbance in winter. There are three good viewpoints.

ACCESS: 1) Turn onto the D91 from the D955 4 km after AZOUDANGE. In 2.2 km from the D91/D955 junction the lake can be seen through the trees. There is a small parking/picnic space on the east side of the road. The lake can be seen from here and by walking on down the road for 100 metres or so, there are clear views over the water both sides of the road.

2) Gondrexange village can be reached by continuing on the D91 for 6 km to Réchicourt, turning left onto the D90 and left again at 8.3 km on to the D89, both signed to Gondrexange. On the outskirts of the village at 14.4 km park by the embankment and canal lock or by the bar-restaurant "de la Plage". There are good views over the water from here. It is also possible to walk along the embankment beside the lake and canal for several kilometres (part of the GR5 footpath) or follow the footpath around the smaller lake. These walks will give better views of birds on the far side of the water.

3) The northern side of the lake can be reached from the D955, where there is a boatyard as the road crosses the canal. From the car-park beyond it footpaths lead along the embankment.

Accommodation: Nancy is central and has hotels in all categories but it is a very large town with heavy traffic, so there are delays getting in and out and it is easy to get lost. Lunéville, the "Versailles of the North" is smaller, has a couple of reasonably priced hotels, several restaurants and is conveniently situated for all the sites above. There is a campsite at Gondrexange and the bar/restaurant "de la Plage" (closed Mondays) beside it can be recommended, not least for its views over the lake if the weather is bad!

Area 2. **THE NORTHERN VOSGES**

The northern Vosges are hilly, rather than mountainous; softly rounded rather than jagged with the highest peaks only reaching 500-600 m. Much of the most picturesque parts are included in the Vosges du Nord Regional Natural Park, which covers 120,000 hectares, of which almost 60,000 hectares are managed for forestry and large areas are cultivated. Beech and Oak are the dominant woodland species, although there are tracts of fir and Scots Pine. The Park forms a rough triangle, the northern edge following the German frontier and the ill-fated Maginot Line of World War II, running south and narrowing after La Petite-Pierre, where the *Maison du Parc* is situated. The Park has been designated one of UNESCO's international biosphere reserves.

The region is fairly wet, with an average precipitation of 700 mm, while temperatures vary from 27°C in July to -15° C in December.

Over 150 bird species have been recorded in the region, a remarkable mixture of forest, mountain and Mediterranean species. These include **Hazel Grouse** and **Capercaillie,** though numbers of both have declined in recent years, **Nutcracker, Tengmalm's Owl, Black, Grey-headed** and **Middle Spotted Woodpecker, Wryneck, Dipper, Pied Flycatcher** (the forests here are one of its most important breeding sites), **Golden Oriole, Hoopoe** (though numbers have declined since the 1970's). **Red-backed** and **Woodchat Shrikes** and **both Common** and **Short-toed Treecreepers.** Raptors include **Red** and **Black Kites, Montagu's** and **Marsh Harriers, Honey Buzzard** and **Peregrine Falcon.**

Other fauna and flora: Red and Roe Deer, Wild Cat, Martens and Wild Boar are found in the forests. Six species of bats are found in the underground military installations at Ramstein including Natterer's, Daubenton's, Greater Mouse-eared and Grey long-eared. Woodland butterflies abound (including High Brown, Silver-washed Fritillaries, White Admiral, Purple Emperor, Large Tortoiseshell, Scarce Swallowtail, Wood White, hairstreaks, blues) and 25 dragon and damselfly species have been recorded around the bogs and lakes.

Six or seven species of helleborines grow in the beech woods and several *Ophrys* species, including Late Spider, as well as Lady, Fly, Lizard and Military, on calcareous grassland. Sundews (*Drosera sp*), Grass of Parnassus *Parnassia palustris* and Butterworts (*Pinguicula sp*) grow in the peatbogs

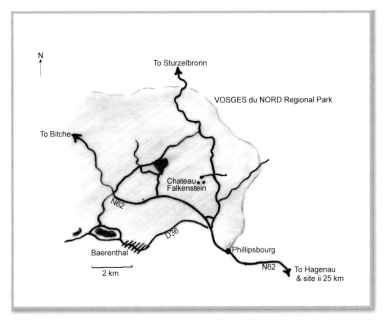

East area 2 sites i Falkenstein

Site i.

FALKENSTEIN CASTLE and the nearby **LAKES BAERENTHEL** and **HANAU** lie at the heart of the Regional Park, very close to the German frontier, in a typical northern Vosges landscape of wooded hills.

The ruins of Falkenstein Castle are on top of a sandstone peak in the middle of mixed deciduous/coniferous woodland. There are beech trees where **Black and Grey-headed Woodpeckers** can be found all year round and a pine wood near it with **Crossbill** and **Crested Tit** as well as other tit species. **Pied Flycatcher** may be found in both woods in summer. Besides the above species there are all the commoner woodland species.

ACCESS: Start in PHILLIPSBOURG, on the N 62 between Bitche and Haguenau. Zero at the D38 turning in Phillipsbourg, signed to Falkenstein Castle. In 1.3 km turn left following the sign to the castle. The road climbs through good forest habitat. Park at 2.8 km by a forest cross-roads, with the main road signed Sturzelbronn/Phillipsbourg. Walk past the map showing all the footpaths and straight on through the short barrier. Climb up the hill following the blue and white marks on trees. The castle ruins are now dangerous and the path peters out just below them but the conifers here are excellent for **Crested Tit** and **Crossbill** and the beeches for **woodpeckers**.

Black Woodpecker can also be found in the trees in the opposite direction from the castle. Walk in the direction of Rothenbourg signed by parcel 210 on a green sign (not towards Landersberg. If facing north towards Sturzelbronn, this is the right-hand road) until you reach the *sauf vehicles authorises* sign. **Black Woodpeckers** are active and noisy in the woods here (by parcel 188). This part of the forest is criss-crossed with footpaths, so if you dip by the castle try walking a circuit around some of them. Beware - the amount of broken glass in the parking areas suggests that car thieves are active in summer. Leave nothing valuable or visible in you car. In early spring the area is deserted.

BAERENTHEL LAKE, a small nature reserve with a hide, can be reached by returning to the crossroads in Phillipsbourg, crossing the N62 and taking the D36 to BAERENTHEL. If you wish to use the hide, the key must be collected from the *Mairie* (closed 12-14h). At the very end of the village turn right towards the signed *Étang de Peche/Reserve Naturelle*. There is parking beside the first part of the lake, which is used by fishermen. The road running along the far side of the lake leads in 1.2 km to the hide, which overlooks a reedbed and the reserve end of the lake. There is flooded woodland next to it and conifers on the slope behind, both good habitats. In summer reeds block views of the open water so it is best to use the hide. (Note: the steps up to it are very steep).

The Étang de Hanau, only 2 km from Falkenstein Castle, can be most easily reached by returning to Phillipsbourg, taking the N62 towards Bitche for 3 km and turning off right (north) onto the minor road also signed to *Château Waldeck*. Zero here. Follow the signs to the Étang. Although Hanau has a Maison de la Forêt and a nature trail running around the lake and the forest here should be as good as around Falkenstein, it is a very popular spot and there is too much disturbance from tourists. It is worth checking out in early spring.

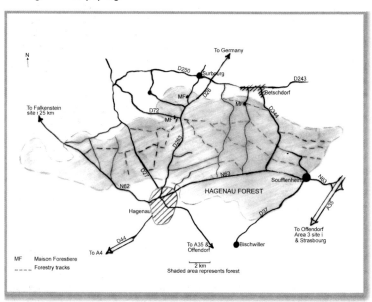

East area 2 sites ii Haguenau Forest

Site ii.

HAGUENAU FOREST, covering over 20,000 hectares, is an area of deciduous and coniferous woodlands, heathland, peatbogs and wet grassland. It is an IBA for raptors **(Honey Buzzard, Red and Black Kites) woodpeckers (Grey-headed, Black** and **Middle Spotted), Nightjar** and **Red-backed Shrike.** In winter check the cleared areas, winter finch flocks of **Chaffinch** and **Brambling** sometimes have **Hawfinch** with them and **Middle Spotted Woodpecker** are often on the edge of these clearings.

ACCESS: The forest lies north of the town of HAGUENAU, just west of the River Rhine and OFFENDORF FOREST (see site i. Strasbourg area 3). Haguenau can be reached from the A4 motorway from the west of the A35 from the south (exits 53 or 55). Roads D27, D263 and N63 run north and north-east from the town through the forest. From them turn off onto any forestry track that is not closed to traffic and stop where there are large, mature trees. The D344 from SOUFFLENHEIM on the N63 to BETSCHDORF on the northern edge of the forest, has a good forestry roads leading off it. There is **Black Woodpecker** near the *Maison forestière de Heuscheuer,* just south of Betschdorf.

Site iii.

The forests to the north of the **COL DE DONON** are an IBA for mountain and forest birds. **Hazel Grouse, Capercaillie, Black** and **Grey-headed Woodpeckers** are all found there, as well as a few **Tengmalm's Owls.** In summer, **Red-backed Shrike** can be found in scrubby areas. **Dipper** can be found in the River Sarre running alongside the D44 down to Abresschviller. There has unfortunately been considerable storm damage to the forests, especially on the west slopes.

ACCESS: The D993, D44, D392 and the D392 meet near the Col and several minor roads and footpaths lead off from them, making this an easy area to explore. The forestry track leaving the D44 2 km after its junction with the D993 and running north to Schneeberg for over 10 km used to be good for forest birds but it was still closed to traffic in early 2002 and the first part is no longer worth walking along, there has been so much storm damage. The long-distance footpath, the GR5 crosses the D44 about half a kilometre nearer the Col and is signed. It could be worth walking along the north-eastern stretch.

At the col, the ski piste and forestry road *R.F. de Prayé/ Haute Abraye* starting almost opposite the Hotel du Donon is worth walking (or driving) along for several kilometres, if the snow has melted. It leads to the Col de Prayé, near where **Black Woodpecker** can be found and **Hazel Grouse** has been heard early in the morning, and continues down through forest for several more kilometres.

Accommodation: There are a couple of comfortable but fairly expensive hotels at the Col de Donon. The Hotel du Donon is a *Logis de France,* closed March and November.

Area 3. **STRASBOURG/ RHINE VALLEY**

The sites in this area are mainly of interest for woodland birds and wintering waterbirds on the River Rhine, where tens of thousands of **duck** (mainly **Gadwall, Pochard** and **Tufted Duck**), **coot** and **cormorants** congregate. Many of the sites are reserves and most are surrounded by riparian and alluvial woodland, excellent for woodpeckers; six species can be found in the Rhine forests. Though interesting birds may turn up at any of the sites below on passage or in winter, Plobsheim Lake (site iii) normally has the greatest number of birds and is the best site. If you have time to visit only one, go to PLOBSHEIM. Offendorf Reserve (site i) is the only one of the sites below that is north of Strasbourg. All the others lie quite close together to the south. A telescope is very useful, if not essential.

WHEN TO VISIT: Sites i - iv below are wintering and passage sites, so November-March are the best months. Site v is best in late spring, but is also worth visiting in winter.

Site i.

OFFENDORF RESERVE lies some 20 km north of Strasbourg. There is some good, wet woodland here (especially in the *Reserve Biologique de Rossdoerfein* section) and it is possible to walk along the *digues* or embankments but for waterbirds, the Rhine is rather disappointing as there does not seem to be a concentration of birds at any one point, as there is at Plobsheim. This is a site for woodland rather than water birds.

ACCESS: Leave the A35 north of Strasbourg at either exit 52 or 53 and take the D468, following signs for OFFENDORF. Drive straight through the town following the signs to *Étang de Peche/Base de Loisirs* and then follow the embankment along to the left, so the forest is on your left and the embankment on the right. Climb up and look at the Rhine or walk into the woods whenever there is access. The road goes on for several kilometres, with several forestry tracks leading into the woods.

Site ii.

ROHRSCHOLLEN ISLAND is a wooded island enclosed by the canal to the west and by the old Rhine on the east. The woodland birds on the island include **Middle Spotted** and **Grey-headed Woodpeckers**. There is a large colony of **Common Tern** by the jetty above the hydroelectricity works. Both the canal d'Alsace and the old Rhine have large numbers of wintering duck, including **Goldeneye** and **Merganser** during cold spells. Access is currently (2002) confusing as there are major road works in this area.

ACCESS: Leave STRASBOURG heading east for Germany along the Route du Rhin. Just before Vauban Bridge, turn right at the traffic lights, direction *Zone portuaire sud* (rue du Havre). At the second set of lights, some 5 to 6 km along the road, where you can see a tall red-and-white chimney, turn left (east) following the sign *Usine hydroélectrique de Strasbourg/Usine d'incineration.* Pass the hydroelectricity plant and keep right (on the tarred road) at the fork.

If coming from Plobsheim and the south, on the D468, zero at the traffic lights at ESCHAU. In 1.2 km at the crossroads, turn right (east) onto the dual-carriageway in the direction of Port de Strasbourg. At 5.0 km at the roundabout turn left, still following signs for Port de Strasbourg. You will see the woodland of Rohrschollen Reserve has been badly storm-damaged here (there is an entrance near the roundabout). Continue on to the traffic lights at 8.2 km and turn right over the railway towards the red-and-white chimney. At 9.5 there is a sign to *Usine hydroélectrique* and a small parking area by a map. Drive up the road towards the works, cross the bridge by the works and bear left. When you reach the substation, drive up the bank to park. Walk along the embankment. In about 500 metres (beyond a wooden hut) there is a good view over a broad stretch of the old Rhine where there are numerous water birds in winter. It is possible to climb down the embankment and walk to the waters edge and back alongside the flooded woodland.

Site iii.

LAKE PLOBSHEIM (sometimes called Krafft/Plobsheim), a large basin used to regulate the flow of the Rhine and the Ill, is an important and protected site for water birds with between 10 to 15,000 duck wintering there (mainly **Tufted Duck, Pochard** and **Gadwall**) but **divers, grebes, Bewick** and **Whooper Swans, Wigeon, Scaup, Goldeneye, Goosander, Smew, Scoters, Red-crested Pochard** can be found among them.   During spring and autumn passage, both **Black-necked** and **Red-necked Grebes** turn up, as well as **Osprey, Little Gull** and **Black Tern.**   It is the best birding site on this stretch of the River Rhine and the most accessible. Birds are normally close to the French side early in the morning and move towards the German bank later in the day.

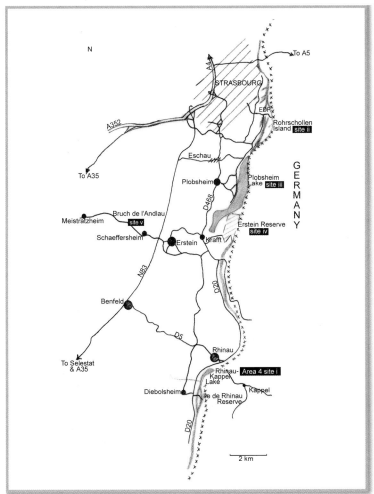

East area 3 Rhine Valley sites ii - iv and area 4 site i

ACCESS: (From STRASBOURG go south on the A 35 motorway, exit at junction 5 and take the D468 south in the direction of PLOBSHEIM). Start at PLOBSHEIM on the D468. Turn east at the traffic lights in the centre of the village and zero. Follow the signs *Plan d'Eau/Base de Rhinland* through the village and past the golf course. At 3.1* turn right towards Rhinland (a boating area and restaurant). At Rhinland, park by the canal, climb up the bank and walk along the footpaths which run along the lakeside.

If it is wet there is even a shelter and covered bridge at Rhinland from where to scope the lake.

If you want to walk further south, a couple of hundred metres or so beyond the Rhinland building, there is another small parking area with a bridge over the canal and steps up to the embankment,

To check the northern part, turn left at the junction (shown with an * above) towards the Marina. In 1km there is another road leading back to Plobsheim and in 2 km there is parking below the *Base Nautique/restaurant* and steps leading up the embankment. This is still a protected area although there are usually fewer duck here.

Site iv.

ERSTEIN NATURE RESERVE covers the woodland between Plobsheim Lake and the Rhine. Like other alluvial forest sites along the Rhine, it is a good spot for **Black, Grey-headed, Lesser** and **Middle Spotted Woodpeckers, Short-toed** and **Common Treecreeper, Firecrest** and many other woodland species. Erstein has 54 breeding species at unusually high densities (210 pairs to every 10 hectares), triple the normal woodland density. There are also good numbers of wintering **Mute Swan, duck, Coot, grebes** on the lake, if not as many as at Plobsheim (see species list for site iii).

ACCESS: From KRAFFT, almost 6 km south of Plobsheim on the D468. Cross the bridge over the Canal Decharge d'Ill in Krafft and in 400 metres turn left (east) signed Reserve *Naturelle/Zone d'Activité*. In 1.3 km there is a car-park by the Polder d'Erstein. Walk some 300 metres to the bridge. There is a large open stretch of water on the left. Check for **Kingfisher** along the bank here. Footpaths lead along beside woodland either side of the canal on the right. It is possible to take a short, circular walk back to the car-park by following the canal to the next bridge and then turning onto the gravel road that leads back to the car-park. The woodland next to the Polder board beyond the bridge can be good for birds.

Site v.

BRUCH DE L'ANDLAU Formerly a huge marsh, this area has long been drained but nowadays the water meadows where **Curlew** and **Corncrake** bred are increasingly being ploughed and planted with maize. **Honey Buzzard** and **Goshawk** still breed in the woods, together with several **woodpecker** species including **Middle Spotted** and many of the passerines typical of eastern France, including **Icterine** and **Marsh Warblers, Lesser Whitethroat** and **Willow Tit. Hen Harrier** can be seen hunting over the meadows in winter and **Hobby** in summer.

ACCESS: From STRASBOURG, take the dual-carriageway N83 south towards ERSTEIN (13 km from the A35 junction) and turn off onto the D426, heading west in the direction of OBERNAI (14 km away) and SCHAEFFERSHEIM. 2.6 km from the end of Schaeffersheim village there is a small bridge over the River Andlau and a wooden sign describing the Bruch. Park off-road just beyond the bridge and walk both left and right along the agricultural tracks that follow the river. There is some good woodland on the north side, inaccessible but easy to bird around the edges.

The D426 runs through good habitat for about 1.6 km beyond the bridge and it is worth taking any tracks that lead off. The best are at the beginning and end of this stretch. Avoid walking across hay-meadows in the spring and summer and do not block agricultural tracks when parking.

WHEN TO VISIT: Spring is best but there is quite a lot to see in winter.

Other fauna and flora: Roe Deer, Badger, Western Polecat and Wild Boar are some of the larger mammals found in the riverine woodland alongside the Rhine. Amphibians and reptiles include three newt species at Erstein (Alpine, Warty and Smooth) as well as Agile Frogs (*Rana dalmatina*). Tree Frogs (*Hyla arborea*) are found in all the woods and the Yellow-bellied Toad (*Bombina variegata*) at Rhinau (Area 5 site i).

Most of the woods are fairly recent, under 200 years old, but dense and festooned with climbers such as Old Man's Beard, Hop and Ivies, giving parts of them a resemblance to a tropical rainforest. In some clearings Lily of the Valley and *Allium ursinum* grow and Bee Orchid in May at Rhinau.

<u>Accommodation</u>: Strasbourg has plenty of hotels in all price ranges but it is a very large and expensive town with heavy traffic. To reach all the sites above it is better to stay in one of the villages beside the N83 south of it. The Logis A La Coronne in Schaeffersheim (on the D426 near Site v above) can be recommended. It is central, reasonably priced, serves good regional food, and all the sites in the Strasbourg and Sélestat areas can easily be reached from Schaeffersheim.

Area 4. **COLMAR AREA**

<u>Site i.</u>

RHINAU-KAPPEL LAKE lies mid-way between STRASBOURG and COLMAR and can be reached from either city (there is a bus service to the ferry from Strasbourg) or from Sélestat. The lake was formed when an old arm of the Rhine was converted in the 1960's to produce hydro-electricity and although on German territory, it belongs to Rhinau parish. Like all other sites along the Rhine, it is important for birds on passage and dabbling and diving duck in winter (including **Pochard, Tufted Duck, Goosander** and **Goldeneye**). **Cormorant, grebes, Coot, Moorhen, Water Rail, Kingfisher** and **Mute Swan** are other species likely to be seen on the river or lake. The nearby forest (a German reserve) holds six species of **woodpecker** (including **Black, Grey-headed** and **Middle Spotted**), breeding **Black Kites, Honey Buzzards** and **Golden Oriole** as well as many woodland passerines.

WHEN TO VISIT: Autumn through to spring; winter (November- February) is best for waterbirds and is also quite a good time for locating woodpeckers, especially February and early March, when they start to call and are easier to find among leafless trees. A telescope is essential.

ACCESS: Coming from either north (Strasbourg) or south (Colmar/Sélestat), take the N83 to BENFELD (respectively 21 or 8 km from the A35 motorway junctions), turn east, go through the village and take the D5 for 13 km to RHINAU (passing through HERBSHEIM and BOOFZHEIM). It is also easy to continue south down the D426 from Plobsheim and Krafft (Area 3 site iii) and turn onto the D20. The car ferry is on the D20 at Rhinau and runs more or less continuously from 6.15 to 18.30 or 19.00 in winter and until 21.00 in summer. (Maximum wait - 15 mins). Check the time of the last boat back on the ferry going over. On disembarking, park either side of the road and follow the river south along the embankment with river to your right and the lake and trees on your left. Stops anywhere along here will give good views of waterbirds in winter. After a kilometre or so it is possible to turn inland, cross by the sluices and walk back on the east side of the old lake, so making a circular walk. Alternatively, continue walking down the river-bank for as long as it takes to find woodpeckers. The riverside woodland here is good habitat.

Another woodland site is the long island in the middle of the river which is the ILE DE RHINAU Reserve. To reach it continue south down the D20 for almost 5 km and turn off towards the *Central Hydroélectricité de Rhinau* at the Diebolsheim junction. Cross the river by the dams in front of the hydroelectricity station and park. Check the river above the lock as there may be waterbirds here. Afterwards follow the road down to the woods. There are walking/cycle tracks (some rather muddy in winter) through the woods on the island.

Flora: Orchids, including Bee, are found in the woods on the German side in May.

Site ii.

ILLWALD FOREST/RIED DE SÉLESTAT. The town of Sélestat has restored and protected the flood plain around the River Ill, creating the Nature Reserve of Illwald/Ried de Sélestat. The area floods regularly in spring and autumn, forming rich water meadows and flooded forests which are classified as an IBA on account of the many waterbirds that winter there or pass through on migration (among them **Greylag** and **Bean Geese**) and the breeding woodland birds, which include **Honey Buzzard, Black Kite, Goshawk, Black** and **Middle Spotted Woodpecker** and **Red-backed Shrike** as well as just possibly a few pairs of **Black Storks.** The latter are often seen in the water meadows in spring. There are always **White Stork** and **Grey Heron** in the meadows, **Great White Egret** occurs regularly. Over 240 species have been recorded in the Reserve since the 1970s and of the 54 species of birds recorded in the forest, some 42 species breed.

ACCESS: From Colmar take the N83 towards SÉLESTAT (20 km north of Colmar) and turn right (east) onto the D424 at the roundabout just outside Sélestat. Zero here. In 1.7 km opposite another turning into Sélestat there is a carpark with a plan of the Reserve. Beyond the meadows you will notice a hide in the reedbed but there does not appear to be any access to it. Walk down the track through the flooded meadows or if short of time drive to the next parking place, over 2 km down the track and then walk right towards the reeds. There are also tracks leading into the woods and it is possible to walk a long circuit through the woods and back to the carpark. Check the plan carefully first.

To drive to the woods, continue east along the D424 for a short way. There is a drivable but rough track leading into the woods directly opposite a large carpark 2 km from the N83 roundabout, just after the bridge and Freiburg sign. It leads to the Chapelle du Chêne. There is a small parking area on the left at the beginning of the woodland. Park here and walk down the track, as between here and the parking/picnic place by the chapel is an excellent area for **Black** and **Middle Spotted Woodpeckers.**

There is another plan of the reserve by the picnic area showing footpaths through the wood.

Anyone wanting more information, or access to the hide, should try contacting the Réserve Naturelle Volontaire du Ried de Sélestat Illwald on 03 88 58 85 00 or on line at http://perso.wanadoo.fr/ill-wald

Further south, nearer to Colmar, is a similar forested area, the Forêt de Colmar. While not as good as Illwald, it has the same woodland bird species and is worth visiting if you have time.

ACCESS: is easy from OSTHEIM, 10 km south down the N83 from Sélestat. Go into Ostheim centre and out again on the D3 towards Jebsheim. 2 km outside the town a forestry road leads off left (north) into the forest and makes a "dog leg" through it, returning to Ostheim. **Middle Spotted Woodpecker** are quite common here, especially near the entrance. Warning: it is used for hunting and closed between 18.00. - 08.00. from 1/10 to 31/3 and 21.00. - 07.00. from 1/4 to 30/9. Do not get locked in! *Other fauna and flora*: Fallow and roe deer and wild boar are found in Illwald forest. The water meadows have a rich flora in spring.

Site iii.

SIGOLSHEIM. North-west of COLMAR, a variety of habitats can be found on the dry, sunny hills around Sigolsheim: Oak (*Quercus pubescent*) woodland, orchid meadows, scrub and vinyards; a combination that ensures a healthy bird population. Species of particular interest in spring and summer are **Hoopoe, Woodlark, Stonechat** and **Lesser Whitethroat**.

ACCESS: Leave the A35 motorway at exit 23 just north of Colmar and take the D4 west to Sigolsheim, just under 6 km. In the centre of town, turn north at the traffic lights by the Mairie-Poste, following the sign to the cemetery (Note: the military cemetery is variously signed *Nécropole or Cimetière*). The road climbs for almost 2 km to a large carpark just below the military cemetery. The track to take leaves the carpark on the right of the cemetery. It is hard-surfaced as far as the cemetery and then becomes dirt, skirting vinyards and eventually climbing the ridge towards the oakwood on the top of the hill to the west.

Other fauna and flora: Orchids include Green-winged, Lizard, Greater Butterfly, Man, Burnt-tip, Late Spider and Military. Butterflies are also numerous in the orchid meadows: Silver-studded, Adonis and Chalkhill Blues, several fritillaries and graylings.

Site iv.

STORK SITES. White Storks are traditionally associated with Alsace but France's north-eastern population had been slowly declining since the 1940s and crashed in the 1970s, from 118 pairs in 1961 to 9 pairs in 1974. Adult mortality caused by the drying up of the Sahel as well as being shot or crashing into power lines when on migration were the principle causes and very wet springs contributed to juvenile mortality. In 1956 Alsace started a reintroduction programme, captive breeding is still continuing, and the number of pairs in this region multiplied by ten between 1980 and 1997 until today there are more than 200 breeding pairs. Since the juveniles have had their migratory instincts suppressed, a great many storks are now sedentary.

The area around Colmar is where the greatest number of White Storks are to be found. Most villages, especially along the "wine route" have at least one breeding pair and nesting platforms have been widely erected. The flooded meadows outside Sélestat are one site where several birds can be seen feeding year round. The Alsace Ecomuseum at Pulversheim, near Ungersheim has nests on many of its old buildings.

It can be reached from the A35, exit at Ensisheim and is signed from the N83 south of Colmar. There has been a reintroduction centre since 1976 at the Parc des Cigognes at Hunawihr, just off the D1 north of Sigolsheim (site iii), where more than 200 birds are fed. Most are free-flying and breed on a forest of nesting poles. Visitors can find out about breeding programmes, raising young birds, etc from April to mid-November, 10-17h30 closed 12-14h except during holiday periods.

<u>Accommodation</u>: This is a very popular area and there are a numerous hotels, in all price ranges, around Colmar. Ostheim is a good centre for all the sites in the Colmar region, being central and small enough for easy access. It is not so "touristy" (i.e. crowded and expensive) as some of the other small towns in the "wine region". *The Logis* "au Nid de Cigognes", right opposite the storks' nest in the square, is recommended.

Area 5. **THE SOUTHERN VOSGES**

The Ballons des Vosges Natural Regional Park covers some 300,000 hectares over three regions (Alsace, Lorraine and Franche-Comté) and four departments, which can sometimes cause difficulties as the level of protection differs from one administrative area to another.

The name "ballons" refers to the rounded summits of the mountains, smoothed by slow erosion. Most peaks are between 1000 and 1400 m high. The highest is the Grand Ballon (1424 m), the second the Hohneck (1363 m).

The climate is one of extremes; influenced both by Atlantic weather from the west and continental from the east. The area around Mount Ventron, which is high enough to stop the clouds coming from the west, is the rainiest in France, with some 2300 mm of precipitation a year. Yet the average rainfall of Colmar is only 500 mm. The average temperature of Altenberg, just east of the Schlucht pass, is only 6.1° C but over much of the region the weather is hot and sunny in summer and cold in winter. Spring and autumn are unpredictable but are usually sunny.

Site i.

Many of the higher peaks can be seen from the famous **ROUTE DES CRÊTES** (Ridge Road) which runs north to south for some 80 km through the Park, crosses several passes, goes through forest for almost half its length and skirts some peat-bog Nature Reserves. Although primarily a scenic route, the road passes through a variety of good habitats and anyone with sufficient time (it will take most of a day, with birding stops) should drive it, stopping and walking wherever looks most promising for birds. Apart from the very high-mountain species, most of the birds listed below for site ii the Hohneck should be seen.

Note: the Route is generally closed by snow from November 15 to March 15 between the Hohneck and the Grand Ballon because it is used for ski de fond. Chains may be needed for the parts that are open.

ACCESS: The Route starts at the Col du Bonhomme, 30 km west of Colmar via the N415 through Kayserberg. At the Col turn south onto the D148 to the Col du Calvaire and turn right towards the Coll de la Schlucht (1135 m). On the way you will pass the Gazon de Faing (1303m). This area is a nature reserve, of botanical interest mainly, although **Water Pipit** and **Northern Wheatear** may be found on the open grassland and **Citril Finch** and **Hazel Grouse** have been seen from the path leading south of Lac Noir. It will take about an hour to climb up.

Back on the road, continue to the *Col de la Schlucht*, cross the main D417 (turn right, then left) and continue south on the D430 for 4 km to the Hohneck (site ii below). Having spent some time at this site, if you wish to continue down the *Route des Crêtes,* keep on the D430 south. Stop at the Parking *de la Duchesse* and explore the area around here. If the road is blocked by snow it may be worth walking from the Hohneck parking as this is a good area in winter. It is under 2 km. For another walk, park at the *Auberge de Breitsouze* and take the footpath in the direction of the *Ferme-auberge du Kastelberg* where you follow the footpath towards Kerbholz (waymarked with yellow crosses) and down to the Fishboedlé lake. From here it is possible to continue to Schiessrothried lake (see site below) and up to the Hohneck or retrace your steps.

Back on the *Route des crêtes* continue south to the ski station at Markstein, then take the D431 continuing south past the Grand Ballon, To walk to the summit, the highest point of the Vosges, leave the car by the hotel and follow the footpath to the left. It will take about 1 hour in all. The Route continues down to Cernay and the N83.

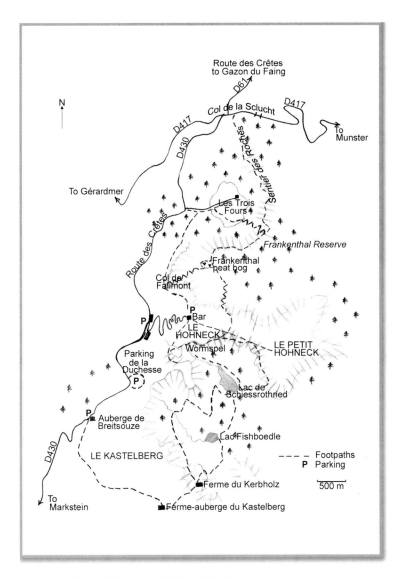

East area 5 sites I and ii Route dees Crêtes and the Hohneck

THE HOHNECK, at 1363 m. the second highest peak in the Vosges, is an excellent site for alpine species, although some are few in number and <u>may take hours of walking and a great deal of searching for.</u>   From the summit can be seen the jagged Frankenthal cirque to the north and the gentler Wormspel cirque to the south. The main habitats are Beech and Fir forests, subalpine meadows and at the highest altitudes, rocky scree.

In the sub-alpine meadows **Sky Lark, Meadow** and **Water Pipits** can be found, **Black Redstart, Northern Wheatear** and **Grey Wagtail** in the rockier zones and **Rock Bunting** (scarce) among the scree on the south-facing slopes of the Wormspel *cirque*. **Raven** and **Peregrine** may be seen above the ridges.

The conifer/beech forests below the peaks hold the expected high-altitude species: **Black Woodpecker, Crossbill and Crested Tit, Goldcrest** and **Firecrest, Nutcracker** (with a little luck) and with even more, **Hazel Grouse. Capercaillie** have been declining at an alarming rate (24% in six years). Both **Common** and **Short-toed Treecreeper** are here. Where the trees thin out at the edges of alpine meadows, **Citril Finch** (at the extreme north of its range) and **Ring Ouzel** can be found. One or two pairs of **Alpine Accentors** have been seen around the Falimont pass and occasionally both **Alpine Swift** and **Crag Martin** fly over the ridges, usually in May-June. **Rock Thrush** (very rare) occurs on the top of the Frankenthal. **Snow Finch** is regularly noted on the meadows near Kastelberg in winter and recently **Common Rosefinch** has been seen on the Frankenthal peat-bog. A few **Tengmalm's Owls** breed in the forests, occupying old Black Woodpecker holes, but are very difficult to find (see note on this species at end of book) and **Pygmy Owl** has been sighted near Machais. **Dippers** will be found in fast-flowing rivers and **Red-backed Shrike** on tall bushes and briars near woodland edges.

ACCESS: Map: IGN 1/25000 no. 3618 OT Col de la Schlucht is advisable if walking any distance. The whole circuit may take most of a day.

Take the D430, the *Route des Crêtes*, from its junction with the D417 at the Col de la Schlucht for 4 km. Park in the carpark beside the Refuge Restaurants and follow the footpath signed to the left to the summit. In fact, it is possible to drive up this very steep track once the snow is cleared. The path leads through some open areas. From the summit, if you want a fairly strenuous walk, join the GR 5 footpath (marked by red rectangles) down the Wormspel cirque to Schiessrothried lake. From there take the Schaeferthal pass back to the summit of the Hohneck or continue down towards the Frankenthal peat bog. At the bottom of the cirque, climb up to the Falimont pass then back towards the Hohneck along the névé footpath.

Some of the footpaths through the **FRANKENTHAL RESERVE,** which lies between the Hohneck and the Col de la Schlucht west of the D430 can be reached from the D417 and this is an option if snow or bad weather make the Hohneck impassable. ACCESS: 9 km from the Orbey/Col de Wettstein junction (6 km west of Munster) and 3 km from the Col de la Schlucht, there is a parking space on the north side of the road with a plan of the reserve and footpaths leading north and south - the latter from 800 m up the road. They lead through good forest for some way. You may not need to walk very far. The clearing beyond the parking might even prove productive; there is **Black Woodpecker** here.

Other fauna and flora: Chamois can often be seen on the slopes of the Wormspel cirque, especially late afternoon. They were introduced to the region in 1956. Red and Roe Deer, Wild Boar and Martens are found in the forest. The abundance of wild ungulates made the Park suitable for the reintroduction of the Lynx in 1983. Northern Bat has been discovered here quite recently. The only other French site is at Bretolet pass in the Alps.

The areas of open grassland, kept that way by grazing, are known as "chaumes" and retain the relics of a boreal-arctic vegetation, while the peat-bogs formed in the glacial cirques have a remarkably rich flora. The alpine meadows have an interesting flora in spring, with Pink Globe Orchid *Traunsteinera* globosa at the northern limit of its French range. In summer the most characteristic plants are perhaps the Great Yellow Gentians *Gentiana lutea* and the small *Viola lutea or Pensée des Vosges; Andromeda,* four species of *Vaccinium* and Sundew can be found in the peat-bogs.

Area 6. **MULHOUSE AREA**

Site i.

The **RHINE ISLANDS RESERVE** (*Réserve Naturelle des Îles du Rhin*), some 20 km south of Mulhouse and close to the Basel-Mulhouse airport, lies between the Grand Canal and the River Rhine. Much of the large island is wooded and good for breeding woodland species such as **Nightingale, Black Kite,** 6 species of **woodpecker** including **Grey-headed** and **Middle Spotted, tits, warblers** and **Golden Oriole.** There are small gravel and rocky islets in the River Rhine, which attract waders on migration; a time when **Osprey** can also be found here.

Winter is probably the best birding season, as the Rhine does not freeze and the nearby hydro-electricity station warms the water so large numbers and species of duck can be seen near the island: **Teal, Mallard, Pintail, Wigeon, Pochard, Tufted Duck, Goldeneye, Goosander** and in very cold spells, **Long-tailed Duck** and **Eider, divers and Red-necked** and **Slavonian Grebes. Cormorants** can be seen all through the year but their numbers increase in winter, as can **Little** and **Crested Grebes, Mute Swan. Kingfishers** are easier to see in winter.

ACCESS: Take the A35, either south from MULHOUSE or north from the Swiss frontier and leave it at the ROSENAU exit, going east. It is 0.9 km to LA CHAUSSÉE and the junction with the N66. Continue straight on at this crossroad and again straight on at the crossroads in ROSENAU village, following the signs for the *Complexe sportive* (do not turn onto the D21A or take the no-through road on the left). At the roundabout turn left (north) for KEMBS. In about 100 metres there is a small car park on the right by the canal and a bridge from where you can climb the bank to see the river. In fact there are several places to stop along this road but the main entrance to the Reserve is at the E.D.F. hydro-electricity works at KEMBS- LOECHLÉ, 2.7 km from the Rosenau roundabout.

At the roundabout with the propeller take the road signed to *Usine Hydraulique, E.D.F. and Isle du Rhin.* Park and the left just before the first sluice and scan the water. At the electricity station follow the road left across the first set of sluices to park again on the grass and look at the river, especially at the bend of the small island, which always seems to have a good concentration of birds. Continue over the canal lock to the small car-park. There is a short circuit around the northern part of the island, which will take about 2 hours, but to walk the complete 12 km circuit will take some 6 hours, even without birding stops. Most birds can be seen from this part of the reserve.

Continue left down the track, which is hard-surfaced for some 300 metres and then becomes a wide gravel track for about 500 metres. Park where it widens out. From here one can look for birds on both the River Rhine and the Canal or walk through the woods on the *circuit jaune* (yellow arrows) following the *sentier de découverte*. The thick, tangled riverine woodland is good for many woodland species.

Site ii.

LA HARTH FOREST covers a huge area north and south of Mulhouse. It is classified as an IBA on account of the raptors and woodpeckers that breed there. These include **Honey Buzzard, Black Kite,** a few **Red Kite, Black** and **Middle Spotted Woodpeckers** (the latter species quite common). Intensive forestry practices and road construction are lessening the site's interest but anyone in the area, visiting the Mulhouse sites, would find it worthwhile to spend some time in the forest, driving along the minor roads, stopping and walking a short distance away from the road wherever the habitat appears suitable.

On their website, LPO Alsace suggest the area around the villages of RIXHEIM AND HABSHEIM, just south of Mulhouse, as one of the best birding areas in Alsace. A variety of habitats and traditional agriculture allows species such as **Little Owl**, **Wryneck**, **Stonechat** and both **Woodchat** and **Red-backed Shrike** to breed. As this area can be easily reached from the southern part of La Harth Forest, it is included in this site.

WHEN TO VISIT: Rixheim Is a spring site and La Harth best in late spring although it is easier to find woodpeckers earlier in the year.

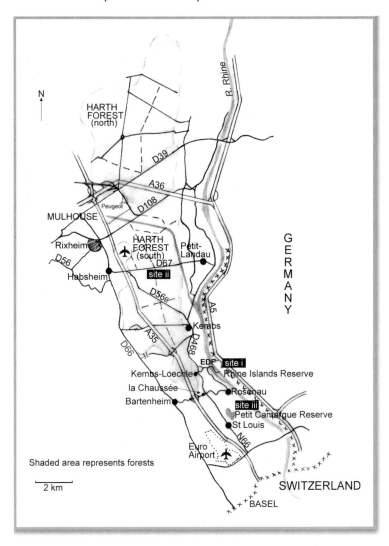

East area 6 Mulhouse sites i - iii

ACCESS: La Harth lies between the A35 motorway and the D468, which runs roughly parallel to the River Rhine. From the D468 north of KEMBS (see site above) take any of the very minor D roads running west through the forest. Stop at the crossroads in the centre and walk along some of the forestry tracks.

HABSHEIM can be reached by taking either the D56 or D57 across the forest from KEMBS, which cross the A35 motorway just by exit 3. From Habsheim take the D56 north towards RIXHEIM and Mulhouse, through the villages of Eschentzwiller and Zimmersheim and explore any of the agricultural tracks leading off alongside fields and woodland.

Site iii.

The **PETIT CAMARGUE ALSACIENNE RESERVE** lies south of ROSENAU, in the areas known as Three Frontiers, right on the French, Swiss, German borders. It is a wetland reserve, as it name suggests, formed on an old bed of the Rhine and its alluvial deposits and underground streams from the Jura which rise here. The pure water has been used for fish farming for over 150 years.

WHEN TO VISIT: A year-round site. Besides a rich wetland flora, 200 plus bird species have been recorded at the Petit Camargue, of which almost 100 breed there. **Nightingales** are abundant in woodland during the breeding season and six woodpecker species, including **Grey-headed** and **Wryneck**, occur. The reedbeds hold **Grasshopper, Savi's** and **Reed Warblers, Penduline Tit** can be seen in autumn; **Water Rail, Snipe, White Stork** and, more rarely, Black, are among passage visitors. In winter duck species are numerous; in the Reserve and the nearby river Rhine, many thousand of waterbirds congregate and there is a Black-headed Gull roost. Besides thousands of **Coot,** the majority of duck species are **Mallard, Pochard** and **Tufted Duck** but, as elsewhere in Alsace, rarities turn up.

ACCESS: The Reserve is signed from the N66 crossroads at LA CHAUSSÉE, just east of the A35 motorway. Turn south here and in 3.3 km, turn left in the village of ST. LOUIS. In 200 metres there is a large notice board with a plan of the Reserve on the left. Just beyond it, on the right, is a large car-park for the sports centre

A footpath leads from the notice-board to the Maison de la Réserve by the fish-farm (*pisiculture*) and continues to make three circuits (one botanical) past reed-beds, trees, arable land, marsh and lakes. The most productive *Grand Circuit,* with a hide overlooking reedbeds, is closed from 15/03 to 01/07 to protect breeding birds. It may be wise to phone 03 89 89 78 59/58 (or 03 89 69 08 47) if making a special visit, to check what can be seen.

Other fauna and flora: Roe Deer, Wild Boar, Badger, Common Dormouse and Harvest Mouse are among the mammals recorded. Plants include Grass of Parnassus, Greater Bladderwort, *Iris sibirica*, White Water-lily and seven orchid species, including Marsh Helleborine, Green-winged, Bee, Late and Early Spider Orchids.

Site iv.

MICHELBACH LAKE, at the foot of the Vosges mountains, some 20 km west of Mulhouse, is a comparatively recent man-made stretch of water, formed by the large Michelbach Dam, which affords the best birding viewpoints. No leisure activities are allowed on the lake, which ensures that birds are relatively undisturbed.

WHEN TO VISIT: Again, this is essentially a winter site for duck and grebe species, though many **waders** and **Osprey** stop off here on passage and **Marsh, Montagu's** and **Hen Harriers** can be seen around the lake. **Great White Egret** regularly turn up in winter and rafts have been erected to encourage **Common Tern** and **Little Ringed Plover** to breed. The nearby woods are good for many passerine species, notably **Bramling** in winter.

Birdline Alsace rates Michelbach as the second most important site in Alsace for rarities. *ACCESS*: Take the A36 motorway southwest from MULHOUSE and leave it at exit 15 (just before the péage or toll-booths), signed BELFORT by RN. Zero here. Turn right (north) onto the N466 for 2 km and then turn off following the direction of MASEVAUX. In another kilometre at the roundabout, turn right, still following signs for MASEVAUX, onto the D466. After 4.2 km in GUEWENHEIM turn right onto the D34 towards MICHELBAD. 8.5 km from the motorway exit, turn right to the village, which is just over 10 km from the exit.

There is a small car park on the right near the beginning of the village, from where one can walk to a 250 metre length of embankment which gives views over the east end of the lake. However, better views and most birds are found at the southwest end, from the large dam. At 10.7 km fork right, signed Barrage and Parking in 700 metres. Drive through the beechwoods (or stop to do some birding there). Park beside the dam and walk along it. There is a plan of the lake, showing footpaths and some information on bird species.

Other fauna: Beavers have been seen in the River Doller, south of the lake.

Area 7. THE JURA - BESANÇON AND DOLE AREAS

The first two sites in this area are along the RIVER DOUBS between Besançon and Dole. The River Doubs follows a strange inverted "u" course, rising southeast of Pontarlier, then flowing north for over one hundred kilometres, forming the French-Swiss border in places, before looping round west and south to Besançon. The slow-flowing stretch of the river south of Dole is listed as an IBA as the surrounding habitats of riverine woodland, marshes, wet meadows and sandbanks support some interesting species. A colony of **Bluethroat,** perhaps 80 pairs, breed here as do some 50 pairs of **Night Heron** with a few **Little Bittern** and **Purple Heron. Marsh, Hen** and **Montagu's Harriers** occur in small numbers as well as **Black Kite.** A few **Corncrake** breed in the wet meadows. Other species likely to be seen include **Little Egret, Buzzard, Kingfisher, Little Ringed Plover, Bee-eater, Nightingale, Golden Oriole,** several tit species including **Willow Tit, Cetti's, Grasshopper, Savi's, Reed, Sedge, Icterine** and **Melodious Warblers, Red-backed Shrike, Serin, Corn** and **Cirl Buntings. Osprey, waders** and **marsh tern** may occur on passage. There are also many waterbirds in winter.

WHEN TO VISIT: As most of these species are summer visitors, April to August are the best months.

The first two sites below should produce many of the species listed above but any part of the river with access is worth exploring if you have time.

Site i.

The **ILE DU GIRARD RESERVE** is an island formed between an old meander of the Doubs, the "Vieux Doubs", and the present river, just at its confluence with the River Loue, some 8 km south of Dole. The Reserve was created to protect its bird life, especially the colony of breeding **Bluethroats,** but it must be said that access to it is not easy and parts are very overgrown - or perhaps this is deliberate and the birds prefer it this way!

WHEN TO VISIT: Spring and early summer (end April-early June) are best though early autumn (end August-September) is fairly good

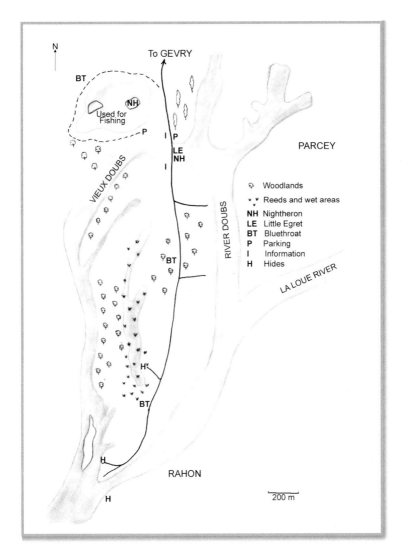

East area 7 site 1

ACCESS: Take the A39 southeast from its junction with the A36 for 7.5 km. Leave at exit 6 for DOLE but at the junction with the N5, take the N73 towards SEURRE for 2 km. Immediately after you have gone under the A39 and just before you reach the airfield, turn left (south) onto the N5 to GEVRY. In about kilometre, turn right into the village. At the first fork go right following the sign *Reserve Naturelle*. By the church, fork left and in 250 metres turn right (both these turnings are signed to the Reserve but then the signs run out). In 600 metres there is a football pitch, go past it and take the left fork. 300 metres on there is a lake on the left, which can be good for birds.

Take the left fork again for I km until you see another lake on the right. There is a notice board with a plan of the Reserve directly ahead and space to park on the right. The total distance is 2 km from Gevry village and 2.8 from the N5 junction.

Before going into the Reserve, it is worth first walking around the lake on the right, which belongs to the Parish of Gevry. Many of the same species can be found here as in the reserve proper, though there is more disturbance as it is popular with local fishermen. Follow the grass footpath around the water. Herons can be seen here, especially **Night Heron** and the bushes beside the grass path are good for **Bluethroat** (see notes under "Special Species" at end). Woodland species can be found in the trees.

To reach the reserve, take the gravel track that leads down on the left, 20 metres before the plan of the Reserve. Take the right fork, which leads to another notice board after crossing an embankment with water both sides. This is another good viewpoint for **Little Egret, Night Heron** and other water birds. The track continues for another 2 km through a series of gateways and should lead to a couple of hides. In summer 2001 it was so overgrown at the confluence end that it was impossible to see the river.

Another view of the confluence can be had from tracks leading from the village of RAHON but there are no signs and it is rather "hit or miss" to find the right part of the river, though the surrounding farmland can be quite productive.

However, if you want to try, return to GEVRY and continue south on the N5, through the village of PARCEY to its junction with the D475, about 8 km. Take this road but almost immediately turn right (west) to RAHON. At the end of this straggling village take the C4, direction MOLAY in 50 metres turn right and in 400 metres fork right onto the Chemin d'Isle. This sounds promising but when you reach the river in 2.3 km, it is difficult to know which track to take. A small track leads off left, leading to a riverside track. It may be worth walking along this for some time in either direction. The trees along the riverbank are good for passerines and there are glimpses of sandbanks and the opposite bank between them.

Other fauna and flora: Roe Deer, Wild Boar and Beech Marten occur on the Reserve. There are some interesting water plants including, at the south of the island, Flowering Rush and Frogbit

Site ii.
The village of **PETIT-NOIR** lies about 15 km downstream from Gevry. There is an old meander of the Doubs here, covered with water-lilies and with a good reedbed, so many of the species listed above can be found there.

ACCESS: Petit-Noir can be reached by minor country roads from RAHON. Take the D46 through St. Baraing to CHAUSSIN, then the D11 to LONGWY and the D13 to Petit-Noir. Otherwise return to the N73, head south-west in the direction of Seurre and turn off at BEAUCHEMIN. *The Rue de Saulois* at the west end of the village leads past some modern house to the *Vieux Doubs*. You can park on the grass beside this reed-covered stretch of water and watch from here or walk down a *Rue Privée* that runs alongside it.

Another stretch of the Doubs can be reached by continuing on the D13 south of the village to where a bridge crosses the river. There is parking on the far bank.

Site iii.
CHAUX FOREST is the second largest in France and has been called "the unending forest". Mainly a beech/oak deciduous forest, with small strands of conifers, several streams cross it forming some wet areas. Finding the **Black** and **Red Kites, Honey Buzzards, Black, Grey-headed** and **Middle Spotted Woodpeckers** that breed there, to say nothing of tits and other woodland passerines, is rather a "needle in a

haystack" search. However, the D31 runs through the east side of the forest with parking areas and forestry tracks leading off from it. There are also some well-marked footpaths leading from the village of ETRÉPIGNEY through a small area of the northern part of the forest and even a short circuit should enable you to see or hear a good number of species.

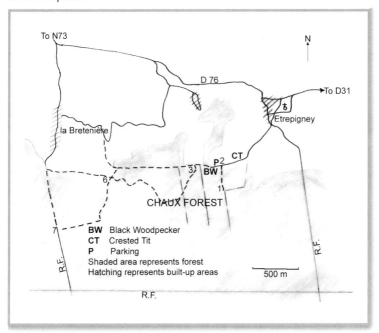

East area 7 site iii Chaux Forest north

WHEN TO VISIT: Late spring is the best season for raptors but woodpeckers are easier to hear and spot earlier, in February and March. Avoid walking in the forest on Thursdays and Sundays from mid-October to February as these are the days when there is shooting. The paths can be muddy after rain.

ACCESS: If travelling on the A36 to or from BESANÇON, leave at exit 2.1 and take the D36 to RANS. Turn right at the crossroads and follow the signs to ETRÉPIGNEY, under 2 km west. From the A39, leave at Dole by exit 6 and take the N73 eastwards round DOLE in the direction of BESANÇON to the village of ORCHAMPS, 13 north-east of Dole, and from there follow the D76 south for 2 km to ETRÉPIGNEY.

From the church at Etrépigney follow the signs *Sentier du Guepier* (<u>Note</u>: the brown signs are not always easy to spot. The first is on a pole by the church) for just over a kilometre up the Rue de l'Eglise, through the village and along a lane to a parking space on the edge of the forest, beside number 2 of the marked trail. There is a notice board by the carpark showing all the trails. The footpath leads off into the forest at number 3, some 300 metres further up the lane. There is a strand of conifers just before the parking. Try here for **Goldcrest** and **Crested Tit**. **Black Woodpecker** has been heard calling near the parking area. The shortest circuit, marked by white and green circular arrows, is about 3.5 km long if you turn back at 6 or you can extend it by continuing to 7 before turning back and so make a longer walk of about twice the distance. A booklet on the nature trail can be bought from the Restaurant La Dolulonne in Etrépigney and Baraque du 14 at Vielle Loye.

If travelling through the forest from south to north on the D31, turn off at the first forestry road leading west to the parking signed 300 metres down it. This is as far as you can drive. **Middle** and **Lesser Spotted Woodpeckers** are around this area as well as plenty of small passerines, including **Willow Tit.** Walk down the road as far as you wish.

Continuing north, turn off at the next main forestry road towards *La Vielle Loye -* Baraques du 14. **Black Woodpecker** has been heard on the left in the *Reserve Biologique* near the wooden hut just before an open area of new growth on the right. This is a good area to look for raptors. Turn off at the crossroads towards ETRÉPIGNEY. There is a plantation of conifers near the crossroads and it is worth walking around the open space, searching the sky for raptors and checking the edges of the forest.

Other fauna and flora: Red and Roe Deer, Wild Boar, Badgers, Wild Cat, Martens are the larger mammals to be found in Chaux. Amphibians and reptiles include Salamander, Yellow-bellied Toad, Common Frog and Slow-worm. Royal Fern *Osmunda regalis* grows in damp hollows and a strange but magnificent toadstool *Clathrus archeri* (=*Anthurus archeri*) whose spores arrived in wool from Australia during the 1914-18 war has spread throughout the forest. It looks a little like an octopus, red spotted with black and belongs to the same order as the strinkhorns and has an equally evil smell.

Site iv.

THE SERRE MASSIF is a wooded granite outcrop to the north of the Doubs valley, 400 m in height. Most of the 4000 hectares of woodland is beech/oak, with an area of Sweet Chestnut and some conifer plantations. The bird list includes breeding **Honey Buzzard, Goshawk, Black** and **Red Kites, Black** and **Middle Spotted Woodpeckers, Golden Oriole** and all the woodland tits including Crested round the conifers. **Nightjars** can be heard at dusk in the clearings. On the forest edges, **Melodious Warbler, Cirl Bunting, Red-backed Shrike** and **Woodlark** (rare in this area) may be found.

WHEN TO VISIT: As for other forest sites in this area (see site iii above).

ACCESS: Either: Leave the Dole-Besancon N73 at ROCHEFORT-SUR-NEVERS, and turn north onto the D10 for 4 km to the village of AMANGE. In the centre of the village, opposite the school, the start of the *Loup-Garou* footpath is signed. It starts 100 metres further on, by the village hall and is marked in sky-blue. There are various information boards along the 4.5 km path, on geology, plants, etc.

To get deeper into the forest, take the D37 than runs north-west through the forest to the village of MOISSEY, 6.5 km away on the D475. Halfway along, turn right (north-east) onto the very minor road that leads to SALIGNEY, stopping and walking wherever the habitat seems suitable.

Site v.

BAUME-LES-MESSIEURS is a well-known beauty-spot near Lons-le-Saunier, some 15 km south of Dole. It is a karstic formation of steep, wooded slopes, rocky scree, towering cliffs and caves, with a more Mediterranean-type climate. For birders, its interest lies in the species found there, some otherwise difficult to see in the Jura, which include **Peregrine, Red** and **Black Kites, Crag Martin, Alpine Swift, Dipper, Bonelli's Warbler, Raven** and **Rock Bunting.**

It is possible to climb up from the village of Baume-les-Messieurs to the top of the cliffs and walk along them before scrambling down near the caves - *Grottes de Baume*. (Park in the village by the abbey and follow the arrows "le Dard".) However the climb up and down is steep and strenuous and birders should see just as many species, especially martins and swifts, by looking up from the foot of the cliffs and then walking for a short way into the woods.

WHEN TO VISIT: Spring or early autumn. There are a great many visitors in summer. *ACCESS:* From LONS-LE-SAUNIER, easily reached by exits 7 or 8 from the A39, take the D471 towards CHAMPAGNOLE for 8 km, then turn off onto the minor road signed to the *Grottes* and *Roches de Baume*. There is an excellent view from here by the *Belvédère*. The road turns back right to rejoin the D471 or continues left towards Sermu where there is parking. The GR 59 footpath circles the cliffs and from near the viewpoint leads into the woods. Follow it for as far as you wish. The D70E from Baume-les-Messiers also affords some good viewpoints both over the cliffs and the River Dard.

Area 8. THE JURA - PONTARLIER AREA

Site i.

The beech/fir forests on the slopes of **MONT D'OR** (1463 m) and the nearby Risol Forest are IBAs for forest birds. **Hazel Grouse, Capercaillie. Woodcock, Nutcracker, Black Woodpecker, Common Treecreeper, Wood** and **Bonelli's Warblers, Siskin** and **Crossbill** are all found here in reasonable numbers and it is one of the rare sites in northern France where **Pygmy Owl** breed (only about 10 pairs over a very large area) as well as **Tengmalm's Owl. Ring Ouzel, Citril Finch** and **Fieldfare** can be found, where the trees thin out as forest gives way to meadows and in the highest areas of open subalpine grassland **Skylark, Water Pipit** and **Northern Wheatear** can be found in summer. A 200 m high cliff, with rocks and scree at its foot, runs along the east side of the massif, a breeding site for **Peregrine, Raven**, a few **Crag Martin** and possibly **Wallcreeper.**

WHEN TO VISIT: Late spring or early summer is best for forest birds though Nutcracker rarely call between mid-March to August. **Tengmalm's Owls** call only March-May, normally just as it is dark, very rarely in daytime. Late August-September is another period when Nutcrackers are noisy again and many young birds are around.

ACCESS: Take the N57 south from PONTARLIER towards the Swiss frontier for 10 km and zero when the D45 turns off right just before LES HÔPITAUX-VIEUX. Follow the signs for LES LONGEVILLES MONT D'OR. Drive through the village and at 6.6 km turn left on a narrow (but hard surfaced) lane which leads towards the summit, signed Mont d'Or. Follow the sign to the Bar Chalet la Grangette 3 km, which you will see on a bend. This road leads through spruce/fir forest with many grassy clearings. It is usually drivable even in winter, unless there is very heavy snow. Park at 8.9 and walk along the forest tracks. **Nutcracker** and **Black Woodpecker** have been heard here. Walk up the road (or drive) towards La Grangette. Eventually the forest gives way to open meadows with signs for skiers pointing to the summit and Métabief. The road leads past la Grangette for another 1 km to a parking place near the summit. From here it is possible to take a circular walk to the highest point of Mont d'Or and then follow the ridge northwards as far as the *Belvédère des Chamois* (Chamois viewpoint) returning through the alpine meadows.

Other fauna and flora: The open grassland and the forest edges have a subalpine/woodland flora lasting well into the summer: Great Yellow Gentian, Martagon Lily, Alpine Sow Thistle, Dark-Red and Narrow-lipped Helleborines. Butterflies are numerous: Apollo, Clouded Yellow, Silver-washed and High Brown Fritillaries.

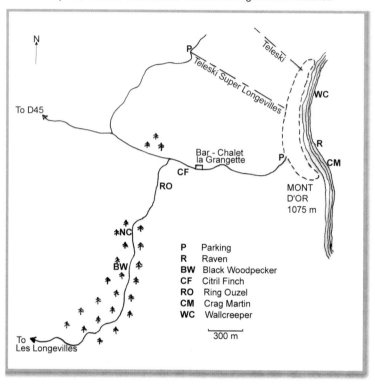

East area 8 site i Mont d'Or

<u>Accommodation</u>: This is a tourist area both winter and summer. There are a number of hotels in Pontarlier and around the Mont d'Or/Métabief ski slopes in Longevilles-Mont d'Or, Labergement Ste-Marie and nearby villages. Summer only, there is a very pleasant campsite right beside Remoray Lake

<u>Site ii.</u>
LAKE REMORAY RESERVE is similar to Frasne (site iii), being a lake and peat-bog, with the eastern part of Grand-Côte forest included in the Reserve. Remoray is a high altitude lake, lying at an altitude of 850 m, surrounded by higher peaks and is split into three areas; the largest, further one being best for birds. Swimming is allowed in summer and a limited number of small boats are on hire for fishing. There is a footpath around the left-hand lake, which gives good views over the larger one and a small hide overlooks the smallest stretch of water.

The adjoining, larger lake of Saint-Point is too much used for water sports to be of much interest but the river and marshy areas linking the two can be very productive.

There is a **Grey Heron** colony at an altitude of 920 m, the second highest in France, in Grand-Côte forest, so **Grey Herons** are numerous around the lake. **Black Woodpeckers** also breed in the forest. **Black** and **Red Kite, Montagu's, Marsh** and **Hen Harriers** and **Hobby** may be seen hunting over the marsh. As at Frasne, **Redpoll** and **Fieldfare** breed at the edge of the peat-bog and **Little Ringed Plover** on the sandbanks. In total, some 180 species have been counted in the area, and some 80 breed, including **Water Rail, Coot, Great** and **Little Grebes, Marsh Warbler, Reed Bunting** and irregularly, **Spotted Crake.** Many waders stop off on the lakeshore during both spring and autumn passage. In winter duck species, for long or shorter stays, may include **Tufted Duck, Goldeneye, Smew, Goosander** and even **Scaup,** with more species on passage. **Curlew** used to breed here; they no longer do so though they still breed nearby, along the Doubs valley and the D9 towards Frasne.

WHEN TO VISIT: Spring (March - May) and autumn (late August - October) are best but there is something of interest all year round, although there is disturbance in summer and the lake is not worth a special journey in winter although well worth visiting if in the area.

If it is open, visit the *Maison de la Réserve* which is situated in an old factory on the outskirts of Labergement-Sainte-Marie on the D437 going northeast. Do not be put off by the rather shabby exterior. Inside there is a good exhibition on the fauna of the areas and helpful staff. Ask what birds are about and the best areas to visit. They organise weekly guided visits to the lake and other nearby areas. Open to the public between 14 - 18h every day in the holiday season, Sundays and bank holidays the rest of the year. Groups by appointment. Tel: 0381693599 Fax: 0381693428 e-mail: lac.remoray@espaces-naturels.fr

ACCESS: Lakes Remoray and St. Point lie alongside the D437 which runs south from Pontarlier, through Oye-et-Pallet and Malbuisson and joins the D45 at the village of GELLIN, south of the Reserve. Turn off to the lake in the centre of LABERGEMENT SAINTE MARIE down *Rue du Lac*, signed to *Base de Loisirs/Aire de Camping*. There is a carpark with an information board by the sports/leisure centre.

To reach the river and marsh between the two lakes take the road signed   *Rive Gauche* at the junction of the D437/D9 just north of Labergement village. Park just before the bridge, by the information boards. Cross the bridge, which gives good views up and down river and then walk right along the D129, the *Rive gauche* of St. Point, on the grass verge for a kilometre or so until the marshy areas and reedbeds give way to the lake proper.

If you turn left after the bridge (by a café), the D46 runs between the Reserve and the edge of Grand-Côte forest. Forestry roads allow you to make a circuit of the forest.
Flora: There is a rich peat-bog flora, which includes Bog Rosemary *Andromeda polifolia,* Cranberry *Vaccinium oxycoccus,* Cowberry *Vaccinium vitis-idaea,* Sundew *Drosera rotundifolia,* Grass of Parnassus *Parnassia palustris,* Great Spearwort *Ranunculus lingua* and *Senecio helenitis*

Site iii.
FRASNE NATURE RESERVE forms part of an IBA, important for wet meadow and forest birds. **Hazel Grouse, Capercaillie** and **Black Kite** breed in the forest to the south of the lake, where **Crossbills** and **Crested Tit** are found in the conifers and both **Woodcock** and **Nightjar** can be heard in the clearings at dusk in late spring. A very few pairs of **Corncrake** and **Spotted Crake** breed irregularly in the water-meadows surrounding the lake; **Redpoll** breed in the birches by the peat-bog and **Fieldfare** in the spruces. **Northern Grey Shrike** may be seen summer and winter. In winter **Smew, Goldeneye** and **Goosander** may be among the wintering **Pochard,** resident **Mute Swan, Coot** and **Great Crested Grebe.**

In April - May and August-September the lake fills up with **grebes, duck** (including **Red-crested Pochard** and **Garganey**), marsh terns **(Black, White-winged Black and Whiskered)** and many species of waders **(Curlew, Godwit, Lapwing, Snipe, plovers, stints)** on passage. This is also the best period for raptors **(harriers, kites, Osprey, Hobby).**

WHEN TO VISIT: Spring or autumn are the best periods though cold spells in winter may be interesting.

ACCESS: If you have visited Lakes Remoray and St. Point first, take the D9 over the bridge between the two lakes. In 11 km you will reach the village of BONNEVAUX. Zero at the junction D9/D47. At 3.5 km there is a map and picnic site (*de Forbonet*). Signed footpaths lead to the peat-bog (*depart Tourbières*) through the forest. Eventually you will arrive at Frasne lake but it may be better to walk as far as you wish through the forest and then return to the picnic area before driving on as described below.

Continuing along the D9, you will see the larger lake on the left. As this is used for fishing and boating, there is disturbance and not usually many birds although it is worth checking it out wherever there is a view. At 5.0 km you will see a small hillock on the right. Walk over the cattle grid by the red sign to the summit from where there is a good view over the eastern part of Frasne lake. At 5.7 km a wooden hut gives another view over the west side. Just beyond the hut and before Frasne village, an unmarked track leads towards a saw-mill. Turn right at the woodyard, then take the right fork to the lake. The birches and shrubs here are good for passerines. **Crested Tit** can be found in the conifers further on. The left hand fork leads to another lake but this is fished and usually birdless.

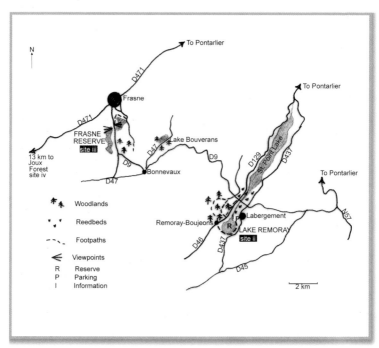

East area 8 sites ii and iii Remoray and Frasne Reserves

From PONTARLIER, go east on the D72, then the D471 for 19km to FRASNE village. At the end of the village turn left (south) onto the D9. Very soon you will see the wooden hut and then the small hillock of the left. (See instructions above).

Some 3 km to the southeast of Frasne Lake is **BOUVERANS LAKE,** where many of the species listed above may also be seen. If you have time it is worth checking it out.

ACCESS: From BONNEVAUX turn north-east onto the D47 in the direction of BOUVERANS. The road runs through woodland   and in 3 km you will see the lake on the left (north side of the road). To view the north side of the lake turn left just before the railway bridge down a narrow road running past the lakeside building,

Site iv.

JOUX FOREST covers a large area some 10 km due west of Frasne (about 14 km by road). It is one of the largest fir woods in France. As in most of the forests in this area, **Hazel Grouse** and **Black Woodpecker** breed, as well as conifer-loving species such as **Crested Tit** and **Crossbill. Tengmalm's Owl** is also found here, nesting in old Black Woodpecker holes. Although this owl is pictured on some of the nature trails in the forest, in fact it is very hard to see. It calls from March to May, normally just as it becomes dark, very occasionally at other times and rarely flies before nightfall. If you find a Black Woodpecker's pear-shaped hole in a tree, it is worth tapping the tree trunk to see if a head pops out! But a lot of luck is needed to see a Tengmalm's Owl, especially in a forest this size. **Hazel Grouse** are also very elusive (they favour the younger conifer plantations) but the other species should be heard and seen by making frequent stops along the route, and taking walks into the forest.

The "*Route des Sapins*" is a signed route through the forest, with well-marked footpaths leading off from it and plenty of parking and picnic areas. Parts may be difficult in winter as the snow is not cleared.

ACCESS: Continue south-east on the D471 from FRASNE, and in 9 km at CENSEAU turn right (north-west) onto the D107 following the signs "Andelot - Route des Sapins". Zero here. In 4.5 km turn right at the *Porte Marine,* a forestry road marked by decorated posts and a map. At 5.4 km you will see the *Reserve Biologique - la Glacière* on the right. A 1200 metre nature-trail, prominently featuring **Tengmalm's Owl,** leads off from the road at this point. It is worth walking the trail but do not be too hopeful. At 6.2 km the road swings left, follow the tarmacked road. The *Route des Sapins* leads to the *maison forestière du Chevreuil* at a clearing, with an arboretum in front. Several more marked walks, varying in length from 0.5 - 4 km in length, start from the left of the building. The itineraries are shown on a plan. Try trail 4, La Vessoye (marked in black) which leads to the *Sapin Président,* the tallest fir in the forest, 1500 m from the maison and then follow *Les Crêtes,* a circular trail around the fir, marked yellow. If you do not want to walk so far, continue driving along the Route des Sapins and you will eventually reach the *Sapin Président.* There are several viewpoints over the forest, either from the trails leading to or from the road near the *Sapin Président.* At 19.5km the *Route des Sapins* signs seem to disappear but two villages are marked. Turn left towards Villiers and then right and you should pick the route up again as it leads to finish near Levier. Alternatively, turn right to Boujailles, then take the D9 to Levier on the D72.

Other fauna: Roe Deer are common throughout Joux Forest. Chamois can be found on the open, rocky slopes near the *Sapin Président.*

Accommodation: There are very few hotels in the north of this area. If you finish the Route des Sapins at Porte Levier, there is a hotel/restaurant in Levier village on the D72 main road to Pontarlier, which is 22 km away to the east.

Area 9. THE HAUT-JURA AREA

Site i.

RISOUX FOREST, part of the Haut-Jura Natural Regional Park, is an important site for forest and mountain species: **Honey Buzzard** (a few), **Hazel Grouse, Capercaillie, Tengmalm's** and **Pygmy Owls** (at least 10 pairs of each, probably many more Tengmalm's), **Black Woodpecker, Ring Ouzel, Crested Tit** and **Crossbill.** Risoux covers over 4000 hectares at an altitude of 1000 - 1300 m. Only part of Risoux lies in France, the larger part is in Switzerland and is also a protected area.

WHEN TO VISIT: There are some cross-country ski and snow-shoe trails but most of this site is only accessible between June and October. Parts are quite steep.

ACCESS: From LES ROUSSES on the N5, take the minor D29E2 to BOIS D'AMONT. In spring or autumn, check the lake des Rousses on the way, as it can be good for passage migrants, both waders and raptors. At BOIS D'AMONT make for LE CRETET to the north-west, park beside the road and take the footpath marked in yellow and red that leads off steeply left at a right-angle to the road. In about 500 metres the path divides, the right-hand one leading to the Roche du Creux viewpoint, the left-hand path, after a hairpin bend, levels out for over 1 km towards a large clearing knows as Chaux-Sèche. There is always good birding on the forest edges round the clearing. Go past the Chalet de la Caserne on the far side of the clearing and continue through the forest towards the Chalet Gaillard. From here you can either returns the same way or join the forestry road des Essarts and then turn left onto the Route de Chaux Sèche which leads back through the clearing towards Les Combettes and Bois-d'Amont. The circuit is about 10 km in length and will take several hours. Map IGN 3327 ET is essential.

Site ii.

MASSACRE FOREST, a little further south, is smaller (under 2000 hectares) but is also an IBA and has a similar bird list, though there are fewer owls.

ACCESS: MASSACRE FOREST can be reached from the D 25, which runs along its western flank. Some narrow minor roads lead off east and twist up through the forest towards Crêt Pela (1495 m) the highest peak and then southwards towards LAJOUX. A long-distance footpath, the GR9, also runs through the forest. A walk into the forest in suitable habitat from anywhere along the minor roads could be productive. From LAJOUX it is easy to reach the COL DE LA FAUCILLE(see next site) via the D936.

Other flora and fauna: The Jura is noted for its flora, both alpine and woodland, which lasts from May until September. Soldanella, Gentiana verna and Anemone alpina appear on the alpine meadows as soon as the snow melts. Later in the season Martagon Lily, centauries, Yellow and Willow-leaved Gentians and Dark-red Helleborine can be found along the forest edges and clearings. Other woodland orchids include Bird's Nest and Narrow-lipped Helleborine with Small White and Black Vanilla in the grassland. Butterflies are numerous and include Apollo, Silver-washed and High Brown Fritillaries, Clouded Yellow, many blues.

Accommodation: See site iii.

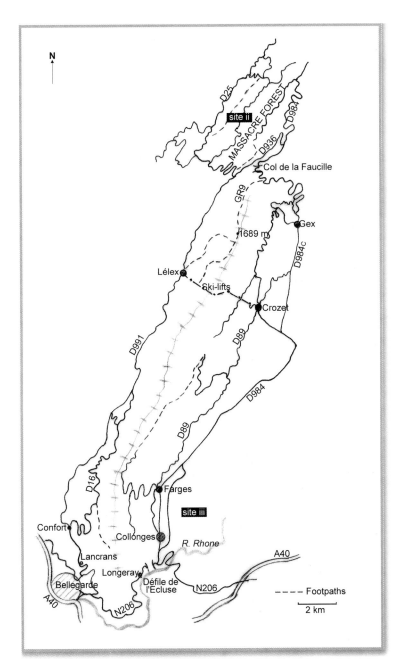

N

D25

site ii

MASSACRE FOREST

D936

D984

Col de la Faucille

GR9

1689 m

Gex

D984c

Lélex

Ski-lifts

Crozet

D991

D89

D984

D89

Farges

site iii

D16

R. Rhone

A40

Confort

Collonges

Lancrans

Longeray

Bellegarde

Défile de l'Ecluse

N206

A40

N206

---- Footpaths

2 km

East area 9 sites ii and iii The Haut-Jura Reserve

THE RÉSERVE NATURELLE DE LA HAUTE-CHAÎNE DU JURA runs south-west down the backbone of the range from the Swiss frontier below Dole mountain in the north to finish above the Rhone, west of Geneva, forming the boundary of the Lake Léman plain. The Reserve is broken in two by the ski installations of Lélex and Crozet. The D991 runs along the western side from Bellgarde in the south to become the D936 after MIJOUX and eventually join the D984, which follows the eastern side from Collonges, at the Col de la Faucille (1320 m) north of Gex.
From both these roads minor roads and forestry tracks lead up through parts of the forest

From the Col de la Faucille a GR footpath, ski and forestry tracks run south down the reserve.

Most of the slopes are heavily wooded and, like the other mountain forests in this area, hold breeding populations of **Hazel Grouse, Capercaillie,** as well as a few pairs of **Pygmy Owls,** with **Crossbills** and **Crested Tits** where there are conifers. Commoner woodland birds include six species of **Tit, Bonelli's Warbler, Jay, Mistle Thrush and Black Redstart.** The southern tip of the chain, where the River Rhône cuts through the Gorge de l'Ecluse, between Bellegarde and Collonges, is a migratory bottleneck where tens of thousands of **Black Kite, Honey Buzzard, Common Buzzards, White Storks, Cranes** and **finches** can be seen overhead in autumn. **Crag Martins** fly around the cliffs by the fort in summer and **Wallcreeper** has been seen there in winter.

This site at the southern end of the Jura is right on the (artificial) boundary between northern France, covered in this book, and France south of the Loire, covered in a previous volume. It is included again, to give more complete coverage of the Jura, as well as being the best and most accessible site in the area.

Capercaillie

WHEN TO VISIT: Late summer and autumn for migration. Late spring or early summer for woodland birds but tracks may be impassable until the end of May.
ACCESS: The southwest part of the reserve can be reached from the D991, which runs from BELLEGARDE through the village of LANCRANS to CONFORT. In the centre of this village turn right onto the D16 signed Menthières. This minor road climbs for 8 km to the Menthières ski station. In 7.2 km turn off onto the forestry track on the right by the sign for Menthières. Follow this road, taking the left fork, until it ends in a clearing where the GR yellow and red marking lead to the Crêt de la Goutte or

down to Menthières. Another little-used footpath, the *Sentier de Varambon* can be found leading up through the woods on the right some 100 metres past the road fork. It is steep and narrow but useful for getting deep into the forest. The right fork forestry road can only be used in summer but might be worth exploring.

The south-east slopes can be reached from the D89E, which runs north from COLLONGES to the next village of FARGES. In the centre of Farges there is a crossroads with one road leading to the D76A and the opposite one called the *Route de Col de Sac*. Take this road, keeping left and climbing up for 7.2 km to a mountain hut at PreBouillet (1045 m). The drivable road ends here but a GR footpath continues up to the top ridge.

The ECLUSE GORGE lies on the D984 east of BELLEGARDE. Two forts guard the narrowest part of the gorge. The lower fort is situated just below the tunnel east of LONGERAY village on the D984. A slip road leads off right just before the entrance to the tunnel if driving east from Bellegarde. There is parking by the entrance. The walls of both this fort and the higher one can be scanned from the entrance. To reach the higher fort, again if coming from the direction of Bellegarde, take a small "no through" road on the left at the entrance to the village of Longeray, called the *Route du Fort*.

It is possible to drive for about half a kilometre to a barred gate. From here it is a 20 minutes walk to the top fort through good oak woodland. The top fort is a good viewpoint from where to watch migrating birds.

Other fauna and flora: Woodland butterflies include Arran Brown, Great Banded Grayling, Black Satyr, Brown Argus and Purple Emperor. Apollo is found on the alpine meadows. Lynx has returned to the Haut Jura from reintroductions in Switzerland but they are unlikely to be seen. There are also Chamois on the highest peaks and Roe Deer in the forest.

<u>Accommodation</u>: This is a popular tourist area both winter and summer. There are hotels in Bellegarde and nearly all the villages mentioned, as well as the Col de la Faucille.

SOME SPECIAL SPECIES -
either birds that are rare in France or those that are frequently sought by British birders

Black-necked Grebe *Podiceps nigricollis.* Common in winter along the coast (especially in Brittany areas 1 and 4) and on passage, several hundred pairs of Black-necked Grebe also breed in northern France, in Nord-Pas-de-Calais (notably in the bassin des Thumeries), in the Sologne (South Central area 8) and Lorraine (East area 1). It is a very rare breeder in (or absent from) Normandy, Brittany, the Paris area and most of the mountainous parts of the east.

Fulmar *Fulmarus glacialis.* The Fulmar is a recent coloniser; the first birds breeding in the Sept-Îles in 1956. They were first noted in Picardie in 1972, started to breed there in 1979 and have continued to expand throughout Brittany, Normandy and along the Channel coast until there are now some 1350 pairs breeding (compared with 570,000 in the British Isles), a thousand of them in Normandy. Sites where they can be seen are les Sept-Îles (Brittany area 7), Brittany cliffs as far south as Belle Isle, Morbihan (area 2), many Normany cliffs and Cap Blanc-Nez, Pas-de-Calais (Channel Coast area 12). The colonies are occupied from January to August. Breeding starts in May; young birds can be seen in the nest sites during July and August and birds can be seen out at sea in every month of the year except October.

Balearic Shearwater *Puffinus maurentanicus.* Now split from both Yelkouan and Manx Shearwaters. Breeds around the Balearic Islands. From June onwards they move into the Atlantic and can be seen from seawatching sites all around the Brittany coastline, returning to the Mediterranean in late autumn.

Manx Shearwater *Puffinus puffinus.* Some 180 pairs breed at 4 or 5 sites around Brittany including les Sept Îles. They can be numerous on passage past the Channel coast sites, Normandy, and Brittany sea-watching sites, especially from September - November.

Cory's Shearwater

Cory's Shearwater *Calonectris diomedea.* Breeds in small numbers off the northern and southern tips of Corsica, the Îles d'Hyères and small islands near Marseilles. The total French population is probably under 1000 pairs. They pass west along the Mediterranean and through the Straits of Gibraltar at the end of October/beginning of November to their wintering quarters in the South Atlantic. They can sometimes be seen in autumn from the southern Brittany seawatching sites.

Northern Gannet *Morus bassanus.* Has only one breeding colony in France, on Île Rouzic in the Sept-Îles archipelago (Brittany area 7), where there are about 15,000 pairs. Tens of thousands of migrants from the north of Europe and Britain pass the seawatching sites (Cap Gris-Nez, Ouessant, etc) between August and October. (Up to 10,000 in a day have been counted at Cap Gris-Nez and Ouessant in early October).

Shag *Phalacrocorax aristotelis.* The Atlantic sub-species breeds around the Brittany coasts, on the îles Saint Marcouf Reserves off the Normandy coast with perhaps very small numbers on-shore. Cherbourg is this species north-east limit although they are quite numerous off the Brittany and Normandy coasts in winter.

Bittern *Botaurus stellaris.* Only some 300 singing males were counted at the end of the 1990s, the majority along the Mediterranean coast. Its most important site in the north is in Lorraine (the Meuse and Moselle river valleys) with about 50 pairs in Picardie (the Somme and Aisne river valleys), 20 in Brière marshes (Brittany area 1). Usually one or two at Romelaere Reserve (Channel coast area 15) and the Sologne (South Central 8) in winter.

Little Bittern *Ixobrychus minutus.* Again about 300 singing males have been counted in France. It breeds in small numbers in reedbeds at wetland sites in Picardie, Pas-de-Calais, the Sologne, Champagne lakes and in the east. On the Channel coast, where the species has undergone a steep decline since the 1960's, it is most likely to be seen at the Romelaere Reserve, near St. Omer (Normandy and Channel coast area 15) and nearer Paris at the St. Hubert Lakes. It is also possible to see them in the Lacs de la Foret d'Orient and Lac du Der areas (North Central areas 5 and 6). Under 300 pairs currently breed in France (compared to 1500 in 1974), mainly in the eastern half of the country.

Night Heron *Nycticorax nycticorax.* Is relatively rare in the north, most birds breeding in the southern two-thirds of the county, where all the large colonies are situated. Over the past 20 years Night Herons have been gradually spreading north, though most breeding sites have only two or three pairs. The Nièvre department of Burgundy (South Central area 6) has about 200 pairs, with about 100 on the Allier river near Mars-sur-Allier (South Central area 9); there are about 50 pairs in the Brenne and the Sologne areas (South Central 8 -Marcilly Lake in the Sologne is a possible site), the same number at Grand-Lieu (South Central area 3), approximately 20 pairs in the Brière marshes (Brittany area 1), a few in the Larchant marshes south of Fontainebleau, Île-de-France (Paris area 6) and 15 or so pairs in the Doubs valley south of Dole (East area 7). There is currently an attempt at captive breeding in Marquenterre Park (Normandy and Channel coast area 10) in the hopes that the species will become a regular breeder there.

Cattle Egret *Bubulcus ibis.* Has been expanding its worldwide range this century but in Europe is still only common in the Iberian peninsular. In France the main breeding colony is in the Camargue, which, following a succession of mild winters, has grown from some 400 to 4000 nests over the past decade. Much smaller, more recently established but growing colonies are expanding up the Atlantic coast. The most northern breeding site at the moment is Marquenterre (Normandy and Channel coast area 10). They may be seen inside the Park or in flooded fields further inland, from the D4 between Le Crotoy and St. Firmin, or anywhere in this area. A few have bred at Lac du Der (North Central area 5) and south Brittany (possibly from Grand-Lieu, near Nantes, where there are over 100 pairs)

Purple Heron *Ardea purpurea.* Is rare in the northern regions covered in this book. It is most likely to be found in suitable habitat (large reed beds) in the Sologne (South Central area 8) (about 30 pairs), the Lac du Der-Chantecoq (North Central area 5), in the Doubs valley in Franche-Comté (East area 7), Grand-Lieu near Nantes (South Central area 3 -100 pairs), the Brière marshes (Brittany area 1) and the River Loire (South Central area 6).

Great White Egret *Egretta alba*. Has recently started wintering in northern France. It may be found near Marquenterre (see under Cattle Egret) or in the Champagne and Lorraine lakes - Lac du Der and the Lac de la Foret d'Orient, when more than 50 individuals have been counted on passage with smaller numbers remaining in winter - and around the Lindre lakes (North Central areas 5 and 6 and East area 1).

Black Stork *Ciconia nigra*. Is a very rare breeder with only 20 to 35 nests counted over the last decade but this figure is possibly underestimated. They breed very locally and sparsely in a broad band from the centre of the Atlantic coast (where the population is expanding) running north-east to the German frontier. The forests of Parroy (East area 1), around Lake Rille (South Central area 2) and Châtillon-sur-Seine (South Central area 10) are three nesting areas in the north. European migrants can be seen crossing France from mid-March to the end of May at lake sites in Champagne, Lorraine and Alsace. Post-nuptial passage peaks end August to mid-September and finishes by the beginning of October. An individual occasionally overwinters in the Jura or at the Champagne lakes.

White Stork *Ciconia ciconia*. Over 600 pairs breed in France, almost half in Alsace where there has been a population explosion in recent years, the others spread along the Atlantic coast up to Normandy but excluding Brittany. Les Ponts d'Ouve centre in the Cotentin marshes reserve (Normandy and Channel Coast Area 4) is an easily observed nesting site. Many reserves in Normany now put up nesting platforms, which has helped the species' expansion. In Alsace, the tourist town of Riquewihr is famous for its storks, the Ecomuseum near Ensisheim encourages them to nest on the old buildings and there are many other villages with nests around Colmar (East area 4). Most French breeders are migratory, many returning to their nest sites by the end of February or during March but migration continues until mid-May. Post-nuptial passage peaks over the last half of August. Some birds overwinter, especially in Alsace where captive breeders have been encouraged to lose their migratory instincts.

Sacred Ibis *Threskiornis aethiopicus*. The feral population in Brittany has grown to well over 350 pairs from the 20 free-flying individuals introduced to the Branféré bird-park in Morbihan, Brittany in 1976, where they nested on an island. They no longer breed there but are frequently observed around this area, especially in winter as well as in the Vilaine estuary, the Brière marshes (Brittany areas 1 and 2), and even further afield. In 1998 over 100 pairs nested in the heronries and Spoonbill colony in Grand-Lieu near Nantes, just south of the River Loire and there were two colonies of 27 nests in the Brière marshes in 1999. Outside the breeding season birds can be seen all along the Atlantic coast of Brittany, the mouth of the Loire and in the Brière marshes.

Spoonbill *Platalea leucorodia*. About 100 pairs breed in France and the number seems to be increasing. The greatest number breed in the colony at Grand-Lieu Lake near Nantes (South Central area 3) and in the Brière marshes(Brittany area 1). There are a couple of other sites in this area as well as a new, small one in Marquenterre Park (Normandy and Channel coast area 10). The species now regularly winters in France down the Atlantic Coast; in Brittany small numbers of wintering individuals can be seen in the Pont-l'Abbé estuary and Molèle, Finistère and a few can often be seen at the Guérande salt marshes and in the Somme estuary, Marquenterre Park and Oye Plage (Normandy and Channel coast areas 10 and 13). The entire Dutch breeding population migrates along the Channel and Atlantic coast end-February-March and August-September so these are the best periods to see this species at any suitable coastal site.

Bean Goose Anser fabalis Taiga Bean A. f. fabalis is a very rare winter visitor in northern France, though they may be found in the Netherlands and Belgium. Puzzlingly, up to the 70s this was the commonest Bean Goose wintering in Champagne, Lorraine and Somme Bay. Nowadays only Tundra Bean A. f. rossicus winter in Alsace and Champagne with fewer in Lorraine.

Garganey *Anas querquedula.* Breeds mainly in the north, in Nord-Pas-de-Calais and Picardie (in the marshes around the Somme bay) as well as in marshes at the mouth of the Loire and nearby (including 50 pairs at Grand-Lieu). A regular migrant from mid-February to the end of March and during August-September when they may be seen throughout the country, but most frequently along the Atlantic-Channel coasts.

Red-Crested Pochard *Netta rufina.* Is an extremely rare breeder in northern France; a few pairs occasionally nesting in the Champagne or Lorraine lakes. It is most likely to be seen on migration or wintering on the Rhine sites in Alsace, especially Plobsheim (East area 3) or possible on the gravel pits in the Seine valley around Paris (Paris area 1). Very cold spells may drive the French wintering population towards Spain but they in turn may be replaced by birds from north Germany or Holland.

Ferruginous Duck *Aythya nyroca* are usually seen on migration October to December or March-April in the Champagne and Lorraine lakes (Der, Orient, Madine), the Rhine sites in Alsace (East area 3) and on the Sologne lakes (South Central area 8).

Goosander *Mergus merganser.* Only breeds in the Haute-Savoie Alps, mainly around Lac Léman, with a very few pairs in the Jura. Also look for them on the Rhone near Bellegarde. They winter on many large lakes in the north-east, and during especially cold spells when the northern and Baltic populations arrive in France may also be found in the west on rivers and lakes along the Channel-Atlantic coast.

Red-breasted Merganser *Mergus serrator.* Winters off rocky shores all along the Channel-Atlantic coasts. There are large numbers in the Gulf of Morbihan (Brittany area 2).

Honey Buzzard *Pernis apivorus.* Nests throughout France, except the Mediterranean coastal area, in all well-wooded areas. The number of breeding pairs varies from year to year (probably affected by climatic conditions in their wintering quarters or late, wet springs in France). They are far less numerous than Common Buzzard, except perhaps in the well-wooded northeast. Southward migrating birds move through France in large numbers during August and the beginning of September, often flying at low altitude. In spring, pre-nuptial migration is late and much less concentrated. Most breeding birds start arriving in mid-April, continue through May and non-breeders can be seen returning as late as mid-June.

Black-shouldered Kite *Elanus caeruleus.* A pair was observed attempting to breed in France for the first time in 1983 and breeding has been confirmed since 1996 at two or three sites in Aquitaine and once in the Grands Causses; there are now at least four or five breeding pairs. Very occasionally a vagrant is spotted in northern France (Maine-et-Loire).

Red Kite *Milvus milvus.* Is widely distributed throughout the eastern half of northern France, though it has been suffering an alarming decline in recent decades (numbers down by 80% in less than 20 years in Champagne-Ardenne; 70% in Doubs; 50% in Alsace), thought in part to be due to poisoning. This decline is not limited to France; numbers have also been dropping in Germany, Spain

Black Shouldered Kite

White-Tailed Eagle

and Portugal. Totally absent as a breeder from the western half of the country. Most birds winter in Spain or North Africa, but increasing numbers are remaining in France throughout the winter and can be seen anywhere in north-eastern France, a few even reaching the Channel coast around Calais. Rubbish dumps are a favourite spot. Most birds leave between August and October, with numbers peaking during the second half of September and many return early, often by the end of February but others only reach their breeding sites at the end of April or even May.

Black Kite *Milvus. Migrans.* Is only absent from the north-west of France (Brittany, Normandy, Picardie, Pas-de-Calais) but seems to be slowly extending its range westwards. It is common around the Champagne lakes east to the Vosges and Jura. A migrant, most Black Kites arrive at their breeding sites in France between March and May and leave by mid-August. Often seen around water, since this is where they find a lot of food items.

White-tailed Eagle *Haliaeetus albicilla.* About 10-20 birds regularly winter in France (most in the northeast, occasionally along the Channel coast). The most famous site is the Champagne lakes - lac du Der-Chantecoq and lac de la Forêt d'Orient (North Central area 5 and 6) where several birds have been seen each year for well over a decade but individuals also turn up regularly at the Lorraine lakes (Lindre especially, East area 1) and the Rhine in Alsace. Birds are sometimes seen in October on passage along the main rivers (Loire, Allier, Rhine) and very occasionally winter there. Most wintering birds are immatures and almost all have left by March. One or two **Spotted Eagles** *Aquila clanga* occasionally winter around the Lorraine lakes (Lindre East area 1).

Osprey *Pandion haliaetus.* A few pairs of Ospreys (currently 11) have been breeding in central France since 1985, after a gap of nearly 50 years. The main breeding area is Orléans forest (South Central area 7). The best time to observe this species is during their spring and autumn migration, especially from the end of March to mid-April when individuals from different European populations can be seen along the river migration routes (the Loire, Allier, Charente) and around the Sologne and other lakes as well as at coastal sites. September is another good month as many birds linger in France for some time before continuing south.

Golden Eagle *Aquila chrysaetos.* Is reasonably widespread and numerous throughout all the southern mountain ranges: the Alps (over 150 pairs), the Massif Central (18 pairs), the Pyrenees (over 40 pairs) and Corsica (37 pairs) but absent from the north with only one or two pairs in the southern Jura and none in the Vosges.

Booted Eagle *Hieraetus pennatus.* Is very rare in the north but a few pairs nest in the Centre and Champagne regions. One site is Orléans forest (South Central area 7) where Osprey also breed. Birds return to their nesting sites from the middle of March to the end of April and leave from the end of August to mid-October.

Short-toed Eagle *Circaetus gallicus.* Breeds only in the southern half of France so is only likely to be seen in the extreme south of the area covered in this book in the Jura foothills, around the Ecluse gorge and just possibly in the Sologne and Orléans forest.

Capercaillie *Tetrao urogallus.* There are small relict populations in all the high mountain areas, stranded since the ending of the last ice-age. This species has suffered much disturbance recently through forestry and the spread of off-piste skiing and snowmobiles and is consequently in decline. They seem to prefer the higher mountain pine forests in the Vosges and the Jura. However, they are very difficult to see except by luck or if you should happen to disturb a roosting bird while walking through the forests. In spring, when they lek, sightings are easier but most leks are protected by wardens who will certainly turn you away. The RSPB has recently issued a code of conduct for watching Capercaillies and Black Grouse in Britain, where there too are in decline. It should also be adhered to on the Continent. Avoid disturbing possible lekking areas from March to May - visit them in autumn instead. Use hides or remain in vehicles wherever possible. Arrive well before daybreak and stay until the lek has finished. Use well-defined paths to avoid disturbing nesting hens and young.

Hazel Grouse *Bonasia bonasia.* This secretive game-bird is found in dense forest in the Jura and Vosges mountains but the populations are very small and scattered. There is a tiny, isolated relict population in the Belgian and French Ardennes but they are difficult to locate there and probably should not be disturbed. The chances of seeing one, even if you spent days walking through the forests, are slight, except with extreme luck. Tracks or droppings are all even the most thorough observer ever sees. In the Vosges Hazel Grouse seem to like young conifer plantations or the birches and rowans at forest edges.

Reeve's Pheasant *Syrmaticus reevesii.* Was introduced and has been breeding in the wild since 1870. There are today a few small, self-sustaining populations which have lasted for more than ten years in 16 forests areas in 10 departments, most in the north-west of the country, in Picardie, Normandie and around the Île de France. The Sologne and Fontainebleau forest are areas where the species has been successful for a long time and they can be easy to see in Hesdin Forest near Boulogne (Channel Coast area 11), especially at the end of summer.

Virginia Quail *Colinus cirginianus.* Has successfully established itself in the Sologne (South Central area 8) where there are perhaps several hundred pairs. Over one hundred thousand birds were released for hunting between 1959-1975 and still continue to be, so it is perhaps not surprising that small populations succeed for a few years.

Spotted Crake *Porzana porzana.* Breeds locally in wetlands across northern France from Pas-de-Calais to Alsace where suitable habitat occurs. Parroy Lake, Lorraine (East area 1) is a possible site in August-September.

Corncrake *Crex crex.* Is a species that is always much easier to hear than to see but it breeds in reasonable numbers in the Cotentin Marshes Regional Nature Park (Normany and Channel Coast area 4), Manneville Reserve near Le Havre and especially near Angers in the Pays-de-Loire region where the LPO manages over 300 hectares of wet meadows especially for the Corncrakes (South Central area 4). This last is the best site in France. Listen for them, at dusk and early morning, from mid-April to June and watch the grass moving with their passage. They sometimes jump up onto a stone or rise to look around.

Stone-curlew *Burhinus oedicnemus.* This bird of dry steppes, dunes and arable land can be found in the central regions of northern France in suitable habitat. It is absent from

Brittany, Normandy (except one small area near Rouen area 9 site ii), most of the Channel Coast and the east, except for a few in the Hardt plain in southern Alsace. Some good sites are the sandy islands on the Loire and Allier rivers (South Central areas 6 and 9), especially the Reserve south of Cosne-sur-Loire (South Central area 6). They start arriving back at their breeding sites mid-March and are especially easy to see from the end of August and through September and October when large numbers flock together before migrating   Listen for its curlew-like call at dawn and dusk.

Stone Curlew

Little Bustard *Tetrax tetrax*. This species, often sharing the same habitat as Stone Curlew, has suffered a drastic decline over the past decade and is currently the object of a LPO campaign to save it and its habitat. From over 7000 pairs in 1980 it was estimated to have declined to only about 1300 individuals in 2000. Modern agricultural practices including the intensive use of insecticides, long mobile irrigation ramps and the abandonment of lucerne *Medicago sativa* as a crop are the probable causes of its decline. There are two main areas where this species can be found, both in the south. The most important site in France is the Crau, on the Mediterranean but in the centre, the greatest number occurs on the flat cereal plains in the west, in Poitou-Charentes, south of the area covered in this book. A few still breed in the central areas of northern France but the species is on the edge of extinction in Champagne, the Ardennes and Île-de-France. The species' stronghold in the north used to be the Beauce plains around Pithiers (north of Orléans and some 40 km south-west of Fontainebleau) but there are now so few here that this site has not been included. The arable fields south of Saumur (South Central area 5) are probably the only place where there is a chance of seeing this species, so though this area is just south of the Loire, it has been included as it is so close to the other Loire sites; look out for fields of Lucerne, the Little Bustard's favourite habitat.

The southern French populations are resident but the remainder migrates (mainly to Spain) between September to November, coinciding with the opening of the shooting season. They flock before migrating and September/beginning of October is often the easiest time to see them. The northern birds return to their nesting sites from March, with most arriving mid-April.

Common Crane *Grus grus*. One of the most impressive birding spectacles is watching skeins of Cranes flying back to roost at dusk at Lac du Der (North Central area 5). During migration (mid-September to early December) there may be over 20,000 at the Champagne lakes but several thousand now remain there all winter. Cranes from the Baltic, Scandinavia, Poland and Germany migrate through France in a broad band from north-east to south-west from the end of October through November and return during February and March when they can be seen at many wetland sites. The Champagne and Lorraine lakes, the Petite-Camargue in Alsace, the Sologne and the Allier river are good sites for this species during migration. It is possible that one or two pairs breed occasionally in Normandy or Lorraine.

Black-winged Stilt *Himantopus himantopus.* A common breeding bird around the Mediterranean and down the Atlantic coast, Stilts are much rarer in the north but they may be seen in the Guérande salt-marshes near Saint Nazaire (Brittany area 1), around Le Havre (Normandy and Channel Coast Region area 8) and the Somme estuary (Normandy and Channel Coast Region area 10) and occasionally in the Sologne (South Central area 8) as well as the pools around the sugar factory on the D927 just west of Pithiviers (35 km north-east of Orléans)..

Kentish Plover *Charadrius alexandrinus.* Is a fairly common breeding bird around the Mediterranean but much rarer in the north, though it can still be found along the Channel and Atlantic coasts where there are sandy beaches, salt marshes and dunes (Oye Plage, Calais, Canche Bay, Somme estuary, Le Havre) and the western estuaries on the Normany peninsular, especially around St. Michael's Mount, and along much of the coastline of southern Brittany. Post-breeding flocks gather at the end of August and through September on the north Brittany coast, especially at Goulven Bay, Finistère (Brittany, area 6). A small number of birds may overwinter in Brittany and Normandy.

Woodcock *Scolopax rusticola.* Is a fairly rare and local breeding bird but a common winter visitor. During this season it can be found in most of the wooded sites in this guide. It favours damp woodland with thick undergrowth. Northern migrants arrive in large numbers during November (there is a heavy passage down the Channel coast this month) and leave during March.

Mediterranean Gull *Larus melanocephalus.* In spite of its name, this is an eastern species with most pairs breeding east of the Black Sea. Since 1965, however, it has started to breed with spectacular success in the Camargue alongside Black-headed Gulls and there are now over 2000 breeding pairs in France. A few pairs nest in the north, in Pas-de Calais, Lorraine, at Gambsheim, Alsace and along the River Loire, always in Black-headed Gull colonies. In winter it can be seen at many Channel Coast sites, especially on the beach at Portel, Boulogne.

Roseate Tern *Sterna dougallii.* Breeds only around the rocky coasts and islands of the north coast of Brittany. Can usually be seen in Morlaix Bay, Finistère but numbers are declining alarmingly and there are now probably under 70 pairs. Post-nuptial dispersal is from mid-August to mid-September in Morlaix Bay, Larmor-Baden in the Gulf of Morbihan and Saint-Gildas Point, Préfailles (south of the Loire).

Black Tern *Chlidonias niger.* About 400 pairs breed irregularly in France, mainly in lakes along the Atlantic coast. In the north the Brière marsh (Brittany area 1) is the main site with up to 200 pairs but there are usually 3-4 pairs in the Sologne (South Central area 8) and more on Grand-Lieu (South Central area 3). However, they are much easier to see during spring migration (first two weeks of May) when varying sized flocks may be seen over many lakes. Good sites are Krafft, Alsace (East area 3), the Champagne Lakes, especially Lac du Der, the lakes around Paris and those in Normandy. In the east a few **White-winged Tern** *Chlidonias leucopterus* may be with them.

Whiskered Tern *Chlidonias hybridus.* Can be found in the same sites as the above species during migration. Over 2000 pairs breed in France: in the Sologne (some 100 pairs), more in the Brenne further south, Brière (200 pairs), Grand-Lieu (400-500) among others. They choose fresh-water marshes with plenty of floating vegetation.

Common Guillemot *Uria aalge.* About 250 pairs breed in Brittany, at Cape Frèhel, Cape Sizun and the Sept-Îles. Can be seen off-shore along the length of the Atlantic-Channel coasts in winter.

Puffin *Fratercula arctica.* This species has suffered an horrific decline over the past half century from some 10,000 pairs to 250 and is now only found at three sites along the north Brittany coast: Ouessant and Morlaix bay, Finistère and the reserve of the Sept-Îles. Oil spills, ocean warming and over-fishing with nets have all played a part in the regression. In 1998, of the 256 pairs counted, 250 were in the Sept-Îles Reserve (Brittany area 7 -Malban and Bono islands) and 2 off Ouessant. The current situation is unchanged. A few Razorbill *Alca torda* may also be found breeding at the same sites, although in winter they are common along the Channel coast.

Rock Dove *Columbia livia.* A fairly genuine article may still be breeding on cliffs along the north Brittany and Channel coasts, from Quimper up to Cape Gris-Nez, but they are probably now all hybrids. You have to go to Corsica to be sure that they are not *urbica* hybrids!

Scops Owl *Otus scops.* A summer visitor, this urban little owl is most numerous around the Mediterranean, and very rare and localised in northern France, most likely to be heard in Burgundy, the Jura or around Mulhouse

Tengmalm's Owl *Aegolius funereus.* In northern France the best populations are in the Jura mountain forests above 800 m, with some in the Burgundy forests and smaller populations in Champagne, Lorraine and the Vosges (between 800-1200 m). The species seems to be slightly expanding its range and occupying sites from where it was absent up to the '90's or it could be that an increasing number of observers with knowledge of the bird's calls have helped locate it. In the mountains, Tengmalm's Owls prefer north-facing slopes with large, old conifers and normally take over a Black Woodpecker's hole as a nest site; the range expansion of this Woodpecker may have contributed to that of Tengmalm's. They also use nestboxes. They call normally only at night and early in the year when their habitat is inaccessible to walkers, breed irregularly and move around frequently. Consequently they are very difficult to find. Any tree with a hole high up in the right habitat is worth tapping with a stick, to see if a head peers out! Sites in this book are the high-altitude forests in the Jura (Risoux and Massacre East area 9) and the Hautes Vosges around Mount Ventron and the lower and more accessible Joux forest (East area 8).

Eagle Owl

Eagle Owl *Bubo bubo.* This can be a very difficult bird to find in northern France as it is confined basically to the south/south-east of the country: the foothills of the Pyrenees, the Massif Central, the Mediterranean hills and the lower Alps and Préalpes. There are only about half a dozen breeding sites in the north, in the Jura, the Vosges (very few) and the Ardennes right on the Belgian frontier near Givet. They call mainly between November and February, at or just before dusk, and are relatively quiet when breeding and feeding young, though they may call briefly before flying from the nest site or roost at dusk. They prefer inaccessible and remote cliff faces, sunny but not necessarily very high, for breeding and though a pair stay in the same territory for many years, they move the nest and roosting sites frequently, so giving precise directions is difficult. The best hope of seeing one is to listen in the right habitat in the Jura.

Pygmy Owl *Glaucidium passerinum.* Only found in the Alps and Jura in coniferous forests up to 1000 m. This tiny owl flies just before dusk and calls throughout the year, which makes it easier to spot than a truly nocturnal owl like Tengmalm's. They are still very hard to find. Try the Risoux Forest (East area 9) but with only 10 pairs in a huge forest...!

Alpine Swift *Apus melba.* This species, which arrives in the latter part of March and leaves in September-October, breeds to the south-east of a line from Biarritz-Mulhouse on high cliff faces. Apart from vagrants, it is only likely to be seen in northern France in the Jura mountains. The best site is Baume (East area 7).

Bee-eater *Merops apiaster.* A few scattered colonies of this typically Mediterranean species can be found in the north: in the Jura, on the south Brittany coast in Finistère (an old quarry inland from Pointe de la Torche on the Baie d'Audierne- Brittany area 3) and south-west of Fontainebleau, where there are some 100 pairs, many in the Gâtinais Française Regional Park. Bee-eaters are present from the beginning of May to mid-August at the colonial breeding sites in holes in soft banks, such as disused sand quarries. 35 km north-east of Orléans, the old pools to the west of the airfield at Pithiviers-le-Vieil is another possible site (turn off the D927 just west of the town, opposite a water tower and you will see a high bank, along which you can walk, overlooking pools.) They can also be reached from the airfield. Also check the old decantation pools at the sugar-beet plant just outside Pithiviers, also on the D927. They have also bred in the chalk quarry at Guillonville, 7 km north of Patay (north-west of Orléans).

Hoopoe *Upupa epops.* Breed throughout France, although they are much more common in the south. They are only missing from north Brittany and the north (northern Normany, Picardie and Nord-Pas-de-Calais as well as the higher parts of the Jura). The southern Brittany coast, the west coast and inland Normandy, around Fontainebleau, along the Loire river and Champagne are all breeding regions.

Wryneck *Jynx torquilla.* Only breeds in any numbers in the hilly, wooded eastern half of northern France. They are not found in Brittany, Normandy, the Channel coast or the extreme north. Areas include Sénart and Fontainebleau (about 10 pairs) forests south of Paris, Compiègne (20 pairs) to the north, the Champagne and Lorraine forests and along the River Rhine in Alsace. In forest areas they are often found around sunny clearings and areas of young oaks.

Grey-headed Woodpecker *Picus canus.* Found in a band across the north of the country from inland Brittany to Alsace. Good sites in the north are the Foret d'Orient, the woods around the Lac du Der (North Central areas 5 and 6), Fontainebleau forests (Paris area 6) and the National Regional Park of Normandy-Maine (South Central area 1). Other sites in this book include the forests of Auberive, Châtillon and Citeaux (South Central area 10), and the woods along the River Rhine in Alsace (East areas 3 and 6). Like Green Woodpeckers, they feed mainly on ants and start displaying and calling as early as January but are most easily heard during February and March. Normally quiet, unobtrusive birds, their "song" is much shorter than the Green's yaffle but their drumming lasts for up to 2 seconds. So check carefully if you see an apparently "Green" woodpecker drumming!

Black Woodpecker *Dryocopus martius.* This large woodpecker is relatively common in mixed and coniferous woodland in all mountainous regions as well as mature woodland throughout northern France, such as St. Germain-en-Laye (Paris area 2), Rambouillet (Paris area 4), Sénart and Notre-Dame (Paris area 5), Fontainebleau (Paris area 6), Châtillon and Citeaux Forests (South Central area 10), Illwald (East area 4), Falkenstein (East area 2) and all the Normandy-Maine forests (South Central area 1). In the north, the woods around Goriaux Lake and Flines on the Belgium border (North Central area 1) are reliable. Anyone finding themselves near Charles de Gaulle airport, Paris with time to spare, might like to look for this species in the Forest de Coye, just 15 km north up the N17. Try the *Route de la Ménagerie* where there are mature beech trees.

This species has expanded its range westwards considerably since the 1960s and is only absent from the Brittany and Normandy peninsulas and part of the Channel coast. Pairs are resident but young birds can fly considerable distances to find their own territories during their first autumn and may then be seen outside known territories. A large bird, the Black naturally only nests in mature trees (at least 30-40 cm diameter) and its nesting hole, often 5 metres or more from the ground, is large and distinctively pear-shaped. Listen out for its very loud drumming and take note of dead trees where they have been feeding; look for large areas of stripped-off bark and deep holes. The Black utters a number of very distinctive calls and is often heard before being spotted. In winter and early spring it calls early in the morning and at dusk, just when coming in to roost. From February to May it is at its most territorial and can be heard at almost any time of day. Whilst in the mountains it is to be found in mixed beech/coniferous or coniferous woods, often in large Scotch Pines, in the lowlands it favours strands of mature Beech in mixed deciduous woodland but it can also be found in large parks or plantations,

Middle Spotted Woodpecker *Dendropocus medius.* Can be found in almost all the woodland sites in Brittany, Normandy to Le Havre, and from Champagne eastwards, where it is most numerous. It is absent from the coastal areas of northern France but can be found in the Compiègne forest north of Paris. Reliable sites are Cerisy Forest, near Bayeux (Normandy and Channel Coast area 6), Perche and Écouves Forests (South Central area 1), Illwald and Colmar forests (East area 4), Chaux and Joux forests (East areas 7 and 8).

Middle Spotted is a species whose numbers fluctuate but it is currently expanding its range, especially around Paris. In many of the sites above it may be more common than Great Spotted. It habitually chooses old oak woodland (though it can be found in Beech or Chestnut woods) but can also be found in smaller coppices and even groups of tree provided they are mature. In mixed deciduous woods look for it in strands of Oaks high up in the canopy. This is easier in winter and early spring when there are no leaves on the trees and the Middle Spotted is at its most vocal and territorial. Its "song" is nasal, raucous and very different from the Great Spotted; it has been described as sounding like a piglet having its throat cut! Some of its loud, repeated cries could be mistaken for a Nuthatch's but its "kick"-call is weak and more like Lesser Spotted's. It does not drum territorially.

Three-toed Woodpecker *Picoides tridactylus.* A very rare breeding bird, at the western limit of its range in the Alps and Jura on the Swiss border. It favours cool spruce/deciduous woods, with clearings and plenty of dead trees on the ground above 1300 m. A nest was found in the Chamonix valley, Haute-Savoie in 1998 but no recent

Black Woodpecker

proof of breeding has been found in the Jura where it is observed occasionally. Almost impossible to see because it is retiring, silent for most of the year and the woods where it is found (the Haute-Griffe and Jura around Gex) are usually inaccessible in spring. There are probably only a few dozen pairs in France.

Crested Lark *Galerida cristata.* Is quite common in the extreme north-west (Picardie, the Channel coast at Nord-pas-du-Calais, down to the Isle-de-France, the east of Normandy, the extreme south of Brittany and along the River Loire to Orléans). Usually found on the outskirts of small towns and villages, industrial wasteland, even around car parks and motorway service stations. It is usually at the Aire de la Fontaine service stations, off the A10 north of Tours. Look for it at Authie Bay (Normandy and Channel Coast area 10) and on the dunes around the Somme estuary, and even at Dunkirk and Calais harbours (Normandy and Channel coast areas 14 and 13). It is more localised throughout the centre of northern France, and around Paris. It is absent from most of Normandy and Brittany (except the south coast), as well as mountainous regions, being essentially a lowland bird. It seems to be in regression especially in Brittany (400 pairs in 1950 to under 50 today), around Paris and in Alsace

Short-toed Lark *Calandrella brachydactyla.* Is extremely rare in northern France and is only found in tiny numbers and with great difficulty on the Beauce plains around Pithiviers, It arrives during the first half of April and leaves at the end of August. Check the areas of dry, uncultivated land where low-growing Mayweed (*Chamomilla*) has taken over around the D927 between Pithiviers and the airfield at Pithiviers-le-Vieil and around the disused sugar-beet basins which lie between the D927 and the airfield. Turn off the D927 opposite a water tower. Pithiviers is some 35 km north-east of Orléans. Birds are sometimes seen at the end of April and in May on passage along the Atlantic coast.

Crag Martin *Ptyonoprogne rupestris.* Is common wherever there are hills and mountains in the south of the country and seems to be expanding its range northwards but can only be found in the extreme south-east of the area covered by this book, in the Jura mountains, where there are about 30-50 pairs. Try l'Ecluse gorge (East area 9 site iii.), or Baume (East area 7).

Bluethroat

Red-throated Pipit *Anthus cervinus*. Is a regular passage migrant through the eastern part of France. Most birds are seen during the pre-nuptial migration, in April to mid-May around the edges of lakes, in wet meadows and marshes.

Water Pipit *Anthus spinoletta*. Breeds in the alpine meadows above the treeline of the Jura and Vosges mountains.

Alpine Accentor *Prunella collaris*. This resident species is an altitudinal migrant; breeding in rocky scree slopes above 2000-2200 m but descending to ski stations and lower areas in winter. The southern Jura mountains are where they are most likely to be seen though a few pairs (perhaps only 10) breed at 1200 m on the Hohneck,in Alsace (East 5).

Bluethroat *Luscinia svecica*. Two subspecies of white-spotted Bluethroat breed in France. The subspecies *namnetum* breeds along the Atlantic coast of France, from the south coast of Brittany down to Arcachon in the south. Sites include the Brière marshes with a few in the Guérande saltmarsh (Brittany area 1), along the south Brittany coast and Grand Lieu (South Central area 3). The subspecies *cyanecula* breeds in the east and north-west, (Nord and Picardie), where it is still expanding its range. This subspecies can be seen at Romelaere Reserve (Normandy and Channel coast area 15), around Le Havre (Normandy and Channel coast area 8) and Mont St-Michel (Normandy and Channel Coast area 1), where both subspecies occur. In the east the subspecies *cyanecula* breeds on the Doubs river south of Dole (East area 7) and the along the Rhine in Alsace (East areas 3 and 6).

April - May, when they are singing, is the easiest time to locate them. Bluethroats are much easier to see at the above sites during migration periods (March-May/mid-August-September) when numbers can be seen almost anywhere along the Atlantic and Channel coasts. Check rank vegetation along wet ditches, around salt-pans and under Tamarisk (and other) bushes near the sea walls at all coastal sites. Bluethroats are shy, skulking birds so watch for furtive behaviour in reed edges and low vegetation.

Rock Thrush *Monticola saxatilis*. A summer visitor to high mountain areas in the south. In northern France only likely to be found in the southern Jura mountains and in the southern Vosges, where it is very rare. (East area 5). It arrives in April or the beginning of May and leaves quietly during September. It can be found in both high mountain areas and the lower foothills between April and September. It likes south-facing, rocky slopes with boulders and a few scattered bushes and often sings from a prominent rock or telephone wires in the last two weeks of May and the beginning of June, which is the easiest time to locate it.

Ring Ouzel *Turdus torquatus*. The race *T.t.alpestris* with broad, pale fringes to wing and body feathers are quite widely distributed in the Vosges and Jura mountains between 1000-1800m (East areas 5 and 8). By July birds will have dispersed and may be seen at higher altitudes. They leave their breeding sites from August to the end of October and return during March and the first part of April. The occasional observation of individuals on the west coast in winter probably refer to migrant birds of the race *T.t.torquatus* from Britain or Scandinavia.

Cetti's Warbler *Cettia cetti.* Is locally common throughout the whole north-west of France. It is rare or absent east of Paris. Always found in dense shrubs close to water.

Fan-tailed Warbler or **Zitting Cisticola** *Cisticola juncidis.* Used to be found mainly along the Mediterranean and Atlantic coasts but during the 1990s its range expanded and it can be seen all around the coast of Brittany with a few singing males along the Loire river, at Le Havre, Seine and Somme Estuaries and Pas-de-Calais (Boulogne). A succession of hard winters could again reduce the northern population otherwise it may continue to gradually expand northwards. Though considered a sedentary species, birds have been noted moving through Ouessant, Finistère in autumn.

Icterine Warbler *Hippolais icterina.* Is a fairly rare species in France. It only breeds in the north from Nord-Pas-de-Calais eastwards through Lorraine to Alsace and Franche-Comté, in effect a broad band along the Belgian and German frontiers, France is very much the south-western limit of its range and in recent years this seems to have contracted somewhat. It rarely arrives before the beginning of May and leaves between the end of July to mid-October.

In France, the widespread *Hippolais* warbler is **Melodious Warbler** *Hippolais polyglotta* which can be found throughout the country except for the highest mountain regions, the extreme north-east and west and the western part of Brittany. The two species are sympatric throughout the northern part of the area covered in this book, so check any "yellow" warbler in young woodland (Compiègne, Crécy-en-Ponthieu) or wooded marshland carefully. Look for Melodious in damp woodland or shrubs, especially brambles, near streams, ditches, etc.

Fan-Tailed Warbler

Marsh Warbler *Acrocephalus palustris.* Breeds mainly in the north-east but is expanding westwards and can be found in Normandy, Île-de-France and good numbers in Nord-Pas-de-Calais. It is very rare in Brittany but can be found in Lillemer marsh and St. Brieuc (area 8). It favours scrub and tall, dense vegetation near water or along ditches or field edges but also dunes on the coast. It does not arrive until May and leaves by the end of August or beginning of September.

Coloured Flycatcher

Great Reed Warbler *Acrocephalus arundinaceus.* Is far less common in the north, where it has been in strong regression during the 1990's, than around the Mediterranean, but this species can nevertheless be found in lowland reedbeds in the north and east, though it is absent from Brittany, Normandy and most of the Channel and Atlantic coasts. Best sites are the Lorraine and Champagne lakes.

Savi's Warbler *Locustella luscinioides.* A rare species in the north of France, where most are found in the Brière marshes - 1400 singing males in 1999 (Brittany area 1) with far fewer in the Somme and l'Authie valleys (Normandy and Channel coast area 10), in Morbihan in southern Brittany, and the Donges marshes east of St. Nazaire in the Loire-Atlantique. Elsewhere it is rare and localised and seems to be declining. It has almost disappeared from Alsace, Île-de-France, the Sologne and even the few pairs that have been at Parroy Lake near Nancy (East area 1) may have gone. The Brière marshes seem the only safe site nowadays. It needs large reedbeds with a few scattered bushes or trees.

Western Bonelli's Warbler *Phylloscopus bonelli.* While this species is one of the commonest warblers in woodland in southern France, in the north it is rarer and more localised being absent from the Channel coast, Nord-Pas-de-Calais, Picardie, most of Brittany and Normandy and most of the north-east. It is found in deciduous and mixed woods as well as pinewoods up to almost 2000 m. in the Île-de France, Centre, Burgundy, Champagne, and Franche-Comté. Some possible sites in this guide are Paris areas 4, 5 and 6, South Central areas 1, 7, 8 and 10, East area 8. It seems to prefer sunny slopes and the edges or clearings of woods but can also be found in plantations, especially of Scots Pines and oak woods. It is most easily located by its two-syllable "hoo-eet" call and short single-note trill. In lower areas its range overlaps with that of Chiffchaff but replaces this species at higher altitudes. It arrives in France at the end of March and leaves during August.

Collared Flycatcher *Ficedula albicollis.* At its western limit in Europe, it only breeds in north-eastern France, mainly in Lorraine (East area 1), with a few in Champagne and Alsace. Mature oak woodland (as in Reine, Parroy and Romersberg forests) is its preferred habitat and the best time to find it from mid-April to mid-June, after which time it seems to vanish.

Pied Flycatcher *F. hypoleuca* can be found in suitable woodland in the north-east from Compiègne Forest (North Central area 3), Fontainebleau (Paris area 6) eastwards to Alsace (East area 2) but it is local and scattered, with the highest density in Alsace.

Bearded Tit *Panurus biarmicus*. A few hundred pairs are found in large phragmites beds along the Atlantic coast of Brittany (try Brittany areas 3 ii and 1 ii). It also breeds at Le Havre (Normandy and Channel Coast area 8) and the Somme estuary (Normandy and Channel Coast area 10). In winter small groups may be found away from these breeding sites along the south Brittany coast, the north Normandy coast and in Pas de Calais as well as a few in Lindre lake, Moselle (East area 1).

Penduline Tit *Remiz pendulinus*. While this species has been contracting its range around the Mediterranean (it has not bred in the Camargue since the 80's), its north-east expansion across Europe means that a few have been breeding in the Ardennes, Alsace and Lorraine. Lakes Parroy and Lindre (East area 1) are two places where they have been seen. Large numbers winter along the Atlantic coast, up to the southern coast of Brittany and can also be seen along the Channel coast when on passage.

Crested Tit *Parus cristatus*. Can be found in most of the forests in this region, provided there are large enough strands of conifers. Along the Channel coast look for it in Normandy and Channel Coast area 6, in Normandy-Maine forests (South Central area 1), as well as the forests in Champagne (North Central areas 5 and 6), the Jura and Vosges forest sites (East areas 2, 5, 8, and 9) nearly always around conifers, although in winter when individuals join mixed feeding flocks of tits and 'crests, it may be found in deciduous woodland or even reedbeds. The race in Brittany is *P.c.abadieri*, which is smaller and redder.

Short-toed Treecreeper (*Certhia brachydactyla*). Both species of Treecreepers can be found in France. However, Short-toed Treecreeper is by far the most widespread and common, found throughout the country from the coast to the eastern mountains in deciduous and mixed woodland, as well as around parks and gardens, up to an altitude of 1500-2000 m., while **Eurasian Treecreeper** (*Certhia familiaris*) prefers the higher, coniferous forests of the Jura and Vosges. In these eastern forests and some of the Normandy, Champagne and Lorraine forests the species are sympatric i.e. there is an overlap where both species occur - see Compiègne Forest (North Central area 3), Parroy Forest (East area 1), and Écouves Forest (South Central area 1). Song is the easiest way to distinguish between them, as their calls can sound similar and the darker flanks of Short-toed are not always easy to spot in the field. In most of lowland France the chances are that you are watching Short-toed.

Wallcreeper *Tichodroma muraria*. One of the "most wanted" continental species. It tends to breed at very high altitudes but also favours narrow, shady gorges close to fast flowing water or by waterfalls at

Penduline Tit

Citril Finch

lower altitudes. In northern France only possible in the Jura mountains on the Swiss border. Fort l'Ecluse gorge (East area 9 site iii.) and the cliffs at Mont d'Or (East area 8) are possible wintering and breeding sites respectively. Listen for their high, thin whistle and watch rock faces and stone facades for a flash of crimson when they flick their wings.

Golden Oriole *Oriolus oriolus.* Is reasonably common throughout northern France except in Brittany and of coastal Normandy. It is a lowland species, found below 600m altitude in mature trees with some shrubby undergrowth. Large poplars beside rivers are another favourite breeding site; Orioles are frequently observed close to water. A late migrant, they arrive in France at the very end of April or the beginning of May and leave, usually with their young, at the end of July or the beginning of August.

Northern Grey Shrike *Lanius excubitor.* Breeds and winters throughout the eastern half of northern France but is absent from Brittany, Normandy, Paris and most of north-west France.

Red-backed Shrike *Lanius collurio.* Has much the same distribution as the previous species but its range extends further west. It breeds throughout the whole eastern half of northern France but is absent from most of Brittany, Normandy (except area 9 ii), the Channel coast, Paris and the north-west.

Woodchat Shrike *Lanius senator.* Is essentially a Mediterranean species, disliking cooler, mountainous climates and so has a more patchy distribution, being found in the eastern half of northern France in warm, sunny hills, often along hedgerows or on tall bushes (East areas 5 and 7).

Nutcracker *Nucifraga caryocatactes.* Though rare, can be found in the Jura and Vosges mountains (East areas 5, 8 and 9) and the Ardennes plateau on the Belgian frontier, north of Charleville (North Central area 2 - the nearest site to the Channel). The race found in the east is *N.c. caryocatactes* but the Ardennes birds probably belong to the race *N. c. macrorrhynchos* from Siberia. There are only some 15 pairs of birds on the French side, more in Belgium, that probably remained after the 1968 irruption. In the northern Alps and Vosges Mountains, Nutcrackers can be found as low as 550 m in forest clearings and valleys wherever there are abundant supplies of hazelnuts and in the Ardennes it occurs between 250 - 500 m. Nutcrackers are probably easiest to see early in the year or just after the breeding season (end-July, August) when pairs fly noisily around, seeking and storing seeds and nuts.

Red-billed Chough *Pyrrhocorax pyrrhocorax.* In northern France there are only a few pairs around the cliffs of western Brittany: the Pointe de Penhir on the Crozon peninsular and Cape Sizun and the Pointe du Van, both on the northern peninsular bordering Audierne Bay (Brittany area 3).

Raven *Corvus corax.* Only occurs in the Jura, where it is fairly common and around the cliffs of Brittany and Normandy, where it is rare and local (Brittany areas 3, 7, 8 and Normandy Area 2 ii)

Rock Sparrow *Petronia petronia.* There is only one site for this species in northern France. This, its most northerly breeding site, and the nearest to Britain, is the old Abbey of Fontevraud near Saumur (South Central area 5) where there are up to fifteen or so pairs. In the same area there are 3 or 4 pairs at Roiffé, Vienne, 7 km south of Fontevraud and 2 pairs at Montsoreau, 2 km to the north. During the breeding season only individual pairs will be found, but from September to March small flocks can be found feeding in fallow and stubble fields, often with other sparrows or finches.

Serin *Serinus serinus.* Is a quite common and widespread breeding bird in northern France, from the Channel coast to Alsace, although it moves out of the colder east and central areas during winter. Look and listen for it in town parks, cemeteries and gardens, including those central Paris. A small number of **Siskin** *Carduelis spinus* breed in conifers in the Vosges and the Jura but it is a common winter visitor throughout the region.

Citril Finch *Serinus citrinella.* This small mountain finch breeds in low vegetation at the edge of the tree line in subalpine areas. They are uncommon in the Vosges, occurring between 600 to 1200 m. and equally scarce in the Jura where they can be found between 800 to 1000 m. In autumn young birds disperse and may be found above the breeding sites and in winter birds often flock with other finches, especially Serins and Siskins, at lower altitudes. They can be found, with some difficulty, in the Jura and southern Vosges mountain sites (East areas 5, 8 and 9 - area 8 Mont d'Or is probably the easiest site).

Common Rosefinch *Carpodacus erythrinus.* This species seemed to be expanding its range westwards and was first noted in France in 1985. In 1994 some 34 to 37 singing males were found in the Doubs, the Jura, Alsace, Haute-Savoie, Pas-de-Calais, the Somme, the Manche. By 1988 the numbers were down to 15 and in 2000 fewer than 10 singing males were heard in the Jura and nowhere else. It may return to its breeding sites on the grassy slopes of Cap Gris-Nez and Blanc Nez (Calais), again or it may disappear as a breeding bird almost before it started to be one. It arrives mid May/June and leaves again end July. **Common Redpoll** *Carduelis flammea* followed a similar pattern. A decade ago it started to breed in some coastal areas in the north of France, now it is again only a winter visitor. **Mealy Redpoll** *C. f. cabaret* breeds in the Jura above 850 m.

Crossbill *Loxia curvirostra.* Breeds regularly in the Vosges and the Jura, usually in Spruce or Pine and in the Ardennes, where it is very rare. It can also be found in coniferous woodland from the Channel coast - Somme Estuary (Normandy and Channel Coast area 10), right across the region, especially following an irruption from the north, although it may only breed irregularly. (Other sites include Paris areas 2, 4, 5 and 6, East areas 2, 4, and 8).

Hawfinch *Coccothraustes coccothraustes.* Breeds and winters throughout northern France, except the Brittany and Normandy peninsulas but is local and not common. It is found in deciduous woodland, beech for preference throughout the Jura, in Alsace, Lorraine, Champagne-Ardenne, Nord-Pas-de-Calais but is rather thin on the ground in Île-de-France and Normandy. The Tillaie reserve area of Fontainebleau is a possible site in this area. In cold winters the most northerly birds may move south but check flocks of finches feeding in eastern woodlands in winter, Hawfinches may be among the Chaffinches and Bramlings as in Haguenau Forest (East area 2)

Rock Bunting *Emberiza cia* breeds in small numbers in the Jura and southern Vosges mountains, but it is very rare (only under 30 pairs in the Jura, between 50-100 in the Vosges). It likes dry, sunny, rocky slopes with shrubby vegetation, mainly between 500 - 2000 m altitudes. In winter, birds from the higher areas normally move down to nearby plains or warmer slopes and often join flocks of other finches. Males sing between February and April and then become rather silent; listen out for their thin, weak, downslurred "tsii" calls.

Cirl Bunting *Emberiza cirlus.* Is reasonably common in Normandy, Brittany and throughout the area south of Paris. It does not breed in the north or the higher areas of the east.

Snow Bunting *Plectrophenax nivalis* winters regularly along the Channel coasts (Normandy and Channel Coast areas 1, 8, 10 and 12 are all good sites) where it can also be seen on passage during October-November.

Black-headed Bunting *Emberiza melanocephala* bred for the first time in south-eastern France in 2000, near Cipières in the Alpes-Maritimes

Red-Billed Chough

BIBLIOGRAPHY AND RECOMENDED BOOKS

Site Guides
Where to Watch Birds in France.
LPO. (Translated by Tony Williams) Christopher Helm.
(I must acknowledge my debt to this book, the first site guide to France. I have used it extensively since the French edition came out in 1989 and it has been invaluable. Inevitably, this book covers many of the same sites but I have tried not to plagiarise too much. I have visited all the sites in this book (most of them several times over many years) and have updated when necessary, corrected any errors that slipped into the LPO book and given what I have found to be the best viewpoints or itineraries. The LPO book includes many extra sites in the northern half of France as well as outside the area covered by this guide. However, it is arranged by departments and lacks maps showing the location of the sites within each department, so they are not always easy to find, nor are the instructions to some sites easy to follow.)

Balades Nature dans... (different regions).
This series published by Dakota Éditions are excellent small paperbacks giving detailed itineraries with clear maps for walks in "the most beautiful natural sites" of different regions of France. These include some of the sites described in this book as well as many others, most of which, though intended for the general naturalist, will be of interest to birdwatchers. Some walks are easy and short, others more demanding. There are full colour illustrated field guides at the end to selected wildlife: birds, mammals, reptiles, amphibians and some insects. Regions covered in northern France include **Paris, Île-de-France, Bretagne, Normandie, Baie de Somme, Pas-de-Calais,** and **Le Jura.** Highly recommended but adequate French needed to follow the text. Can be bought from the LPO.

Wildlife Travelling Companion: France
Gibbons & Davies. Crowood 1992.
Gives details of many more sites, some of them better for flowers or insects than birds. Instructions not always sufficiently detailed but good photos.

Birds
The Birds of Britain and Europe. New Edition.
Heinzel, Fitter and Parslow. Harper Collins

Birds of Europe.
Jonsson. Helm. (French edition available)

The Birds of Prey of Britain and Europe.
Gensbol. Collins

Collins Bird Guide.
Mullarney et al (French edition available)

Guide des Oiseaux d'Europe.
Peterson et al. Delachaux & Niestlé (The English Peterson gives French names also)

Flowers
Alpine Flowers of Britain and Europe. New Edition.
Blamey/Grey-Wilson. HarperCollins

Wild Flowers of Britain and Northern Europe.
Fitter/Blamey. HarperCollins

Guide des Fleurs Sauvages.
Fitter/Blamey. Delachaux et Niestlé (The above guide in French)

The Illustrated Flora of Britain and Northern Europe.
Blamey/Grey-Wilson. Hodder & Stoughton

Orchids of Britain and Europe.
Buttler. Crowood

Animals
Mammals of Britain and Europe.
Macdonald/Barrett. HarperCollins

Reptiles and Amphibians of Britain and Europe.
Arnold/Burton. Collins

Insects
Butterflies.
Whalley. Mitchell Beazley.

Butterflies and Day-flying Moths New Generation Guide.
Chinery. Collins

Collins Photographic Guide to Butterflies of Britain & Europe.
Chinery. Harper Collins

Guide to the Insects of Britain and Western Europe.
Chinery. Collins.

Guide to the Dragonflies of Great Britain.
Powell. Arlequin Press. (Equally useful in France).

Bibliography

Les Zones Importantes pour la Conservation des Oiseaux en France. LPO & Ministère de l'Environnement.

Important Bird Areas in Europe: Priority sites for conservation. Vol 2. Southern Europe Eds. Heath & Evans et al. BirdLife International.

Guide des Reserves Naturelles de France. Cans, Chantal & Reille, Antoine Delachaux et Niestlé

Guide des Parcs Naturels Régionaux. Reille, Antoine Delachaux et Niestlé

Dubois, P.J. et al. Inventaire des Oiseaux de France. Nathan 2000.

Rapaces de France. Suppléments nos. 1-4. L'Oiseau magazine. 1999-2002.

Où Voir les Oiseaux en France. LPO. Nathan. 1989

Atlas des Oiseaux Nicheurs de France. Yeatman-Berthelot & Jarry. S.O.F. 1995

Atlas des Oiseaux de France en Hiver. Yeatman-Berthelot & Jarry. S.O.F. 1991

Crozier, P & Dubois, P.J. Brignogan Ornithos 6-3 1999.

Flohart, Guy. Le cap Gris-Nez. Ornithos 2: 124-127 (1995)

Hervé, Michel, LPO Lorraine. L'étang de Lindre et les étangs mosellans. Ornithos 8-3:108-115 (2001)

Leclercq, Jacques-André. La jetée du Clipon et les environs de Dunkerque. Ornithos 7-3 133-138 (2000)

Le Maréchal, Pierre & Lesaffre, Guilhem. Les Oiseaux d'Île-de-France. Delachaux et Niestlé

Portier, Bruno. Autumn seawatching in northern France in the 1990s. Birding World 12 - 6 August 1999

Sériot, J et al. Les Oiseaux nicheurs rares et menacés en France en 2000. Ornithos 9-6. 2002

Rock Sparrow

BIRDS

The following check list follows the sequence and nomenclature of the List of Birds of the Western Palearctic (British Birds Ltd 1997), which follows those adopted for the new Concise Edition of Birds of the Western Palearctic. Extreme rarities and very occasional visitors have not been included but most of the American and eastern vagrants that turn up in Britain have also occurred in France. The order in which the symbols are given indicates the normal status (for example, if the majority of birds are winter visitors but a few may remain to breed, then WV comes first, followed by OB).

Key to Symbols:

RB = Resident Breeder   OB = Occasional Breeder   WV = Winter Visitor
MB = Migrant Breeder   PM = Passage Migrant   AV = Accidental Visitor

Status	English Name	French Name	Scientific Name
WV	Red-throated Diver	Plongeon catmarin	*Gavia stellata*
WV	Black-throated Diver	Plongeon artique	*Gavia arctaica*
WV	Great Northern Diver	Plongeon imbrin	*Gavia immer*
RB	Little Grebe	Grèbe castagneux	*Tachybapus ruficollis*
RB	Great Crested Grebe	Grèbe huppé	*Podiceps cristatus*
WV	Red-necked Grebe	Grèbe jougris	*Podiceps grisegena*
WV	Slavonian	GrebeGrèbe esclavon	*Podiceps auritus*
RB,WV	Black-necked	Grebe Grèbe à cou noir	*Podiceps nigricollis*
RB, PM	Fulmar	Fulmar boréal	*Fulmaris glacialis*
RB, WV	Cory's Shearwater	Puffin cendré	*Calonectris diomedea*
WV, PM	Balearic Shearwater	Puffin de Baléares	*Puffinus mauretanicus*
RB, PM, WV	Yelkouan Shearwater	Puffin de Mediterranée	*Puffinus yelkouan*
PM	Leach's Storm-petrel	Océanite culblanc	*Oceanodroma leucorhoa*
RB, WV	European Storm-petrel	Océanite tempête	*Hydrobates pelagicus*
RB, WV, PM	Northern Gannet	Fou de Bassan	*Morus bassana*
RB,WV	Great Cormorant	Grand Cormoran	*Phalacrocorax carbo*
RB, AV, WV	Shag	Cormoran huppé	*Phalacrocorax aristotelis*
RB, MV, WV	Great Bittern	Butor étoilé	*Botaurus stellaris*
MB	Little Bittern	Blongios nain	*Ixobrychus minutus*
MB	Night Heron	Bihoreau gris	*Nycticorax nycticorax*
MB, PM	Squacco Heron	Crabier chevelu	*Ardeola ralloides*
RB	Cattle Egret	Héron gardeboeufs	*Bubulcus ibis*
RB	Little Egret	Aigrette garzette	*Egretta garzetta*
AV	Western Reef	Heron Aigrette des récifs	*Egretta gularis*
WV, PM	Great White Egret	Grande Aigrette	*Egretta alba*
RB, WV	Grey Heron	Héron cendré	*Ardea cinerea*
MB, PM	Purple Heron	Héron purpré	*Ardea purpurea*
PM, RB	Black Stork	Cigogne noire	*Ciconia nigra*
RB, PM	White Stork	Cigogne blanche	*Ciconia ciconia*
AV, MB	Glossy Ibis	Ibis falcinelle	*Plegadis falcinellus*
RB (intro)	Sacred Ibis	Ibis sacré	*Threskiornis aethiopicus*
PM, MB	Eurasian Spoonbill	Spatule blanche	*Platalea leucorodia*
RB	Greater Flamingo	Flamant rose	*Phoenicopterus ruber*
RB	Mute Swan	Cygne tuberculé	*Cygnus olor*
WV	Bewick's Swan	Cygne de Bewick	*Cygnus columbianus*
WV	Whooper Swan	Cygne chanteur	*Cygne cugnus*
WV	White-fronted Goose	Oie rieuse	*Anser albifrons*
WV, PM	Bean Goose	Oie des moissons	*Anser fabalis*
AV	Greylag Goose	Oie cendrée	*Anser anser*
WV	Barnacle Goose	Bernache nonette	*Branta leucopsis*
WV, PM	Brent Goose	Bernache cravant	*Branta bernicla*
AV	Red-breasted Goose	Bernache à cou rouge	*Branta ruficollis*
RB	Common Shelduck	Tadorne de Belon	*Tadorna tadorna*
WV, PM, OB	Eurasian Wigeon	Canard siffleur	*Anas penelope*
RB, WV, PM	Gadwall	Canard chipeau	*Anas strepera*
RB, WV, PM	Common Teal	Sarcelle d'hiver	*Anas crecca*
RB, WV, PM	Mallard	Canard colvert	*Anas platyrhynchos*

Status	English Name	French Name	Scientific Name
WV, PM, OB	Pintail	Canard pilet	*Anas acuta*
PM, MB	Gargany	Sarcelle d'été	*Anas quequedula*
WV, PN, RB	Northern Shoveler	Canard souchet	*Anas clypeata*
RB, WV, PM	Red-crested Pochard	Nette rousse	*Netta rufina*
WV, RB, PM	Common Pochard	Fuligule milouin	*Aythya ferina*
AV, PM	Ferruginous Duck	Fuligule nyroca	*Aythya nyroca*
WV, RB, PM	Tufted Duck	Fuligule nyroca	*Aythya fuligula*
PM, WV	Greater Scaup	Fuligule milouinan	*Aythya marila*
WV, PM, OB	Common Eider	Eider à duvet	*Somateria mollissima*
PM, WV	Common Scoter	Macreuse noire	*Melanitta nigra*
PM, WV	Velvet Scoter	Macreuse brune	*Melanitta fusca*
WV	Goldeneye	Garrot à oeil d'or	*Bucephala clangula*
WV	Smew	Harle piette	*Mergus albellus*
WV, PM, OB	Goosander	Harle bièvre	*Mergus merganser*
WV,PM	Red-breasted Merganser	Harle huppé	*Mergus serrator*
PM, MB	European Honey-buzzard	Bondrée apivore	*Pernis apivorus*
AV, RB	Black-shouldered Kite	Elanion blanc	*Elanus caeruleus*
PM, MB	Black Kite	Milan noir	*Milvus migrans*
PM, MB, WV	Red Kite	Milan royal	*Milvus milvus*
WV	White-tailed Sea-eagle	Pygargue à queue blanche	*Haliaeetus albicilla*
PM	Osprey	Balbuzard pecheur	*Pandion haliaetus*
RB	Lammergeier	Gypaète barbu	*Gypaetus barbatus*
MB	Egyptian Vulture	Vautour percnoptère	*Neophran percnopterus*
RB	Griffon Vulture	Vautour fauve	*Gyps fulvus*
RB	Monk Vulture	Vautour moine	*Aegypius monachus*
MB, PM	Short-toed Eagle	Circaète Jean-le-Blanc	*Circaetus gallicus*
RB, WV, PM	Marsh Harrier	Busard des roseaux	*Circus aeruginosus*
WV, RB, PM	Hen Harrier	Busard Saint-Martin	*Circus cyaneus*
PM, MB	Montagu's Harrier	Busard cendré	*Circus pyrargus*
RB, PM, WV	Northern Goshawk	Autour des polombes	*Accipiter gentilis*
RB, PM, WV	Eurasian Sparrowhawk	Epervier d'Europe	*Accipiter nisus*
RB, PM, WV	Common Buzzard	Buse variable	*Buteo buteo*
WV	Spotted Eagle	Aigle criard	*Aquila clanga*
RB	Golden Eagle	Aigle royal	*Aguila chrysaetos*
MB, PM	Booted Eagle	Aigle botté	*Hieraeetus pennatus*
RB	Bonelli's Eagle	Aigle de Bonelli	*Hieraeetus fasciatus*
PM	Osprey	Balbuzard pêcheur	*Pandion haliaetus*
MB	Lesser Kestrel	Faucon crécerellette	*Falco naumanni*
RB, WV	Common Kestrel	Faucon crécerelle	*Falco tinnunculus*
AV, PM	Red-footed	Falcon Faucon kobez	*Falco vespertinus*
WV, PM	Merlin	Faucon émerillon	*Falco columbarius*
MB, PM	Hobby	Faucon hobereau	*Falco subbuteo*
AV	Eleanora's Falcon	Faucon d'Eléonore	*Falco eleonorae*
RB, WV, PM	Peregrine Falcon	Faucon pèlerin	*Falco peregrinus*
RB	Ptarmigan	Lagopède alpin	*Lagopus mutus*
RB	Hazel Grouse	Gélinotte des bois	*Bonasa bonasia*
RB	Black Grouse	Tétras lyre	*Tetrao tetrix*
RB	Capercaillie	Grand Tétras	*Tetrao urogallus*
RB	Red-legged Partridge	Perdrix rouge	*Alectoris rufa*
RB intro.	Chukar	Perdrix choukar	*Alectoris chukar*
RB	Rock Partridge	Perdrix bartavelle	*Alectoris graeca*
RB	Grey Partridge	Perdrix grise	*Perdix perdix*
MB, PM	Common Quail	Caille des blès	*Cortunix cortunix*
RB intro.Cors.	Californian Quail	Colin de Californie	*Callipepla californica*
RB	Common Pheasant	Faisan de Colchide	*Phasainus colchicus*
RB intro.	Reeves's Pheasant	Faisan vénéré	*Symaticus reevesii*
RB, PM, WV	Water Rail	Râle d'eau	*Rallus aquaticus*
OB, PM, WV	Spotted Crake	Marouette ponctuée	*Porzana porzana*
OB, AV	Little Crake	Marouette poussin	*Porzana parva*
OB, PM	Baillon's Crake	Marouette de Baillon	*Porzana pusilla*

Status	English Name	French Name	Scientific Name
PM, MB	Corncrake	Râle des genêts	*Crex crex*
RB	Moorhen	Gallinule poule-d'eau	*Gallinula chloropus*
RB (few)	Purple Swamp-hen	Talève sultane	*Porphyrio porphyrio*
RB, WV	Common Coot	Foulque macroule	*Fulica atra*
PM,WV,OB	Common Crane	Grue cendrée	*Grus grus*
RB, MB	Little Bustard	Outarde canepetière	*Tetrax tetrax*
RB, PM, WV	Oystercatcher	Huîtrier pie	*Haematopus ostralegus*
MB, PM	Black-winged Stilt	Echasse blanche	*Himantopushimantopus*
MB, PM, WV	Avocet	Avocette élégante	*Recurvirostra avosetta*
MB, PM, WV	Stone-curlew	œdicnème criard	*Burhinus oedicnemus*
MB (few),PM	Collared Pratincole	Glaréole à collier	*Glareola pratincola*
MB, PM	Little Ringed Plover	Petit Gravelot	*Charadrius dubius*
RB, PM, WV	Great Ringed Plover	Grand Gravelot	*Charadrius hiaticula*
RB, PM, WV	Kentish Plover	Gravelot à collier interrompu	*Charadrius alexandrinus*
MB,(few) PM	Dotterel	Pluvier guignard	*Charadrius morinellus*
WV, PM	European Golden Plover	Pluvier doré	*Pluvialis apricaria*
WV, PM	Grey Plover	Pluvier argenté	*Pluvialis squatarola*
RB,WV, PM	Northern Lapwing	Vanneau huppé	*Vanellus vanellus*
PM, WV	Red Knot	Bécasseau maubèche	*Calidris canutus*
PM, WV	Sanderling	Bécasseau sanderling	*Calidris alba*
WV, PM	Little Stint	Bécasseau minute	*Calidris minuta*
PM, AV	Temminck's Stint	Bécasseau de Temminck	*Calidris temminckii*
PM	Curlew Sandpiper	Bécasseau cocorli	*Calidris ferruginea*
PM,WV	Dunlin	Bécasseau variable	*Calidris alpina*
PM, WV	Ruff	Combattant varié	*Philomachus pugnax*
PM, WV	Jack Snipe	Bécassine sourde	*Lymnocryptes minimus*
RB,PM,WV	Common Snipe	Bécassine des marais	*Gallinago gallinago*
RB, PM,WV	Woodcock	Bécasse des bois	*Scolopax rusticola*
WV, PM	Black-tailed Godwit	Barge à queue noire	*Limosa limosa*
PM, WV	Bar-tailed Godwit	Barge rousse	*Limosa lapponica*
PM	Whimbrel	Courlis corlieu	*Numenius phaeopus*
WV, PM, RB	Eurasian Curlew	Courlis cendré	*Numenius arquata*
PM, WV	Spotted Redshank	Chevalier arlequin	*Tringa erythropus*
PM, WV, RB	Common Redshank	Chevalier totanus	*Tringa totanus*
AV	Marsh Sandpiper	Chevalier stagnatile	*Tringa stagnatilis*
PM, WV	Greenshank	Chevalier aboyeur	*Tringa nebularia*
PM, WV	Green Sandpiper	Chevalier culblanc	*Tringa ochropus*
PM	Wood Sandpiper	Chevalier sylvain	*Tringa glareola*
AV	Terek Sandpiper	Bargette du Terek	*Xenus cinereus*
RB, PM, WV	Common Sandpiper	Chevalier guignette	*Actitis hypoleucos*
PM, WV	Turnstone	Tournepierre à collier	*Arenaria interpres*
PM	Red-necked Phalarope	Phalarope à bec mince	*Phalaropus lobatus*
PM, WV	Grey Phalarope	Phalarope à bec large	*Phalaropus fulicarius*
PM, WV	Great Skua	Grand Labbe	*Catharacta skua*
PM	Pomarine Skua	Labbe pomarin	*Stercorarius pomarinus*
PM, WV	Arctic Skua	Labbe parasite	*Stercorarius parasiticus*
WV, PM, RB	Mediterranean Gull	Mouette mélanocéphale	*Larus melanocephalus*
WV, PM	Little Gull	Mouette pygmée	*Larus minutus*
RB, PM, WV	Black-headed Gull	Mouette rieuse	*Larus ridibundus*
RB, PM	Slender-billed Gull	Goéland railleur	*Larus genei*
RB, PM	Audouin's Gull	Goéland d'Audouin	*Larus audouinii*
WV, PM, RB	Common Gull	Goéland cendré	*Larus canus*
WV, RB, PM	Lesser Black-backed Gull	Goéland brun	*Larus fuscus*
RB, PM, WV	Herring Gull	Goéland argenté	*Larus argentatus*
RB, PM, WV	Yellow-legged Gull	Goéland leucopheé	*Larus michalelis*
WV, RB	Great Black-backed Gull	Goéland marin	*Larus marinus*
RB,WV, PM	Kittiwake	Mouette tridactyle	*Rissa tridactyle*
PM, MB	Gull-billed Tern	Sterne hansel	*Sterna nilotica*
PM	Caspian Tern	Sterne caspienne	*Sterna caspia*
RB, PM, WV	Sandwich Tern	Sterne caugek	*Sterna sandvicensis*

Status	English Name	French Name	Scientific Name
PM, MB	Common Tern	Sterne pierregarin	*Sterna hirundo*
PM, OB	Arctic Tern	Sterne arctique	*Sterna paradisaea*
RB, PM	Roseate Tern	Sterne de Dougall	*Sterna dougallii*
MB, PM	Little Tern	Sterne naine	*Sterna albifrons*
PM, MB	Whiskered Tern	Guifette moustac	*Chlidonias hybridus*
PM, MB	Black Tern	Guifette noire	*Chlidonias niger*
PM	White-winged Black Tern	Guifette leucoptère	*Chlidonias leucopterus*
PM, WV, RB	Common Guillemot	Guillemot de Troil	*Uria aalge*
WV, PM, RB	Razorbill	Pingouin torda	*Alca torda*
RB, WV, PM	Atlantic Puffin	Macareux moine	*Fratercula arctica*
RB	Pin-tailed Sandgrouse	Ganga cata	*Pterocles alchata*
RB	Rock Dove	Pigeon biset	*Columba livia*
RB, PM, WV	Stock Dove	Pigeon colombin	*Columba oenas*
RB, PM, WV	Wood Pigeon	Pigeon ramier	*Columba palumbus*
RB, PM	Collared Dove	Tourterelle turque	*Streptopelia decaoto*
PM, MB	Turtle Dove	Tourterelle des bois	*Streptopelia turtur*
MB	Great Spotted Cuckoo	Coucou geai	*Clamator glandarius*
MB, PM	Common Cuckoo	Coucou gris	*Cuculus canoris*
RB, WV, PM	Barn Owl	Effraie des clochers	*Tyto alba*
MB	Eurasian Scops Owl	Petit-duc scops	*Otus scops*
RB	Eagle Owl	Grand-duc d'Europe	*Bubo bubo*
RB	Pygmy Owl	Chevechette d'Europe	*Glaucidium passerinum*
RB	Little Owl	Chouette cheveche	*Athene noctua*
RB	Tawny Owl	Chouette hulotte	*Strix aluco*
RB, PM, WV	Long-eared Owl	Hibou moyen-duc	*Asio otus*
WV, RB, PM	Short-eared Owl	Hibou des marais	*Asio flammeus*
RB	Tengmalm's Owl	Chouette de Tengmalm	*Aegolius funereus*
MB	European Nightjar	Engoulevent d'Europe	*Caprimulgus europaeus*
MB, PM	Alpine Swift	Martinet à ventre blanc	*Tachymarptis melba*
MB, PM	Common Swift	Martinet noir	*Apus apus*
MB, PM	Pallid Swift	Martinet pâle	*Apus pallidus*
RB, WV	Common Kingfisher	Martin-pêcheur d'Europe	*Alcedo atthis*
MB, PM	European Bee-eater	Guêpier d'Europe	*Merops apiaster*
MB, PM	European Roller	Rollier d'Europe	*Coracias garrulus*
MB, PM	Hoopoe	Huppe fasciée	*Upupa epops*
MB, PM	Wryneck	Torcol fourmilier	*Jynx torquilla*
RB	Grey-headed Woodpecker	Pic cendré	*Picus canus*
RB	Green Woodpecker	Pic vert	*Picus viridis*
RB	Black Woodpecker	Pic noir	*Dryocopus martius*
RB	Great Spotted Woodpecker	Pic épeiche	*Dendrocopus major*
RB	Middle Spotted Woodpecker	Pic mar	*Dendrocopus medius*
RB (very local)	White-backed Woodpecker	Pic à dos blanc	*Dendrocopus leucotos*
RB	Lesser Spotted Woodpecker	Pic épeichette	*Dendrocopus minor*
RB rare	Three-toed Woodpecker	Pic tridactyle	*Picoides tridactylus*
RB rare	Calandra Lark	Alouette calandre	*Melanocorypha calandra*
MB	Short-toed Lark	Alouette calandrelle	*Calandrella brachydactyla*
RB	Crested Lark	Cochevis huppé	*Galerida cristata*
RB rare	Thekla Lark	Cochevis de Thékla	*Galerida theklae*
RB, PM, WV	Wood Lark	Alouette lulu	*Lullula arborea*
RB	Sky Lark	Alouette des champs	*Alauda arvensis*
WV rare`	Horned Lark	Alouette haussecol	*Eremophila alpestris*
MB, PM	Sand Martin	Hirondelle de rivage	*Riparia riparia*
RB, WV	Crag Martin	Hirondelle de rochers	*Ptyonoprogne rupestris*
MB, PM	Barn Swallow	Hirondelle rustique	*Hirundo rustica*
AV, OB	Red-rumped Swallow	Hirondelle rousseline	*Hirundo daurica*
MB, PM	House Martin	Hirondelle de fenêtre	*Delichon urbica*
MB, PM	Tawny Pipit	Pipit rousseline	*Anthus campestris*
MB, PM	Tree Pipit	Pipit des arbres	*Anthus trivialis*
RB,WV, PM	Meadow Pipit	Pipit farlouse	*Anthus pratensis*
MB, PM, WV	Water Pipit	Pipit spioncelle	*Anthus spinoletta*

Status	English Name	French Name	Scientific Name
PM, WV, RB	Rock Pipit	Pipit maritime	*Anthus petrosus*
PM rare	Red-throated Pipit	Pipit à gorge rousse	*Anthus cervinus*
PM, MB	Yellow Wagtail	Bergeronnette printanière	*Motacilla flava*
RB, PM, WV	Pied (White) Wagtail	Bergeronnette grise	*Motacilla alba*
RB, PM, WV	Grey Wagtail	Bergeronnette des ruisseaux	*Motacilla cinerea*
WV rare	Waxwing	Jaseur boréal	*Bombycilla garrulus*
RB	Dipper	Cincle plongeur	*Cinclus cinclus*
RB	Wren	Troglodyte mignon	*Troglodytes troglodytes*
RB, PM, WV	Hedge Accentor	Accenteur mouchet	*Prunella modularis*
RB	Alpine Accentor	Accenteur alpin	*Prunella collaris*
PM rare	Rufous-tailed Scrub-robin	Agrobate roux	*Cercotrichas galactotes*
RB, PM, WV	Robin	Rougegorge familier	*Erithacus rubecula*
MB, PM	Rufous Nightingale	Rossignol philomèle	*Luscinia megarhynchos*
MB, PM, WV	Bluethroat	Gorgebleue à miroir	*Luscinia svecica*
RB, PM	Black Redstart	Rougequeue noir	*Phoenicurus ochruros*
MB, PM	Redstart	Rougequeue à front blanc	*Phoenicurus phoenicurus*
RB, PM, WV	Common Stonechat	Tarrier pâtre	*Saxicola torquata*
MB, PM	Whinchat	Tarrier des prés	*Saxicola rubetra*
MB, PM	Northern Wheatear	Traquet motteux	*Oenanthe oenanthe*
MB	Black-eared Wheatear	Traquet oreillard	*Oenanthe hispanica*
RB v.rare	Black Wheatear	Traquet rieur	*Oenanthe leucura*
MB	Rock Thrush	Merle de roche	*Monticola saxatilis*
RB, PM	Blue Rock Thrush	Merle bleu	*Monticola solitarius*
MB, PM	Ring Ouzel	Merle à plastron	*Turdus torquatus*
RB, PM, WV	Blackbird	BMerle noir	*Turdus merula*
RB, PM, WV	Fieldfare	Grive litorne	*Turdus pilaris*
RB, PM, WV	Song Thrush	Grive musicienne	*Turdus philomelos*
PM, WV	Redwing	Grive mauvis	*Turdus iliacus*
RB, PM, WV	Mistle Thrush	Grive draine	*Turdus viscivoris*
RB	Cetti's Warbler	Bouscarle de Cetti	*Cettia cetti*
RB, PM	Zitting Cisticola	Cisticole des joncs	*Cisticola juncidis*
MB, PM	Grasshopper Warbler	Locustelle tachetée	*Locustella naevia*
MB	Savi's Warbler	Locustelle luscinïoïde	*Locustella luscinioides*
RB	Moustached Warbler	Locustelle à moustaches	*Acrocephalus melanopogon*
MB, PM	Sedge Warbler	Phragmite des joncs	*Acrocephalus schoenobaenus*
MB, PM	Marsh Warbler	Rousserolle verderolle	*Acrocephalus palustris*
MB, PM	Reed Warbler	Rousserolle effarvatte	*Acrocephalus scirpaceus*
MB, PM	Great Reed Warbler	Rousserolle turdoïde	*Acrocephalus arundinaceus*
MB, PM	Icterine Warbler	Hypolaïs ictérine	*Hippolais icterina*
MB, PM	Melodious Warbler	Hypolaïs polyglotte	*Hippolais polyglotta*
RB Corsica	Marmora's Warbler	Fauvette sarde	*Sylvia sarda*
RB, PM, WV	Dartford Warbler	Fauvette pitchou	*Sylvia undata*
MB	Spectacled Warbler	Fauvette à lunettes	*Sylvia conspicillata*
MB	Subalpine Warbler	Fauvette passerinette	*Sylvia cantilans*
RB	Sardinian Warbler	Fauvette mélanocéphale	*Sylvia melanocephala*
MB	Orphean Warbler	Fauvette orphée	*Sylvia hortensis*
MB, PM	Lesser Whitethroat	Fauvette babillarde	*Sylvia curruca*
MB, PM	Common Whitethroat	Fauvette grisette	*Sylvia communis*
MB, PM	Garden Warbler	Fauvette des jardins	*Sylvia borin*
MB, PM, WV	Blackcap	Fauvette à tête noire	*Sylvia atricapilla*
MB, PM	Western Bonelli's Warbler	Pouillot de Bonelli	*Phylloscopus bonellii*
MB, PM	Wood Warbler	Pouillot siffleur	*Phylloscopus sibilatrix*
MB, RB, WV	Common Chiffchaff	Pouillot véloce	*Phylloscopus collybita*
MB, PM	Willow Warbler	Pouillot fitis	*Phylloscopus trochilus*
RB, PM, WV	Goldcrest	Roitelet huppé	*Regulus regulus*
RB, PM, WV	Firecrest	Roitelet triple-bandeau	*Regulus ignicapillus*
MB, PM	Spotted Flycatcher	Gobemouche gris	*Muscicapa striata*
MB, PM	Collared Flycatcher	Gobemouche à collier	*Ficedula albicollis*
MB, PM	Pied Flycatcher	Gobemouche noir	*Ficedula hypoleuca*
RB, WV	Bearded Tit	Panure à moustaches	*Panurus biarmicus*

Status	English Name	French Name	Scientific Name
RB	Long-tailed Tit	Mésange à longue queue	*Aegithalos caudatus*
RB	Marsh Tit	Mésange nonnette	*Parus palustris*
RB	Willow Tit	Mésange boréale	*Parus montanus*
RB	Crested Tit	Mésange huppée	*Parus cristatus*
RB, WV	Coal Tit	Mésange noire	*Parus ater*
RB, WV	Blue Tit	Mésange bleue	*Parus caeruleus*
RB, WV	Great Tit	Mésange charbonnière	*Parus major*
RB Corsica	Corsican Nuthatch	Sitelle corse	*Sitta whiteheadi*
RB	European Nuthatch	Sitelle torchepot	*Sitta europaea*
RB, PM, WV	Wallcreeper	Tichodrome échelette	*Tichodroma muraria*
RB	Short-toed Treecreeper	Grimpereau des jardins	*Certhia brachydactyla*
RB	Eurasian Treecreeper	Grimpereau des bois	*Certhia familiaris*
RB, PM, WV	Penduline Tit	Rémiz penduline	*Remiz pendulinus*
MB, PM	Golden Oriole	Loriot d'Europe	*Oriolus oriolus*
MB, PM	Red-backed Shrike	Pie-grièche écorcheur	*Lanius collurio*
MB (local)	Lesser Grey	Pie-grièche à poitrine rose	*Lanius minor*
RB, WV, PM	Northern Grey Shrike	Pie-grièche grise	*Lanius excubitor*
RB, WV, PM	Southern Grey Shrike	Pie-grièche	*Lanius meridionalis*
MB, PM	Woodchat Shrike	Pie-grièche à tête rousse	*Lanius senator*
RB, PM, WV	Eurasian Jay	Geai des chênes	*Garrulus glandarius*
RB	Magpie	Pie bavarde	*Pica pica*
RB	Nutcracker	Cassenoix moucheté	*Nucifraga caryocatactes*
RB	Red-billed Chough	Crave à bec rouge	*Pyrrhocorax pyrrthocorax*
RB	Yellow-billed Chough	Chocard à bec jaune	*Pyrrhocorax graculus*
RB, PM, WV	Eurasian Jackdaw	Choucas des tours	*Corvus monedula*
RB, WV	Carrion/Hooded Crow	Corneille noire/ mantelée	*Corvus corone*
RB, PM, WV	Rook	Corbeau freux	*Corvus frugilegus*
RB	Common Raven	Grand Corbeau	*Corvus corax*
RB local	Spotless Starling	Etourneau unicolore	*Sturnus unicolor*
RB, WV, PM	Common Starling	Etourneau sansonnet	*Sturnus vulgaris*
RB, PM, WV	House Sparrow	Moineau domestique	*Passer domesticus*
RB local	Italian Sparrow	Moineau cisalpin	*Passer italiae*
RB, PM, WV	Tree Sparrow	Moineau friquet	*Passer montanus*
RB	Rock Sparrow	Moineau soulcie	*Petronia petronia*
RB	Snowfinch	Niverolle alpine	*Montifringilla nivalis*
RB, PM, WV	Common Chaffinch	Pinson des arbres	*Fringilla coelebs*
WV, PM	Brambling	Pinson du Nord	*Fringilla montifringila*
RB, PM, WV	European Serin	Serin cini	*Serinus serinus*
RB	Citril Finch	Venturon montagnard	*Serinus citrinella*
RB Corsica	Corsican Citril	Venturon corse	*Serinus corsicanus*
RB, PM, WV	Greenfinch	GreeVerdier d'Europe	*Carduelis chloris*
RB, PM, WV	Goldfinch	Chardonneret élégant	*Carduelis carduelis*
WV, RB, PM	Siskin	Tarin des aulnes	*Carduelis spinus*
RB, PM, WV	Linnet	Linotte mélodieuse	*Acanthis cannaina*
RB, PM, WV	Common Crossbill	Bec-croisé des sapins	*Loxia curvirostra*
PM rare	Parrot Crossbill	Bec-croisé perroquet	*Loxia pytyopsittacus*
OB rare	Common Rosefinch	Roselin cramoisi	*Carpodacus erythrinus*
RB, WV	Common Bullfinch	Bouvreuil pivoine	*Pyrrhula pyrrhula*
RB, WV, PM	Hawfinch	Grosbec casse-noyaux	*Coccothraustes coccothraustes*
WV	Lapland Longspur	Bruant lapon	*Calcarius lapponicus*
WV	Snow Bunting	Bruant des neiges	*Plectrophenax nivalis*
RB, PM, WV	Yellowhammer	Bruant jaune	*Emberiza citrinella*
RB, PM	Cirl Bunting	Bruant zizi	*Emberiza cirlus*
RB	Rock Bunting	Bruant fou	*Emberiza cia*
MB, PM	Ortolan Bunting	Bruant ortolan	*Emberiza hortulana*
RB, WV, PM	Reed Bunting	Bruant des roseaux	*Emberiza schoeniclus*
OB	Black-headed Binting	Bruant mélanocéphale	*Emberiza melanocephala*
RB, PM, WV	Corn Bunting	Bruant proyer	*Miliaria calandra*

FRENCH-BIRD NAMES

The second check list is in alphabetical order of the French name for the bird. It is hoped that this will help those whose knowledge of French does not include all the French names as it will be an aid to translating the name quickly when reading information boards at reserves etc. Some birds have been shown twice to take into account alternative French names.

English Name	French Name
Alpine Accentor	Accenteur alpin
Hedge Accentor	Accenteur mouchet
Rufous-tailed Scrub-robin	Agrobate roux
Booted Eagle	Aigle botté
Spotted Eagle	Aigle criard
Bonelli's Eagle	Aigle de Bonelli
Golden Eagle	Aigle royal
Western Reef Heron	Aigrette des récifs
Little Egret	Aigrette garzette
Calandra Lark	Alouette calandre
Short-toed Lark	Alouette calandrelle
Sky Lark	Alouette des champs
Horned Lark	Alouette haussecol
Wood Lark	Alouette lulu
Northern Goshawk	Autour des polombes
Avocet	Avocette élégante
Osprey	Balbuzard pecheur
Osprey	Balbuzard pêcheur
Black-tailed Godwit	Barge à queue noire
Bar-tailed Godwit	Barge rousse
Terek Sandpiper	Bargette du Terek
Woodcock	Bécasse des bois
Curlew Sandpiper	Bécasseau cocorli
Temminck's Stint	Bécasseau de Temminck
Red Knot	Bécasseau maubèche
Little Stint	Bécasseau minute
Sanderling	Bécasseau sanderling
Dunlin	Bécasseau variable
Purple Sandpiper	Bècasseau violet
Common Snipe	Bécassine des marais
Jack Snipe	Bécassine sourde
Common Crossbill	Bec-croisé des sapins
Parrot Crossbill	Bec-croisé perroquet
Grey Wagtail	Bergeronnette des ruisseaux
Pied (White) Wagtail	Bergeronnette grise
Yellow Wagtail	Bergeronnette printanière
Red-breasted Goose	Bernache à cou rouge
Brent Goose	Bernache cravant
Barnacle Goose	Bernache nonette
Night Heron	Bihoreau gris
Little Bittern	Blongios nain
European Honey-buzzard	Bondrée apivore
Cetti's Warbler	Bouscarle de Cetti
Common Bullfinch	Bouvreuil pivoine
Snow Bunting	Bruant des neiges
Reed Bunting	Bruant des roseaux
Rock Bunting	Bruant fou
Yellowhammer	Bruant jaune
Lapland Longspur	Bruant lapon
Ortolan Bunting	Bruant ortolan
Corn Bunting	Bruant proyer
Cirl Bunting	Bruant zizi

English Name	French Name
Montagu's Harrier	**Busard cendré**
Marsh Harrier	**Busard des roseaux**
Hen Harrier	**Busard Saint-Martin**
Common Buzzard	**Buse variable**
Great Bittern	**Butor étoilé**
Common Quail	**Caille des blés**
Gadwall	**Canard chipeau**
Mallard	**Canard colvert**
Pintail	**Canard pilet**
Eurasian Wigeon	**Canard siffleur**
Northern Shoveler	**Canard souchet**
Nutcracker	**Cassenoix moucheté**
Goldfinch	**Chardonneret élégant**
Greenshank	**Chevalier aboyeur**
Spotted Redshank	**Chevalier arlequin**
Green Sandpiper	**Chevalier culblanc**
Common Sandpiper	**Chevalier guignette**
Marsh Sandpiper	**Chevalier stagnatile**
Wood Sandpiper	**Chevalier sylvain**
Common Redshank	**Chevalier totanus**
Pygmy Owl	**Chevêchette d'Europe/**
	Chouette chevêchette
Yellow-billed Chough	**Chocard à bec jaune**
Eurasian Jackdaw	**Choucas des tours**
Little Owl	**Chouette chevêche/**
	Chevêche d'Athèna
Tengmalm's Owl	**Chouette de Tengmalm**
Barn Owl	**Chouette effraie**
Tawny Owl	**Chouette hulotte**
White Stork	**Cigogne blanche**
Black Stork	**Cigogne noire**
Dipper	**Cincle plongeur**
Short-toed Eagle	**Circaète Jean-le-Blanc**
Zitting Cisticola	**Cisticole des joncs**
Thekla Lark	**Cochevis de Thékla**
Crested Lark	**Cochevis huppé**
Californian Quail	**Colin de Californie**
Ruff	**Combattant varié/**
	Chevalier combattant
Rook	**Corbeau freux**
Shag	**Cormoran huppé**
Carrion/Hooded Crow	**Corneille noire/ mantelée**
Great Spotted Cuckoo	**Coucou geai**
Cuckoo	**Coucou gris**
Eurasian Curlew	**Courlis cendré**
Whimbrel	**Courlis corlieu**
Squacco Heron	**Crabier chevelu**
Red-billed Chough	**Crave à bec rouge**
Whooper Swan	**Cygne chanteur**
Bewick's Swan	**Cygne de Bewick**
Mute Swan	**Cygne tuberculé**
Black-winged Stilt	**Echasse blanche**
Barn Owl	**Effraie des clochers**
Common Eider	**Eider à duvet**
Black-shouldered Kite	**Elanion blanc**
European Nightjar	**Engoulevent d'Europe**
Eurasian Sparrowhawk	**Epervier d'Europe**
Common Starling	**Etourneau sansonnet**
Spotless Starling	**Etourneau unicolore**
Common Pheasant	**Faisan de Colchide**
Reeves's Pheasant	**Faisan vénéré**

English Name	French Name
Common Kestrel	Faucon crécerelle
Lesser Kestrel	Faucon crécerellette
Eleanora's Falcon	Faucon d'Eléonore
Merlin	Faucon émerillon
Hobby	Faucon hobereau
Red-footed Falcon	Faucon kobez
Peregrine Falcon	Faucon pèlerin
Spectacled Warbler	Fauvette à lunettes
Blackcap	Fauvette à tête noire
Lesser Whitethroat	Fauvette babillarde
Garden Warbler	Fauvette des jardins
Common Whitethroat	Fauvette grisette
Sardinian Warbler	Fauvette mélanocéphale
Orphean Warbler	Fauvette orphée
Subalpine Warbler	Fauvette passerinette
Dartford Warbler	Fauvette pitchou
Marmora's Warbler	Fauvette sarde
Greater Flamingo	Flamant rose
Northern Gannet	Fou de Bassan
Common Coot	Foulque macroule
Common Pochard	Fuligule milouin
Greater Scaup	Fuligule milouinan
Ferruginous Duck	Fuligule nyroca
Tufted Duck	Fuligule morillon
Fulmar	Fulmar boréal
Moorhen	Gallinule poule-d'eau
Pin-tailed Sandgrouse	Ganga cata
Goldeneye	Garrot à oeil d'or
Eurasian Jay	Geai des chênes
Hazel Grouse	Gélinotte des bois
Collared Pratincole	Glaréole à collier
Collared Flycatcher	Gobemouche à collier
Spotted Flycatcher	Gobemouche gris
Pied Flycatcher	Gobemouche noir
Herring Gull	Goéland argenté
Lesser Black-backed Gull	Goéland brun
Common Gull	Goéland cendré
Audouin's Gull	Goéland d'Audouin
Yellow-legged Gull	Goéland leucopheé
Great Black-backed Gull	Goéland marin
Slender-billed Gull	Goéland railleur
Bluethroat	Gorgebleue à miroir
Common Raven	Grand Corbeau
Great Cormorant	Grand Cormoran
Great Ringed Plover	Grand Gravelot
Great Skua	Grand Labbe
Capercaillie	Grand Tétras
Eagle Owl	Grand-duc d'Europe/ Hibou grand-duc
Great White Egret	Grande Aigrette
Kentish Plover	Gravelot à collier interrompu
Black-necked Grebe	Grèbe à cou noir
Little Grebe	Grèbe castagneux
Slavonian Grebe	Grèbe esclavon
Great Crested Grebe	Grèbe huppé
Red-necked Grebe	Grèbe jougris
Eurasian Treecreeper	Grimpereau des bois
Short-toed Treecreeper	Grimpereau des jardins
Mistle Thrush	Grive draine
Fieldfare	Grive litorne
Redwing	Grive mauvis

English Name	French Name
Song Thrush	**Grive musicienne**
Hawfinch	**Grosbec casse-noyaux**
Common Crane	**Grue cendrée**
European Bee-eater	**Guêpier d'Europe**
White-winged Black Tern	**Guifette leucoptère**
Whiskered Tern	**Guifette moustac**
Black Tern	**Guifette noire**
Common Guillemot	**Guillemot de Troïl/ marmette**
Lammergeier	**Gypaète barbu**
Goosander	**Harle bièvre/Grande harle**
Red-breasted Merganser	**Harle huppé**
Smew	**Harle piette**
Grey Heron	**Héron cendré**
Cattle Egret	**Héron gardeboeufs**
Purple Heron	**Héron purpré**
Short-eared Owl	**Hibou des marais**
Eagle Owl	**Hibou grand-duc/ Grand-duc 'dEurope**
Long-eared Owl	**Hibou moyen-duc**
Eurasian Scops Owl	**Hibou petit-duc/ Petit-duc scops**
House Martin	**Hirondelle de fenêtre**
Sand Martin	**Hirondelle de rivage**
Crag Martin	**Hirondelle de rochers**
Red-rumped Swallow	**Hirondelle rousseline**
Barn Swallow	**Hirondelle rustique/ de cheminée**
Oystercatcher	**Huîtrier pie**
Hoopoe	**Huppe fasciée**
Icterine Warbler	**Hypolaïs ictérine**
Melodious Warbler	**Hypolaïs polyglotte**
Glossy Ibis	**Ibis falcinelle**
Sacred Ibis	**Ibis sacré**
Waxwing	**Jaseur boréal**
Arctic Skua	**Labbe parasite**
Pomarine Skua	**Labbe pomarin**
Ptarmigan	**Lagopède alpin**
Linnet	**Linotte mélodieuse**
Savi's Warbler	**Locustelle lusciniöide**
Grasshopper Warbler	**Locustelle tachetée**
Golden Oriole	**Loriot d'Europe**
Moustached Warbler	**Lusciniole à moustaches**
Atlantic Puffin	**Macareux moine**
Velvet Scoter	**Macreuse brune**
Common Scoter	**Macreuse noire**
Baillon's Crake	**Marouette de Baillon**
Spotted Crake	**Marouette ponctuée**
Little Crake	**Marouette poussin**
Alpine Swift	**Martinet à ventre blanc**
Common Swift	**Martinet noir**
Pallid Swift	**Martinet pâle**
Common Kingfisher	**Martin-pêcheur d'Europe**
Ring Ouzel	**Merle à plastron**
Blue Rock Thrush	**Merle bleu**
Blackbird	**Merle noir**
Rock Thrush	**Merle de roche**
Long-tailed Tit	**Mésange à longue queue**
Blue Tit	**Mésange bleue**
Willow Tit	**Mésange boréale**
Great Tit	**Mésange charbonnière**

English Name	French Name
Crested Tit	Mésange huppée
Coal Tit	Mésange noire
Penduline Tit	Mèsange rèmiz
Marsh Tit	Mésange nonnette
Black Kite	Milan noir
Red Kite	Milan royal
Italian Sparrow	Moineau cisalpin
House Sparrow	Moineau domestique
Tree Sparrow	Moineau friquet
Rock Sparrow	Moineau soulcie
Mediterranean Gull	Mouette mélanocéphale
Little Gull	Mouette pygmée
Black-headed Gull	Mouette rieuse
Kittiwake	Mouette tridactyle
Red-crested Pochard	Nette rousse
Snowfinch	Niverolle alpine
Leach's Storm-petrel	Océanite culblanc
European Storm-petrel	Océanite tempête
Stone-curlew	Oedicnème criard
Greylag Goose	Oie cendrée
Bean Goose	Oie des moissons
White-fronted Goose	Oie rieuse
Little Bustard	Outarde canepetière
Bearded Tit	Panure à moustaches
Rock Partridge	Perdrix bartavelle
Chukar	Perdrix choukar
Grey Partridge	Perdrix grise
Red-legged Partridge	Perdrix rouge
Little Ringed Plover	Petit Gravelot
Eurasian Scops Owl	Petit-duc scops/
	Hibou petit-duc
Grey Phalarope	Phalarope à bec large
Red-necked Phalarope	Phalarope à bec mince
Sedge Warbler	Phragmite des joncs
White-backed Woodpecker	Pic à dos blanc
Grey-headed Woodpecker	Pic cendré
Great Spotted Woodpecker	Pic épeiche
Lesser Spotted Woodpecker	Pic épeichette
Middle Spotted Woodpecker	Pic mar
Black Woodpecker	Pic noir
Three-toed Woodpecker	Pic tridactyle
Green Woodpecker	Pic vert
Magpie	Pie bavarde
Lesser Grey Shrike	Pie-grièche à poitrine rose
Woodchat Shrike	Pie-grièche à tête rousse
Red-backed Shrike	Pie-grièche écorcheur
Northern Grey Shrike	Pie-grièche grise
Southern Grey Shrike	Pie-grièche méridionale
Rock Dove	Pigeon biset
Stock Dove	Pigeon colombin
Wood Pigeon	Pigeon ramier
Razorbill	Pingouin torda
Common Chaffinch	Pinson des arbres
Brambling	Pinson du Nord
Red-throated Pipit	Pipit à gorge rousse
Tree Pipit	Pipit des arbres
Meadow Pipit	Pipit farlouse
Rock Pipit	Pipit maritime
Tawny Pipit	Pipit rousseline
Water Pipit	Pipit spioncelle
Black-throated Diver	Plongeon artique

English Name	French Name
Red-throated Diver	**Plongeon catmarin**
Great Northern Diver	**Plongeon imbrin**
Grey Plover	**Pluvier argenté**
European Golden Plover	**Pluvier doré**
Dotterel	**Pluvier guignard**
Kentish Plover	**Pluvier à collier interrompu**
Ringed Plover	**Pluvier grand-gravelot**
Little Ringed Plover	**Pluvier petit-gravelot**
Purple Gallinule	**Porphyrion bleu/**
	Poule sultane
Western Bonelli's Warbler	**Pouillot de Bonelli**
Willow Warbler	**Pouillot fitis**
Wood Warbler	**Pouillot siffleur**
Common/Iberian Chiffchaff	**Pouillot véloce/**
	iberique
Cory's Shearwater	**Puffin cendré**
Balearic Shearwater	**Puffin de Baléares**
Yelkouan Shearwater	**Puffin de Mediterranée**
Manx Shearwater	**Puffin des Anglais**
White-tailed Sea-eagle	**Pygargue à queue blanche**
Water Rail	**Râle d'eau**
Corn Crake	**Râle des genêts**
Penduline Tit	**Rémiz penduline**
Goldcrest	**Roitelet huppé**
Firecrest	**Roitelet triple-bandeau**
European Roller	**Rollier d'Europe**
Common Rosefinch	**Roselin cramoisi**
Rufous Nightingale	**Rossignol philomèle**
Robin	**Rougegorge familier**
Redstart	**Rougequeue à front blanc**
Black Redstart	**Rougequeue noir**
Reed Warbler	**Rousserolle effarvatte**
Great Reed Warbler	**Rousserolle turdoïde**
Marsh Warbler	**Rousserolle verderolle**
Gargany	**Sarcelle d'été**
Common Teal	**Sarcelle d'hiver**
European Serin	**Serin cini**
Corsican Nuthatch	**Sitelle corse**
European Nuthatch	**Sitelle torchepot**
Common Redpoll	**Sizerin flammé**
Eurasian Spoonbill	**Spatule blanche**
Arctic Tern	**Sterne arctique**
Caspian Tern	**Sterne caspienne**
Sandwich Tern	**Sterne caugek**
Gull-billed Tern	**Sterne hansel**
Little Tern	**Sterne naine**
Common Tern	**Sterne pierregarin**
Common Shelduck	**Tadorne de Belon**
Purple Swamp-hen	**Talève sultane**
Siskin	**Tarin des aulnes**
Whinchat	**Tarier des près**
Common Stonechat	**Tarier pâtre**
Black Grouse	**Tétras lyre**
Wallcreeper	**Tichodrome échelette**
Wryneck	**Torcol fourmilier**
Turnstone	**Tournepierre à collier**
Turtle Dove	**Tourterelle des bois**
Collared Dove	**Tourterelle turque**
Northern Wheatear	**Traquet motteux**
Black-eared Wheatear	**Traquet oreillard**
Black Wheatear	**Traquet rieur**

English Name	French Name
Wren	**Troglodyte mignon**
Northern Lapwing	**Vanneau huppé**
Griffon Vulture	**Vautour fauve**
Black (Monk) Vulture	**Vautour moine**
Egyptian Vulture	**Vautour percnoptère**
Corsican Citril	**Venturon corse**
Citril Finch	**Venturon montagnard**
Greenfinch	**Verdier d'Europe**

MAMMALS

English Name	Scientific Name
Western Hedgehog	Erinaceus europaeus
Pyrenean Desman	Galemys pyrenaicus
Mole	Talpa caaeca
Common Mole	Talpa europaea
Pygmy Shrew	Sorex minutus
Millet's Shrew	S. coronatus
Alpine Shrew	S. alpinus
Water Shrew	Neomys fodiens
Miller's Water Shrew	N. anomalus
Lesser White-toothed Shrew	Crocidura suaveolens
Greater White-toothed Shrew	C. russula
Pygmy White-toothed Shrew	Suncus etruscus
Lesser Horseshoe Bat	Rhinolopus hipposideros
Mediterranean Horseshoe Bat	R. euryale
Greater Horseshoe Bat	R. ferrumequinum
Daubenton's Bat	Myotis daubentonii
Whiskered Bat	M. mystacinus
Long-fingered Bat	M. capaccinii
Natterer's Bat	M. nattereri
Geoffroy's Bat	M. emarginatus
Bechstein's Bat	M. bechsteinii
Greater Mouse-eared Bat	M. myotis
Lesser Mouse-eared Bat	M. blythi
Common Pipistrelle	Pipistrellus pipistrellus
Nathusius's Pipistrelle.	P. nathusii
Kuhl's Pipistrelle	P. kuhlii
Savi's Pipistrelle	Hypsugo savii
Leisler's Bat	Nyctalus leisleri
Noctule	N. noctula
Greater Noctule - rare	N. lasiopteris
Serotine	Eptesicus serotinus
Northern Bat	Eptesicus nilssoni
Parti-coloured Bat - rare	Verpertilio murinus
Barbastelle	Barbastella barbastellus
Grey Long-eared Bat	Plecotus austriacus
Brown Long-eared Bat	P. auritus
Schreiber's Bat	Miniopterus schreibersi
Free-tailed Bat	Tadarida teniotis
Brown Hare	Lepus europaeus
Rabbit	Oryctolagus cuniculus
Cotton-tail Rabbit (intro.)	Sylvilagus floridanus
Red Squirrel	Sciurus vulgaris
Alpine Marmot	Marmota marmota
European Beaver	Castor fiber
Bank Vole	Clethrionomys glareolus
Southern Water Vole	Arvicola sapidus

English Name	Scientific Name
Northern Water Vole	A. terrestris
Muskrat (intro.)	Ondatra zibethicus
Alpine Pine Vole	Pity;mys multiplex
Field Vole	Microtus agrestis
Common Vole	M. arvalis
Pyrenean Pine Vole	Microtus pyrenaicus
Snow Vole	M. nivalis
Garden Dormouse	Eliomys quercinus
Fat (Edible)Dormouse	Glis glis
Common Dormouse	Muscardinus avellanarius
Wood Mouse	Apodemus sylvaticus
Yellow-necked Mouse	A. flavicollis
Harvest Mouse	Micromys minutus
Brown Rat	Rattus norvegicus
Black Rat	R. rattus
House Mouse	Mus domesticus
Coypu (intro.)	Myocastor coypus
Wild Boar	Sus scrofa
Chamois	Rupicapra pyrenaica/rupicapra
Alpine Ibex	Capra ibex
Mouflon/ Sardinian Mouflon	Ovis orientalis/musimon
Red Deer	Cervus elaphus
Fallow Deer	Dama dama
Roe Deer	Capreolus capreolus
Wolf	Canis lupus
Red Fox	Vulpes vulpes
Racoon Dog (intro.)	Nyctereutes procyonoides
Brown Bear	Ursus arctos
Weasel	Mustela nivalis
Stoat	M. erminea
European Mink	M. lutreola
American Mink (intro.)	M. vison
Western Polecat	Mustela putorius
Pine Marten	Martes martes
Beech Marten	M. foina
Badger	Meles meles
Otter	Lutra lutra
Genet	Genetta genetta
Wild Cat	Felis silvestris
Lynx	Lynx lynx
Striped Dolphin	Stenella coeruleoalba
Common Dolphin	Delphinus delphis
Bottle-nosed Dolphin	Tursiops truncatus
Killer Whale	Orcinus orca
Fin Whale	Balaenoptera physalus
Minke Whale	Balaenoptera acutorostrata
Sperm Whate	Physeter macrocephalus
Risso's Dolphin	Grampus priseus
Long-finned Pilot Whale	Globicephala melaena
Cuvier's Beaked Whale	Ziphius cavirostris
Mediterranean Monk Seal	Monachus monachus
Common Seal	Phoca vitulina
Grey Seal	Halichoerus grypus

AMPHIBIANS and REPTILES

English Name	Scientific Name
Hermann's Tortoise	Testudo hermanni

English Name	Scientific Name
European Pond Terrapin	*Emys orbicularis*
Moorish Gecko	*Tarentola mauritanica*
Turkish Gecko	*Hemidactylus turcicus*
Large Psammodromus	*Psammodromus algirus*
Spanish Psammodromus	*P. hispanicus*
Oscellated Lizard	*Lacerta lepida*
Green Lizard	*L. viridis*
Sand Lizard	*L. agilis*
Viviparous Lizard	*L. vivipara*
Iberian Rock Lizard	*L. monticola*
Pyrenean Lizard	*L. bonnali (L. aurelioi)*
Common Wall Lizard	*Podarcis muralis*
Iberian Wall Lizard	*P. hispanica*
Slow Worm	*Anguis fragilis*
Three-toed Skink	*Chalcides chalcides (C. striatus)*
Monpellier Snake	*Malpolon monspessulanus*
Western Whip Snake	*Coluber viridiflavus*
Aesculapian Snake	*Elaphe longissima*
Ladder Snake	*E. scalaris*
Grass Snake	*Natrix natrix*
Viperine Snake	*N. maura*
Smooth Snake	*Coronella austriaca*
Southern Smooth Snake	*C. girondica*
Asp Viper	*Vipera aspis*
Adder	*V. berus*
Seoanei's Viper	*V. seoanei*
Fire Salamander	*Salamandra salamandra*
Alpine Salamander	*S. atra*
Pyrenean Brook Salamander	*Euproctus asper*
Corsican Brook Salamander	*E. montanus*
Marbled Newt	*Triturus marmoratus*
Warty Newt	*T. cristatus*
Alpine Newt	*T. alpestris*
Smooth Newt	*T. vulgaris*
Palmate Newt	*Triturus helveticus*
Yellow-bellied Toad	*Bombina variegata*
Midwife Toad	*Alytes obstetricans*
Western Spadefoot	*Pelobates cultripes*
Common Spadefoot	*P. fuscus*
Parsley Frog	*Pelodytes punctatus*
Common Toad	*Bufo bufo*
Natterjack	*B. calamita*
Green Toad	*B. viridis*
Common Tree Frog	*Hyla arborea*
Stripeless Tree Frog	*H. meridionalis*
Grass (Common) Frog	*Rana temporaria*
Agile Frog	*R. dalmatina*
Pool Frog	*R. lessonae*
Edible Frog	*R. esculenta*
Marsh Frog	*R. Ridibunda*

BUTTERFLIES

PAPILLIONIDAE	
Swallowtail	*Papilio machaon*
Southern Swallowtail	*P. alexanor*
Corsican Swallowtail	*P. hospiton*
Scarce Swallowtail	*Iphiclides podalirius*

English Name	Scientific Name
Spanish Festoon	*Zerynthia rumina*
Southern Festoon	*Z. polyxena*
Apollo	*Parnassius apollo*
Clouded Apollo	*Parnassius mnemosyne*

PIERIDAE	
Black-veined White	*Aporia crataegi*
Large White	*Pieris brassicae*
Small White	*Artogeia rapae*
Southern Small White	*A. manii*
Mountain Small White	*A. ergane*
Green-veined White	*A.napi*
Black-veined White	*Aporia crataegi*
Bath White	*Pontia daplidice*
Peak White	*P. callidice*
Freyer's Dappled White	*Euchloe simplonia*
Dappled White	*E. ausonia*
Corsican Dappled White	*E. insularis*
Mountain Dappled White	*E. simplonia*
Orange Tip	*Anthocharis cardamines*
Moroccan Orange Tip	*A. euphenoides*
Mountain Clouded Yellow	*Colias phicomone*
Moorland Clouded Yellow	*C. palaeno*
Clouded Yellow	*C. crocea*
Pale Clouded Yellow	*C. hyale*
Berger's Clouded Yellow	*C. australis*
Brimstone	*Gonepteryx rhamni*
Cleopatra	*G. cleopatra*
Wood White	*Leptides sinapis*
Eastern Wood White	*L. duponcheli*

RIODINIDAE	
Duke of Burgundy	*Hamearis lucina*

LIBYTHEIDAE	
Nettle-tree Butterfly	*Libythea celtus*

NYMPHALIDAE	
Two-tailed Pasha	*Charaxes jasius*
Purple Emperor	*Apatura iris*
Lesser Purple Emperor	*A. ilia*
Poplar Admiral	*Limenitis populi*
White Admiral	*L.camilla*
Southern White Admiral	*Limenitis reducta*
Camberwell Beauty	*Nyphalis antiopa*
Large Tortoiseshell	*N. polychloros*
Small Tortoishell	*Aglais urticae*
Comma	*Polygonia c-album*
Southern Comma	*P. egea*
Map Butterfly	*Araschnia levana*
Painted Lady	*Cynthia cardui*
Red Admiral	*Vanessa atalanta*
Indian Red Admiral	*V. indica vulcania*
Peacock Butterfly	*Inachis io*
Map Butterfly	*Araschnia levana*
Cardinal	*Pandoriana pandora*
Silver-washed Fritillary	*Argynnis paphia*
Corsican Fritillary	*A. elisa*
Dark Green Fritillary	*Mesoacidalia aglaja*
High Brown Fritillary	*Fabriciana adippe*

English Name	Scientific Name
Niobe Fritillary	*F. niobe*
Queen of Spain Fritillary	*Issoria lathonia*
Twin-spot Fritillary	*Brenthis hecate*
Marbled Fritillary	*B. daphne*
Lesser Marbled Fritillary	*B. ino*
Shepherd's Fritillary	*Boloria pales*
Mountain Fritillary	*B. napaea*
Cranberry Fritillary	*B. aquilonarais*
Bog Fritillary	*Proclossiana eunomia*
Pearl-bordered Fritillary	*Clossiana euphrosyne*
Small Pearl-bordered Fritillary	*C. selene*
Titania's Fritillary	*C. titania*
Weaver's Fritillary	*C. dia*
Glanville Fritillary	*Melitaea cinxia*
Knapweed Fritillary	*M. phoebe*
Spotted Fritillary	*M. didyma*
Lesser Spotted Fritillary	*M. trivia*
False Heath Fritillary	*M. diamina*
Heath Fritillary	*Mellicta aathalia*
Njickerl's Fritillary	*M. aurelia*
Provençal Fritillary	*M. deione*
Meadow Fritillary	*M. parthenoides*
Marsh Fritillary	*Eurodryas aurinia*

SATYRIDAE	
Marbled White	*Menanargia galathea lachesis*
Esper's Marbled White	*M. russiae*
Western Marbled White	*M. occitanica*
Woodland Grayling	*Hipparchia fagi*
Rock Grayling	*H. alcyone*
Corsican Grayling	*H.neomiris*
Grayling	*H. semele cadmus*
Southern Grayling (Corsica)	*H. aristaeus*
Tree Grayling	*Neohipparchia statillinus*
Striped Grayling	*Pseudotergumia fidia*
The Hermit	*Chazara briseis*
Black Satyr	*Satyrus actaea*
Great Sooty Satry	*S. ferula*
Great Banded Grayling	*Brintesia circe*
False Grayling	*Arethusana arethusa*
Alpine Grayling	*Oeneis glacialis*
Dryad	*Minois dryas*
Large Ringlet	*Erebia euryale*
Sudeten Ringlet	*E. sudetica*
Yellow-spotted Ringlet	*E. manto*
De Prunner's Ringlet	*E. triaria*
Mountain Ringlet	*E. epiphron*
Scotch Argus	*E. aethiops*
Silky Ringlet	*E. gorge*
Gavarnie Ringlet	*E. gorgone*
Spring Ringlet	*E. epistygne*
Common Brassy Ringlet	*E. cassioides*
Spanish Brassy Ringlet	*E. hispanica rondoui*
Ottoman Brassy Ringlet	*E. ottomana tardeneota*
Woodland Ringlet	*E. medusa*
Water Ringlet	*E. pronoe*
Lefèbvre's Ringlet	*E. lefebvrei*
Larche Ringlet	*E. scipio*
Autumn Ringlet	*E. neoridas*
Bright-eyed Ringlet	*E. oeme*

English Name	Scientific Name
Piedmont Ringlet	*E. meolans*
Dewy Ringlet	*E. pandrose*
False Dewy Ringlet	*E. sthennyo*
Arran Brown	*E. ligea*
Meadow Brown	*Maniola jurtina*
Dusky Meadow Brown	*Hyponephele lycaon*
Gatekeeper	*Pyronia tithonus*
Southern Gatekeeper	*P. cecilia*
Spanish Gatekeeper	*P. bathseba*
Ringlet	*Aphantopus hyperantus*
Small Heath	*Coenonympha pamphilus*
Corsican Heath	*C. corinna*
Dusky Heath	*C. dorus*
Pearly Heath	*C. arcania*
Chestnut Heath	*C. glycerion*
Spanish Heath	*C. iphioides*
False Ringlet	*C. oedippus*
Scarce Heath	*C. hero*
Speckled Wood	*Pararge aegeria*
Wall Brown	*Lasiommata megera*
Large Wall Brown	*L. maera*
Northern Wall Brown	*L. petropolitana*
Woodland Brown	*Lopinga achine*

LYCAENIDAE	
Brown Hairstreak	Thecla betulae
Purple Hairstreak	Quercusia quercus
Spanish Purple Hairstreak	Laeosopis roboris
Sloe Hairstreak	Nordmannia acaciae
Ilex Hairstreak	N. ilicis
False Ilex Hairstreak	N. esculi
Blue-spot Hairstreak	Strymonidia spini
Black Hairstreak	S. pruni
White-letter Hairstreak	S. w-album
Green Hairstreak	Callophrys rubi
Chapman's Green Hairstreak	C. avis
Provence Hairstreak	Tomares ballus
Violet Copper	Lycaena helle
Small Copper	L. phlaeas
Large Copper	L. dispaar
Scarce Copper	Heodes virgaureae
Sooty Copper	H. tityrus
Purple-shot Copper	H. alciphron
Purple-edged Copper	Palaeochrysophanus hippothoe
Long-tailed Blue	Lampides boeticus
Lang's Short-tailed Blue	Syntarucus pirithous
Short-tailed Blue	Everes argiades
Provencal Short-tailed Blue	E. alcetas
Little Blue	Cupido minimus
Osiris Blue	C. asiris (or sebrus)
Holly Blue	Celastrina argiolus
Green-underside Blue	Glaucopsyche alexis
Black-eyed Blue	G. melanops
Alcon Blue	Maculinea alcon
Large Blue	M. arion
Scarce Large Blue	M. telejus
Iolas Blue	Iolana iolas
Baton Blue	Pseudophilotes baton
Panoptes Blue	P. panoptes
Chequered Blue	Scolitantides orion

English Name	Scientific Name
Silver-studded Blue	Plebejus argus
Reverdin's Blue	P. argyrognomon
Idas Blue	Lycaeides idas
Geranium Argus	Eumedonia eumedon
Brown Argus	Aricia agestis
Southern Brown Argus	A. cramera
Mountain Argus	A. artaxerxes
Alpine Argus	Albulina orbitulus
Silvery Argus	Pseudaricia nicias
Glandon Blue	Agriades glandon
Gavarnie Blue	A. pyrenaicus
Mazarine Blue	Cyaniris semiargus
Furry Blue	Agrodiaetus dolus
Forster's Furry Blue	A. ainsae
Damon Blue	A. damon
Escher's Blue	A. escheri
Amanda's Blue	A. amanda
Chapman's Blue	A. thersites
Ripart's Anomalous Blue	A. ripartii
Turquoise Blue	Plebicula dorylas
Meleager's Blue	Meleageria daphnis
Chalk-hill Blue	Lysandra corydon
Provence Chalk-hill Blue	L. hispana
Spanish Chalk-hill Blue	L. albicans
Adonis Blue	L. bellargus
Common Blue	Polyommatus icarus
Eros Blue	P. eros

HESPERIIDAE	
Grizzled Skipper	Pyrgus malvae
Large Grizzled Skipper	P. alveus
Oberthur's Grizzled skipper	P. armoricanus
Foulquier's Grizzled Skipper	P. foulquieri
Olive Skipper	P. serratulae
Carline Skipper	P. carlinae
Cinquefoil Skipper	P. cirsii
Yellow-banded Skipper	P. sidae
Rosy Grizzled Skipper	P. onopordi
Safflower Skipper	P. carthami
Alpine Grizzled Skipper	P. andromedae
Dusky Grizzled Skipper	P. cacaliae
Red Underwing Skipper	Spialia sertorius
Sage Skipper	Syrichtus proto
Mallow Skipper	Carcharodus alceae
Marbled Skipper	C. lavatherae
Southern Marbled Skipper	C. boeticus
Tufted Marbled Skipper	C. flocciferis
Dingy Skipper	Erynnis tages
Large Chequered Skipper	Heteropterus morpheus
Chequered Skipper	Carterocephalus palaemon
Large Chequered	Heteropterus morpheus
Lulworth Skipper	Thymelicus acteon
Essex Skipper	T. lineola
Small Skipper	T. flavus
Silver-spotted Skipper	Hesperia comma
Large Skipper	Ochlodes venatus
Pigmy Skipper	Gegenes pumilio
Mediterranean Skipper	Gegenes nostrodamus

NOTES

NOTES

OTHER TITLES AVAILABLE
FROM ARLEQUIN PRESS

A Birdwatching Guide to MALLORCA *by GRAHAM HEARL*

Written by the RSPB representative on the Island this guide is unsurpassed in its detailed coverage of the area with maps and clear directions. Includes colour photographs and full checklist of the 309 documented species recorded on the Island over the last 20 years. Now 92pp.

£9.95 +p&p

A Birdwatching Guide to THE ALGARVE
by KEVIN & CHRISTINE CARLSON

A poular holiday destination and plenty to see for any person interested in nature all year round. This book will be of use to those just wishing to have just a day or so birdwatching and for those who wish to spend more time exploring the rich fauna and keen to pick up some of the rarities. Details of day trips to see Black shouldered Kites, Little Bustards etc. 62pp, checklist, colour habitat photos.

£8.95 +p&p

A Birdwatching Guide to MENORCA,
IBIZA & FORMENTERA
by GRAHAM HEARL

This guide covers the smaller Balearic Islands, all important staging posts for migrants crossing the mediterranean. Menorca is especially good for seeing Egyptian Vulture, Red Kite and Booted Eagle. Ibiza which hosts all the typical Balearic resident specialities and Formentera is important for its breeding colonies of Mediterranean Shearwater. 56pp, site maps, colour habitat photographs.

£8.95 +p&p

A Birdwatching Guide to SOUTHERN SPAIN
by MALCOLM PALMER

Covering the provinces of Almeria, Grand, Jáen, Málaga, Cadiz, Murcia and part of Cordoba and Sevilla. Sites which offer the most interesting birdwatching opportunities are included. Specific list and habitat guide, checklist, maps, colour habitat photographs. 92pp.

£9.95 +p&p

A Birdwatching Guide to MOROCCO
by PETER COMBRIDGE & ALAN SNOOK

Morroco remains an exciting and interesting country to visit. This guide is aimed at those with limited time and want to see a cross section of habitats and find a good selection of species. 64pp, maps, checklist, colour habitat photographs.

£9.95 +p&p

A Birdwatching Guide to CYPRUS
by ARTHUR STAGG & GRAHAM HEARL

Ideally situated in the Mediterranean the Cyprus bird list is long, it currently stands at 363 species. Notable among the endemics and resident species are Cyprus Warbler, Cyprus Pied Wheatear and Griffon Vulture. Summer visitors include Eleonoras Falcon and Red rumped Swallow. In winter Flamingo and a wide variety of wildfowl. In all respects Cyprus is a truly a year round birdwatching venue. 88pp.

£9.95 +p&p

A Birdwatching Guide to THE PYRENEES
by JACQUIE CROZIER

Written by a resident of the area, this excellent guide covers the entire area from the Atlantic to the Mediterranean. Not only detailing the best sites to visit for birdwatching but includes information about other flora and fauna. 92pp.

£9.95 +p&p

A Birdwatching Guide to CRETE
by STEPHANIE COGHLAN

Crete offers a great deal to the birdwatcher, botanist and general naturalist. It is very mountainous and many of the mountains are cut by impressive gorges which from the birdwatchers point of view offer breeding areas for Griffon Vultures, Lammergeier and Blue Rock Thrush as well as good observation points. This guide features the most productive birding sites on the Island, includes maps, checklists for birds, mammals, amphibians, reptiles, butterflies and orchids.

£9.95 +p&p

A Birdwatching Guide to FLORIDA
by DEREK MOORE & DAVID HOSKING

Florida is an ideal family holiday destination. The opportunities to combine some fantastic birding whilst giving the family every chance to enjoy Disneyworld, the beach etc. are enormous. This book concentrates on describing some of the best sites close to Orlando and Miami which provide a good chance of finding most of Florida specialities. Maps, colour identification photographs, full checklist.

£9.95 +p&p

A Birdwatching Guide to EXTREMADURA
by JOHN MUDDEMAN

The essential guide to the area including illustrations by John Busby, colour habitat photographs and checklists.120 pp.

£10.95 +p&p

A Birdwatching Guide to FRANCE
South of the Loire including Corsica
by Jacquie Crozier

This is the most comprehensive Birdwatching Site Guide to the area published in the English language. 240 pages including 8 pages in colour, Illustrations by John Busby
Size: 215mm x 135mm,

£15.95 +p&p

A Birdwatching Guide to EASTERN FRANCE
by Malcolm Palmer & Luis fidel

This book covers the whole of the coastal strips from the frena frontier down to the Southern tip of the Alicante Province and those sites within a comfortable day trip inland.
120 pages including 8 pages of colour.

£10.95 +p&p

A Birdwatching Guide to BERMUDA
by Andrew Dobson

If you are going to Bermuda this is a must for you.
176 pages including 16 pages of colour.
Size: 215mm x 210mm.

£13.95 +p&p

BUTTERFLIES & DRAGONFLIES 'A Site Guide'
by Paul Hill & Colin Twist

The guide features 116 sites enabling you to find every U.K. breeding species of Butterfly and Dragonfly. The guide contains maps for each site, details of target species, status of site, optimum time to visit and information regarding the areas other notable flora and fauna. The authors Paul Hill and Colin Twist are experts in their fied, this guide shares their undoubted knowledge with you. The appropriate conservation bodies have been consulted whilst preparing the guide so you can be confident that you will be welcome at each site featured.

£12.95 +p&p

All of the above titles measure 148.5mm x 210mm unless otherwise specified.

Prices as of 31st March 2003.

Available from all good book shops *or* direct from Arlequin Press, 26 Broomfield Road, Chelmsford, Essex CM1 1SW.
Tel: (01245) 267771 Fax: (01245) 280606
www. arlequinpress.co.uk